African Women

Social Change in Global Perspective
Mark Selden, Series Editor

Exploring the relationship between social change and social structures, this series considers the theory, praxis, promise, and pitfalls of movements in global and comparative perspective. The historical and contemporary social movements considered here challenge patterns of hierarchy and inequality of race, gender, nationality, ethnicity, class, and culture. The series will emphasize textbooks and broadly interpretive synthetic works.

African Women: A Modern History, Catherine Coquery-Vidrovitch, translated by Beth Raps

Human Families, Stevan Harrell

Portraits of the Japanese Workplace: Labor Movements, Workers, and Managers, Kumazawa Makoto, translated by Mikiso Hane

Capital, the State, and Late Industrialization: Comparative Perspectives on the Pacific Rim, edited by John Borrego, Alejandro Alvarez Bejar, and Jomo K. S.

Power Restructuring in China and Russia, Mark Lupher

The Challenge of Local Feminisms: Women's Movements in Global Perspective, edited by Amrita Basu, with the assistance of C. Elizabeth McGrory

The Transformation of Communist Systems: Economic Reform Since the 1950s, Bernard Chavance

African Women

Women

A Modern History

Catherine Coquery-Vidrovitch

UNIVERSITY OF PARIS-7 DENIS DIDEROT

Translated by
Beth Gillian Raps

Westview Press
A Member of the Perseus Books Group

Social Change in Global Perspective

Grateful acknowledgment is made to the French Ministry of Culture for assistance in translating this book.

Originally published in France as *Les Africaines: Histoire des femmes d'Afrique noire du XIX au XX siècle* by Éditions Desjonquères
Copyright © 1994 by Éditions Desjonquères
English translation copyright © 1997 by Westview Press, A Member of Perseus Books, L.L.C.

Augmented new edition published in 1997 in the United States of America by Westview Press, 5500 Central Avenue, Boulder, Colorado 80301-2877, and in the United Kingdom by Westview Press, 12 Hid's Copse Road, Cumnor Hill, Oxford OX2 9JJ

Library of Congress Cataloging-in-Publication Data
Coquery-Vidrovitch, Catherine.
  [Africaines. English]
  African women: a modern history / Catherine Coquery-Vidrovitch;
translated by Beth Raps.
    p. cm.—(Social change in global perspective)
  Includes bibliographical references and index.
  ISBN 0-8133-2360-6 (hc).—0-8133-2361-4 (pbk)
    1. Women—Africa, Sub-Saharan—History—19th century.   2. Women—
Africa, Sub-Saharan—History—20th century.   I. Title.
II. Series.
HQ1787.C6613   1997
305.4'0967—dc21
      96-47847
      CIP

The paper used in this publication meets the requirements of the American National Standard for Permanence of Paper for Printed Library Materials Z39.48-1984.

10   9   8

PERSEUS
POD
ON DEMAND

*To two historian friends
and pioneers in the field,
Natalie Zemon Davis
and Marcia Wright*

*To my children Natacha, Marina,
Sarah, and Julien*

*For the new generation,
the history of women is part of
the history of the world*

Contents

Part Four
Women and Modern Life

Illustrations

Photographs (following page 139)

Queen mother, Benin City, early fifteenth century
Mother and child, Bambara, Mali
Women and apartheid in Johannesburg, 1977
Women selling crafts at the pier, Ganvie, Benin
Women at Ganvie, Benin: A water-village on the lagoon
A Christian cult at Dissin, Burkina Faso
Anyi chief's wives attending yam festival at Asouba, Côte d'Ivoire
Rice harvest in Casamance, South Senegal
Washing near a rice field in Casamance
The first wife of a Senegalese civil servant, Dakar, 1975
A girl in Kaolack selling peanuts
Chad marketplace, Djamena
Market women offering their produce at a railway station, Côte d'Ivoire
Cartoon from Na Zona da Frelimo
Poster from Na Zona da Frelimo
Portrait of a couple, Bamako, Mali, 1950s

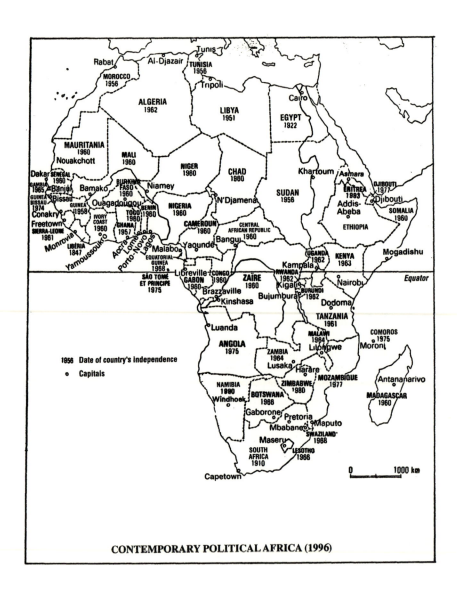

CONTEMPORARY POLITICAL AFRICA (1996)

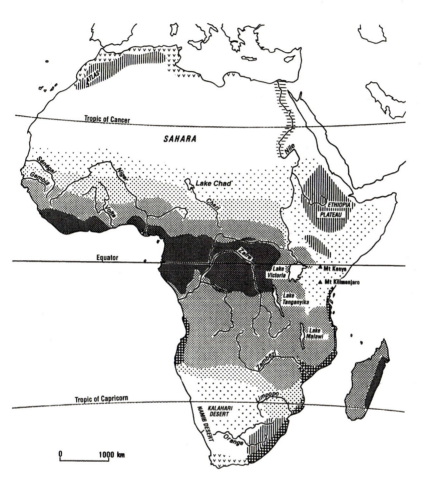

REGIONS OF AFRICA

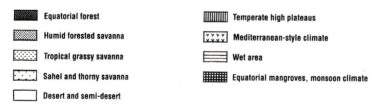

■ Equatorial forest

▨ Humid forested savanna

⣿ Tropical grassy savanna

⣿ Sahel and thorny savanna

☐ Desert and semi-desert

▥ Temperate high plateaus

∨∨∨∨ Mediterranean-style climate

☰ Wet area

▦ Equatorial mangroves, monsoon climate

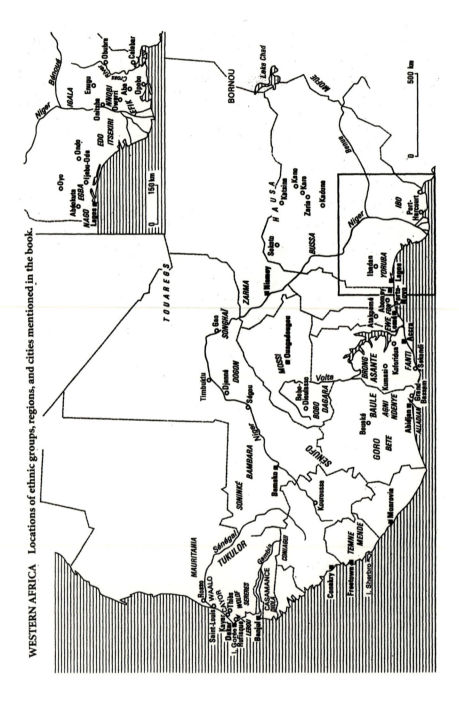

WESTERN AFRICA   Locations of ethnic groups, regions, and cities mentioned in the book.

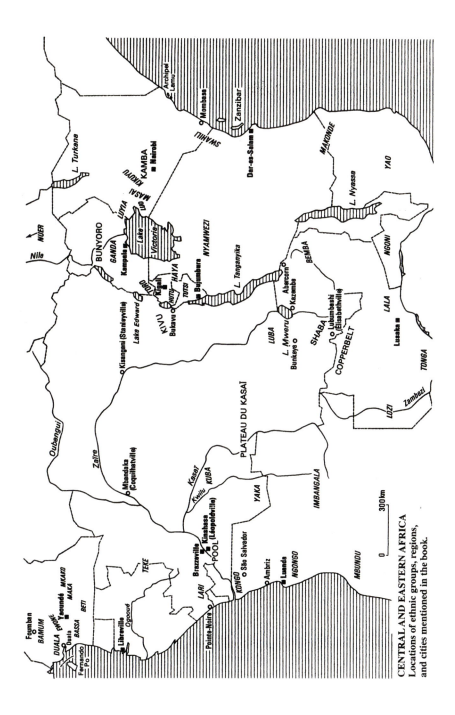

CENTRAL AND EASTERN AFRICA
Locations of ethnic groups, regions, and cities mentioned in the book.

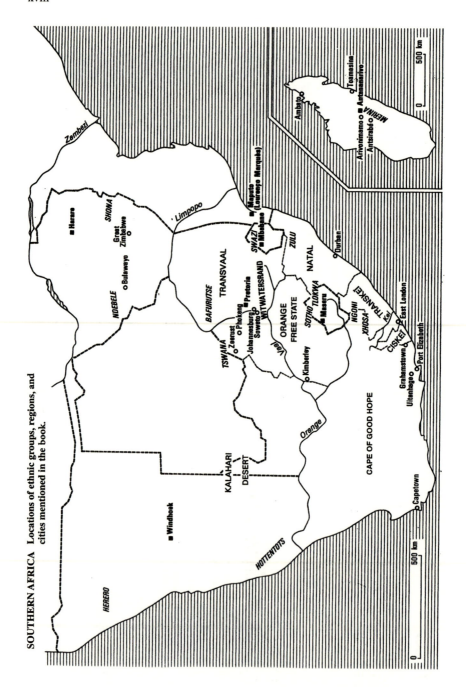

SOUTHERN AFRICA Locations of ethnic groups, regions, and cities mentioned in the book.

Introduction

In different ways at different times, the women of sub-Saharan Africa have led, and continue to lead, difficult lives. In barely a century, their situation—or, rather, situations, because the subcontinent is huge, and widely divergent in types of social organization—has changed drastically. Ancient and modern ways mingle uniquely in each case.[1]

Femaleness is of course a common factor, but the woman is also a peasant or a city-dweller, intellectual or working-class, overburdened and overworked mother, independent, single, or divorced; all these factors play their role. And these life circumstances are experienced differently by women in Africa than in Western societies.

African women have at least one other point in common: they have no time. They have always worked more than men (which is not to say that men did nothing, a false idea that is widespread). Today they work differently but, with few exceptions, just as hard. They are so overburdened with tasks of all kinds that they hardly have time to bemoan their fate or even to wonder about it. Their image of themselves remains cloudy.

The image that African men have of them—and African men, like men throughout the world, love to watch women—has been the more distorted for having been perverted by others, particularly but not exclusively Western observers. All these observers have been men, for it is men who have traveled to Africa from earliest times. Thus, even more than that of women in general, the image of African women is stereotyped: from the fertile and nurturing Earth Mother to the lazy, debauched young beauty. These images do not interest me.

The point of this work is primarily to understand why African women have lacked the leisure and often even the right to observe themselves. How have they used the time so parsimoniously allotted to them, and how would they like to use it? I have learned about these women through their lives and their activity. They have been and are still the nurturers. What did they do in nomadic and sedentary societies, in pastoral and agricultural ones? What do they work at today, in the countryside and the city? How have they—or have they not—been prepared for it? From birth to death, via the almost obligatory act of marriage and until very recently the birth of as many children as possible, how have they been trained, what have they learned, how have they changed, and, ultimately, what do they want? Along with women all over the world, they have begun to make their voices heard. Yet they do not speak as one, and this is why men often do not hear them.

What I would like, then, to show is not women's life unto itself—there is no such thing. Here too, women are only half of humanity. They participate in all activities and all events; they make up part of society. What is important is to understand their role and function in society as partners and participants in the collective whole. Women's history thus provides us with a constant that cuts across time and space, and this is how it should be read in this book. Of course, for convenience's sake, I assume that the broader history of Africa is known, or at least better known, and address mainly women's history in this book. There was almost nothing written about African women until the United Nations Women's Decade of 1975–1985. African women were rarely spoken of—especially in French, where the generic masculine can be so deceiving, but in English too; who but an expert would think, reading "African farmers" or "African slaves," of women? And "children"—half of them are specifically *girls.*[2] That is why this book, more than providing a history of women, highlights a perspective: the history of the whys and wherefores of society from women's viewpoints.

In attempting to embrace the entire subcontinent as I did in an earlier volume (on the history of African cities), I run the risk of unfair generalization. I have discussed this elsewhere and will not do so here again,[3] except to emphasize that the most significant points are not the similarities but the innumerable variants in women's condition in African societies that are similar and different. We have many case studies, especially in English. Their unfortunate tendency is to conclude, using an example specific in time and place, with a description of "the" African woman. Only comparative history allows us to keep in mind that reality is always more complex than that. Confronted with specific situations, one cannot summarily say, for example, that colonialism lowered living standards or advanced women's emancipation. The many facets of a social and historical reality in flux urge us to subtler understandings.

Such is the vast territory I set out, without any hope of being exhaustive, to explore in this work. I have chosen to highlight several meaningful themes that seemed essential to an understanding of the changes in women's condition in the countryside and the city from just before colonialism to the present: work, education, labor migration, economic activity, marriage, divorce, sexuality, political action, and artistic awakening. One could certainly write about others, starting with a history of women's images and representations. We will have to wait a little longer for that, because, except for a few activist leaders, too-rare female social scientists, and superb women novelists, African women have seldom spoken for themselves except via anthropologists, usually foreign ones.

Women's condition in ancient times is little known and easily, often unfairly, generalized because research sources are lacking. In addition, the daily lives of women, in African history as elsewhere, have been of scant interest to foreign or native observers. Written sources, more plentiful than one might expect, have almost without exception been foreign in origin—Arab since the tenth century, European since the fifteenth. For centuries their authors were men—merchants, explorers, political men—coming from male-dominated societies and mainly concerned with men's affairs. Women in these sources appear as stereotypes: princesses and chiefs' mothers, slaves and concubines. These travelers mainly experienced the ruling classes and scarcely looked at women except to use them.[4] The most curious were missionaries, though their critical observations mainly stigmatized what they considered pagan attitudes: bare breasts, an often exaggerated sexual freedom, polygamy. Colonists of every nationality were imbued with the Victorian heritage of their age. For them, the world of work was male. All failed to see how often physical labor in Africa fell to women. Their opinions caricatured women; one has only to examine satirical works of the period on the subject to notice this.[5]

There was at least one feminist work about women at the dawn of the twentieth century,[6] but things did not change until after the 1930s, when women's and children's health also became of concern. Under colonialism the medical establishment, like everything else, was designed for the male workers recruited by the colonial officials, and therefore it did not trouble itself with measles until after World War II. The illness was seldom diagnosed as such before that, supposedly because it was impossible to detect on black skin—though it meanwhile ran rampant among children.[7]

Oral traditions are often more eloquent in recognizing women and recall several heroines, like Queen Amina of the Zaria Hausa in the sixteenth century, Beatrice of the Congo in the eighteenth century, and the priestess Nongqause in southern Africa in the nineteenth century. Matrilineality was very widespread and, at times, valued. Historical anthropology studies women's lives in certain societies at different periods, but what is often rather glibly and sweepingly referred to as "the precolonial era" actually spans two millennia and a very vast and disparate landscape from desert to dense forest. Such generalizations can thus only oversimplify.

Among free peoples, tradition was better preserved by men, particularly by the professional storyteller-musicians (griots) of West Africa, whose job it was to sing the genealogy and praises of the notables for whom they worked. They were rarely female, but this may be because women's role in the transmission of collective memory has been underestimated by researchers influenced by the weight of male ideology as much in their own societies as in the ones they studied.[8] Certain queen mothers and older women held important roles, for example, among the Yoruba of Nigeria, transmission of the *oriki,* both literary and historical texts.[9] In Dahomey "the most secret traditions were transmitted by women, some of whom were the real historians" of the country.[10] There were also the erudite Ndenye women in what is now Côte d'Ivoire, but by and large women were kept from knowing their country's history.[11]

Those most able to resist this inferiority were slave women. Slave men were mere progenitors, easily sold and often separated from their offspring. Women were more stable, living with their daughters and doing domestic labor beside them. Mamadou Diawara has described the transmission of various kinds of songs that were often more open than the works of free men and women.[12] An enormous task awaits women historians and anthropologists, because what remains of this culture can more easily be told to a person of the same sex as the informant. Interesting as it may be, however, this literature is hardly informative on women's condition, for women also transmitted the prevailing tradition of male dominance. More revealing are the life stories collected by missionaries in the past or from women born with the century, within which the impact of the interviewer/interviewee relationship has yet to be decoded.[13]

The recent explosion of feminist historiography in English, especially from the United States, has increased the frequency of publication of case studies with titles that can be extrapolated ad infinitum: "Women and ____" (fill in the blank: Work, Class, the City, Patriarchy, Power, the State, Development, Imperialism, etc.).[14] In other languages, high-quality research continues to ignore issues affected by gender differences concerning, for example, the birth of black churches or the process of conversion.[15] The present work will have its own weaknesses, even silences, simply because so much about African women remains to be explored.

The objective is to detail not what *women's* lives were like on the eve of the colonial period but the major areas of difference between men and women on these many topics. To the nonspecialist, the book's first section may seem unpleasantly exhaustive in its detail about what historical anthropology has already told us on the subject. Yet in order to evaluate the later changes it is important to determine one's point of departure, and this in fact is the object of the entire first part of the book. In the twentieth century, the sources are more expressive and suggest how women's fate and function changed, sometimes slowly and sometimes brutally, with the beginning and then the traumas of colonial and postcolonial "modernity."

Distinctions between the colonial period and independence turn out not to be significant; cross-cultural influences and overlays have become stronger since the beginning of European domination, and decolonization had no special effect on women's condition. The turning point was instead the early 1980s, when through the combined impact of years of crisis and the expanded influence of the Western media, the shift in women's status began to seem likely to become a radical one. Each theme in the present work is treated as a continuous thread while emphasizing the overall, gradual shift of social focus from the country to the city. In each case, I seek to examine not only the causes but the diverse rhythms of a shift that is common but not simultaneous throughout the continent. The chronological thread therefore changes throughout the book because it depends on the personalities of peoples, the influences they have experienced, and the divergent reactions these influences have generated.

The commonplace that women's situation has deteriorated during the twentieth century must be approached with more subtlety by examining social class, gender relationships, and differences in site and time period. Thus we can ask if it is absolutely true that in the countryside women were relegated to subsistence work while men were able to produce for export. The role of independent young women in the migratory movements of the turn of the century has been greatly underestimated. Very early on, women had an effect on city life through their work (trade, markets, domestic service, prostitution (which arose because of great concentrations of men in urban areas), their creative enterprise (interregional wholesaling, buying and selling cloth or dried fish), and their social and political influence (changes in matrimonial and property laws, resistance movements).

All this results, whether one likes it or not, in a heightened consciousness that is manifested in a variety of ways, ranging from recent explorations of personal liberty—with a possible shift from being perceived as an "independent" woman to being perceived as a "free" woman—to the dawn of artistic self-expression, with women finally asserting the right and taking the time to express themselves by themselves; written literature, a relatively recent importation, appears to be the chosen terrain of women's recaptured creativity.

TOPONYMIC DECOLONIZATION

Colonial Name	Modern Name
Nations	
Gold Coast	Ghana
Ubangi Chari	Central African Republic
French Sudan	Mali
Ruanda	Rwanda
Urundi	Burundi
Nyasaland	Malawi
Northern Rhodesia	Zambia
Bechuanaland	Botswana
Basutoland	Lesotho
Southwest Africa	Namibia
Fernando Po and Rio Muni	Equatorial Guinea
Belgian Congo	Zaire
Portuguese Guinea	Guinea-Bissau
Dahomey	Benin
Western Sahara	Sarhaoui Democratic Arab Republic[a]
French Territory of the Afars and Issas	Djibouti
Southern Rhodesia	Zimbabwe
Upper Volta	Burkina Faso
French Guinea	Guinea
Cities	
Fort Lamy	Djamena
Leopoldville	Kinshasa
Elisabethville	Lubumbashi
Stanleyville	Kisangani
Coquilhatville	Mbandaka
Bathurst	Banjul
Salisbury	Harare
Lourenço-Marques	Maputo
Tananarive	Antananarivo

[a]Not internationally recognized.

SOURCE: Hélène d'Almeida-Topor, 1993, *L'Afrique au XXe Siecle,* (Paris: Colin), p. 228.

PART ONE

Nineteenth-Century Women

1

Peasant Women

For centuries the family was at one and the same time the locus of production, consumption, and domestic life. This was not the limited family called "nuclear" of the contemporary Western world (father, mother, and children, with perhaps grandparents and at most a few close cousins) but a larger group known as a lineage. A lineage is a group of individuals who recognize themselves as descendants of a *known* common ancestor. Where knowledge is transmitted orally, the lineage can be extremely extensive; one can with reasonable accuracy trace one's descent back nine or ten generations, involving a considerable number of relatives in a long series of lineage branches or segments. But the term "lineage" can be misleading: it exaggerates the importance of biological affiliation, whereas over the course of generations the extended family incorporated a large number of social allies, whose descendants then became part of the family: children and adolescents given to the family to work against forgiveness of a debt or an offense, adoptees (far more common than in our modern societies, with their exacting regulations), slaves, dependents, and others.

Women, Family, and Household

To understand women's place in ancient African societies, we must of course examine their place in the family as just defined. But the African continent, with its vast expanses and its multitude of historical-social-cultural or "ethnic" groups, spans a broad spectrum of types of familial communities. There is no one model that describes "the African family," much less a "position of women" in such a family. Nonetheless, one can discern certain main tendencies, colored by regional differences.

If we exclude the early colonization of South Africa, which created cities and mining towns, until about the middle of the twentieth century the great majority of Africans were rural people. They were cattle herders, farmers, and occasionally hunter-gatherers and foragers, such as the Mbuti Pygmies of the Ituri Forest or the Kalahari Desert San. A clear but not rigid division of labor existed between men and women. Usually, men were responsible for war and long-distance trade, helped clear land, hunted, and ran political affairs. Women took care of agriculture, household tasks such as supplying water and firewood, nearby gardening, and small-scale subsistence and neighborhood trading. At the same time, women were entirely responsible for the work connected with reproduction and had an almost biologically maximal fertility rate—an average of one child every three years.[1]

Inheritance of goods and power was unequal between men and women. The great division was the opposition between patrilineality and matrilineality, with many local variations dependent on whether the couple went to live with the husband's family (patrilocal) or (less commonly) with the wife's (matrilocal). In matrilineal traditions, where inheritance passed not from father to son but from uncle to sister's son, rather than enjoying power women passed it on to the men in their families and were sometimes privileged as "mother of the chief."

Polygamy, doubtless linked with women's important dual role as producer and reproducer, was very widespread. This position, glorified—as in all agrarian societies—as both symbol and reality of fertility, was one of the pillars of marriage. In contrast to the situation in ancient Chinese society, the birth of girls was valued, although less than that of boys. For the family receiving her, whether birth family (for matrilocal societies) or future in-laws (for patrilocal ones), a girl was a source of wealth—a promise of work and a guarantee of children. Thus women had social value, and with the monetarization of the economy this became market value. In any case, women always had political value if their fathers employed it judiciously. They were used by society and thus objectified.

Ordinary polygamy meant only two to ten wives, if only because of their cost. It contrasted with the more extensive polygamy of chiefs, which was used for political domination. The king of the Ganda, in central Africa, is said to have possessed several hundred and even thousands of wives; Mutesa, in the nineteenth century, had three or four hundred. Any lineage aspiring to political office did well to give several of its daughters to the king. The man who wanted a favor or pardon for an offense would offer one or two daughters. In addition, once a year the king sent his agents to gather female attendants for his wives in every province, keeping the best for himself. He also chose wives and slaves from among war prisoners, gathering around him a female elite of *bakembuga*, a tangible expression of his power.[2] He might then give some of them to his chiefs, using women as prizes within the political hierarchy. On the Niger plateau around 1832–1833, the chief of the Igala is said to have had 2,000 wives. At the beginning of the twentieth century King Njoya of the Bamum of Cameroon had 1,200, of whom at least 120 were precisely identified. At his death in the early 1930s he left 163 living children of the 350 he had apparently fathered.[3] In 1960 the Kuba's sovereign in Zaire had 600 wives.[4] Women of the aristocracy were not a workforce for the great chiefs. Although occasionally invested with administrative or military functions, they commonly lived together in a special place, conducted royal ceremonies, and at most supervised an army of female servants and slaves who took care of the palace's and the king's daily needs. Women in this category were of course an exception.

Daily Life

Africa is too large and its types of social organization too varied to allow a detailed description of "the" African woman's tasks. As in all societies, male supremacy was both ideologically and effectively a reality, and the public sphere, considered the most prestigious, was reserved for men. Women's domain was domestic life in the broadest sense: not just the house, as in the West, but the whole household's subsistence—the household being the basic unit of production and consumption. In eastern and southern Africa, where human settlements were widely scattered, the household usually consisted of a woman and her children, possibly including her dependents and slaves; the husband came to visit each of his wives in turn. It might, however, be a group of households in a village, usually small in forested parts of Africa (at the most a few hundred inhabitants) and larger in western Africa (where numbers could exceed a thousand). In both cases, each wife, autonomous to some degree, had her food stores and her kitchen; she managed her own fields and sometimes her own herd of cattle. Yet she remained tied to the head of the family, who was responsible for overall production.

Whether in forest or savanna, in nation-state or decentralized society, or among farmers or herders, peasant women's work was organized in the same way. First, it was mainly women who farmed. Today field work is largely done by men in only a few regions, mainly in West Africa, and this has probably always been true. Men traditionally used the hoe for subsistence production only along the southern border of the Sahara, for example, among the Songhai of Mali or the Hausa of Nigeria, where women were allowed outside only after sunset. Among the Hausa, women were even secluded according to a peculiarly urban custom that is said to have been introduced by the sultan of Kano in 1485 but became more common as Islam spread. Men were farmers among the Yoruba of southwestern Nigeria, but among their Igbo neighbors to the southeast it was women who worked in the fields.[5] Among the Fon of Benin, working the land, while not forbidden, was considered improper for women because their jobs beyond gardening were trade and handicrafts, especially indigo dying, and, long ago, transporting goods as needed for trading. Everywhere else, even where field work was done by both sexes, as on the Tonga plateau (in what is now southern Zambia),[6] the hoe was generally a women's tool. Men used axes to chop down trees and sometimes another tool called the *nton*, a kind of shovel with a very long handle used by the Beti of forested Cameroon.[7] Can we conclude from this that hoeing made agriculture women's work and that the introduction of the plow (as in North Africa and Asia) almost automatically implied men's participation in it?[8] In sub-Saharan Africa, men's turning to agricultural work was a late consequence of "modernization." Mechanized and skilled labor was monopolized by men because it required some capital, while hand labor fell to women, who needed only their centuries-old knowledge in order to do it.

Gender division of labor was still the rule. In nineteenth-century Kikuyuland (now Kenya), for example, as in most of central and eastern Africa, over vast grassland plateaus, women and girls cultivated and prepared food while men and boys mainly kept herds of goats and sheep and later cattle. It was always women, however, who milked the cows and made butter, as among the Nuer (now in Sudan) or among the Fula of western Africa.

Men were responsible for making war, which was often connected with agriculture; the long fallow periods required by poor soils (fifteen or twenty years if not more) meant a semi-itinerant form of agriculture and the occasional wresting of new lands from neighbors. Some kinds of agricultural work were done by men because of the physical strength required, such as the heavy labor of clearing land for planting; cutting down a single tree could take two men an entire day. Other tasks were performed by men and women together, for example, preparing the soil after clearing and sometimes even the first planting. Men, with the possible help of their wives, grew particular foods such as sweet potatoes, sugarcane, and bananas among the Kikuyu, yams and watermelons[9] among the Beti, yams among the Baule of Côte d'Ivoire, and peanuts in Senegal. It was also their task to dig trenches and build drainage systems, bridges, and trails.

In Kenya, Masai men, as in other herding cultures, kept raising and selling of herd animals to themselves, though their wives had to milk. A Luo proverb has it that "herding is better than farming as the man is better than the woman."[10] To women were relegated all other tasks: sowing grain and beans, daily hoeing, harvesting, transporting and storing surplus, milking cows and caring for smaller animals, pounding millet and preparing cassava flour and millet beer.[11] Women also did the laundry for the entire household and the daily chores of supplying water and firewood for the kitchen. Water was often located at the bottom of a ravine and wood in the bush where it had to be gathered with the help of children (little boys included). Everywhere in Africa where water is not piped into homes (that is, in most rural areas), the best one can hope for is a trip to the village water faucet. Women and children make these daily supply trips to this day. Everything tells us that these are centuries-old female tasks, even though, as we shall see, women's work in rural areas has gotten harder since colonization. The only relative respite in all this activity is the dry season, which lightens agricultural burdens. It is a time for celebrations, marriages, harvest feasts, and socializing between villages and families—but here again, women make most of the preparations.

Beasts of Burden: The Tswana Example

Comparing pastoral societies with very different social structures at two opposite ends of Africa, the Kikuyu of Kenya and the Tswana of southern Africa,[12] subject to the same ecological constraint of rainfall, one is struck by the similarities in women's condition. The rains are more irregular in Tswana country, which receives less than four hundred millimeters of rain annually—a meaningless average, since several dry and good seasons alternate over cycles of about fifteen years. Such vulnerability requires the development of alternative ways to survive: herding and growing staple grains (mainly corn for the Kikuyu, sorghum for the Tswana) and drought-resistant plants such as chickpeas and pumpkins. To this food base may be added the products of the hunt, brought in by men, and of foraging by women. In cases of prolonged drought, as in 1820 and 1834 in the Tswana area, gathering may become the only recourse against famine.

Here, women appear to be beasts of burden, especially within the strict patrilineal order of Tswana society. The political structure was decentralized to large villages, each of which might have 5,000–10,000 residents. Each neighborhood or "ward" was a microcosm, encompassing several lineage groupings each with its own chief. Each ward was subdivided in turn into households organized around their head within the same walled compound, made up of basic units that might be reduced to one wife and her dependent children. Each wife was the subject both of her husband and of her own mother, who never lived too far away and who stored the shares of the harvest that in principal belonged to each of her daughters but that she could use in their stead. Therefore the young wife lacked any personal right to the fruits of her labor twice over, except occasionally for two or three head of cattle that her father had given her when she was married. She had no hope of increasing what she owned, with nothing more to sell than the perishable foodstuffs she gathered daily.

Women had a negative image of themselves. This image was the result of the society's refusal to recognize them as individuals, an entire existence devoted to the domestic economy, and training from their earliest years in humility and acceptance as normal of an ideology that was entirely based on labor. Men, in contrast, participated in complex networks of dependence between lineages and within their own families, but they had two other options: accumulating wealth in cattle and land and trading for profit. They tanned hides and exchanged them for copper, the second-most-important source of wealth after cattle. A little copper jewelry was given to women, serving above all as coin in matrimonial exchanges conducted to the advantage of the lineage heads rather than their wives.

The ward was the effective unit of production, and each of its households could call on all the others to work if need be. Herds were given to the care of boys collectively, and women organized much of their hoeing, sowing, and harvesting in teams. This also diffused their individual responsibility for the harvest's products, which were, like land, shared according to the rank of the family head, the head of a particular family branch, the lineage chief, and the village as a whole. The title of chief, as translated in 1927 by a missionary, was "owner of the town and the country adjoining."[13] Women were thus officially excluded from power, and in fact their presence was forbidden in the men's debating courtyard. At best, they could participate by calling out from their own doorways or from the edge of the courtyard.

Women often worked longer hours than men. Despite irregular rainy seasons (from October to May or June), agricultural labor, including protecting grain harvests from predatory birds or other animals, kept women in the fields about eight months out of twelve from sunrise to three or four in the afternoon. Then they went back to work around the house. In contrast to the situation in other regions, in the Tswana area they were also responsible for building and repairing houses and cellars. Pottery, weaving, and other activities took the rest of their time, and they also had to care for children.

Missionaries emphasize that women had to endure extreme privations. From a very young age, men and boys took priority over women and girls, especially during times of scarcity. Observers may have emphasized certain aspects that particularly shocked them, given their stereotypes of Western housewives, but their reports are consistent enough to be convincing. From the age of five or six, while boys were beginning to roam the pastures with cattle and playing with their first weapons, girls were at work with their mothers, and by ten or twelve they were considered almost self-sufficient.

To this harsh childhood was added apprenticeship in docility and submission to men. No social sanction limited fathers' or husbands' right to beat dependent women. The height of this was initiation, which essentially consisted of verifying girls' virginity. Female sexual relations outside marriage were considered bad luck, potentially keeping away rain and requiring purification rites. Training sought to teach a girl her role as a woman—that is, as wife and mother. The first phase of initiation was deflowering the girl with a tuber shaped like a phallus (the Makonde in northern Mozambique used a phallus made of clay). The girl was instructed in her sexual role by an older woman, preferably a widow, and then violently beaten to give her a sense of the pains of childbirth. All this was sufficient to teach passivity and idealize subordination. During the first month of the ceremony the little girl was given to a poor family to be treated like a low-caste servant, required daily to carry water and wood, and beaten on her return. This period ended with a public ceremony in which the girls insulted men and accused them of being lazy and refusing to work for their own families. The apology for servitude was reemphasized during the second month, when girls put on vests woven of wet grasses that rubbed their skin raw as they dried. A missionary went so far as to add that the final trial consisted of making the initiate grasp a piece of burning metal in order to show that "her hands were ready for the hardest labor."[14]

Missionaries have probably made things sound worse than they were. Yet this climate of passive feminine obedience, pushed to its ultimate among the Tswana, was hardly better among other ethnic groups, especially the Yao or the Shona of eastern Africa, where sexual mores made woman an object both submissive to and trained to please men.[15] Only one conclusion is possible: Although it might vary greatly from society to society, the fate of the African peasant woman was not an enviable one. This is likely the reason that women in rural areas readily accepted polygamy, which allowed them to organize and divide labor among co-wives.

Was women's burden heavier or lighter before colonization? Despite many case studies, it is hard to arrive at an opinion, given the lack of direct information from the distant past. Tradition says little on the subject and may embroider the memory of times "before the whites came." Travelers' tales, hardly eloquent regarding precolonial rural areas, also say little. The most detailed information, still weighted with much prejudice about women's role, comes from the earliest missionaries or colonial military personnel who arrived when change had already begun to accelerate, on the eve of or at the beginning of the European invasion.

Gender and the Hierarchy of Work

The lot of rural women has always been hard. Whatever the ecology of the region or its dominant religion, animist or Muslim, rural society had the same broad outlines almost everywhere. The basis of agrarian social organization was gender division of labor—assigning to men labors requiring strength, such as warfare, the building and rebuilding of houses and cellars (except among the Tswana), hunting and fishing (but among the Bete of Côte d'Ivoire, fishing was a subsistence activity of women only), and politics[16] and to women subsistence activity and child rearing. Women had many obligations but also a few prerogatives and a certain autonomy. Most of the time they worked, ate, and amused themselves in a group. Women and young children lived apart from the world of men, who worked and ate meals prepared for them by the women separately.

Organization by gender was visible not only in the way in which tasks were divided but in the standards according to which each sex was evaluated and evaluated itself. A woman's value and status depended first on her fertility and second on her cooperativeness, initiative, and ability to work. A man was judged in terms of his courage and even capacity for aggression, his ability with words, and his physical prowess. The major distinction was that men made the rules whereas women had power only over themselves. Conversation between men and women was rare, and polygamy did not encourage it. The couple's relationship consisted mainly of spending the night together and intercourse. Male supremacy was omnipresent, even in matrilineal societies, where transmission of the family's line and goods was *by* women but not *for* women.

Matrilineal theory and practice did not alter women's everyday tasks. At best they helped balance the division of responsibilities between the sexes and created more hierarchy within the community of women. Older women, the husband's mother in particular, gained particular authority because of their role in transmission. Their power was recognized when they reached menopause, which excluded them from the reproductive cycle. They exerted this power over their daughters-in-law, their younger co-wives, and, of course, slave women, who might also be co-wives. The result was that older women reproduced, within the community of women, the same hierarchical relations that governed relationships between elders and their many dependents—younger people, women, and slaves. They organized and supervised work done mainly by younger people and servant women. In essence, this was work done *in their stead* and not *for* them but for the lineage head. This form of organization occurred at all levels, from the basic family unit to the state.

In hierarchical societies, where a political structure including an aristocracy coexisted with a kinship system, things were more complex. Here women's economic roles varied with their husbands' social positions. Some aristocratic women worked little or not at all. Early in this century, the Germans suggested to the Bamum King Njoya that he should make use of his wives. He responded by having them make weavings to supply the shop he had opened, but they continued to depend materially upon him.[17] The main task of women of the aristocracy, like that of older women in purely kinship-based societies, was supervising the work of their dependents and slaves. In central Africa's aristocratic societies of Rwanda and Burundi, where a ruling class of herding Tutsi dominated a lower class of Hutu farmers, Tutsi noblewomen supervised the Hutu's work, and Hutu women worked hard at agricultural subsistence while the labor of their husbands in their fields or at war was monopolized by the aristocracy. Yet a Hutu man, despite his miserable position, remained no less a patriarch within his own family, where his wife had to kneel to offer him beer.[18]

Another extreme example was the state of Garenganze, which was organized at the end of the nineteenth century in Katanga (today Shaba, in southern Zaire) by a Nyamwezi slave trader named Msiri. His state was composed of several autonomous groups among whom he had personal representatives—wives and other kin of both sexes. This allowed him to contract diplomatic marriages with various noblewomen from surrounding areas or between women of his family and local Yeke or Swahili chiefs under his authority. These women gave him their loyalty and efficiency and became powerful civil servants. Beyond revenues from ivory and the slave trade, the state's economy depended on tribute paid in foodstuffs. This ensured the subsistence of Msiri's warriors and caravans, especially when they were staying in the capital. The capital was a group of forty-two villages with about 25,000 inhabitants. Msiri's wives administered a vast semiurban complex with the authority he delegated them. Large farms were cultivated by slave women, the main workforce. During critical periods in the agricultural cycle these women were joined by teams of men directly supervised by men. Thus the permanent inhabitants of the capital were mostly women. The frequent movements of caravans and warriors offered them much sexual opportunity, and the reported frequency of polygamy and divorce implies the relative emancipation of the dominant class of women.[19]

But Msiri's system merely extended what were basic household systems. At all points up and down the social ladder, subsistence was ensured by women, with the most dependent ones working the hardest. As a rule, the smaller the social grouping, the more women who had to work. Only aristocratic societies could allow the development of a female hierarchy based on age and status. The chief's princesses or women of the court, where there was one, made the other women work, but such women remained a tiny minority.

From Production to Reproduction: The Role of Marriage

These subsistence societies, with their mediocre or nonexistent surpluses threatened (except in rain-forest areas) by the vagaries of rainfall, were based on food production. This was generally the job of the women in a family, but that might depend on their number. No individual, male or female, can work more than five acres a year with a hoe. More women meant more land worked, and this gives women intrinsic value as instruments of both production and reproduction. More women meant more children and greater numbers of kin. Girl children would become producers in turn; men would attract wives who would expand the circle and the group's social impact while expanding its productive force.

If women were at once employed and despised in production, they were valued, even glorified, in reproduction.[20] Today it is said that African women are defined by the three S's: silence, sacrifice, and service. In Benin, women were referred to as "the enclosure of another man's compound" or "the in-laws' horse." The rich man was not one who accumulated wealth or lands; land was a sacred gift of the gods, inalienable, and the only rights to it were for its use. In earlier African societies, where land was seldom scarce, the concept of landownership was meaningless. Accumulating wealth derived from production meant little as well—ultimately, such wealth meant owning a hoe, and almost anyone could own one. What mattered was the ability to work land and the control of enough hands to do so. Women and the children they guaranteed constituted real wealth, just as cattle did in pastoral societies. Ownership of women was ordinarily reserved for men, who were permitted to acquire wives by bride-price. The more animals, the more wives and the more children—which made one wealthy.

In contrast to the dowry, a contribution made by the prospective bride's family, the bride-price is paid by the *groom's* family to the family of the bride-to-be for their loss of the double wealth in work and children that she represents. This practice, though transformed, corrupted, and in some areas forbidden by governments, remains deeply rooted in African society. That it was indeed a question of *compensation* was underscored among the Wolof, where goods received as bride-price were used immediately to procure a wife for one of the brothers of the woman being given up—that is, to replace her.[21]

In rural societies, the infrequent use of money was reserved for long-distance trade, controlled by chiefs and rulers; it was marital alliances that controlled these societies' economic, social, and even political balance. Agreements were made by those responsible for the group—elders, family heads, and kin chiefs—between families whose alliance was sought or even whose alliances were due to or dependent on other people. The bridegroom gave goods, utilitarian or prestigious: cattle, copper bracelets, cloth. That cattle were so often given under these agreements is significant: The family giving the woman could become wealthier at the same time as the family receiving her. The prospective groom, usually young, did not own enough to provide these goods himself. For this he depended on his lineage head. Sometimes, especially in southern central Africa or in rain-forest areas such as that of the Igbo (southeastern Nigeria), the bulk of his contribution was made in labor. He joined his in-laws by agreeing to take part in various tasks, and this could be part or all of his debt. A bridegroom was sometimes reduced almost to servitude by his future mother-in-law.[22]

The woman was mainly expected to be a good childbearer. Whereas in the western Sahel unmarried pregnant women encountered strong disapproval and were even chased out of the village,[23] in Ogooué-Maritime, Gabon, a young woman had to prove her fertility by becoming pregnant before marriage. If the child was male, the future husband's family took care of it and awaited the arrival of a daughter before ratifying the marriage by paying the bride-price. Only then had the young woman proven her "high quality."[24] This indicates that though the birth of a daughter (a guarantee of continuity of the labor force) may not have been prized, it was not a dishonor. Even recently, the father of a well-off family in Accra who had just had twin girls was congratulated by relatives: "So now you are rich!"[25]

If the wife left the conjugal home for one reason or another and returned to her own family, the family had to give back the gifts received. The contract was broken, and the family recovered the force represented by the woman, often to use it for another engagement. Wives (especially in matrilineal areas, where their rights were better protected) would not hesitate to return home, perhaps only for brief periods, whereupon their families would be prepared to renegotiate for them.[26] Husbands, in contrast, rarely sent their wives back; doing so was unlikely to lead to recovery of the bride-price. A husband could, however, complain to his in-laws about his wife's services and enlist their help in getting her back on course.

There are some exceptions to all this. Thus, for example, the peoples, few but diverse, of the Niger plateau practiced wife swapping. The first British observers, shocked by a practice so far from conventional Western models, saw only an absence of decency, morality, and propriety. To them, these peoples were "so to speak, a cultural cul-de-sac characterized by a series of interesting archaic traits ranging from widespread complete nudity to certain utterly unique marriage" practices.[27] In fact, their exchanges were governed by strict and complex rules. The wife, who had to be a virgin for her first marriage, had to contract several more marriages thereafter, on the condition that she live with only one husband at a time. As for the husband, he was required to offer his wife to his brothers and his sisters' husbands and allowed access to his brothers' wives. Of course, such marriages included the payment of bride-prices to the wives' families. It was sometimes assumed that the wife would have a special relationship with a lover—himself married, the notion of bachelorhood being nonexistent—on the condition that, once accepted by the husband, he pay the husband a ritual compensation. The lover owed the woman protection, even more than her husband did. Children generally went to the first husband, who gave them to their fathers in exchange for payment. The system was expensive, and the richer the man the more he could participate. Such a man developed his "clientele," with the lover and his wives becoming his dependents in the same way as the other husbands and brothers of his wives. Without going this far, many central African societies considered the woman a commodity that the husband could offer to honor a visitor—a blood brother or kinship ally. This practice existed in Buganda, but the young woman still had to be a virgin when she first married.[28]

Marriage was an economic, social, and political affair. Negotiations were conducted by the elders, who alone held bargaining power and control of the group's wealth. Still, this was not, properly speaking, trading any more than dowry was in the West, especially because payment could have more a symbolic than a real value. Still, we shall see that in these exchanges a woman was really a commodity to be used. Marriage, which was both a social and a political commitment, became completely mercenary only with the rise of the market economy.[29]

2

Slave Women

The marriage pattern described earlier applied to free women, but some societies also captured women from other tribes or bought slaves for marriage.

Slaves, Marriage, and Social Hierarchy

Wife capture or purchase was widespread in the ancient kinship-based societies of what is today southern Côte d'Ivoire. These groups (the Ani, the Guro, the Alladian, and others), ranging in size from several thousand to several tens of thousands, lived in the forest or on its edges and along the coastal lagoons. From at least as early as the nineteenth century they had high mortality rates that threatened their survival and their productive capacity. The genealogies of the dominant lineages reveal that succession was often a problem because of a lack of survivors. Seeking slave women through force or purchase was considered worthwhile both to increase reproductive capacity (although it did not always do so) and, especially in matrilineal societies, to strengthen the father's line—the children of a female slave belonging without question to the father's family. Slave mothers, in contrast to free women, were permitted neither to leave nor to have extramarital relations. Similar customs have long prevailed in some of the small kinship-based societies of central Nigeria (the Cross River Basin area), where as late as the 1930s the Obubra were observed to capture children and purchase slaves. The pretext of paying bride-price for early marriages kept anyone from being prosecuted for purchasing slaves. In 1944, the price of a girl was about £30 (compared with £25 for a boy). The children came from large, poor families in nearby districts, and the custom was encouraged by the traditional authorities, who saw it as a means of fighting a decline in population due to labor migration and a defense against the frequent instability of marriages involving free women in that matrilineal society.[1] Other forest societies (the Igbo, for example) took slaves as well but forbade marriage between free

men and slave women,[2] a luxury that they could probably afford because of
their steady population growth.

Sahelian ranked societies were hostile to mixed marriages. There a slave
was at most a concubine. Besides, slaves produced fewer children than free
women because of their servile status. Slaves were denied family life and
treated as objects—strong disincentives to reproduce. Infanticide and aban-
donment of children were more common among slave women than among
others.[3] Thus they were sought after less for their reproductive abilities than
for their productive capacity.

Most slave women—wives or not—were important as laborers in the
fields. Pawning a child to repay a debt or settle some past departure from
right behavior was common practice. Little girls were particular targets because they were subordinate in their own kin groups and their households
would suffer less from losing them and because they promised more work
for the family receiving them. If the little girl's kin group failed to redeem
her she ultimately became the source of a new line of dependents or slaves
for her new protector.

Islamic West Africa, extremely hierarchical, had several categories of slave
women—in Soninke country (now Mali), everything from the chief's servant
women to common slaves. The former were relatively integrated into leading
families, had certain privileges, and were used more for domestic work such as
spinning, caring for children, water bearing, or storytelling. As in the emirates
of northern Nigeria, they were almost the only slaves who could be emancipated and regain all the social and political prerogatives of a free person. This
treatment was normally accorded concubines who had provided children to
the master. But origin's indelible stain was rarely forgotten and was kept more
or less secret. Even now it is repellent to a free man to think of marrying his
daughter to a person of slave origin. In the past, the marriage of a free woman
and a slave man was unusual but not forbidden. Baba of Karo, born in 1890 in
the emirates of northern Nigeria, indicated that in this event the children were
born free because they had "sucked the milk of a free woman."[4]

Women were less often sold or given as gifts or killed than men for two
reasons: their worth as workers and their necessary role in reproducing the
slave "stock." But even if the slave woman was given to a slave man, she was
not properly speaking "married," because the man had no paternity rights
unless he had the means to purchase her and their children. This was a rarity
because the price was high—almost the entire agricultural production of all
the active persons of both sexes in the family. Normally, increase in females
belonged to their owners, just as with animals. Slaves' children in Senufoland
were normally inalienable. They were circumcised at twelve or thirteen at
the master's expense and became privileged slaves (*worono*), sometimes very
closely connected to the family. According to the Hausa, "the slave man is a
stallion,"[5] and his children "follow the milk side."[6]

The master or his dependents could have intercourse with slave women. Similarly, the young free man who was entrusted to a privileged slave to be taught how to work would receive his sexual initiation at the same time with his host's daughters or wives, and if the slave were to surprise the young man with one of these women, he had the right only to strike him with his fist symbolically.[7] A woman's slave status was commonly handed down from generation to generation in varying ways according to the society. Memory was longer in matrilineal societies, where a woman passed on her status to her daughters, than in patrilineal societies. In the latter, descent was traced through the free man who had bought his slave wife.

In these societies, free young women in well-to-do families lived surrounded by slaves. As Baba of Karo described it, her mother was a secluded wife raised by a slave nurse. Each man in her family possessed at least twenty slaves, and buying a female one cost two males.

There were more slave women in Africa than men, but attributing this to the supposed preponderance of males taken in the Atlantic slave trade may be mistaken. A recent study seems to show that the ratio of men to women was more balanced than has been assumed, because labor on American plantations was essentially the same for all slaves, at least as late as the eighteenth century.[8] Even where cultivation mainly depended on men, as among the Hausa, the wealthiest families might own several hundred slaves, almost all used in the fields regardless of their gender.

Slave Women in Central Africa

In the nineteenth century, central and south-central Africa especially experienced unprecedented growth in the slave trade with the Indian Ocean in exchange for increasingly sought-after firearms and Western manufactured products imported by Arab and Swahili traders. Insecurity caused by slave raids was even greater here than in the Sahel, where Baba of Karo described pillagers attacking women and girls first, with the despoiled husband owing high ransoms for them if he could find them. In the case Baba of Karo describes, the man paid 400,000 cowries for a woman, 400,000 for each of three children, and 400,000 for a child in the womb. Baba does not specify the price paid for the ten slaves taken at the same time or even if they were recovered.[9]

Prey to aggressive slave trading, people in these areas also began to use slaves much more intensively themselves. Men began taking slave wives. Among the Bemba of what is now Tanzania and southern Zaire, matrilineal beliefs and low bride-prices explain the relative marital mobility of free women. Early colonial judges' reluctance to approve the emancipation of women in the region whose "excessive freedoms" had to be repressed is instructive: "recently Chief Mporokoso, after touring his villages, told me that the women of the country were growing out of hand, and that the results were becoming apparent in a decrease in the birthrate. The character of the Wemba woman must be borne in mind. . . . Always notably independent—more or less a shrew—and prone to unfaithfulness. . . ."[10] Using slaves as wives meant stability because the women could not be taken back, since no bride-price had been paid for her. The vagaries of their status caused them to be sold in times of need and made them veritable walking hoes, with each protector getting the most from them every time.

Bwanika, for example, was sold and married ten times between 1886 and 1911. Her tribulation had three phases. The first was under Msiri, a great trafficker in slaves who died in 1891. The second was in a period of turbulence and insecurity in which male protection was an absolute necessity, and the final phase came after the Christian mission took her in. Born in the early 1870s in Luba country, she was sold into slavery by her father, a man with twelve wives who was required to pay his in-laws three slaves to marry a deceased wife's younger sister and could come up with only two. In adding her to make three, he promised to come back for her, but he never found the money to do so. Bwanika was sold again, this time for a package of cannon powder. Traded from man to man several times because she was too young to serve as a wife and to work in the fields, she ended up in the capital city, Bunkeya, as the wife of a slave trader who kept her for himself (apparently because she was beautiful). Msiri's death threw the empire into disarray and left the capital in ruins. Bwanika's master fled to Kazembe, where the chief, Mukoka, managed to acquire her, only to sell her himself to a band of slave traders from the western coast. Bwanika escaped and married a man who worked as a mason for missionaries settling on the banks of Lake Mweru, but he too sold her to Arab traders, this time from the east coast.

Escaping again, Bwanika took refuge with an old civil servant from Msiri's government who had converted and entered the service of the mission. He bought her for the price of a gun and then married her. She became the trusted assistant of a missionary's wife and worked making pottery and raising chickens until she could buy her freedom by repurchasing the gun. The author of this account, a missionary, noted the change in the couple's relationship from that point on. As a free woman, Bwanika went to the fields at her husband's side rather than behind him and ate at the same time he did. "They sat and chatted together on the veranda of their house, and speaking of each other to outsiders there was the tone of deference and respect formerly lacking."[11]

Bwanika must have been a woman of remarkable energy and intelligence. Yet suffering from her slave status for more than twenty years, immersed in her environment, adhering to its customs, she did not recognize herself—and was not recognized—as free until she had bought her freedom herself. This was common for the era and region, according to a number of missionary and police accounts and reports of the British judiciary from the beginning of the twentieth century.

The most disturbing case was that of a woman who repeatedly sought permission from the British authorities to pay a price for herself that no one was asking her to pay. Her case was exceptional, because what emerges from several slave women's stories collected during that time by missionaries is the great extent to which networks of neighbors and kin spread word about women, despite the turbulence of events. Thus in the corridor from Lake Nyasa to Lake Tanganyika (central-eastern Africa) we know that women were brought back to their homes, despite breaks in their lives caused by their having been sold or taken prisoner and then running away, sometimes across sixty miles or more. Because they were traded at least as often as cows, ivory, and guns, they had value, and very few were willing to let them escape.

Narwimba, Chisi, and Meli were three women taken young from their families. They had many masters and husbands before ending up at the mission. Each was finally found by her first protector and went to end her days with him voluntarily, so intense was her need to remain part their society of origin. Once home, they picked up the agricultural and domestic tasks that had always been their lot, permanently submissive (despite the energy with which they had fought adversity) in a kind of social conformism not untinged with fatalism. In such hard times, young men who were uprooted could find other paths open to them. New opportunities for work within the colonial world were theirs. Quite simply, they felt group pressure less because they had the power to found new lineages, albeit inferior ones. Women were denied even that modest freedom; slaves or not, they always belonged to someone—their lineage, their husband, or their master.

We see this clearly in the life of Narwimba, who was born in the midnineteenth century to a family of chiefs. Her noble birth did not spare her the common fate of women from her region. Her life, marked by extremes, began in the normal way of a chief's daughter. She was married to a man to whom she gave six children, one of whom survived. Widowed when still young, she became the wife of her husband's nephew Mirambo. Decades later, he became one of the main slave-trading chiefs in the area. She again had six children, of whom two survived. Mirambo grew less interested in her as she grew older (she was about forty), and she came to be among the captives of a neighboring chief, who tried unsuccessfully to sell her. After making the rounds several times from man to man she was given back to Mirambo without her children, who remained in slavery. As an old, neglected woman, her social status became more and more delicate, and she could only marry her daughter to a slave. She managed with great difficulty to keep her granddaughter from being pawned to Mirambo as compensation for a peasant dispute. In despair, she took refuge in her natal village, where she was only barely tolerated because she had no man able to clear a field for her to cultivate. This was why she eventually came to the mission to finish out her life.

Chisi, born around 1870, had an even harder life. Captured as a slave with her elder sister when she was just a child, she was sold several times and passed from man to man as Swahili caravans passed through Nanwanga country. She escaped and was hidden and taken in by a chief who gave her to an adoptive father who eventually married her. Mistreated by his other wives, she refused to follow the family when it sought protection with a nearby chief. Of course, she had to leave her children behind, but she managed to get them back again later. On her ex-husband's death, she married a peddler. His frequent absences allowed her to live more independently but were also a hardship because she had no protector. At one point she was penalized with a heavy fine and had no other recourse than to seek protection within her second husband's family. She spent her last days between the mission and one or the other of her children.

Meli belonged to the generation following Chisi's. At five she was captured during a raid by Bemba for revenge against his father, a petty local chief. Taken as a slave with a group of women who abandoned all the children when they managed to flee, she embarked on the hard life of a young female domestic slave. She was finally sold to a Swahili elephant-hunter for four pieces of ivory. Resold several times for ivory or cloth, she went from caravan to caravan. At about ten she was freed by whites and brought to the mission. A passing woman, hearing her name, made contact with the men in her kinship group. Married at the turn of the century by the missionaries (who received her bride-price), she was baptized in 1910; eventually she anchored twice over into her society of origin when she was recognized by her paternal family and adopted by her husband's family. Yet the latter meant to profit from this and applied customary law with the result that, on the death of her husband, she was successively married to two of her relatives. The second one, polygamous, lived with her for over ten years before her death.[12]

Was Every Woman a Slave?

In practice, the distinction between the duties of a free woman and those of a slave was tenuous—to the point that almost all the first travelers, missionaries, and explorers referred to slaves as male. "True slavery"—servile work and lack of inheritance rights—was a male condition. Deprived of free ancestors, free wives, and children and thus unable to father a lineage, neither the manhood nor the adulthood of male slaves was recognized. They could even be required to perform female tasks such as carrying water. A slave man was an individual made to do a job that a woman would normally do. There is no clearer way to describe the condition of women, slave or free, at the dawn of colonization.

A slave woman's status was usually defined as "domestic." She was more a member of the family or at least more able to become a member because of a certain ambiguity in the different tasks she was called upon to perform. For this reason, her position was far less difficult socially than the male slave's. Among the Nuer,[13] a free man asserted his superiority and independence by keeping a certain distance between his real needs and his role as master of production. For example, he controlled cattle, but women milked them. This allowed him to retain his prestige. Because of their function as providers of foodstuffs, women mediated between a man and his animals, between man and nature, and between a man's social dignity and his physical needs.

Whatever has been written about them in the past, African women's condition was hard in the nineteenth century, perhaps even harder than it had been before because of the political and social disturbances inside Africa. In the west, the dwindling Atlantic slave trade led to a glut of slaves, who were then used across the western Sudan by the new conquerors' armies. These slaves also served there as tools of production in a slave system of cloth weaving and in the forest areas for the harvest of new export products, mainly palm kernels. A parallel shift occurred in eastern Africa with the Arab and Swahili plantations encouraged by the Zanzibari sultans—clove plantations on the islands of Zanzibar and Pemba and sugarcane plantations on the coasts of what are now Kenya and Tanzania. On the eve of colonial conquest at the turn of the century, slaves probably were at least a quarter of the population of western Africa and even more numerous in eastern and central Africa. There is no doubt that female slaves were numerous if not in the majority, although the earliest Western observers showed little interest in them and traditional African sources remained silent on them. In fact, the trend until very recently has been to minimize the slavery of "domestic captives" in comparison with international slave trading.[14]

Women and Slavery in South Africa

Slavery among women in South Africa is a special case. Almost all the women slaves there were foreign, imported by Dutch slave traders in the eighteenth century to compensate for the very small number of colonial women—a few hundred at most, almost entirely stemming from migrations prior to 1717, the wives and daughters of the French Huguenots or girls from the Rotterdam orphanages. Of the 65,000 slaves brought to the Cape before 1815, about 15,000 were women from the eastern coast, Madagascar, the Indonesian islands, and India.[15] Their servile condition lasted into the nineteenth century as natural increase may have doubled their numbers.

Dutch-owned port slaves rented their "wives" to sailors in port briefly or for what were called "six-week contracts," the duration of a sailor's stopover. The result was a great many "colored" children. Since white women were few, white soldiers and sailors in need of wives had no choice. They first purchased the freedom of a slave, preferably a "colored" woman, and then married her. This was the primary way in which women were freed; alternatively, wet-nurses were often freed when they had grown old. A genealogical survey conducted by the Institute of History of the University of the Western Cape revealed that many of today's nationalist Afrikaners have ancestors of color dating to the first generations of the conquest.[16] Marriage criteria for slaves were precise: of 191 slaves married by German descendants through the mideighteenth century, almost 60 percent were girls born in the Cape, preferably "colored" (of white fathers and Asian mothers) or "mulatto" (of white fathers and black mothers). These women also spoke Dutch. One-fourth were Indonesian, and 15 percent were Bengali. Only 3 percent of men married Malagasy or black women, but black women were the largest percentage of imported female slaves, almost 19 percent. Only very exceptionally did a white woman free a male slave in order to marry him. Only two such cases were noted, and both concerned "colored" persons, born of black and white couples: the document of the period uses the pejorative term "half-bred."

For the white settlers, according to the Roman law introduced by the Dutch, a child inherited servile status from the mother.[17] The effect of this was far-reaching—a slave's owner could simply "rent" a concubine to another settler or offer a slave to a passing guest, though in the early nineteenth century any children resulting belonged to the mother's owner. These abuses ended only in 1827 when Steyntje, an Asian-white woman of great beauty and no less courage, after more than a decade of perseverance and humiliation before the courts, won her own freedom and that of the various children she had had, each with a different father, depending on her "rent" or sale.[18]

These practices spread polygamy-like uses among white settlers. There are only a few examples, however, of relations between a white woman and a slave man. One case was denounced by a local church in 1717 and another later in the eighteenth century. A report from the 1770s mentions, in the case of a dubious birth to a settler's daughter who had had relations with a domestic slave, that she was hurriedly married and the father sold far away. The tale is silent about the fate of the child.

Until emancipation in 1834, it was common to keep light-skinned women enslaved for use by settlers' wives as reliable maids. These women considered it beneath them to go with black men or bear a child with darker skin. There is an odd text from 1822 defining them as a privileged "class" and "race" of slaves named "Afrikanders."[19] Female slaves and their children were so sought after that they were far less often freed than men. The ratio among slaves, which until this point had been well over 150 men for every 100 women, reversed after 1808. To put it bluntly, few settlers would have thought to free their own daughters. Keeping women enslaved meant preservation of the stock of slaves their descendents would produce.

The attitude toward free African women (only 118 in 1765) was especially harsh. The city council forbade them that year to wear colored silks, embroidered hats, curls, or even earrings. They were to wear cotton fabrics only and, if they were married or Christian, black silk for church. A generation later, in 1798, when mixed marriages were on the rise, Dutch ladies so thoroughly rejected a young quadroon woman engaged to be married (whose grandmother had been a slave) that she eventually emigrated.

As was true of free people in the rest of sub-Saharan Africa, Cape white families had far more children than slaves did, according to population studies done using the core of French Huguenots present. It was white families' custom to marry off girls very young, between fourteen and eighteen, and to use black wet-nurses to feed white ladies' young; therefore white women did not benefit from this natural form of contraception. Between 1700 and 1808, the average number of children born to white women increased from 5.3 to 6.2. Slave fertility was low for many reasons ranging from malnutrition to venereal disease, abortion, and infanticide (probably more common than the historical record indicates). Marriage between slaves was not officially recognized: where two slaves lived together, the woman at best could be called *wiifie*, which meant simply "female." Thus slaves developed their own ceremonies, which were not recognized by white settlers, especially with the spread of Islam in the nineteenth century. In 1823 the colony began to recognize Christian marriages only, but eight years later, only three "legal" marriages in a population of 35,000 slaves were noted.

This long history of slavery clearly shows why South Africa is the African society in which the various peoples mixed the most, to white nationalists' great chagrin.

3

Women and Trade
at the Dawn of
Colonialism

Women's situations varied by region and society. Whereas the central and eastern areas of Africa were particularly ravaged by the slave trade, in West Africa some women enjoyed a certain autonomy because, in addition to working the land, they produced handicrafts and sold goods in the market. Such was the case in the Yoruba area, which had long been urban, and in areas with cash crops such as palm oil in what is now Benin or kola nuts in Bete country (now western Côte d'Ivoire) and Ghana.

Trade: A Tradition Rooted in West Africa

In the old kingdom of Abomey (or Danxhomé, now Benin), trading in cash crops began in the midnineteenth century. The cultivation of oil palms on royal plantations was the job of slaves. Gathering the palm nuts was perilous, requiring a climb up the high, smooth tree trunk with a rope about one's waist holding one to the tree, and was a male task. Little is known about regional trade in the nineteenth century, but there is some information for the early twentieth, when, after slavery had been abolished, large intact plantations remained.[1] Production and harvest were organized by village. Women participated in the production of palm oil and in transporting it by caravan to Western companies' coastal warehouses. According to a system that had probably begun the century before, husband and wife each had their own property and kept separate accounts, and the woman bought what she produced on credit from her husband and reimbursed him after making a profit from it. Polygamy made holding property in common unworkable, as each wife supported her own children. Because of this and because they had more control of marketing the product than men, women entered the money economy early on. It would be interesting, though difficult, to ascertain what changes in gender relations occurred between the time of the slave trade (a market controlled by men) and the time when products began to be traded. We do know that women gained a certain economic independence that colonialism tended to diminish.

The Sherbro women of Sierra Leone[2] and the Lebu women of Senegal fished and then bought the catch from their husbands to dry and sell in the market. They and others more directly in contact with European traders, such as the female vendors of fresh produce in nineteenth-century Sierra Leone, profited from the opportunities available to them, but the Sierra Leonean women were out of their element three times over—as wives in their husbands' lineages, as members of ethnic minorities, and as market women functioning in an urban environment. All this made them more open than men to change; they were quick to ask for British protection in the port of Freetown (a crown colony since 1807) to facilitate their trading there but were nonetheless able to maintain their identity through membership in the *bundu* (women's secret society).[3]

A form of female enterprise less connected to the Western market was the sale of kola nuts in Bete country.[4] The kola nut comes from a tree that grows in the forest of the Ghanaian interior and is still very popular with the Muslim groups of the Sahelo-Sudanese savanna.[5] The product of a complementary region, from its origins it implied interregional trade that contributed to the wealth of the Asante empire. What we know of kola trading from the early colonial period leads us to suppose that the women involved, who were the active traders, had developed a system similar to the one described for palm nuts. Bete women traded with the caravans and combined prospecting for gold in the mines of the Volta Valley with transport of their produce. For this they recruited almost entirely female staffs of younger dependents and slaves as porters. Women today tell of the exploits of their grandmothers or great-grandmothers, themselves under the direction of their own mothers, crisscrossing the country at the end of the nineteenth century. Such a level of organization suggests significant profits, even if they were not monetary and depended largely on the interdependence of female relatives. Guro women had a trading system that was less dependent on men's production because their crop was cotton and they retained control of it when they gave it to men to weave. Guro businesswomen enjoyed relative independence and real prestige, although oral tradition has scarcely recorded it. They were eliminated by more modern technology, especially in the 1920s, when they lacked the means to purchase trucks.

Among the Yoruba, women helped their husbands in the fields in planting, harvesting, and transporting the crops, but most of their time was spent trading foodstuffs and producing their diverse handicrafts. Different areas specialized in different products, for example, palm oil and palm soap, millet beer, baskets, pottery, and cotton and indigo-dyed cloth. In contrast to the Guro women, women here wove cotton grown by men. Men's only handicraft was metalwork (ironwork or jewelry). Women also traded salt along the Benue River and were organized into guilds that covered activities from production to marketing. Thanks to their relatively considerable profits, women enjoyed influence in negotiating bride-prices, which they used to favor sons who would later ensure their subsistence. But here again, their autonomy was limited by the household head's control. He divided agricultural and handicraft tasks among all his dependents, men and women, and decided how what they produced would be used.

Trade: A Forgotten Tradition in East Africa?

Until recently, these autonomous female market activities were thought to exist only in West Africa. Women in the rest of Africa were thought to be more limited in type of work and more male-dominated. In central Africa, men accumulated wealth through cattle and trading in connection with hunting or warfare (ivory or slaves). There is nothing, however, to suggest that women's condition in the past was like what they endured later under colonialism. Colonial reports emphasize Kikuyu women's submissiveness and dedication to subsistence tasks, but recent research suggests that colonialism, especially harsh in these regions, may have stripped women of prerogatives they once held.[6] Trade, including peddling, was very early taken over by the Indians who came to Kenya after the British. Before, however, trading was essentially handled by Kikuyu women, if only because they could travel more safely than men, who were always suspected of being on the warpath. Their being women and their production of domestic handicrafts would have in some sense protected them. This was indeed long-distance trade; the journey from Kikuyu territory to the Kamba country of the Masai took several days. The Masai particularly liked the flour, beans, corn, sugarcane, honey, tobacco, and pottery that the Kikuyu women traded them for skins, copper wire, beads, goats, sheep, and cows. Despite male privilege in matters of cattle, nothing could be done with the cattle women had traded for without their agreement. This trading required periodic peace negotiations, and in these instances women served as go-betweens and their presence was a sign of peace.[7] These travelers were experienced women who had to have at least one initiated daughter before beginning their tour of duty. They ranked among the elders, and their status as menopausal women was the source of their authority.

Locally, women also controlled trade in foodstuffs; men could not use the food reserves stored in special granary huts without their agreement.

Women also played a special role in distributing meals and beer to young men working under their elders to clear land for women to cultivate. Among the Kikuyu, the Gondo of Uganda,[8] and the Tonga of Zambia, millet beer was an important payment for work. A household's prestige depended on its ability to gather the most laborers possible. Lineage heads could thus display their wealth and contract better marriages for their descendants.

Here it becomes difficult to separate men's world, based on prestige, and women's world, based on subsistence. Men's power clearly resided in their central role as organizers of labor, but women were vital to that organization. Did women control resources, or were they themselves resources controlled by men? In the event of famine, for example, or simply poverty, a wife might certainly, in an extended polygamous group, be reluctant to open her food stores to the entire household. Among the Tonga, where women were protected by the option of matrilineality, a widow did not have to go back to her husband's family; she could establish her own household and be recognized as head of it by her brothers. Generally, however, women's authority over food, which they had to make sure was sufficient to last from one harvest to the next, was mitigated by their limited autonomy. Among the Beti of Cameroon, where men's agricultural labor was significant, relatively equal workloads were not reflected in equal division of the harvest. Instead, the husband divided up shares that he distributed to each wife and her dependents for their subsistence—even peanuts, which were grown only by women. He stored the rest with his favorite wife but retained exclusive use of it for ceremonies and marriage payments.

Among the Hausa and on the Benue plateau, women had no access to food stores, and in times of hardship or the absence of a husband their only recourse was to grow more food.[9] In any case, co-wives' explicit task was to contribute to making their husband rich. On his death, their contributions in children, agricultural work, and handicrafts were the subject of public discussion and entered into the account as their distribution as wives to this or that brother or relative of the deceased was decided. Women were important enough to the group's survival that their role was not limited to that of mere objects, but their inferiority was no less evident.

4

Powerful Women

Women's reproduction and agricultural work are often linked in fertility-based religions. Procreation not only gives women prestige but through rituals fosters their identification with vital forces. Because power was defined in Africa by authority not over inert, limited factors of production such as land but over one's own life and that of others, women's power depended greatly on their children. A woman without descendants was by definition powerless. In contrast to men, whose identity came from their ancestors, women's identity came from their children. Among the Nuer and elsewhere, a man was called "son of so-and-so," while a married woman was called "mother of so-and-so" (normally her first-born son). Even today, the value given to procreative capacity and motherhood (female identity linked to fertility) is probably a major difference between concepts of women's emancipation in Africa and the West. In Western society to associate woman with nature in opposition to man, the symbol of culture, is to condemn her to inferiority.[1]

Women Chiefs

In subsistence societies, where women's role was key to survival, men certainly asserted their political supremacy, but women always retained opportunities for power. These were particularly clear in matrilineal societies. Offices and wealth were passed down through the female line. Men's power was more diffuse as a result; life was organized around the mother. The maternal line was so important that real power sometimes fell into the hands of women. Even among the Tonga, where women's submission was great, there were women chiefs who had power over very limited units of production in this area of widely scattered homes. One woman chief, Namulizili, divorced her husband and established her own village around 1900 with five of her unmarried children, a married daughter and her husband, a sister and her son, another sister and her husband, her daughter and daughter's husband,

34

and six other groups. In this instance, kinship ties among the women were clearly the important ones. Another divorced woman, Civi, kept her gardens after the divorce and created a new village with her sons, brothers, and other male relatives and various daughters- and sons-in-law. There was also Matimba, who ruled the fifteen adults and six children who worked her fifteen acres.[2]

There is a tradition of women chiefs in West Africa, in pre-German central Cameroon, among the Flup of Casamance in southern Senegal,[3] and among the Mende and Sherbro of Sierra Leone. In 1787, a Sherbro woman, Queen Yamacouba, ceded the first lot of the peninsula to a British company.[4] Two other women a century later signed similar treaties in 1889.[5] Mammy Yoko (ca. 1849–1906) led a veritable Mende confederation that became the most powerful group in the Sierra Leonean interior. After divorcing her first husband and being widowed by her second, she married a powerful chief from the western part of the country. As his first wife she played an active political role, and on his death in 1878 she took over from him. Renowned for both her charm and her diplomacy, she built a vast confederation with her neighbors and allied herself with the British against her main enemies. When the protectorate was established, her loyalty won her power through the British system of indirect rule. She supposedly committed suicide to avoid the ravages of aging.[6]

Between 1914 and 1970, of the 146 chiefs recognized in Sierra Leone ten were women, despite an ancient, fairly patrilineal tradition.[7] But the explanation is perhaps not kind to women, because, properly speaking, there were no chiefs, except war chiefs, before colonization. The British, in imposing indirect rule, created a network of salaried civil servants, so-called warrant chiefs, out of whole cloth and charged them with transmitting colonial demands. Sherbro and Mende women had relatively high status in traditional society, the connections they forged during their initiation into the *bundu* lasted all their lives, and finally, the new positions being offered by the British may have seemed suspect to the traditional elders. This may be why several women chiefs were able to take advantage of this opportunity following in the footsteps of Mammy Yoko, to achieve more political and economic power.

The Baule of what is now Côte d'Ivoire displayed remarkably egalitarian sharing between the sexes.[8] Baule women had the right as members of their lineages to inherit the position of lineage elder, village chief, or even chief of a cluster of villages. According to tradition, the privilege dated back to the groups' founder, Queen Pokou, of Asante origin, who in the eighteenth century brought with her a stream of political refugees.[9] Women chiefs were fewer than men but not uncommon before colonization, which was in fact hostile to them. In order to become chiefs women had to remain within their maternal line. Marriage was patrilocal, so women sometimes maintained dual residence or divorced their husbands. Divorce was easy in this region, where the bride-price was very low and may even have been abandoned in precolonial times. Thus some women of the families from which chiefs were commonly selected could not marry. Even today, one meets women who decline to marry or whose families refuse marriage for them because they are heirs to a power that today is clearly only potential.

For the opposite reason, until the nineteenth century Ganda princesses (in eastern Africa) were forbidden to marry. In a strictly patrilineal society, the *kabaka* (ruler) was wary of female royal blood that might lead to a male heir from the women's line. Princesses could not marry, much less have children. It was Mutesa I, in the nineteenth century, who felt it more politic to engage the princesses in matrimonial alliances with his primary chiefs in order to consolidate his power. Before him, when a princess was pregnant she had to abort or kill the newborn if she was unable to give it to a commoner. Adoption was common and made easier by the common practice of moving children, mainly sons and daughters of sisters, from adult to adult. The practice drew a moralizing cry from missionaries, who understood nothing of women's social structures. Each woman took turns staying in the compound to watch over the brood and prepare meals for the others who had gone to work the fields. But missionaries pitied these poor children with so many mothers that they were "no longer even capable of recognizing their own!"[10]

In matrilineal societies like the Baule, the dominant woman might be surrounded by dependents from her mother's line and her own slaves, even if she was married. If so, she also benefited from her daughters' work. To her husband she owed respect but not allegiance. As for him, he generally lived with his father's family, through which he could not inherit. On his father's death, he often returned to his mother's family, where he lived with or brought back his sisters, from whom he would later inherit. Here, the marriage was a temporary association of productive and reproductive interests. Both parties had a right to the children and goods produced: men wove the cotton grown by women, women helped husbands grow their yams. Women's profit-making activity was an economic guarantee of their enjoying real power.

Ironically, a woman wielded this power only once she had lost the source of her original power, her ability to procreate. More than the others, young women had to bow both before female elders and before men regardless of their age. Menopause made women asexual, in a sense, and thus similar to men. It allowed their claim to and exercise of power. A woman's turning point was often marked, as among the Nuer, by her youngest son's initiation, which for her meant the end of the first cycle of her life. For example, Igbo women (Nigeria) ruled among themselves by an assembly or *ikporo-ani* of related women, widowed, married, or not. The woman married the longest presided. They heard spousal disputes, adultery cases, and quarrels between groups and villages. Exogamous practices gave the privileged role of arbiter to married women outside their village and their lineage, which sometimes meant that women could prevent war. The existence of this body meant women could also impose rules on their village's political authorities.

Queen Mothers and Female Regents

The important role played by queen mothers or their equivalents, whether in a matrilineal or patrilineal society, is the clear sign of real female power. Women also sometimes acted as regents in Africa, as they did elsewhere.

Powerful Women in Tropical Africa

Around 1563–1570, in the Kanuri kingdom of Bornu, Queen Aisa Kili Ngirmaramma, the deceased ruler's daughter, ensured royal continuity until the famous Idriss Alaoma was able to take power. Celebrated by local oral tradition, her story was later excised by Arab historians, who apparently lacked interest in recognizing a preeminent female head of state.[11] In Ethiopia, the most famous of these women of power was Empress Menetewab (ca. 1720–1770). On her husband's death in 1730 she became regent in her son's name. He continued to give her the reins of power after he came of age. When he died, she returned to the regency in her grandson's name but was ousted by a new candidate to the emperor's throne. It was at this point that she met the traveler James Bruce, who encouraged her to write her story.[12] Akengbuwa, *olu* (chief) of the Itsekiri kingdom (in Yoruba country), had a half-sister, Queen Dola, who established a state council in order to ensure continuity of the regime. She died in 1848 without having achieved political unity.[13]

We find a central African regent in Mamochisane, daughter of Sebitwane, king and founder of the Kololo people in what is now Zambia. Captured during a war against the Lozi and returned to her father around 1840, she was then charged by him with administering its central province after he conquered the Lozi. Before his death he named her his successor, but she soon abdicated in favor of her brother Sekeletu, supposedly so that she could marry and devote herself to her family.[14] But this kind of reasoning certainly has a distinctly Western ring. Was it not rather a way for the male heir to seize the power that had at first escaped him?

In the court of King Agonglo (Danxhomé), according to the little we know about her, Na Wanjile supported the faction hostile to him and would have assassinated him in 1797 because he was about to convert to Christianity to expand his ability to trade with the Portuguese. When the plot failed, she was burned alive with the other conspirators, and it was the dead king's son, Adandozan, who was crowned.[15]

Among some western Igbo groups, the *omu* or queen of the village or a group of villages had a position similar to that of the *obi* or king. Yet she was not his mother or his wife or even his female relative; she was the female equivalent of male power in the community, known for her wealth, intelligence, and character. She directed the women's association, the *ikporo-ani*.[16] Like the king, she wore a headdress denoting her power, in some areas a white felt hat or a red cap. She chose her own aides and counselors and gave them titles similar to those of their male counterparts.

Market women, active in business, ruled the marketplaces, set rates, settled lawsuits, and even imposed fines. They took care of widows and performed the rituals necessary for the proper functioning of the market as a whole. It is not surprising that at first, British indirect rule gave some women a certain opportunity to increase their influence. Okwei d'Onitsha, known as Omu Okwei (1872–1943), used her business relationships with foreign companies in this way and had her husband named a member of the native court. She became a kind of foreign affairs minister for her people to European businessmen and colonial officers.[17]

Among the Oyo, in Yoruba country, power centered around the *alafin* (king) whose administration was a complex hierarchy of priests, lineage heads, military chiefs, and judges. It was run by his many wives or "palace ladies." Called "his eyes and ears," they also functioned as spies using their business opportunities. There were eight women priests and eight women dignitaries. First among them was the king's "official mother" or *iya oba*. She was not his biological mother, who was more or less kept away from power once he was selected.[18] The *iya kere* was the guardian of the treasury, which included the royal insignia; she crowned the king, and she could refuse him access to the insignia if she deemed him undeserving of them. Another important woman was the *iyalagbon* or mother of the crown prince, who ran part of the capital city. The *yamode* had a more religious function, protecting the king's spiritual health, guarding the royal tombs, and interceding between the king and the spirits of his ancestors. The king's deference to her was such that he called her *baba* (father) and knelt to greet her.

Among the Edo, we find Yoruba women in the same eminent role. Traditionally, three years after the *alafin's* accession, he gave his mother the title of *iyoba*. She then went to rule at Uselu and sat with four of the king's main counselors in the royal executive council. This custom was apparently introduced in 1506 by the *oba* Esigie, who appreciated his mother Idah's wise political and military counsel. The custom was abandoned in 1889 under British pressure[19] but was revived after independence, and the first secondary school for girls in the city of Benin was named for Queen Idah.

Among the Hausa, many political-origin myths give queens and some princesses an important role. For example, in Zazzau, the *magajiya* (king's mother) ran the palace and attended the king's audiences. This title appears elsewhere and later, usually given to an elder daughter. According to the *Chronicle of Abuja*,[20] female dignitaries date far back in time, but their functions apparently ceased with Fula conquest in the nineteenth century, which reinforced the seclusion of women, especially those of high rank. The *Chronicle of Kano* mentions no such women.

We also know about the important role played by the mother of the Ganda *kabaka*. Muganzirwazza (ca. 1817–1882), one of the *kabaka* Suna II's 148 wives, saw her son, Mutesa, among the youngest of the sixty-one competitors eligible, named to succeed his father, surely with her help, and contributed to his successful reign. Though he needed her help less and less, she retained an eminent position throughout his term.[21]

Queen mothers were also important, as we shall see, among the Asante and the Fon.

Powerful Women in Southern Africa

In southern Africa, women seem to have played a relatively important political and military role among the Zulu, where we know that Shaka, their formidable ruler at the beginning of the nineteenth century, had both girls and boys in his military forces. (Psychoanalysis might explain this in terms of the castrating conduct of his mother, Nandi, and his alleged homosexual tendencies.) The first Shaka princess clearly to play a political role was Mnkabayi, the elder sister of Senzangakhona, who was the father of three Zulu kings. In the 1780s she was regent during her brother's childhood and became an intimate of one of his wives, Nandi. She took Nandi's side when Senzangakhona repudiated her and supported the accession of Nandi's son Shaka when his father died around 1815. It is said that she blamed Shaka for having his mother killed in 1827 and joined in a plot to ensure that one of his half-brothers, Dingane, acceded to the throne. She died very old in about 1835.[22]

Brother-sister rivalries, with the male winning out, also appear in the case of Mawa (ca. 1770–1848), Senzangakhona's youngest sister. Until 1840 she held the position of chief of a military encampment and town. In that year, on Dingane's death, she became involved in rivalries for succession among the lineage's princes. Her favorite candidate was executed in 1842, and she fled at the head of several thousand Zulus. She later achieved recognition by the British of her installation at Natal.

A woman serving as leader of a *mfecane* (or *difaqane*), as the great migratory movements of expansionist Zulu factions in this period were called, was not unusual. In what are now Orange and KwaZulu/Natal, Queen Mma Ntatise or Mmanthatisi (ca. 1781–ca. 1836), the first wife of chief Mokotjo (who died in 1817), took the regency for her son, then thirteen, at the expense of her brother-in-law, who would normally have inherited this power. She asserted the independence of a group of Tlokwa against other Sotho peoples of southern Africa and declared war on Moshweshwe, the Zulu chief who founded Lesotho.[23] As early as the 1820s she led the Tlokwa west, beginning the first great Sotho and Tswana migrations. Around 1822 her energetic leadership and the relentless resistance of another woman, Meseile, apparently kept her marchers from being routed and turned the tide in their struggle, known as the Battle of the Pots because of the many kitchen utensils destroyed in the Tlokwa camp. Known for her intelligence and quick action, she was able several years later to repel an unexpected attack in Lesotho despite the absence of most of her troops, fighting elsewhere; behind her few available men she lined up an army of women and children with hoe handles instead of spears and straw mats for shields.[24]

It is said that Mma Ntatise's reputation earned her the right to maintain a prominent role during the reign of her son, who assumed power at about nineteen. Without literally heading the army, she incontestably directed several of its campaigns. Her unusual character as a female chief inspired tales about her destructive powers. A derivative of her name, "mantatee," became the generic name for the bands of thieves that ravaged the area between the Orange and Vaal Rivers, making her responsible for all the robberies committed in the region. She eventually moved to the north of Lesotho, where her son gave her responsibility for Tlokwa affairs.[25] She died after 1835 and was buried in Joalaboholo, a site that has become sacred to Tlokwa who gather there annually to commemorate their history.[26]

Nyamazana, who may have been the great chief Zwangendaba's niece, followed him north to what is now Zimbabwe around 1819. Later she led a group of migrating Ngoni because, according to oral tradition, he had refused to allow her to accompany him beyond the Zambezi River in 1835. She and her troops apparently lived by pillaging in Shona country until the Ndebele led by Mzilikazi arrived there. He took over from her and married her around 1839—a logical action by a conquering chief to ensure the submission of a woman. She is said to have died at the turn of the century.[27]

Eminent Women of Ancient Times

In Africa as elsewhere, collective memory records only a few women, about whom very little is known. All over Africa they have left their mark by being great war chiefs or resisting white domination in political or religious terms.

Nzinga of Angola

Queen Nzinga Mbande (or Mbundu), "heroine of the slave trade," resisted the Portuguese advance on the southern Kongo kingdom for many years. She was born around 1582, apparently the daughter of a slave and the king (*mbande a ngola*) of Ndongo. (The Portuguese turned his title into the name of the country, "Angola," which despite its intense resistance became a colony in 1575.) Nzinga began her political activism under her elder half-brother's reign. He was an active slave trader in northwestern Angola, ready to submit to the Portuguese. One brilliant action, probably embellished by the Portuguese chroniclers and the Italian Capuchin monks, our primary sources,[28] made her famous forever. After many years of war, she was sent to Luanda in 1622 to discuss peace terms with the Portuguese governor there. As a necessary preliminary (which for a time won her Portuguese goodwill), she had herself baptized Dona Ana de Souza. In exchange for temporarily opening her country to missionaries and especially to the Portuguese slave trade, she managed to have a fortress that was located too close to her lands evacuated and certain chiefs whom the Portuguese had made their vassals freed. Most important, she won the recognition of her dominion over Ndongo. The freed chiefs were probably little inclined to accept this, given the double handicap of her precarious political ascendancy and her being a woman.

The next year, disappointed with the Portuguese, she broke with Christianity and allied herself with the Jaga, a marginal group of warriors recently arrived from the southern Kwanza River plateaus. The legend of her cannibalism perpetuated by the Portuguese arose partly from the mores of these new allies and partly from her having had her brother's son poisoned (as he had her own son some years earlier). It is said that she won the Jaga over by guaranteeing freedom for slaves who managed to escape Portuguese hands. Whether or not this is true, she did categorically refuse to return fugitive slaves. She also had the Portuguese army infiltrated by her men to incite the Africans within it to desert. Thus she was able to increase her forces and obtain sufficient arms to plunge the country into open warfare. The Portuguese, aided by perhaps most of the Mbundu, managed to rout her, and this led to a protracted guerrilla war. The Jaga's mobile tactics helped to foil many Portuguese attempts to capture her dead or alive. In 1629 she consolidated her power as a *tembanza* (a Jaga title reserved for powerful women) by arranging a ritual marriage (actually a political alliance) with the Jaga's chief, the *kasanje*.[29] In the early 1630s, she finally managed to establish sovereignty over the neighboring kingdom of Matamba to the east, where there was a useful ancient lost tradition of female chiefs. She broke with the Jaga when they allied themselves in their turn with the Portuguese and came to pillage her capital.

Both warrior and diplomat, Nzinga was also a great slave trader. Her apparent political twists and turns came from her need to establish her authority over external allies, since she lacked kinship support and especially men's legitimacy. She controlled the back-country slave-trading networks so thoroughly that the Portuguese had to resume fighting. So she bargained with the Dutch—who occupied Luanda from 1641 to 1648—to weaken her enemies, only giving in partially in 1656 by signing a treaty like the one she had signed almost thirty-two years earlier. She resumed slave trading with the Portuguese in Matamba, which had become the main regional slave marketplace. Once again she accepted missionaries, who gave her, in her final six years, the chance to shore up what remained of her power.

The Dutch soldier who was briefly her attaché described her in this male, warrior world as a chief who dressed like a man and maintained a harem of young men garbed as women acting as her "wives." Toward the end of her life, she returned to Christianity. At eighty-plus she is said to have sent a deputation to the pope and celebrated the event on the spot, finally dressed as woman—but an Amazon! She died a Christian death in 1663 at over eighty-two, still independent. As successor she had chosen one of her sisters, also Catholic and recently purchased from the Portuguese for 130 slaves after eleven years in captivity. Yet Catholicism survived them only a short while in Matamba.[30]

Nzinga's story, relatively well known to Europeans, is very similar to what was probably the first African novel written in French, published in 1769. Highly embellished and combining fact with fiction, it incited the indignation and fascination of readers throughout the Enlightenment, apparently even inspiring the Marquis de Sade.[31]

Queen Amina of Zaria

The legendary history of the sixteenth-century Queen Amina (or Aminatu) of Zazzau (which she renamed Zaria after her sister) is much like that of Nzinga. Doubt was later cast on her existence, probably because Muslims were hardly prepared to accord such importance to a woman, but tradition reports that the emergence of the Hausa city-states was preceded by a dynasty of seventeen queens. It is known, in any case, that during her reign (in the early fifteenth century, according to the *Chronicle of Kano,* but more probably around 1536 to 1573 or even later than 1576), Amina was a great conqueror. Helped by her sister Zaria and heading an army of 20,000 men, she tried to annex several surrounding cities up to Nupe and ruled Kano and Katsina, at the cost of thirty-four years of almost uninterrupted warfare. The ruins of several castles in the region still bear her name, and the idea of surrounding Hausa cities with fortifications is attributed to her even though many seem to date to the twelfth century. It is said that she never married but chose a lover in every conquered city. Expanding her kingdom made it the trading center for all of southern Hausa country spanning the traditional east-to-west trans-Saharan axis and guaranteeing Zaria's prosperity. Amina brought unheard-of wealth to the country; one description cites a tribute payment of forty eunuchs and 10,000 kola nuts. The modern state of Nigeria has enshrined her by erecting a statue to her, spear in hand on a horse, in the center of Lagos.

The Queen Mother of the Asante

The last woman to lead resistance to British conquest was one who assumed the role of queen mother of the Asante in what is now Ghana. In 1896 the true queen mother was deported to the Seychelles with her son Prempeh I and the one male relative who remained loyal to her—Nana Afrane Kuma, chief of Edweso province, some ten miles from the capital, Kumasi. Nana Afrane Kuma's mother, Yaa Asantewa, unlike her son, refused to be subjugated. From 1900 on, under the British protectorate established in 1897, she inspired and led a group of malcontents demanding Prempeh's return. She assembled 40,000 to 50,000 Asante for a siege of Kumasi that lasted two months. The British had to mobilize 1,400 men with the latest in weapons to break the siege, and it took them three more months and 1,200 more men to capture the queen and the last of her loyalists. She is said to have spit in the face of the British officer who arrested her. She died in exile in 1921 at the age of fifty to sixty.

Kimpa Vita, Beatrice of the Congo

Other women used the weapon of religion. For example, tradition keeps alive the memory of the Mujaji, a seventeenth-to-nineteenth-century female dynasty of Sotho country, some of whose members were venerated as rainmakers.[32] The best known of the religious resisters was Kimpa Vita, born around 1682 and known by her Christian name as Beatrice of the Congo. An astonishing mix of Christianity and messianism, she was not the first of her kind in the Kongo kingdom. Often in decadent periods such as the eighteenth century, prophecies called for the restoration of political order through religious regeneration. Christian conversion in the region began as early as the sixteenth century, and missionaries (Portuguese Jesuits or Italian Capuchins) had remained active. Before Kimpa Vita there had been other visionaries: one woman reported having had a vision of the Virgin Mary, who was upset at what had become of the Kongo; a young man predicted chastisement by God if the capital São Salvador was not restored and inhabited anew by the Manicongo; and an old woman, Ma-Futa, declared that she possessed the head of Christ disfigured by human wrongdoing (in reality a stone from the River Ambriz).[33]

Dona Beatrice, of noble birth, felt the ruin of her country, and while she was living in the capital around 1704, Saint Anthony appeared to her during an illness. He was a Portuguese saint particularly revered by local settlers, and he appeared to Dona Beatrice as an African—one of her own brothers. For two years she preached a kind of anti-Catholic Christianity rooted in Kongo cultural symbolism. She created an African church inspired by biblical teachings—Kongo was the holy land, Christ was born in São Salvador, the fathers of Christianity were Africans. Although she had a certain black consciousness, she taught that blacks and whites were of different natures: whites were born of soapstone, blacks of a fig tree. She incited blacks therefore to find their roots by rejecting European clothing and values. This also explains her support of polygamy. Like many mystics, she renounced earthly pleasures, and many of her followers believed that like Christ she would die on a Friday and be reborn the following Sunday. Pushing the analogy even further, she gave birth around 1706 to a son proclaiming that she was a virgin. Beautiful and inspired, she predicted the day of the Last Judgment. Under pressure from missionaries, the ruler of the Kongo kingdom, Pedro IV, who needed Portuguese support against a competitor, had her burned as a heretic that same year with her baby at the age of about twenty-four. But the Antonianist church that she created gave rise to a brief renaissance of the Kongo kingdom during the years that followed. As a kind of local Joan of Arc, she inspired a play by the Ivoirian writer Bernard Dadié.[34]

Nehanda (ca. 1862–1898) of Shona country in what was once Mutapa or Monomotapa (now in Zimbabwe) was born to a highly respected family and early on acquired great religious renown (as a witch, say European texts). When in 1890 Cecil Rhodes began his conquest of the country in the name of the British South African Company, Nehanda opposed the massive land expropriations and preached resistance, along with Kagubi, another great *féticheur* (priest) of the period. The first war of liberation or *chimurenga* began in 1896 under the direction of Mkwati, the greatest of the religious chiefs preaching unity between Shona and Ndebele. Nehanda became a formidable war chief from her Musaka fortress, although she only occasionally joined in the fighting herself. She had the whites spied on and targeted their farms, mines, and factories (trading posts) for attack. Her troops were well organized, and she forbade pillage except for weapons. Guns and projectiles were assembled with telegraph wire and broken glass. The British finally captured her and Kagubi in December 1897. She was executed some months later in a place kept secret so that it would not become a site of worship.[35]

In the twentieth century, notably during World War I, these women founders of churches increased as always during times of crisis.

5

Female Identity and Culture

We know almost nothing about precolonial women's world. Did they have a certain way of looking at themselves and their place in this world? What forms did their affectivity and their sexuality take? What were their sexual beliefs and practices? The only observers who approached women in the early colonial period were missionaries and the occasional civil servant—teacher or health worker. The early missionaries' views were distorted by their prejudices; they found the traditional African kinship model and methods of upbringing incompatible with Christianity and emphasized women's apparent "licentiousness and shamelessness . . . and the atrocious disorderliness into which [each woman] throws herself entirely."[1] This image draws heavily on the Christian and particularly Catholic notion of woman as demoniacal seductress and tool of Satan. Colonial novels also abused the stereotypically agreeable African woman by portraying her as impure and hedonistic. The error of these judgments became clear only with the arrival of the first anthropologists, and by this time profound shifts had occurred in African societies.

Individual accounts passed down by women themselves are rare. They exist, as we have seen, especially among slave women, less subject to patriarchal ideology than others, but even these tend to celebrate the great deeds of male heroes. This is the case with the *Tanbasire* of the Soninke (Mali), a group of songs composed and sung by women that dates to the late fifteenth or early sixteenth century. It was said to be the work of the six sisters of Hammadi, immortalizing their brother. These first women composers' names have not come down to us, and with one exception the rare women cited in the songs are identified only as female relatives or descendants of male heroes.[2]

Women and Religion

Women's fertility is at the core of African beliefs, but women's role in ancestral religions appears to have been small. Perhaps it is simply that not enough research has been done, most anthropologists being male. For matrilineal societies, the sacredness of women's fertility was an absolute, but men tended to minimize it in religious belief and practice. The Kikuyu, for example, believed in a tyrannical matriarchy passed down by the female descendants of an original couple, against whom men one fine day revolted after having impregnated all the women, making it impossible for them to respond. This tale is based on the conviction that power and motherhood are incompatible. Another tale says that women are forbidden to own cattle because women are cruel and arrogant. Similar myths exist in many societies. Among the Nuer, warfare is said to have begun when men killed the mother of cows and buffalo.[3]

Among the Bete of Côte d'Ivoire it is said that men and women originally lived apart, each sex in its own village. They were constantly at war, and women, the better warriors, always won. The men therefore turned to trickery to defeat their adversaries. Appealing to women's insatiable love of food, they put palm kernels in their path and waited until the women set their weapons down to pick them up. Then they killed Zikai, female authority incarnate, and appropriated both weapons and women. The vanquished women were taken to the men's village to become their wives, but marriage only paved the way for endless secret vengeance in the form of adultery, witchcraft, and tricks of all kinds.[4] The Nnobi (Nigerian Igbo) believed that the first man married a goddess, Idemili, who demanded that she and her daughter Edo be worshipped throughout the land even though she had been domesticated by men.[5] The Ganda's origin myth says that Nambi came from afar to marry Kintu on his clan lands. She took pity on him because he lived alone and gave up her freedom and the beauty she had enjoyed in Gulu (the kingdom of Heaven) to work hard and watch over his household.[6]

All these myths justify the patrilocal principle and woman's subjugation. Deep belief in both the sacred powers of the forces of fertility (primarily woman's arena) and in men's exercise of political and religious power is widespread.

Men have often worshipped female figures, for indeed, they have feared a power that they needed but could not control: the ability to give life, to obtain good harvests for the community through fertility rituals, to intervene as mediators in the complex marriage strategies and social relations among neighboring groups and villages, to defuse quarrels, and to heal. It was generally women who were felt to be endowed with religious power as healers. Every illness was held to have a human cause: vengeance, the desire to harm (connected with witchcraft), or ancestral punishment for some misdeed. For healing to be effective, either the one who cast the spell or the patient had to expiate the sin.

In societies that were very oppressive to women, such as the Tswana, witchcraft was women's only escape, whether they were practicing or receiving it. Women were both maleficent and necessary in every ritual of propitiation that used dance and song to attract rain. Women were also called on in cases of poisoning clearly linked to witchcraft, but they most often served as occasional oracles prophesying rain, war, or famine. Men, priests or rainmakers, retained the day-to-day management of religion.

Yet women had a power of intercession that could change the course of events: women could make peace. This indispensable yet dangerous power, so similar to witchcraft, was feared by men, who created appropriate rituals and techniques both to avail themselves of it and to protect themselves from it.[7] Hence the famous "masquerades" of the western Yoruba, developed since the beginning of the nineteenth century as the *gelede*. These dances and songs about masks celebrate the most revered mask of all, that of Great Mother Inyanla, surrounded by numerous dancers and singers most particularly portraying market women and foreign Muslim traders.[8] Yet among the Yoruba, worship of the earth divinity, the goddess Onile, is above all practiced by women, although most agricultural work is done by men.[9]

Among the great female religious figures the best-known was Beatrice of the Congo. Another eighteenth-century woman, Fumaria, is said to have had visions of the Virgin Mary and the gift of perceiving and punishing sin. Similar figures appear during the nineteenth century—no mere coincidence in this crisis period of colonial conquest. Some women, such as Nehanda, played an important religious role less in their own names than as intermediaries for an inspired leader. Thus in nineteenth-century South Africa the Xhosa medium Nongqause translated the visions of the prophet to whom she was attached, her uncle Mhlakaza. These young female diviners were quite common in a region traumatized by the brutal advances of colonialism. In 1856 Nongqause began communicating with her ancestors, who told her what her people had to do to save themselves: sacrifice animals and destroy the harvest to calm the gods' anger and see the whites thrown into the sea. Following this prescription, the Xhosa killed 150,000 cows and burned their fields and their stores of food in one vast ten-month-long movement of purification in the expectation that this would deliver them of the whites for a thousand years. Those who survived the resulting famine had no choice but to enter into the white settlers' service. Nongqause was arrested by the British, who judged her a victim of her uncle and imprisoned her along with another young prophetess, Nonkosi. She was later allowed to return to the eastern province of the Cape, where she died forgotten sometime between 1898 and 1905.[10]

The ability to transmit the spirits' wishes allowed a number of inspired twentieth-century women to create their own churches, drawing in large part on ancestral beliefs. These movements were especially successful during times of crisis. In contrast to men such as Matswa in Congo or Kimbangu in Zaire, they rarely engendered religions that survived them. Their power was no doubt inseparable from their personal abilities as healers of women and children. One of the most remarkable of these women was Maï (Mother) Chaza, a charismatic figure in Zimbabwe and probably the equal of the great Shona religious leaders. Of Methodist background, she was believed to have died and risen again, in the course of which experience she received the gift of healing. Like Moses, she received rules for living (forbidding alcohol and sex) along with the secrets of traditional medicine on a mountaintop. Her mission was to treat women who were possessed, sterile, or blind. By the end of the 1950s she seems to have had some 70,000 worshippers. She created "God's villages," especially near Harare and Bulawayo, where treatments mainly consisted of exorcism and public confessions. A man succeeded her on her death and effected extraordinary cures in her name.[11]

Alice Lenshina Mulenga, born in 1924, founded her own church in Northern Rhodesia (today Zambia). Raised by Scots Presbyterians, she started a purification movement based on witchcraft following a vision in 1953. She also is said to have died and been resurrected. She promised health and a better life to her disciples if they would abandon their magical practices. She created a holy village, "New Zion," and declared it politically and religiously autonomous. Between 1957 and 1963 her followers increased from 50,000 to 100,000. Excommunicated at last, she created the Lumpa (Bemba for "supreme") church, which took a stand in favor of the African National Congress. Although she participated in the anticolonialist struggle, she refused to recognize the independent state and denied access to her village to Kenneth Kaunda, who had become the first president of independent Zambia in 1964. The resulting repression was intense; her followers were expelled from Zambia in 1970, and from that point on Mulenga spent most of her time in prison. She was released only in 1975, three years before she died.[12]

Marie Dahonon Lalou founded Deima, an offshoot of the Harris movement (introduced to Côte d'Ivoire in 1913) based on the curative virtues of water supposedly provided by snakes, in 1940. She claimed the privileges of a priest to some degree, imposing celibacy and sexual abstinence on the woman leading the faith, but the cult eventually died with her.

Aoko, a member of the Legion of Mary faith (inspired by Catholicism) that appeared in 1963 and spread like wildfire among the Luo of Tanzania and Kenya (assembling some 90,000 followers around 1970), launched an antiwitchcraft crusade in her own name. She sought the support of a local Luo prophet, who baptized her, and then, crucifix and rosary in hand, she began her fight against evil spirits and illnesses. She particularly addressed women, inciting them to resist pressure from their husband's kin. But once again, the movement soon foundered.

These women of faith, although clearly part of an ancient tradition, were reacting to missionary teachings, and they remained fewer and less influential than their male counterparts. Women are healers and witches in many regions today, but this role seems traditionally to have been held especially by men. Male witches often have more power than female ones, at least more than in the Christian West, so quick to identify woman with the devil (probably because of different cultural attitudes regarding sexuality).

As we approach modern times women tend to lose their power in religion as elsewhere. The apostolic movements established in the early 1930s in eastern Rhodesia (now Zimbabwe) by two prophets, John Masowe and John Maranke, clearly illustrate this. In both cases, weekly worship (*kerek*) is the main ritual. The preacher, always a man, has the main role, but women, as a choir, can interrupt the preaching by songs or chants that comment on it, correct it, and sometimes even guide it. In Maranke's faith some especially gifted women, often but not always the wives of important men, are named choir leaders (*maharikro*) and enjoy the prerogatives and sometimes the gifts of prophetesses. In Masowe's faith a special group of "sisters," the master's spiritual wives and more or less doomed to celibacy, have a certain importance.[13] Yet in both religions their roles are secondary. Here as in other areas, women have more prestige than power.

Women in the City

The religious life of women before colonialism is so little known that we have to look at very modern phenomena such as the messianic movements of this century for hints of what might have inspired women in the past. Yet we know even less about city-dwelling women than about peasant ones.

Women Warriors of Dahomey

The women warriors of the Dahomeyan king's army may have begun in the seventeenth century as a company of elephant hunters who were gradually called into service more and more toward the end of the eighteenth century to remedy a shortage of male soldiers or at least to reinforce them in case of threatened attack. In the first half of the nineteenth century, during Ghezo's reign, these women became a unit of elite regulars. Recruiting them at a barely pubescent age was not easy. Although it was an honor to become one of the "king's women," it seems that families did not jump at the chance. In the beginning, girls of noble birth were exempt. Enrollment began as a punishment for delinquent or willful females, war captives, and wives convicted of adultery. At that point volunteering was encouraged, but when it did not suffice, recruiters came through villages requiring lots to be drawn.

Ghezo organized systematic recruitment every three years, and under Glele, who succeeded Ghezo in 1858, it became an annual event. Little by little, the troop structure began to resemble the men's. The most fearsome of these warriors were armed with rifles, and each woman was accompanied by a female munitions assistant. There were also archers, hunters, "razor women," and spies. Clothed like local women and selected according to the local language, they seduced important men to gain secrets that might lead to a victory. Their expeditions took place during the dry season, a good time for campaigns, and produced prisoners for sale as slaves on the transatlantic market. Travelers' estimates of their number vary between 14,000 (in 1845) and 2,000–4,000 (in 1890). In the final moments of Behanzin's resistance to French conquest in 1894 there were only a little over 1,500, and they were massacred in heroic fashion; as an elite corps, they were on the front lines, renowned for their ardor and even ferocity.

When not in combat, the women warriors were housed in the capital, Abomey, unlike the men, who went home to their villages. Women lived in barracks in the royal palaces, which they guarded day and night. They participated in all festivities and were very much a part of the sovereign's official and private life. They went about their daily tasks under the surveillance of female officers and might supplement their daily rations with what they grew in their fields or purchased with the proceeds in their trade in pottery and calabashes. They were not, by the way, warriors for life: after about twenty years, when they could no longer function as soldiers, they returned to civilian status. In the villages one might meet old women warriors who told tales of their heroic days.

Their daily life was organized around physical training for combat. They tailored their bodies and their spirits to this, for example, by dipping their nails (filed to points) in ox urine for more effectiveness in hand-to-hand combat. Every woman warrior had to make a blood pact with her sovereign and drink from a human skull a special potion to prevent her betraying it. Women warriors were in principle celibate and committed to this with a vow—any children they might bear had to disappear immediately after birth. The case of Tata Ajache, a war captive who became queen through marriage around 1857 to King Glele, was an exception.[14]

These women's social condition remained ambiguous; they rejected women's condition but were proud of being women beyond the norm. In attempting to look, act, and sound more virile, their ideal was not to look like men but to surpass them in courage and action. They sought to reverse gender roles:

> *Men, men, stay!*
> *May the men stay!*
> *May they raise corn*
> *And grow palm trees . . .*
> *We go to war.*[15]

This troop of warrior women was unique in ancient Africa; Shaka's female soldiers are not really comparable.

Urban Slave Women and Cultural Hybridization

The largely urban Swahili culture, developed along the Indian Ocean between the twelfth and fifteenth centuries, combined foreign Arab and indigenous Bantu influences. This cultural hybridization can be seen in the language, in which both origins can be detected. This happened over time through cross-cultural contact between Bantu and Arab individuals. In all probability (we lack written sources), almost all the sailors and merchants who settled in the port cities were men, and they put down roots with native women. Who were these women, and where did they come from? Some women were certainly attracted to these new centers of wealth, and many were simply purchased or conquered in the developing slave trade. Domestic, "feminine" terms in the language are generally Bantu in origin and terms for "masculine" business and public affairs Arabic.[16]

Slave women did most of the domestic labor in the capital of the Kuba kingdom in what is now Zaire. Until the nineteenth century, they alone had the right to work the land, which meant that they were in charge of supplying the city with foodstuffs, water, and firewood.[17]

Ultimately, the slaving past explains the high degree of hybridization in urban areas where the confrontation of cultures began earliest, as in South Africa and the Portuguese-speaking countries of Angola and Mozambique.

The Beautiful Creoles: Women with Sense and Spirit

The scarity of women created alliances that were, if not more durable, at least based on something other than a master-slave relationship. From these alliances emerged a privileged class of women, the core of a creolized elite that at certain points played an important role.[18] These were the *signares* of Saint-Louis, the British or Portuguese creoles, and the Afro-Brazilian women of the Gold Coast, Benin, Luanda, and Lourenço Marques (now Maputo). These women learned early on that they could profit from relationships with European traders and settlers. They were often (but not necessarily, particularly in Muslim areas) converts to Christianity, sometimes educated, and always shrewd. They tended to be concubines or courtesans rather than prostitutes. Despite their very small number, they are the women we know the most about. Closest to the Europeans' world, they rubbed shoulders with travelers and sometimes left behind writings and archives of their own. Some of these women were native; many were creole in culture only. It was to the slave traders' advantage to forge personal connections with the chiefs of the interior, their suppliers of human and other merchandise, by marrying their daughters. These women learned the mores of each side well and were clever at exploiting the commercial networks linking them.

Before the colonial period proper, when relations with Africa were monopolized by a few royal trading companies, a whole mythic tradition developed around the *signares,* with their beauty, Western-style clothes, and relative wealth. Their unions with passing slave traders lasted only until the
latter returned to Europe to marry in the only way recognized by their religions and countries.[19] The custom began with the Portuguese; flourishing in
the eighteenth century, the women were known as *nhara* in upper Portuguese Guinea, *senora* in the Gambia, and *signare* in Senegal—all terms derived from the Portuguese word for lady, *senhora.* In fact, it was under Portuguese domination that Senhora Philippa, described as a "Portuguese lady"
in 1634, controlled European access to trade in the port of Rufisque. Another Portuguese woman whose name is unknown enjoyed the same privileges in 1669. In 1685 Senhora Catti, the African widow of a Portuguese
slave trader, became the commercial agent of the ruler (*damel*) of Cayor, the
Wolof kingdom in that region. Another Euro-African, Marie Mar, especially
looked after stranded sailors.[20] The most famous of all was Bibiana Vaz, who
between 1670 and 1680 built a veritable commercial empire between the
Gambia and the Sierra Leone River. She kept Captain de Cacheu, who held
the post there, captive for fourteen months from 1684 to 1685 and briefly
created a kind of métis republic in the region. It is hard to know the true origin of these women, who sometimes played vital roles as cultural brokers;
they owned many slaves, maintained courts and sometimes griots of their
own, and were extremely good at business.

The wealth of the *signares* of Saint-Louis, a trading post established by
the French on the island of the same name at the mouth of the Senegal
River, became significant at the beginning of the eighteenth century, when
these women began to serve as intermediaries and auxiliaries in the river
trade. They were especially useful because the Compagnie du Sénégal theoretically forbade its agents to trade in their own names—thus the women
served as figureheads. It was precisely for this reason that the Compagnie
refused for so many years to recognize its agents' marriages and particularly
the right of their children to inherit. Some *signares* chartered their own
transport ships. They began to own houses on the island and up to several
dozen slaves whom they rented to the Compagnie. Through official agents
(in whose interest it was to associate with the most influential of them), the
women obtained unofficial preferential treatment that undermined official
trading privilege.

The expatriate men were generally older than their wives and greatly affected by a climate that they ill withstood. Most died young and left their
wives to manage their affairs. The process was facilitated by de facto advantages accorded the *signares* by the Compagnie du Sénégal, particularly when
around the middle of the century it rescinded the rule forbidding inheritance
by their sons. This measure formed the basis of enduring creole mercantile

and real-estate fortunes. In 1747 ten of thirteen private properties declared on Gorée Island belonged to people with cross-cultural backgrounds, nine of them women. In 1767 the wealthiest *signare* of Gorée Island, Caty Louette, then associated with a Captain Aussenac, owned twenty-five male and forty-three female slaves. In 1779, of eighteen concessions (grants of use-rights to land) controlled by the French administration eleven were held by *signares.*

We have the most information on the *signares* of Gorée and Saint-Louis, often embellished and romanticized by the European men, mostly French, who associated with them in the eighteenth and nineteenth centuries. It is likely that most of these women were former slaves engaging in what was considered (first by Europeans and finally by their compatriots) a means of social advancement. In the beginning, the highly hierarchical local Wolof, Tukulor, and Peul societies did not allow free girls to compromise themselves as slaves or at best "castes."[21] Many of these women belonged to griot families whose function was to flatter the master to whom they were attached. Orginally black, sometimes purchased and then freed by their masters, who made them their wives, after years of unions of this kind the *signares* became lighter and lighter in color. There is a single mention in the region of a Walo "princess" who apparently married the governor of Gorée in 1758.[22]

It was very much the intelligence and lifestyle of these strong-willed women that won out over the reservations of many, including the Compagnie du Sénégal, whose directors had taken a vary dim view of the inevitable miscegenation. To venture a comparison, Dutch authorities absolutely forbade immigration to the Netherlands by the Indonesian wives of agents of the East India Company, and these wives were commonly abandoned by departing settlers. For the French, who were theoretically required by the Compagnie to remain unmarried and forbidden to bring French wives to Africa, trading and particularly living with native women were also forbidden until the 1730s. Agents going upriver, however, had many opportunities for sexual relations with African women. We find no trace, however, of children of mixed parentage in the interior; they would not have been accepted, and abortion or infanticide were probably commonly practiced.[23]

In the cities, European men began to enter into local marriage, observing its customs but abandoning their wives and usually their children when they returned to Europe whether they had married in church or "in the local fashion." This "local fashion" consisted, among the Wolof, of obtaining prior agreement by the wife's family, giving gifts, and entering into the ritual of marriage. The woman took her husband's name and passed it on to her children even when the man's return to France caused the de facto dissolution of the marriage. It became common for a woman to marry her husband's professional replacement in the Compagnie. Children were baptized by the Compagnie's chaplain or a passing priest and often entered in turn into the service of the Compagnie, contributing to the continuing creolization of Saint-Louis culture. From the mideighteenth to the midnineteenth century a unique Franco-African lifestyle developed in Saint-Louis within the minority merchant upper class, cross-cultural and unsegregated. The *signares'* wealth, their charm and elegance, their jewelry, their receptions, and the balls (or *folgars,* Portuguese for "festivities")[24] they gave set the tone, and the highest officials attended. The Chevalier de Boufflers, the last royal governor of Senegal before the British occupation, became famous for his commercial and amorous alliance with Anne Pépin, reputedly the city's most beautiful *signare* and probably its best businesswoman. The colonization that began with the arrival of Louis Faidherbe (who had fathered a child out of wedlock himself in 1857) caused these practices to be abandoned in favor of simple cohabitation. Métis society became a closed caste and ended up intermarrying, creating more and more obvious inbreeding. Its daughters in particular, Catholics of color, could either find takers among lower-class whites or choose celibacy or Africanization, to the degree to which they were not rejected by a majority Muslim society.

Still, this was the basis of a real Francophilic tradition that continued beyond the end of the slave trade. The Saint-Louis creole milieu produced nineteenth-century businessmen devoted to trading in peanuts and rubber, and their children became lawyers, journalists, and doctors. These descendants, suffering from the social regression that colonial restrictions imposed, by the turn of the century had become the most ardent defenders of a political reformism for the benefit of this nascent bourgeoisie. The same thing took place in the British Gold Coast, where, although the shift itself has been much studied, women's probably comparable role has been less so.

In Luanda, a very Catholic city colonized by the Portuguese early on, creolization began as early as the sixteenth century. Two types of wives existed there, those who had received a Christian education, who more or less led a life of ease (which still meant they could be passed from hand to hand as upper-class concubines), and those who had managed to become businesswomen. The former (a census around the end of the eighteenth century set their number at forty-eight) lived in the residential neighborhoods of the lower city in semiseclusion in beautiful two-story houses and went out only for church—in palanquins, surrounded by slaves in livery and clothed in sumptuous fabrics. Their aristocratic lifestyle required imported luxury items such as cloth and silver for the interiors of their homes and churches and for the embellishment of their tombstones. Their role increased in importance during the eighteenth century, both because they were more sought after in marriage and because their husbands had to go farther and farther from the capital in order to trade. In contrast to what took place in West Africa, the idea of invaders marrying princesses was not rejected by slave-trader chiefs, who saw advantage in it for themselves.[25] One of these women, Dona Ana Joaquima dos Santos e Silva, held real commercial power in the interior during the nineteenth century.[26] Most of the wealthy creole widows, however, lived in the upper city, which was more mixed. The 1777 census counts sixteen "white" women and five "mulattas," reflective more of prestige than skin color, in the parish of Sé. Each woman had more than seventeen slaves, accounting for more than two-thirds of slaves in the neighborhood.[27]

Although hardly any Afro-Brazilian women are mentioned in the literature, male slaves who had been taken to Brazil and then freed returned to the west coast (Benin, Togo, southern Nigeria) from the eighteenth century onward, some of them to become flourishing slave traders themselves. Many of these men must have brought women with them. Were these women only their wives? We also know of a Yoruba woman in Ibadan around the middle of the nineteenth century who ran a farm with 2,000 slaves.[28] Some Yoruba businesswomen achieved eminence, among them Madame Tinubu, who had made her fortune in the slave and tobacco trades with Brazil. Through her wealth and tact she contributed to the return of *oba* Akitoye, who had been exiled when the British established their protectorate over Lagos in 1851. Driven from Lagos, where she had worried the local authorities, Madame Tinubu sought asylum in Abeokuta, where her weapons trade was a powerful help to the Egba in their war against the Dahomeyans during the 1860s. She received the title of *iyalode* (first lady) in thanks.[29]

Autonomy and Subjugation

The women entrepreneurs of the western coastal region, who had long confronted the vicissitudes of trade, enjoyed a certain autonomy. This was manifest above all in their solidarity and even complicity with the world of men, from which they generally lived apart. The vigorous matrons of West Africa, who can today be seen to some extent in other African cities as well, are continually surprising men. They have become strong through their economic power and are transforming the social game.

The rules of this game were once very limiting. Women could escape them only occasionally and in special cases. Among the Igbo of Nigeria, for example, when the survival of the lineage was imperiled by lack of a male heir, a daughter might be turned into a "woman-man" to head the household until a son could take over from her. This move was not readily accepted by the other men of the father's line. Nwajiuba, the daughter of a famous *féticheur*, complained bitterly that witchcraft was being used against her and her mother in an attempt to get rid of them.[30] Substituting a daughter for an absent son was also practiced in other regions whenever population decline threatened descent. Among the Toro of Uganda (a thoroughly patrilineal society), a daughter could inherit her father's herd and rights and have her husband live on her lands without ceding him those rights.[31]

Yet, as a general rule, girls' education was an apprenticeship in subjugation to male power. They were taught from their earliest years never to speak in public, never to speak to a man before being spoken to, never to look a man in the eye (an insolent affront), and to speak to him softly and discreetly unless they were alone together or in a ceremonial situation. Contrary to what might be imagined, this is not limited to Islamic cultures; respectable Hausa and Swahili women are increasingly reticent with strangers, and little Fula girls are trained to these customs from a very young age.[32] These rules are still more strictly observed in central (Zaire, Uganda, Tanzania) and southern Africa, where a convergence of traditional female submission and Christian sexual phobia continues to create havoc.[33] It would be wrong to attribute women's condition entirely to an indigenous past. But it is clear that among peoples as different as the Kikuyu of Kenya, the Haya of Tanzania, the Tswana of southern Africa, and the Zairean women of Kwilu or Kivu, the rules of female submissiveness transmitted from generation to generation continue to weigh heavily, especially in the countryside but, ironically, also within the Westernized city-dwelling bourgeoisie.

PART TWO

*From the Country
to the City*

6

⚸

Rural Women and Colonialism

Whatever their prior status, peasant women's fate worsened under colonial rule, which upset the fragile balance between dependence and autonomy in relations between the sexes in work as at all levels of social organization. The imbalance increased for two reasons: the intensification of cash-crop cultivation (peanuts, coffee, cocoa) and the production of surplus foodstuffs (corn, yams, rice) for sale, which took up part of the cycle of subsistence cultivation, and the collection of these latter for sale by foreign companies, which often destroyed preexisting female networks.

The Twentieth-Century Trend: Cash-Cropping for Men, Subsistence for Women

Female overwork was the common trend. During the early colonial period, the cultivation of new crops (peanuts, cotton, cocoa, coffee, etc.) was imposed on men. Men volunteered for this as soon as they realized that they could make a profit from it and thus were the first to benefit from the money-based economy. To women went the task of ensuring all the rest—growing all the foodstuffs, even more than before. Women also had to help their husbands as needed in keeping up the new plantations. In other words, they worked harder without compensation.

Later on, at first in South Africa, where mining began before the end of the nineteenth century, and then between the World Wars in tropical Africa, men went to work on the railroad and in the mines. Women remained in the countryside and found themselves running their families' farms, and their work increased again. Some women were able to profit from this by learning management and even amassing savings that might allow them to win battles of will with their husbands. But most of the time they remained illiterate and broken by work and watched their fates worsen. Colonial law did not help matters by promoting marital authority—recognizing the family head as the sole owner of goods whose value had been created by women. Protected by colonial officers and missionaries, men were also the first to benefit from the technical innovations they gradually introduced.

Disruption of a Delicate Balance

Among the Sotho (in what is now Lesotho) the plow, harnessed and pulled by oxen, was introduced by missionaries as early as the midnineteenth century. By 1875 there were already nearly 2,800 plows in the country, and there were more than 10,000, or one for every twenty inhabitants, by 1891. The plow became a common tool used mainly by men, women in theory having no access to oxen. It soon became a medium of exchange in marriage payments, allowing husbands to work more land but increasing the workloads of wives, who did everything else including sowing, proportionately. This technical innovation had little influence on the distinction between cash-cropping and subsistence cultivation; the sexual division of labor remained the same regardless of the plant being grown, and sorghum, for example, was eaten as a subsistence food as well as sold to nearby cattle herders. Men's need to help their wives, overwhelmed by work, helped break down the sexual division of labor. As time went on, women began to take over agriculture as a whole. This situation lasted until Boer pressure drove the Sotho onto the least fertile lands and repeated droughts intensified men's migration to the mining centers in the 1880s and 1890s.[1]

The introduction of the plow had similar results a little later among the Tonga. Until this point, matrilineal custom had granted relative autonomy to women, who did most of the field labor. Some women farmers even managed to purchase slaves and acquire cattle for themselves. As in southern Africa, the development of intensive agriculture under the colonial system deprived women of men's help in subsistence agriculture. Thus Adventist missionaries, the first to arrive at the turn of the century, created huge corn farms (on the order of 5,000 acres) that attracted young men. The future mothers-in-law to whom these men had provided work as part of the bride-price thus lost part of their available supply of manual labor. Similarly, among the neighboring Lala, Jehovah's Witnesses introduced tobacco growing, which was reserved for men but caused much extra labor for the women who harvested and dried it. Jesuits brought the plow to the Tonga in 1905 and taught the men to farm using harnessed animals. The early settlers obtained from the colonial authorities the right to force rural men to work for them at least four months a year. The construction of the railroad and then the opening of the Katanga copper mines in the 1920s actually caused an increase in the number of corn plantations, which were needed to supply the laborers concentrated on the job sites. The settlers' ever-increasing demands for cattle led men to enter the monetary economy. Whether they accepted the very low salaries offered them or chose migrant labor, the result was the same: Men helped their wives less and less with the growing of staple foods.[2] World War I aggravated the poverty of the men hired as porters by the British during military operations against the German colonies of Tanganyika, Cameroon, and Togo.

In southern Rhodesia in the 1920s, the demand for foodstuffs was such that white settlers could not keep themselves supplied, and the government began encouraging native production. Africans acquired new technical knowledge by working on white farms. Some went to mission schools, where they learned the use of fertilizers and the horticultural basics. The government offered them easier credit, and they began producing like the settlers. Two hundred light plows, each drawn by two oxen, were by then in use in the area. The wages of farm laborers gradually rose to the level of salaries, labor migration declined, and men went into plantation farming. Up until this point, women's work had certainly increased, but their profits had also increased because they were supplying nearby urban centers with fresh foodstuffs.

Around the 1930s the balance between the sexes was definitively destroyed by the removal of most Africans to newly created Bantustans, which temporarily upset production. The Great Depression had had its effects on the white settlers, and they had begun to worry about such low-cost competition. At the same time, governmental agencies, alarmed at the rate at which the soil was being depleted, imposed crop rotation among corn, peanuts, beans, and sorghum, paying more for corn to men who produced it this way. In doing so they completely ignored the way in which work was divided between women's subsistence agriculture (sorghum and beans) and men's cash-cropping (corn and cotton). This policy ate away at women's land rights. Simultaneously, an antiwoman policy in the cities and in the Bantustans shut women out of the urban markets. As early as 1936, to protect white settlers, the Maize Control Board reserved two-thirds of grain production for them. Rising demand allowed African men who succeeded in being hired as farmhands to attain a certain material ease. In the south, men organized and pooled their technical resources, equipping themselves with wells and hand-carts. In the Bantustans retail selling was forbidden to whites, but women's lack of capital kept them from opening shops or improving their agricultural techniques.

By about 1945 the change was complete, and an agricultural hierarchy had been established. The wealthiest included no women. On the contrary, women were the majority of the poorest, those who worked less than an acre, insufficient even for their own subsistence; at the risk of severe malnutrition, they were still forced to sell part of their production to obtain a little cash. In the early 1950s the wealthiest peasants, monogamous Seventh-Day Adventists, petitioned to be able to have their sons inherit. The matrilineal system was indeed dead, although by the beginning of the 1960s the Adventist core was outnumbered by a rising middle class of planters who held onto polygamy in order to increase their workforce. The bride-price more and more became the price of a woman's labor. When, during a village debate, a missionary suggested that men might work a little more to relieve their wives, he was told that they would die if they had to work like the women.

Ironically, it was among the poor (where traditional customs had survived) that women were least ill-treated. When after 1966 the independent government of Zambia created family farms among the Tonga to relieve the land shortage caused by overpopulation, it was able to achieve the more equal sharing of hard labor between men and women and extension to women of the use of the plow. Organization, accounting, and relations with development organizations were, however, monopolized by men, of whom 50 percent were polygamous in 1980 and only 18 percent monogamous with the intention of staying that way.

In the rest of Zambia, male supremacy was even stronger. The government created a school to train agricultural technicians for the whole country and then increased the number of training centers primarily benefiting men, although women were taught how to raise poultry. It had become common in the event of divorce or the death of a husband for all agriculture materials to be taken by the man or his family. Men's productivity tended to improve and women's to decline among well-to-do farmers because women worked the fields less and less and among the poor because they lacked equipment.[3] Often the only commercial recourse women had was brewing millet beer. Many women were barely aware of their unequal treatment, declaring that they were not exploited and that if they had been they would have divorced. But others reacted to the loss of their traditional land rights by refusing to participate in heavy labor, for example, choosing harvest time to visit their mothers or even emigrating to the city.

Similar processes occurred elsewhere. Even without constraints, export agriculture and the supplying of cities and job sites also became more common, for example, among the Luo of western Kenya. Men began to produce a surplus of salable grains to meet the settlers' demands, using their profits to increase their stock of sheep and goats. Women found themselves excluded even more by a series of food taboos that kept them away from cattle. They were forbidden to eat milk, mutton, rabbit, chicken, eggs—in other words, almost any protein—and this may have had an effect on their health, fertility, and agricultural productivity.[4]

Palm-oil producers on the Nigerian coast (the Ngwa, neighbors of the Igbo) also saw a trade economy shift revenues and some work from women to men. In the nineteenth century, palm-oil preparation meant boiling palm nuts and filtering the oil by hand, apparently by women. Women made a profit from selling the oil and also knew the secrets of extracting it from the palm kernel, which they crushed themselves. By the turn of the century, however, the burden of work on these women was so great that they could no longer meet the needs of expansion, and manual production of palm oil declined. The men developed a simpler process for manufacturing palm oil, replacing the boiling with fermentation. This allowed them to produce more oil, which was less refined, of course, but which Europeans accepted by mixing it with the finer oil produced by women. Men profited and stopped growing yams. Women once again had to increase their subsistence activity by beginning to grow cassava, introduced during World War I. Although easier to grow than yams, cassava called for more preparation to make it edible—even longer when city dwellers began to want it in the form of flour (*gari*). With technical improvements, men began to manufacture and especially to market *gari* in the 1920s. In the 1950s, men controlled all the long-distance trade in the area. They invested most of their profits in bicycles and in wives, to increase production. Once again, women were preferred to machines and used more but paid less for their work.[5]

Women, Forgotten by Colonialism

Generally, the colonial administration ignored women, and for a long time development "experts," African and foreign, did as well. The colonizers focused on men, from whom they demanded a tax in silver and compulsory cash-cropping, privileging men's entry into the monetary economy. Cash-crop production was a determining factor in keeping men on the land while profoundly changing how the land was worked. For example, among the Beti of Cameroon, women were the main cocoa growers at the beginning of the century, but this quickly became men's work between the World Wars because of the head tax imposed and because it required that land rights be made inflexible and permanent. In this patrilineal society, men had land rights. In addition, this type of farming required clearing the forest, one of their customary tasks, and had the same harvesting calendar as yams and watermelon seeds,[6] which they also grew.

In practice, the plantations belonged to the elders protected by the administration, who made the villagers under their authority work; forced labor was not explicitly forbidden until 1946. Until World War II some of these polygamous village chiefs had thirty to a hundred wives. These women had to do extra agricultural work while remaining outside the money economy. Their lack of money condemned them to grow foodstuffs in their own fields (yams and peanuts among the Beti, for example) just as they had in the past, the only change being an increase in their work hours. Among the Yoruba, where men worked the fields, they quite naturally turned to cocoa. Women had to help them to care for the young trees and to harvest and transport the

harvest, receiving almost no compensation. The only difference in this between Beti and Yoruba was that Beti women continued and even intensified
the subsistence cultivation they had done in the past, whereas Yoruba men
cut into this greatly, preferring supplies from external sources thanks to their
cocoa revenues. In the former case, women's fate worsened, whereas in the
latter the increase in trade was beneficial to them.[7] But in any case, the number of hours they had to work remained greater than for men. A survey done
in the Gambia is revealing. In this area, where agricultural work done by
men was hardly negligable, women spent an average of 159 days per year in
their fields, as against 103 days for men. Women worked 6.8 hours per day in
the fields compared with 5.7 for men but also devoted 4 extra hours daily to
carrying wood and water, cooking, washing, and caring for children.[8] Thus
in many regions of Africa, during high-activity periods women's workdays
may be 15 hours long.

Access to Land

What remained the determining factor was land rights. For women they diminished as the matrilineal tradition declined; in that tradition marital dominance had been counterbalanced by women's continuing to belong to their
own lineage of origin. Colonial ideology, shaped by the moral precepts of
Christian inspiration and Roman law, adhered to traditions of male supremacy. Before, no distinction had been made between the male right to al-
locate familial lands (which were not private) and the mixed right of *access* to
the land to which women acceded as daughters, wives, and mothers. The expansion of private property privileged men and proportionally reduced
women's access to land.

To counter women's desire to escape their peasant condition by flight or
urban migration, customary chiefs and colonial power forged a de facto alliance destined to reinforce male authority. It became more and more difficult for a woman to get land, to keep her children or even to benefit from
part of her work without being under the control of her husband. The means
to this end was a legal manipulation undertaken by agreement in the 1930s.
The colonial administrators, both British and French, sought to make alleged precolonial laws permanent by calling on traditional authorities to
help them. In French West Africa, this was the origin of the *Grands Coutu-
miers,* the "Great Customary Laws," published in three volumes at the end
of the 1930s; in French Equatorial Africa it was the source of more narrowly
focused works by French or African agents of colonial administrations such
as Léon Mba, Gabon's future president, who is known to have written this
kind of memoir. These volumes were designed to serve as the bases of jurisprudence for the native authorities. Chiefs took advantage of women in

these documents; with the abolition of slavery they saw their authority threatened by female initiative. Women might profit from the new farming opportunities to improve their domestic condition and increase their savings or take advantage of the attentive ears of civil servants and missionaries in the cities. Chiefs were ingenious in rethinking to their own benefit customs and prerogatives that up to that point had been much more flexible. "Customary law" was law manipulated and rigidly codified.

Through a colonial land law of 1904, the French decided to recognize only private property attributable to an individual and duly registered. Given the Napoleonic Code, all property automatically belonged to the head of the family—the husband. British law evolved according to the jurisprudence of the territory in question. An analysis of the conflicts and the judgments delivered by native councils and by British law demonstrate the degree to which men and women were rivals in achieving or retaining control of their households' goods. This jurisprudence was often favorable to individual women, for example, regarding slavery, repudiation, and divorce. As a disaffected Zambian chief observed in 1916 about adultery, "The women should be punished [but] when we punish them they run to the Magistrate to complain."[9] Similarly, in the 1930s a Swazi official accused the colonial courts of "protecting women and witches."[10]

In the absence of a code, British courts referred freely to the writings of early ethnographers. Everything depended on the curiosity, intelligence, and prejudices of those researchers, who had mainly talked only to local chiefs. These chiefs, almost always men and frightened by the "liberties" that the women of their country seemed to them to be taking, were not kind to the women. This can be seen in societies as different as the Luo of Kenya and the Ndebele of Zimbabwe.

Patrilineality and the Plunder of Land in Central and Eastern Africa

That women had lost ground legally was obvious in Zimbabwe. Patrilineal affiliation favored expropriation. From the end of the nineteenth century white settlers had monopolized the best land, and by 1902 they controlled three-quarters of it. The Land Appointment Act of 1930 ratified this de facto condition by reserving half the land for whites. Black men went to seek income in the mines, and their wives remained on the plantations. Yet until very recently the courts depended on the land regulations established by Child, a government officer of the Rhodesian era, one of which was the exclusion of women from direct access to land.[11] According to a "customary law" that he reshaped, an African woman remained a perpetual minor in relation to her husband. Ndebele women enjoyed property rights concerning cattle, the only wealth recognized then, but they could also increase their small herds with cows given them by their fathers or received from their sons-in-law as marriage payments. Yet married women lost the fruits of these gains, which of course created problems in cases of divorce.

The rights of women among the Tonga, a matrilineal society, were more generous; they could own wealth originating in the dowry, given in compensation for wrongdoing, or even purchased or inherited. In the 1940s, however, they lost this right. Claims made by African men resulted in their restriction to 8 percent of the land. A 1951 law opened the land market to individual men only, but this ruling was abolished when the White Nationalist party took power in 1962. A woman was not accepted as a head of household unless she was "single, widowed, divorced, or officially separated"—in a word, without a man, even if only temporarily. At most 10 percent of women were in this category.

Everything was interpreted in a restrictive light. In Rhodesia common-law marriage was made official, but according to civil law (for which "married" meant monogamous and recorded) the African married woman had no right to what the couple owned. She could not inherit from her husband (her brothers benefited here instead, a relic of the levirate)[12] and did not have custody of her children, who belonged by right to the husband's family as soon as the regular bride-price payments began. This legislation caused many problems, because, according to Child, "should a woman go out to work with the approval of her husband while under his marital control, any money she earns belongs to him under both Shona and Ndebele law."[13] Reinforced by this, as recently as a few years ago one could still see nurses' husbands lined up at the hospital exit on payday to receive their wives' checks.

Beginning in 1982, despite much of African land's being "recolonized" and the persistent increase in the numbers of independent women, the government continued in the same spirit by giving priority to "family groups," which obviously favored male heads of household. A 1981 declaration by the deputy minister of lands was an example of this: "We cannot give land to the employed since they will not have time to work that land. . . . At the moment they have a lot of land belonging to the unemployed [i.e., their wives!], lying idle."[14] From this point on, married women did almost all the agricultural work without enjoying the protections afforded by customary laws that made the man responsible for the survival of his wives and their children. The fate of widows was especially hard. Widows and divorced women made up most of the approximately 10 percent of landless peasants. We can now understand why Zimbabwean women called so energetically for a reform in the status of women that had been "forgotten" at independence. But they were far from true emancipation because of the "moral discourse" characteristic of the colonial legacy.[15]

The careless adoption of Western concepts brings us to the measures taken by the white South African government that, starting in 1946, halved the number of rural jobs by eliminating rural women, now to be considered "housewives," from its statistics. Yet women were a majority of those who worked the land, because they were not allowed to follow the men to their contract job sites. Women's agricultural work remains invisible because it is unpaid and thus has not yet truly become part of national economies. This attitude regarding women's land rights is not unique to southern Africa but nearly ubiquitous. Women's situation worsens with lack of land and the rise of a primarily male agrarian bourgeoisie.

In Kenya, women are responsible for almost 80 percent of agricultural production. The property rights of the Luo, Gusii, and Luyia women in the west of the country were always very limited. Because these societies were patrilineal, women did not inherit from their fathers and were not allowed to own land, cattle, or other goods except through their husbands. Outside marriage, with few possibilities of divorce and the custom being, in the event of widowhood, to marry the husband's brother, they had no option other than to take refuge in a mission or in the city. This explains their early desire to migrate. When they managed to accrue a little savings from cattle they had been given or from the sale of weaving or pottery, their profits were very fragile because any accumulation of wealth returned to their husbands as the sole legal owners of their families' goods. The situation worsened in the 1950s when the authorities codified traditional law. Luo chiefs themselves recognized a little later that "the substantive content of 'customary law' was being altered through . . . the expressed desire of African elders to reestablish norms of control over young women." In particular, they were unalterably opposed to registering individual properties, because this might have favored women, the de facto users of the lands that they worked in the absence of their labor-migrant husbands.[16]

The situation has hardly improved. Today Kenyan women are responsible for one-fourth of the parcels worked, the smallest and worst, because it is there that men's urban migration is highest. At the same time, women owned only 5 percent of the 7.5 million hectares registered as individual property in 1978. The government had started a women's program in 1966 that was designed to improve their participation in development. The government's 1977 development plan suggested that a special effort be made on behalf of women agriculturalists who headed families, offering no specifics about the details. Nevertheless, in 1984, a local official argued, during a preparatory session for the UN conference on women to take place the following year in Nairobi, "Although women do not have title deeds on the family land, they make a lot of decisions concerning the use of that land. We should not therefore waste a lot of time talking about land ownership or title deeds for women as an instrument of increasing food production."[17]

A Kikuyu woman who did almost all the subsistence work for her household answered this assertion with "Without land, we are nothing." Yet, as elsewhere, men controlled the cash crops, cocoa, tobacco, tea, and rice, and women the staples, peanuts, manioc, and vegetables. Earlier, in this patrilineal region women worked up to ten different parcels of land that they had obtained through marriage. Today they may have only two or three very small parcels. They have no access to farm loans to improve their equipment or buy land because these loans require as security land that their husbands own. Thus it is the husbands who benefit and increase their cash-crop plantings, which women work as well. Women are reduced to using their share of what they have produced, given them by the men for their subsistence purchases. They no longer produce enough to feed their many children in this nation where birthrates are among the highest in the world, still 54 per 1,000 in 1984.[18] The unmarried or divorced woman remains in or returns to her father's house. He lends her a parcel while waiting to marry her off; giving it to her outright would reduce his sons' shares. Later she will receive her parcel in the same fashion from one of her brothers and eventually from her children. If the man she depends on is working elsewhere and wants to sell some land in order to build himself a house in town, she remains defenseless in the face of the loss of her breadwinning ability and a diminished sense of the respect and duty due her, a casualty of the expansion of the land market. Recently women have tried to organize into cooperatives to gather the capital needed to buy equipment or land to ensure their subsistence, but only 11 percent of women are part of these women's groups. For the others, all that remains is to migrate to the city.

Land Laws and Matrilineality in Western Africa

In western Africa, the regression of women's condition is even more noticeable in the light of the remarkable autonomy they had once enjoyed. The question has been closely examined among the Igbo women of Nigeria, who were able to put collective pressure on men by shaming them.[19] The case of the Asante and Fanti women of the Gold Coast (now Ghana) is also interesting. Cocoa production became widespread in the region in the early part of this century. Work on plantations was fairly well shared between men and women until the early 1930s, when women farmers clearly outnumbered men, who were being swallowed up by the city in increasing numbers. Even where they were present, men did not rule over all, and the society's matrilineality favored the women who, married or not, headed farms. Yet between the World Wars, a patrilineal offensive was mounted and began to erode women's rights. The native authorities themselves, incited by the colonial powers but also by small growers who wanted to pass the fruit of their labors on to their descendants, ratified the idea of a shift from matrilineal to patrilineal transmission of wealth.[20] Women, however, resisted the change. In some regions almost half the women were still heads of farms in 1962, although the latter were smaller than men's. Ten years later, fully into independence, male farmers had become far fewer than female ones and were often absentee owners of the most and the largest plantations. Women had access only to a small workforce made up of their unmarried daughters and other female relatives. They themselves also worked their husbands' lands without any reciprocity.[21]

Fieldwork done in 1972 specifically identified 163 male compared with 103 female farmers. Men owned an average of two acres of cacao trees each compared with only half that for women. Men over forty-five owned at least half the land. Men over sixty-five owned one-fourth of it while women in the same age-range owned only one-twentieth. This situation, handed down from a fairly ancient matrilineal past, was still much more favorable to women than that in regions that had been recently cleared, in which the workers were all migrants. Where workers had been uprooted and relocated, male supremacy became overwhelming. In regions where new lands had been opened to production since the end of the 1950s, all the owners were men.[22] In the case studied in the Dominase area, all the women except six (five of whom were unmarried and originally from the area) had followed their husbands to help them work their lands and were doing all the subsistence cultivation. These were young women, 40 percent under fifteen and only 6 percent over forty-five.

Women, fully occupied with their reproductive and productive functions, were economically and socially regressing. Over time, however, female autonomy recaptured some rights: The oldest planters eventually gave their wives and children small parcels of land (two to three acres) in remuneration for their services, and on these the women established their own farms. In the Dominase example, of sixteen women studied closely five began cultivating independent farms.

The variety in these examples points to one general observation: the social status and economic function of rural women have tended to be devalued since the turn of the century. What autonomy they had had in the ancient societies was weakened and nothing was offered them in exchange. They were long excluded from Western capitalism and denied a Western-style education.

The Future: Women's Revenge?

Little by little, the labor market took over the cities and construction sites. This process accelerated around the 1920s as wages became increasingly necessary and over time came to exceed agricultural returns. Peasant women remained in the countryside and for lack of a labor force had to assume all the work in subsistence farming and cash-cropping themselves. Their lack of capital forced them to continue to work with almost as limited means as they had had in the past. Spread thin among field work, carrying water and wood, domestic labor, and caring for the elderly who remained in the village and for children, they lacked the time to go to school, listen to agronomists, or try out new farming methods. They remained trapped in a production system designed for a domestic market that depended only slightly if at all on cash. In contrast, men were able to work for the international market. At independence, development programs in the Gambia, Burkina Faso, Mauritania, Senegal, and Zanzibar only excluded women all the more from productive resources.[23] Whatever property laws there were, men received the training and obtained the plots of land. Only recently have national governments and international organizations seriously considered women's fate, noting in fact that not only did women suffer more than they needed to but that what was at stake was the entire continent's having enough to eat.

The New Women Farmers

This realization was late in coming, but now the failures of the systems described are challenging assumptions. Traditional cash crops (peanuts, coffee, cocoa) are no longer very profitable, and the domestic urban market has begun to experience a shortage of foodstuffs. Peasant women nearly everywhere have become entrepreneurs. The increase in the number of women rejecting marriage, almost unthinkable before, is an unmistakable sign of this. In Beti country, the villages studied reveal that in 1971 one-third of the men lived at a distance and only 56 percent of women over sixteen were married. Women farmers' new independence should be seen as parallel to the breakdown of the complementarity of agricultural work between the sexes and to the new importance of supplying foodstuffs for the cities.[24] We see a role reversal in the face of recent development in the informal economies of urban areas, where male unemployment has risen to levels heretofore unknown. Women today, whether farmers or city dwellers, bring home more money than their husbands. The most active women are those who, like men but without men's protection, have begun to create urban market gardens, regaining a little of the cash they lost with the decline in the marketability of traditional products such as peanuts in Senegal or the Gambia. In the Gambia, dry-season vegetable production, encouraged by the government and by nongovernmental organizations, has been integrated with no trouble into what was an off-season. But these gardens require watering twice a day, and produce must be transported to urban markets often more than fifteen miles away. Wells are dug by humanitarian organizations or if need be by men (but in that case women pay for them). And there is little or no technical progress. Women continue to work with hoes, to carry water, and to water the crops by hand. Their often minimal gain is accompanied once again by an increase in their workload.[25] In fact, except in a few cases, women's role in development programs has barely been conceived of. Yet in some regions the awareness women have of their own work is changing rapidly. The change is particularly noticeable where women have been self-sufficient for a long time in the absence of their husbands, but it is also observable in areas where they appear to remain very much subject to their husbands. Two examples will illustrate this.

Hausa Women and Women of Transkei

Hausa women live cloistered, and Islam teaches them that men should satisfy their needs. Although women's seclusion tends to be more intense where modern Islam is stronger, peasant women often flout that seclusion. All women, young and old, abandon it when heavy work in the fields requires them to—during the harvest, gleaning, and sorting of grain—but they remain under their husbands' control. The Kano River Project in 1971 created irrigated areas for growing wheat or tomatoes. Most agricultural workers there were men, but for some kinds of labor, especially planting bean seedlings, the company preferred to hire women. Most of these women were fairly old, menopause allowing them to leave their homes more readily. Some were widowed or divorced and had no choice. They were preferred to men because they received 30 to 36 kobo per day (1 naira = 100 kobo) for their work whereas men received an average of 2.2 naira. These women, reputedly docile and passive, in 1977 organized a surprising demonstration. More autonomous toward their employer than in their households, having discovered that one of the company's officials had offered them twice as much to work during the weekend on his farm they went on strike for a pay increase. The company refused them and broke the strike by hiring women from a little farther away who knew nothing of the affair. These women soon learned of it from their comrades and struck in turn. The company had to give in and doubled their wages.[26]

The change in women's thinking is particularly noticeable where they have more responsibility. This is the case in eastern Africa, where men's migration and the inability of women to follow them have made women the majority of the population in the countryside. A study done in Transkei showed that 79 percent of women farmers were married but 60 percent were de facto heads of businesses.[27] It may seem surprising that so many women whose husbands were migrant workers should have preferred this system, but the reasons were above all economic. The men who remained at home were elderly. Forty-five percent of women had attended rural schools for fewer than four years, and almost as many could neither read nor write. Yet of those who had gone to school, many had participated in extracurricular religious groups that played an important role in their future organizational life. The youngest ones recognized the vicious circle of poverty that oppressed them (60 percent of households suffered from malnutrition). In general, they considered the land they had sufficient—because they lacked the time to cultivate any more—but wanted help in equipping themselves and increasing their livestock and their harvests and recognition of their autonomy. Eighty-seven percent said that they would like to go to night school, and 60 percent were ready to organize to participate in self-development programs. This is evidence that the education of girls, hardly widespread even now, is of primary importance for the future.

7

Women and Urban Migration

Population movements are nothing new in Africa, where peoples throughout time have been remarkably mobile. Ancient migrations, while less widespread than has been thought, were usually collective moves by families or groups of families motivated by internal readjustments or security concerns. They periodically increased during periods of crisis such as rain shortfall, internecine warfare, and slave raids. Individual migration was exceptional for men but common for women because patrilocal residence predominated. Thus young wives were dislocated, even uprooted—although this usually took place within a limited area. Individual male migration began with the need to look for opportunities for wage earning and increased as the labor market created by colonial operations developed.[1] Research on these migrations has focused on men because employers were primarily concerned with men. Studies have emphasized the economic attraction of the city, where the labor market was open and wages were higher. Women remained "the second sex in town"[2] until at least the end of the colonial period, but the gender imbalance was less pronounced than is believed. It has been imagined that women were either only following their husbands or had only prostitution in mind.

Women merely followed their husbands, however, much less often than is believed and then only over short distances as was often the case in southern West Africa, the colonizers' "useful Africa." In countries with racial and residential segregation such as Kenya, South Africa, Namibia, and Rhodesia, legislation on contracts for temporary work addressed only men, the only ones admitted to the mining compounds under apartheid. Until recently it was against the law for mining companies to provide family housing for more than 3 percent of their African workforce. In other countries, in particular in western and central Africa, women were too useful in the fields for men to agree to their being plucked from the countryside. Polygamy was sometimes a way to resolve the problem. In 1965, for example, a Gabonese diplomat, his country's ambassador to the United Nations, had a wife in New York, another in the capital of Libreville, and a third, very young, far up-country in Gabon, where she was relegated because of her sterility.

In general, women remained in the countryside. Their survival in the city was uncertain, and their presence at home guaranteed continuity of land rights and the family's subsistence. Urban salaries until recently were calculated only on a supposedly unmarried individual's needs. Only in the early 1950s did minimum wage calculations in Nairobi officially take the worker's household into account. Women's rural work was therefore essential to the survival of the group.

In the Beginning: Colonial Migration

Female migration, especially by young women, was much greater than might have been expected. Their situation in rural areas was, as we have seen, particularly difficult. Female slaves and young wives were dependent and exploited and thus were among the first to seek out the opportunities of colonialism's urban centers, especially given the climate of political instability, insecurity, and social disorganization prevailing at the end of the nineteenth century.

Recourse Against Forced Marriages

Rare documents fortunately preserved by a conscientious magistrate posted to the limits of northeastern Rhodesia between 1897 and 1903 reveal how commonly women and children were hired out or enslaved. For them, refuge in the tiny, newly created administrative center where this particular civil servant worked was their only recourse. The cases he adjudicated clearly show the many reasons women migrated: Some had left husbands simply because another suitor's urban salary seemed more promising; others had come to the city to marry men of their own choosing without waiting for their suitors' families to pay the bride-price or to avoid unions planned by their families with older polygamous men. But most often the complaint reaching the magistrate was one of some form of mistreatment: battering, pressure to accept a deceased husband's brother against one's will, slavery, or extreme exploitation.[3] What he observed in this forgotten corner of Africa must have often happened elsewhere. We know, for example, from interviews with old prostitutes why they came as teenagers to Nairobi at the turn of the century. Most often they had refused to be married to a man they rejected; sometimes, too, they had followed a lover into the city.[4]

In some cases (notably in western Africa) the young unmarried mother was fleeing disapproval, because in many societies virginity before marriage was the rule.[5] There were also women who had married badly, unhappily, or who had divorced.[6] Some young Hausa women also fled the family home to escape marriage against their will. In the city they became independent women and perhaps *karuwai* (courtesans).[7] It was often by accident that they became prostitutes. Little girls from poor families often came to the city to help their better-off female relatives with domestic work and child care; in Nairobi they were called ayahs. To these economic and social pressures we should add the attraction that grew for them the more they heard about a chance at a new life, free from the pressures of rural customs.

The anthropological literature from the period 1950 to 1970 tended to exaggerate this latter reason.[8] According to this literature, women would have been only too happy to go to the city to escape their traditional household tasks, for in the city women had only to sit and chat. Except for a then exceedingly limited fringe of a tiny bourgeoisie and, even so, only at the very end of the colonial era, these statements are highly inaccurate. Daughters of the elite came to the city to work as midwives or nurses and, later on, as teachers—a job long reserved for men, who had more years of education. (The first training school for teachers was created in French Africa in 1938.) School played a role, as did Western notions introduced by missionaries and, after World War II, the messages of modernity of the radio, the movies, and popular fiction: that love is the most important part of marriage and that the partners should be equal within the relationship. Toward the end of the colonial era, universal suffrage (in 1956 in the Union Française)[9] exerted its influence in this quest for freedom under the cities' seductive power.

Young women's migration was self-initiated, encouraged neither by the colonizers nor by African tradition. The bourgeois Victorian spirit of the former could scarcely accept female independence. Missionaries emphasized woman as mother, responsible for care of the household, cooking, and children, supposedly leaving the house only for church, unemancipated from either father or husband. Colonial administrations blocked girls' urban migration as much as they could, more or less assimilating it to prostitution. In Kampala the laws of 1914 against prostitution and of 1918 against "adultery and fornication" were invoked to limit girls' travel. New laws in the early 1950s authorized repatriation to the region of origin without trial for any unmarried woman caught wandering the city.[10]

Africans knew only too well how much women were needed in the village and in the fields. They also feared the pernicious effects of the city on children's upbringing. Both conservative Muslim and missionary ideology reinforced these predispositions. At the beginning of independence, five Ghanaians out of six thought it proper for a young man to spend a little time in the city, but only half accepted the same idea for girls.[11] A comedy by the Nigerian novelist Wole Soyinka illustrates in amusing fashion the common view of girls' freedom; in it an educated man dazzles a young village beauty with the allure of life in one of the Nigerian metropoles.[12] Only very slowly, and hardly at all before the 1930s, did arguments in favor of the city begin with regard to school and health, especially for lower- and upper-middle-class girls.[13] Not until World War II did such ideas reach the working classes; until then, a kind of African and European consensus kept girls from migrating.

South African Women's Surprising Freedom of Movement

In one part of Africa, however, female migration became common: South Africa. From the end of the nineteenth century on, more and more detailed legislation managed to limit male urban out-migration to the mining compounds. Control increased when in the 1930s industrial growth led a growing mass of rural workers to move to the city to try their luck. To limit this movement to the real demands of the Western labor market, the South African authorities established complicated pass laws. Passes were pamphlet-like working papers that could be demanded of any African male in his travels. Less well known is that women were not subject to these constraints until after the apartheid regime took power and even then not until the early 1950s. The Orange Free State after 1912 was an exception, but women managed to have the law abrogated in 1920. Earlier the movement of women had been almost as free as in the rest of Africa.[14]

Women were not nominally the subject of the Urban Areas Act of 1923, the basis of later residential segregation. This demonstrates the minimal importance attributed to their presence in the city. Two measures were, however, introduced to limit their movements: from 1930 on, as perpetual legal minors, they were in theory admitted to the city by the urban authorities only if their fathers or husbands had worked there at least two years *and* were able to house them. In 1937 a federal law added that they must obtain the agreement of the local authorities in the area they were leaving. But because these restrictions were not supported by the requirement of a pass, they were difficult to enforce. Despite their legal status as minors and a miserable selection of jobs to choose from, women cleverly took advantage of this tolerance. When nationalists tried on several occasions to take it from them, women fought for their freedom of movement and succeeded in keeping it.[15]

The result was that between the World Wars South Africa was the only nation on the continent in which the numbers of women in cities increased faster than the numbers of men.[16] This essentially uncontrollable influx is explainable in terms of the sophistication of the controls on the male labor market. Despite the clandestine presence of a certain number of wives, the hordes of unmarried men could not survive in the city without a whole series of services—from washing and ironing to cooking and dressmaking and, of course, prostitution. An entire informal urban sector arose in which women early on had a choice position.

The Feminization of the Service Trades

It is very interesting to observe the shift in the gender balance in most of the service trades. Under colonialism and to this day, many subaltern jobs in the cities were held by men. Often these were service tasks directly supporting the white authorities, for example, such as interpreters, secretaries, couriers, and postal workers. This is hardly surprising when we realize that colonial administrations essentially sought to make men their auxiliaries. The gender shift was slow, and the number of male typists and secretaries is still surprising to the Western observer. The same phenomenon is observed in the private sector: male tailors at their sewing machines, cooks and *totos,* (kitchen help), houseboys and children's nurses, washermen and ironers, etc.

Several explanations for this have been suggested. It has been claimed that men were the ones who benefited from the minimal instruction likely to make them able to understand the whites' demands. It has also been thought that Islam may have played a role. Neither argument is satisfying, particularly if we realize that ignorance and religion did not keep mainly women from being used in domestic tasks in North Africa and if we recall the economic activity of the extremely secluded Hausa women. The truth is that at the start of the colonial era men were more available than women. Women were always overwhelmed with work. Their daily subsistence tasks left them less and less free time, as we have seen, and men's migration had put cash-crop cultivation on their shoulders as well. Always indispensable in the fields, where their work at least nearly guaranteed the family a minimum of food, their departure for the city represented a severe loss to the household. Men were more available and had been defeated in the wars of conquest and removed from public affairs; everything spurred them to take salaried jobs, because, in brief, they had nothing else to do.

Thus that men were the majority of migrants at the beginning of colonialism is easily explained. It is not surprising, then, that in the South African cities of Natal colony in 1904, for example, almost all of the domestic work was done by nearly 33,000 men.[17] These jobs had earlier been held by women in the Rand, doubtless as men went to the mines and factories. In the cities of the Cape colony and in Johannesburg, launderers, food vendors, and tailors were all men at first. Only after the 1930s did women, mostly young ones, begin taking up these trades and developing others. They became clandestine beer brewers—a role that they had already held in traditional society.[18] It has been suggested that trades that are becoming less profitable and that no longer require initial capital (which women do not have) tend to become predominantly female.[19] This was true of hand laundries when the first home steam washing machines became available at the start of World War II and of sewing when renting an old machine became more affordable. The suggestion is plausible and is singularly reinforced in South Africa by the free migration of women more able to do these jobs because their movements were less controlled, but it is hard to generalize. Indeed, the shift was precisely in the other direction in nearby Lourenço Marques (today Maputo). Women had been the first ones there to take in laundry and sell goods in the streets, starting in at least the early 1900s, but they had lost their monopoly in the 1930s following repressive legislation that was hostile to their migration. The Portuguese administration required them to obtain licenses that they could not afford, and settlers' families began to join together to pay for a man to wash their clothes. Soon all that remained for women was the physical labor that they were so used to in rural areas. They became wood carriers and dockers, finding the work more easily because they were paid half what men were paid. As everywhere in the world, their social status was deemed inferior, and this simply reinforced the Western assumption that their earnings were a mere adjunct to a man's.[20]

Migration After World War II

Attitudes toward women's migration gradually changed after the Great Depression and even more during World War II. Africans understood that they could no longer do without the cash from women's work in the cities; Europeans recognized that work done by people in stable households was more profitable.

Belgian Paternalism

The first Europeans to address the scarcity of women in the cities were the Belgians. Officials of the Union Minière du Haut Katanga (Upper Katanga Mining Company) sought in the late 1920s to stabilize their hard-to-find workforce in mining cities such as Elisabethville (now Lubumbashi). In an effort to counter the instability of poorly qualified workers, alcoholism, and malnutrition, they decided that they should encourage couples to move together. Recruiters were asked to bring in couples, and the company encouraged marriages by advancing the money for marriage payments. This advance was absolutely necessary because the cost of a wife in the 1930s was between 600 and 3,000 francs, while the lowest salary was 4.4 francs per day and the highest 162.6 francs per month. Thus, in order to compete with the polygamous cotton planters, whose production depended on the number of their wives, a worker had to go into debt for at least a year to obtain a wife.

The women newly arrived from the countryside had to be controlled. Missionaries rose to the task in association with the mining company's "protective committee," a consultative body established to handle "native" health and welfare and social and religious activities. The clerics preferred Christian and professional gatherings to tribal associations or dance groups, deemed dens of perversion. The Circle of Saint Benoit, a group of elite African men, was the first to propose a women's section. There was also a married women's association, the Union de Familles Katangaises (Katangan Families' Union—UFAKAT), founded around 1948 on women's initiative (although the president was helped by her husband). The group had a female board of directors, commissioners, treasurer, and secretary and monthly dues received by the female director of the social center. It also had a flag, and its members wore a colorful uniform that conferred on its wearers its connotation of social advancement. The group lasted about ten years. Other associations, "family circles" both educational and Catholic in nature, were sponsored by whites. There was even a Zambian-inspired Methodist group, the *kipendano*, founded by a minister's wife.[21] But the most interesting groups were of course those founded by African women themselves. These were disliked by the colonial authorities because their members tended to be independent women, either businesswomen or prostitutes, whom they sought to marginalize as much as possible.

Imbalance Between the Sexes in the City

Though the cities gradually filled with migrant women as well as men, the gender shift was sometimes slow in coming. Numbers of men and women balanced out rather quickly in the native population, but the disparity remained great among foreigners.[22] In 1960 there were 102 Ganda men (from around Kampala, Uganda's capital) for every 100 women, whereas almost all immigrants were male. In Leopoldville (now Kinshasa) in Zaire barely ten years earlier, there were 2 men for every woman. The imbalance was worse in Nairobi; in 1965, only 5 percent of inhabitants were native to the city, and 95 percent had arrived less than ten years before. After apartheid had slowed the flow of South African women into the cities, the influx of men was greater than that of women throughout Africa. This was particularly true in Rhodesia, Kenya, and Namibia, where controls were harsher. Thus in 1960 for every 1,000 women there were 1,268 men in the cities of Namibia, 1,386 in those of Kenya, and 1,412 in those of Zimbabwe. Nine years later, women were hardly one-third of the adult population of Nairobi and Mombasa.[23]

The only country where, oddly enough, migration balanced out between the sexes by independence was Madagascar. In Tananarive in 1965, of a total population of 320,000, 170,000 were female and 150,000 were male, with slightly more women among adults.[24] This can be explained by consensus in favor of family immigration and substantial female autonomy dating to ancient times, with less frequent polygamy and fairly easy divorce. Girls could inherit as well as boys (one-third versus two-thirds) and had rights to cattle, which were symbolically, ritually, and economically of considerable importance. There was also no strict rule regarding patrilineality or matrilineality but some freedom to choose between the two. Thus in Madagascar the right to migrate to the city and the motives and associations created by the move, whether based on family, job, or neighborhood, were shared by individuals of both sexes. Unmarried, widowed, and divorced men and women had similar outlooks that fostered an early gender balance in the city.

City Women Today

Urban migration is now gender-balanced throughout Africa. Many women have become city dwellers, and more women migrate than men. This is a recent phenomenon that has two causes. The first is that rural living and working conditions have become impossible for farm women; they are exhausted, and their children are hungry. The second is that upper-class women now have greater access to schooling.

On average throughout the continent, the number of girls attending school doubled between 1960 and 1970. In Tanzania since the *ujamaa* revolution (at the end of the 1960s) and in Zimbabwe since independence in 1980, for example, education has encouraged women to come to the city. A 1971 Tanzanian survey showed that after six years of schooling a girl was seven to eight times more likely than an uneducated girl to move to the city for work. It is thus no surprise that for the past two decades the rural exodus has consisted largely of women.[25]

Independent Women

Independent women's migration has become significant in the past twenty years. A Ugandan survey done during the 1970s and 1980s on Luo and Ganda women migrants to a neighborhood on the outskirts of Kampala (Namuwongo) helps us to understand these women's motivations. Of the 162 women in this survey, only one-fourth had accompanied their husbands, and 27 were visiting them one to three times per year for an average duration of a month. Wives' migration was in fact recent (dating back ten years at the most), because before that point only men had migrated. All the other women had moved to the city for personal reasons. One-third of them had come very much alone; 15 had taken the opportunity to visit relatives, and 18 were born nearby. The reasons invoked were both negative and positive. In addition to the predictable widows and divorced or "betwitched" women there were many who were "tired" or blamed polygamy, but the one who spoke to this most strongly had saved the money for her departure long before her husband brought in his new wife. Married or independent, they had come with the clear intention of profiting from the opportunities offered by the city, and most of them had been successful. One had opened a hairsalon, and others had little by little become owners of businesses; one was a tailor, another the owner of a snack bar, and still another the owner of a distillery. One of them, who had arrived illiterate at eighteen with the desire to go to school, had almost reached her goal with the help of religious organizations, working at the same time in a textile mill. The most effective were the 25 women who by stages had acquired experience in small towns before coming to pursue their careers in the capital. They worked hard, but they clearly considered their prospects, linked to the market economy and the reality of the monetary system, better than in the country. Participating in religious or informal economic activities, they especially liked feeling autonomous in their work and earnings.[26]

The timing of this migration of women has varied from one country to another. In Mozambique women and their dependent children set out for the capital en masse as early as World War II. By 1945 the influx of women from the countryside was one of the colonial administration's main problems, even though it had imposed a tax on each woman, employed or not. Migration increased especially between 1950 and 1962, when women took the place of men attracted to the South African mines and industrial cities.[27] Elsewhere, the prevalence of female migration is much more recent: 1970 for Tanzanian cities[28] and 1978–1979 for Nairobi and Mombasa.

Most women migrants are young, with more women aged fifteen to thirty-nine than men of the same age.[29] The majority are unmarried, widowed, divorced, separated, sterile, or elderly, lacking support at home and seeking both independence and a livelihood. Polygamy encourages this situation, as does the extreme age difference between husbands and wives. Widows have almost no options; taking refuge in their birth families can only be temporary, and staying with their families-in-law is against their best interests because the levirate is no longer the custom. Defenseless, in rural areas they may be held responsible for misfortune and death.[30] "Witch killings" in the villages of northwestern Tanzania have increased to the point that several hundred old women have fled to the city in fear of being accused. In the city a woman feels more protected if one of her sons has preceded her and she can find new things to do—taking care of her grandchildren, for example, as older women often do in southern Nigeria and elsewhere.[31]

Cities Populated by Women?

Contrary to popular opinion, there are more women than men in many black African cities. For every 1,000 women in Brazzaville (where nearly one-quarter of the Congolese population lives), for example, there are 988 men. In Maseru, the capital of Lesotho, the migration rate for the past ten years has been 100 women for every 49 men under the age of twenty-four.[32] In Ethiopia,[33] Togo, and Burkina Faso,[34] majority female migration is obvious. Saint-Louis du Sénégal has the lowest percentage of men of any tropical African city, 877 per 1,000 women. Women's role has always been important here, and migration increased after independence. Making Dakar a political capital meant a loss of administrative jobs; for the past thirty years the city has essentially run on female labor.[35] Lesotho is again a typical example, although the balance is closer to equal in the countryside (992 men per 1,000 women). In all these countries, female majority migration can be explained by high male migration to other countries; in Burkina Faso, for example, Mossi men go to Côte d'Ivoire and Ghana, and in Lesotho men went to apartheid's gold mines. Togo's economy and political situation condemn more than 20 percent of working men to live outside the country.

In Botswana, in contrast, the gender balance more closely approaches equality in the city (942 men per 1,000 women) than in the country (just 840 men per 1,000 women). Addis Ababa is even more intriguing: for the past twenty years it has had far more women than men.[36] True, prostitution is high there but no more so than in other cities. It has been suggested that the frequency of divorce in the mountainous massifs of the central part of the country drove unmarried women to migrate to urban areas.[37] There has also been a great increase in women's work at home and the generalized use of women for work that is as difficult as it is necessary, such as manually supplying the city with firewood.

In general, the sexes tend to be present in African cities in equal numbers, even in nations that have had an exceptional influx of immigrants such as Côte d'Ivoire. Yet, very unusually, in Lagos men's numbers grew a great deal toward the end of the colonial period because of rapid industrialization.[38] Countries in which men remain in the urban majority—Mauritania, Burundi, and Rwanda (probably because of very late urbanization)—are becoming the exception. In addition, men in these countries have more and more difficulty finding jobs abroad, and there is massive return migration.

Women's migration to the city differs from men's in another way: Women tend to migrate permanently. Men migrate for practical reasons, the most obvious being to earn money. Although they cannot always return home, they almost always dream of doing so. Women's reasons for leaving are more complex and more existential: above all, leaving is a survival strategy, but it is also a personal and even a social response to their status in society. Only married women enjoy recognition comparable to that of men in the village. To women who are widowed or divorced and, even more, sterile or unmarried, the village offers no security. Their rejection of rural society, whatever its cause, is permanent.

A survey done in Nairobi shows clearly that the connection between the city and the countryside is much weaker, when not entirely broken, among women city dwellers than among men.[39] Interviews revealed that the number of men who wanted to retire in their native village was much higher than the number of women. The exceptions were men born in the city or those who were completely disillusioned about what they could expect from the land. Women preferred to settle permanently in the city, where they had developed neighborhood networks and new affinities based on religion (Christian in western and central coastal Africa, Muslim in Nairobi and in the cities of the Sahel). Men remained more attached to their ethnic groupings.

All this contributes to freeing women from their rural yoke. In Calabar, a little city on the coast of Niger, many married women decide to remain in the city all their lives.[40] In southern Africa, where in the sterile countryside girls' frustration is as great as their confusion, the percentage in the capital of Lesotho is much higher. In 1978 almost half (43 percent) swore that they would never return to working the land. Two-thirds of farm women are de facto heads of household, but only half can hope to receive some subsidy from their labor-migrant husbands.[41] The fate of women who follow their husbands to the city is no better.

Women's Rights in the City

The dawn of the twentieth century for many women meant relative autonomy with regard to the constraints of marriage and farming. Yet Christianity, Roman law, and Western education also had their constraints. If the expansion of international trade and the introduction of colonial law facilitated the mobilization of capital and a workforce, it was because of their control of the land market. Rural landownership did not shift in women's favor at all. Urban landownership followed suit and for the same reasons: the collusion of male traditional officials and colonial administrators.

Lagos is an example. A protectorate in 1851 and a crown colony since 1861, this city (which the British had wanted to make an international port) benefited from British law. The native women of Lagos enjoyed real economic autonomy for many years, with formidable competition from Saro women (Christian immigrants from Sierra Leone) and Afro-Brazilian women (returned slaves and slavers), who were accustomed to the Western patriarchal model. Often advised and aided by Protestant missionaries in cases of divorce or inheritance, Lagos women did not hesitate in the early years to submit their troubles to colonial justice. But far fewer women than men were given ownership of land or buildings by the crown.[42] Responsibility for the land, if it was granted collectively to the family, was assumed by the man of the family. Only a handful of women, widowed or divorced, benefited from such grants, and then for land and goods very inferior to those of men. King Dosunmu, who reigned in the 1850s, granted seventy-two plots in writing, only four of them to women. The percentage hardly varied.[43]

The consequences were numerous. Starting in the 1860s, businessmen and banks developed the practice of giving advances based on a promissory note against assets or even mortgages. Without credit, almost all women were thus excluded from international trade. Toward the end of the century the two richest businesswomen of Lagos, Fanny Barber and Rebecca Phillips, respectively owned only nine and six plots in Lagos, whereas Taiwo Olowo, an illiterate salesman, had fifty-eight in the best neighborhood and Sunmonu Animasaun, a Muslim merchant of servile origin, had amassed thirty-seven. To compensate for their lack of capital and official credit, women resorted to tontines, whose members contributed to a pool that each in turn might later win by drawing lots.

One might think that in Ghana matrilineality would have protected women more, but this has been less and less the case, and patrilineal inheritance has won out almost everywhere.[44] True, growing food more for her own kin than for her husband's ensured a woman more solid support, but in the city, as these old kinship connections died, maintaining this system was difficult. The old custom had the woman bearing full responsibility for the children in her own line, her husband being connected to his sisters' children. The two kept separate accounts, and the husband had almost no financial obligation to his wife once he had given her a little money to start her business. Among the Akan in Accra, the capital of Ghana, almost 60 percent of couples, even among the bourgeoisie, maintain this pattern.[45] Wives are too afraid that their assets will be siphoned off by their husbands' families to risk joining them in their investments, except when they have the legal protection of contracts properly recorded (true of only a tiny segment of city dwellers). Women prefer to keep their interests and earnings within their birth families. The result is that to maintain their financial independence almost all married women continue to ply their trades.

The situation of widows is the most tragic. A deceased husband's wealth goes (according to custom) to his sisters' children. The Confederation of Akan Chiefs had suggested in 1938 that widows and their children might inherit one-third of the deceased's assets, but the British governor at the time did not countersign the proposal. It was enforced only ten years later.[46] The problem is the same when the woman has divorced or becomes pregnant without being married, and it is no better in polygamous households when the woman is neglected for a younger wife and the husband no longer lives under the same roof. Until recently, a female head of a single-parent family had no legal way to demand assistance from her children's father.

Since December 1981, women faced with such obstacles have been able to bring family-related problems to special family courts. The economic depression of the 1980s hastened this evolution; before then it was almost unthinkable to talk about domestic problems outside the lineage. Such trials have increased in recent years. Almost half the women who use the courts are employed in the informal sector, and 20 percent are unemployed. They ask for child support, help with school fees, or assistance in the case of illness—an understandable request if we remember that the infant mortality rate is on the rise.

The legal system's effects reach much farther than simple social measures. They are changing the whole society. Now when the man shares in children's upkeep he claims a right to control over them. This is completely new, especially among the Fanti, where the father's role is more prominent than elsewhere. One consequence is the father's and his lineage's claim to custody of his children. Because paternity brings with it costs, however, many men are not prepared to admit it; they may decline to marry the women they have made pregnant and, worse, refuse to recognize their offspring. This goes against the ceremony of welcoming, which consists of "naming" the newborn (presenting it officially as a member of the family), and does serious harm to the child. Finally, this law can have a perverse effect, causing the mother to lose her traditional matrilineal rights by favoring the Western conception of her as the man's dependent. Many Akan women fear this change in mind-set, which will reduce their autonomy over time.

The cities are largely composed of young adults and their many children. Old men still end their days in the village; it is mainly old women, the poorest and least adaptable of all, who remain in the city. Today, people aged fifteen to twenty-five make up almost a fourth of the urban population.[47] The migration of couples to the cities is increasing more rapidly than the migration of single men, but independent women have become real and increasingly visible actors, often numerically a majority. Some are poor village girls seeking work, and some are young unmarried women who come to the city for the diploma they need for their social and professional advancement. Only among the marginal European-style urban bourgeoisie does one encounter the Western model of the supposedly dependent woman at home.

PART THREE

Women in the City from Colonization to Independence

8

The Urban Condition

One conclusion can clearly be drawn: the presence of so many women in the city can only partially be explained by their husbands' migration. The major shift of the twentieth century was the emergence in the cities of a very specific new category of independent women who could meet their own needs and the needs of their families—particularly their children—without help from anyone and without depending on a man unless under accepted social arrangements that lacked any economic relation.

Much attention, perhaps too much, has been given to prostitution. It is not that it should be denied or that it is not a relatively profitable profession, but studies of it tend to accord it disproportionate importance, at least historically. Certainly, urban prostitution was encouraged in the early twentieth century by colonizers who preferred (or, as in Kenya, the Rhodesias, and South Africa, demanded) that the only workers admitted to the cities be men under contract, treated as bachelors. Despite everything, women were able to find many other kinds of work in the city. Lacking training and means, they chose jobs that required little capital and great adaptability to local markets. They held a privileged place in petty merchant capitalism in the informal sector and later in domestic labor.

Deterioration or Progress?

When we look at the question of the urban woman, once again it is impossible to generalize. The factors at play are many. Beyond the cultural heritage unique to each region, women's ages, geographical and social origins, and urban class, as well as relations between the sexes unique to each society, created noticeable differences. It has been observed that city women's status rose or fell in *inverse* relationship to their class origins. For middle-class women, city life meant increased dependence. Working-class women found conditions favoring relative emancipation. The peasant women who came to live in the suburbs of Accra, for example, were remarkably able to draw benefits from the small-scale supply and trade opportunities available to them.[1] In contrast, middle-class women mimed the Western model of the housewife, and even if they had jobs their salaries were generally lower than their husbands'. They progressively lost the domestic advantages that matrilineality had offered and became prisoners of the European patriarchal model—dependent on their husbands for pocket money, support for their family, and, consequently, for their entire existence. In addition, inveterate polygyny (even where legally forbidden, as was the rule in English-speaking countries) and the ease of divorce made fragile the conditions and the prospects of women's survival.[2]

This line of reasoning should, however, be adopted with caution. One might also claim that in some societies the condition of rural women was so poor that coming to the city was always a kind of liberation. Among the Tswana, for example, wives of chiefs, while supervising their daughters' and female servants' work, worked nearly as hard themselves. Among the Kikuyu, all wives owed their husbands very humble deference. One might also argue that women (in western Africa especially) of every social class have always worked outside the home. In Accra as in Lagos, middle-class women without jobs seldom existed under colonialism—almost all were market women. Bourgeois Hausa women lived secluded but still worked for pay and disposed of their profits as they saw fit.

It is not clear that coming to the city was necessarily an improvement for working-class women. Men, especially the better-trained ones, most readily entered urban life. They were better able than women to multiply their starting capital, establish useful contacts, and acquire professional training. Under colonialism, almost all salaried jobs were held by men. And colonial laws favored the urban family head's control of the household profits and property. Even recently, quite extraordinary situations of social alienation can still be found: in the late 1960s, for example, there was the case of a Luo man who used the salary of his wife (a schoolteacher) to pay for a second wife.[3] His case came to light when his educated wife took him to court. But how many illiterate working-class wives have been exploited by their husbands?

We can also reverse this argument. Although rural women were generally subject to men, they once enjoyed a female solidarity and relative autonomy that were lost on their arrival in the city.[4] In sum, women's poverty in the city was probably worse than in the village.

Clearly, attempts at overgeneralization become meaningless. Instead, leaving aside the very small number of privileged women living Western-style urban lives, we must try to understand how the majority of African women have entered the urban workforce since the beginning of colonization.

Between Value Judgments and Reality:
Independent Women and Free Women

City women's various heritages have affected not only the future of their roles in the city but the way in which they were thought of by both the colonizers and the colonized. An abundant literature makes clear that African men themselves and, in consequence, most researchers, historians, anthropologists, and sociologists in Africa have propagated divergent moral judgments regarding women's urban work. For example, small-scale women street vendors are despised in Nairobi but lauded in Nigeria. Social scientists have tended to wax compassionate over the sad fate of the former but extol the enterprising spirit of the latter. In all of central-eastern Africa, from Kenya to Mozambique, women who work in the cities are more or less despised, but, ironically, their work is considered normal in the countryside. Two factors come together to give women's independence a bad name in this part of Africa. In traditional society, a free woman was a serious challenge to the laws of seniority and affiliation founded on ritual and reciprocal exchange of gifts (among which marriage payments played a preeminent role). Most complaints argued before early colonial judges were to obtain the repayment of the bride-price when a woman had abandoned her husband or village. Europeans early on assimilated the *independent* woman with the *free* or prostituted woman.

In the Belgian Congo, the assimilation of the two was even upheld by law. From 1920 to 1925, the Elisabethville (Lubumbashi) mining company encouraged wives to come with their mining husbands to help stabilize their workforce. Yet at the same time, the number of young unmarried women in mining cities increased, although they were theoretically forbidden access by the colonial administration unless they had managed to acquire an identity card. In practice in cities (referred to administratively as "centers beyond customary law" [*centres extra-coutumiers*]) the card was compulsory for adult women over sixteen and "theoretically living alone" (*vivant théoriquement seules,* or VTS), who paid a special tax. The few widows and elderly women were exempted from this tax. The card was proof that the woman lived legally in town and was required for membership in any leisure, dance, or self-help organization. This administrative ruling often confused prostitutes and unmarried women. Young women labeled "VTS" were usually in fact simply the partners of men—wives for whom the men had not paid a bride-price. This was very common in Elisabethville, where the price of a wife was particularly high and might be equivalent (as we have seen above) to ten months of salary at the Union Minière. These "free" women were subjected by the city to double taxation—a residency tax and a tax on their estimated income. Miscarriages of justice were frequent, and it was often hard to decide who was or was not a prostitute. The community needed these moneys: 55 percent of Elisabethville's urban revenues depended on them, and probably as much in Stanleyville (Kisangani), where one-third of adult women during World War II were registered "free women." The authorities were divided between the desire to keep these reportedly dangerous independent women from coming in and the satisfaction of exploiting them, since they were soon vitally necessary both for the work they did and for the percentage of city revenues they brought in.

In this specific case, independent women became so numerous that they organized their own associations, some of which remain famous. Diamant, an organization of merchant women that began in Leopoldville (Kinshasa), recruited only women who were unmarried or married outside tradition (i.e., without a bride-price). Its goal was to find husbands for its members and help organize marriage celebrations. Sami was more complex. It was an organization of "friends" (*des-amies*, elided, produced the name "sami") that served as a kind of marketing agency for small-scale merchant women. These clever women hired young apprentices, preferably straight from their own villages and nice-looking, to hawk their wares among the bachelor miners who made up the bulk of their clientele. Members often brewed beer in clandestine dives where other illegal activities also took place. To combat their bad reputation—though some of their recruits came directly out of Catholic schools—they went so far as to change their name to the Association des Jeunes du Sacré Coeur (Sacred Heart Young Women's Association). We cannot seek to clear their bad name entirely, but it would be simplistic to reduce this organization to a mere prostitutes' cooperative.[5]

From this point on, whatever was thought of them, most poor urban African women had the same demographic profile and worked at the same types of jobs, often leaving them below the poverty line. Except when they were sterile, young women had often been married several times and were responsible for young children. Many were divorced, widowed, or abandoned, and the number of young unmarried women has sharply increased in the last few years. Female-headed households in town are today at least one-third and often half of all family groups. These women have not necessarily gone astray or been abandoned. It is simply often easier for women to keep their rights to their children if they are not married. In Senegal, for example, under Muslim law a widow goes back to her birth family, but her children go to her husband's. In Tanzania, a 1971 law stipulates that in cases of divorce, custody will be determined by a community's social customs. Thus the courts tend to give children over six or seven to their father, observing patrilineal practice. We can better comprehend mothers' desire for independence from such examples.

Most women have very little or no capital and tiny profits. Almost all end up in the informal economic sector, which must not be misunderstood. Although until recently this sector was neither observed nor controlled by official accounting, it consists of a precisely organized, hierarchical, and sometimes quite remunerative set of activities, very much a part of the Western capitalist market both "upstream" (in primary materials used) and "downstream" (in the outlets of its market).[6]

9

Women and Trade

Trade that is not integrated into the Western market economy is called "informal." This "informal sector" is many city women's universe today. Once this varied by region. For example, city women in western Africa had a long trading history in sharp social and ideological contrast to the rest of women on the continent. In eastern and southern Africa, most cash-and-carry and retail trade were quickly monopolized under colonialism by immigrants, for example, Indians in English-speaking African countries, Greeks in Madagascar, and Portuguese in central Africa. In Johannesburg and Nairobi there were no African market women until World War II, and in Lusaka (Zambia) they hardly existed before independence.[1] But in western Africa, the increasingly important Lebanese and Syrian communities were almost nowhere able to gain entry into the regional trading networks supplying the cities that the old networks, often female, had taken over. These were often very large networks operating even internationally, dealing both wholesale and cash-and-carry in salt, fish, palm and kola nuts, shea butter, cloth, and gold.

West African Market Women

Moral rejection of women's independence in the name of Western puritanism and traditional prejudice only makes many western African women's real, ancient economic autonomy the more remarkable. Muslim and Christian, in areas colonized by Catholic and by Protestants, on the savanna and in the forest, except in some Sahelian societies such as the Songhai of Mali, we find market women almost everywhere.

Because religion was not a determining factor, we must look for other, more profound reasons for this cultural feature unique to western Africa. In some areas, for example, among the coastal Ga and Akan, women's trading has a long history. Sometimes the antiquity of cities helped to integrate women's economic activity into urban life, for example, in Hausa country. In port cities, creolization played a role, as we know for Saint-Louis, Freetown, Accra, and Luanda. In most cities, long-standing commercial and urban ways of life have long given women in these areas a unique position. In cities like Djenné or Timbuktu on the Niger River, city wives of rich merchants began discreetly trading in luxury products very early on; other wives participated in caravan expeditions. René Caillé described how Mandingo expeditions were organized in the early nineteenth century: While doing all their domestic work, women managed small personal businesses—trading kola nuts received from their husbands for cotton, which they wove before reselling it for cowries, which allowed them to buy salt or glassware.[2]

Among the many kinds of businesswomen, we can cite at least two types, one encompassing women of the West African coast—the women of Saint-Louis, the Ga and Akan of Ghana, the Fon of Benin, and the Mina and Ewe of Togo[3]—and the other the secluded Hausa women.

Except along the lagoons of Côte d'Ivoire, where trade was the domain of foreigners coming from what is now Ghana or elsewhere, coastal women worked in markets long before colonialism. There is no clear link between the early women trading in kola nuts and palm oil and the twentieth-century market women of cities in Ghana, Togo, Benin, and Yoruba country, but it is likely that the traditions of the former encouraged expanded trading by the latter. Women who had worked in markets and caravans were able very early on to seize opportunities to supply the growing colonial cities with village produce.

The cities, built and first inhabited mainly by whites, soon had six to ten times as many Africans as white settlers. Destitute urban Africans needed cheap consumer goods in small quantities in order to survive: food, hand-crafted household articles, and locally manufactured cloth, none of which foreign companies offered them. From the 1930s on, a local petite bourgeoisie developed that sought fancier but still African-style articles such as wrap-skirts and boubous of cotton cloth hand-dyed with indigo or kola nut, the cloth itself increasingly being imported from Europe.

Women continued to use the marketplace for their business. At one time, markets took place regularly, on set dates that varied according to the area and punctuated the local calendar, usually twice weekly. In Yoruba country, the larger wholesale and cash-and-carry markets took place only once a week because they required traveling a greater distance. These were held near larger urban centers, generally close to borders, and sold products of complementary exchange value. Retail markets were held in smaller towns twice weekly. City markets quickly became daily affairs.

The sexual division of labor in trading varied by region. At one time, Fanti men (Ghana) controlled trade in gold, slaves, ivory, skins, and even kola nuts and cloth. Their role in business diminished as most of these products gradually disappeared, and the male workforce went into salaried jobs. Today, as a general rule, food is traded entirely by women, and so is cloth, where it is not controlled by Lebanese or Syrian middlemen. As for handicrafts, the closer to home an article is produced, the more likely its trade is handled by women, and this is especially true of pottery. On the other hand, any kind of metal product (forged or jewelry) and imported product is usually traded by men. Imported products include the baubles sold by Lebanese and Syrian wholesalers, inexpensive Asian items such as Chinese tin and hardware or small audiovisual equipment from Hong Kong and elsewhere. In essence, trade in articles that require capital and direct connections to international markets is usually male; everything to do with daily subsistence and local markets is usually female. Again, the reason is the limited cash resources available to women. We know of a few remarkable exceptions—Togolese women and Ghanaian or Yoruba matrons who wholesale cloth, Wolof women gold traders connected to the Mecca pilgrimage network, and women trading in contraband diamonds from Sierra Leone and Zaire.

Ghanaian Market Women

In Ghana (formerly the Gold Coast), women traders have a long history. Ga (or Fanti) women living in the oldest section of Accra, Ussher Town, have inherited a long line of contact with the West, having long shuttled between the coast and the Asante empire. Throughout the nineteenth century, men were trained in missionary schools. At the very beginning of the twentieth century, in what was still just a tiny town, almost the country, they became colonialism's auxiliaries while their wives conducted business as they had learned to do from their mothers and grandmothers. The 1911 census showed that three-quarters of the 4,000 women working in that section of Accra were market women. Most worked in family enterprises that included mothers, daughters, and sisters.

The percentage has remained surprisingly stable; in 1970, 79 percent of Ussher Town women were in business,[4] though trade practices had changed. British law freed slaves and individuals pawned to repay debt or dishonor (usually girls) in 1874. Another law allowed ill-treated wives to leave their husbands. Both measures favored women's emancipation. During and after World War II, helped by the war effort and urban population boom, masses of women took advantage of their nascent independence to start trading in fish and cloth. But here again, conditions had changed. At first, many women were producers, making beads locally from bauxite, dying cloth, and preserving fish. The massive increase in production brought about by motorized pirogues and industrial drying techniques was highly advantageous to some women.

Yet they had to stay within a more and more piecemeal woman-to-woman distribution system, from purchasing the fresh fish to selling it retail, including its preparation, transportation in trucks, and wholesale and cash-and-carry sale. Their dependence on industrial suppliers, the proliferation of middlemen, and the fragmentation of family support created serious problems for women traders when economic downturns dramatically worsened after 1970, leaving them impoverished and alone. They worked even harder at small-scale food businesses and at cooking food for sale or resigned themselves to seeking support from men who had been able to enter modern capitalist society through education. This kind of support often paved the way to prostitution.

There are many, many small businesswomen in the cities. The trade a woman goes into depends on her assets and her ability to obtain credit. Most often, a market woman's only capital is the little cash her husband gives her if he has a salary. Akan husbands hand over this money every day or week; some husbands prefer to do so just once, when the couple marries, as is done among the Yoruba of Lagos, with a sum of 10 shillings before the war that rose to £2–5 in the early 1950s.[5] This gift permitted the woman to start a business that she alone owned. Some particularly skilled women could begin retail operations because they enjoyed bank credit in the several thousands of pounds sterling in the 1950s. It is usual in Akan country for the wife to have her own finances and, within a matrilineal framework, to assume responsibility for her own subsistence and that of her children. In 1952 in Koforida, a town of 30,000, one observer counted about 3,000 market women in the marketplace, or 10 percent of the total population, with perhaps 40 percent of adult women present, not counting those doing only occasional business. The percentage remains constant and large: in the late 1970s it was estimated that about 70 percent of adult women were traders.[6] A survey conducted in Koforida revealed that a not insignificant minority of these women were "foreigners," without lands nearby. Most were or had been married; only a few were widowed or abandoned. Almost all were working to feed their children. The 78 women in the sample were supporting 224 children, an average of almost 3 children per woman. They acknowledged working between six and eleven hours per day in the marketplace. Those who worked the least number of hours on-site were the ones cooking food for sale. All these activities were within urban female social norms.

The Nago of Lagos

The same observation can be made of the Yoruba of Lagos.[7] Women stated in 1951 that all women "who are neither sick nor disabled" worked.[8] Of a sampling of 207 mothers, 170 worked at an activity that kept them away from home several hours per day or several days per week; fewer than 20 percent stayed at home.[9] Almost all wives in polygamous households worked, and almost all the housewives were non-Yoruba in monogamous households. Here again, women's working away from home is part of a long-standing cultural tradition. Among Yoruba the father takes responsibility for his children's subsistence, buys their everyday clothes, and pays their school fees. The mother supports herself and assumes all other costs of the children's upkeep: dress-up clothing, school uniforms and supplies, toys, and even bus tickets. The husband has to feed his wife only "if she doesn't do her work well" and owes her only one dress a year, on New Year's Day.

Almost all these women (95.5 percent) were market women, and the few others—mainly Saros (from or with parents from Sierra Leone)—worked as dressmakers, hairdressers, washerwomen, nurses, schoolteachers, etc.

To open a shop, a woman needed at least £50, although the size of this sum did not mean that thousands of shops were not owned by women. Some shops had considerable stock, worth at least £5,000, and one very exceptional case was cited of a woman merchant whose stock was valued at £20,000. These businesswomen did not have to show their accounts or have a license unless they were selling spirits. Taxes were estimated for women who were assumed to have over £200 in net income. The colonial administration was fairly flexible on this count, no doubt because it remembered the violent riots that had occurred since the 1930s by the institution of the tax.[10]

Husbands and the small businessmen's union complained about women's individualism, yet there was no question in these women's minds of giving one cent in profits to the couple's joint assets. They instead put their money into their maternal line, where the woman as a little girl had been apprenticed to her mother. A large-scale trader in fabric boasted that she had earned £100 plus jewels and fabrics since before her marriage and that she had lied to her husband about these savings (left with her mother) and then begged him to give her the ritual £5 when they married: She claimed that she wanted to start the printed-fabric business she was already engaged in from scratch.

In Lagos, there were four hundred merchant women, each of whom owned between three and five rental houses, most refusing to pay taxes on the income from them even though the properties were in their own names. Like their mothers in ancient times, many of these women were constantly on the go, traveling to the interior to obtain the merchandise they sold. Other women had female relatives from the village keep them supplied. Most had started at the age of ten or twelve in a time when there was no question of their going to school. Yoruba women specialized in cloth, deemed very profitable. Beautiful cloth for skirts was made locally by traditional weavers, and white or off-white imported fabric was hand-dyed or encrusted with embroidery, called *bazin*, which sold for quite a lot, often on commission. The weaver or importer would give a certain quantity to the market woman, and it would be up to her to get the best price she could for them, with her profits taken out only after she had earned back the purchase price. The advantage of this process was that the market woman could return unsold merchandise—if she bought on credit or for cash in advance, she had to make up any losses herself. Many producers, to keep orders for their wares coming in regularly, resorted to brokers.

Some women regularly traveled to neighboring colonies such as Dahomey (Benin), the Gold Coast, Fernando Po, or even the Gambia, buying the best they could find while prospecting for clients. They would sometimes establish permanent regional offices run by female relatives who handled cloth procurement. Most of these assistants ultimately left to set up their own businesses once they had amassed the necessary petty capital. The most industrious of these women owned one or two trucks. In 1961 the richest was a Muslim woman of sixty-five, Mrs. Rabiatu, who had received from the *oba* of Lagos the title of *iyalode,* head of the markets. She had inherited her mother's business, while her husband, now retired, had had a modest career as an agent for a European firm.

In contrast to the situation in Ghana, none of these Nigerian women had any connection with a European expatriate firm as employee, manager, or independent head of a business. Perhaps the Europeans, especially the Lebanese and Syrians, had developed a habit of working with men. Or were women stopped by their informal methods of doing business and their illiteracy? Business associations were rare and confined to the familial level; husbands would hardly have liked any other kind. Associations of market women rarely lasted longer than a year, at the end of which the group had to divide the profits.

The wealthiest of these women also traded in money, though this trade, lending, was male. It virtually went underground when the colonial government imposed a license on lenders at the official rate of 3 pence per pound per month (15 percent annually). For amounts under £100, lending rates amounted to outright usury—from 30 percent to 150 percent, with the loan guarantee of cloth or jewelry often being sold again on the market by the woman lending.

Igbo women, who were often newcomers to Lagos, stuck to the food trade. Foodstuffs were almost always directly purchased from producers. Often, market women simply stopped farm women walking to the city at prearranged places and purchased some of their goods to sell. Competition existed, although the rule was first come, first served.

The gender division in trade gradually changed. Today, trade in household articles, hardware, enameled metal washbasins, and plastic articles that require an initial advance of capital are controlled by men in many markets, especially in Senegal or in the Sahelian cities. At one time in Lagos this was women's trade, just as the job of herbalist was. Women selling herbal remedies often had male experts in their employ who would to go the forest or bush to find the leaves, herbs, and roots that local healing traditions recommended.

In Lagos's fifteen markets, women were very clearly a majority of traders. In 1948 they numbered about 8,000, plus all of their assistants and apprentices, both regular and occasional, four or five to one nominal market woman. Trade in each item was organized by section: fish, *gari* (cassava flour), dishes, cloth, etc. Each section had its rules. For example, no merchant could sell fish purchased directly from the producer; all had to go through a broker. Shellfish, in contrast, could be sold by the person gathering them. Women in theory could not butcher or sell meat, but some women could be seen doing so. Each section head reported to the market's general manager, who was chosen by consensus and recognized by the *oba* (chief of the town). Almost all differences were resolved by the women themselves without recourse to the usual courts. Heads and managers met regularly over drinks and food to discuss the group's social cohesion, yet never sought to organize any further, for example, by taking action on retail price-fixing.

The markets' organization was highly structured and early on began to play a political role. Market women's associations had their say in who was designated *oba*. In 1923 Herbert Macaulay brought them into his National Democratic party. The Igbo "women's war" showed the colonial government their strength. It started recognizing their associations, the market women's unions. These entered the political scene in May 1944, when they joined the Lagos Women's party.

Currently, Yoruba women's adventurous spirit has led some of them to exercise their talents in overseas trade. In 1991, in Britain, of 267 women arrested for drug trafficking, 81 were Nigerian.

The "Nana Benz" of Lomé

The extensive female trading so striking among the Yoruba was not unusual; there are so many cloth wholesalers from Lomé in Togo that they have been the object of a number of case studies.[11] Trade in cloth has become very well developed since the early days of transatlantic slave trade. It increased after 1880 on the initiative of a Glasgow trader who introduced mass-printed cottons throughout the Gold Coast, competing with local production of hand-dyed imported cotton. The printed-cotton fashion spread because the African soldiers who had served for the Netherlands in the East Indies enjoyed great prestige among the people and liked the patterns of the Indian and Javanese textiles.

The expansion of cocoa farms held by men (in 1911 the country became the top cocoa exporter in the world) contributed to women's entering the market. Trading in cloth started with the Gold Coast *mammies,* and until 1950 Lomé wholesalers went to them for supplies. Trade spread to neighboring Togo, in part with profits from contraband. As early as the turn of the century, we see cloth wholesalers in Lomé—Mina or Ewe women who, like Yoruba and Fon women, seldom did fieldwork. Traditionally, they had free use of the income from their own businesses, despite their cultures' patrilineality and their supposedly receiving from their husbands what they needed to support their families. While their men worked salaried jobs, the boldest Mina and Ewe women seized opportunities to save small sums in their own names so that in the event of divorce, which was quite frequent, they could buy custody of their children.

The cloth business took off in 1930. In 1940 there were about forty wholesalers. By the end of the 1970s, 6,000 female licensed merchants almost monopolized the business, except for European imports (*java* and *cover,* plus higher-quality Dutch *wax* or *tchiganvo*) and cloth from the Dadja textile mill a few miles from Atakpamé, which employed 13,000 people at the time and produced less expensive *fancy* or *tchivivo.*

These Lomé wholesalers were not a homogeneous class. Togolese women have a reputation for commercial ardor and organizational hierarchy. In the 1950s there were at least three categories of wholesalers. The first were those with incomes over 10 million CFA francs. The wealthiest, with import-export connections, could get exclusive representation rights to certain designs after seeing samples, which was one of their key advantages in competing within this relatively closed profession, involving only a privileged fraction of the Togolese bourgeoisie. These women were at the top of an international hierarchy that stretched from Côte d'Ivoire and Niger to Zaire. They organized the business very cleverly, for example, by refusing to sell the most sought-after fabrics unless the buyer also took a certain number of *azo* or hard-to-sell fabrics in the lot.

The second group of wholesalers were the cash-and-carry businesswomen, who bought some of their supplies from the first group and some from expatriate companies. Their workplace, like that of the first group, was the marketplace.

In the third category were retailers who worked both in villages and in the city, often for someone else. In 1967 there were just 6 women in the first group, 33 in the second, and 546 in the third.

We can chart their ascent from the beginning of the colonial period. Most today belong to wholesaling dynasties, either through their family line or by entering the family's network as assistants, for example, having been invited by a maternal aunt to come from the village to work. More recently, some women have bought shops with their savings or with the help of their husbands, who may then become the company's agents. These women run every inch of the two floors of a quite grand concrete building built in 1967 that is overflowing with impressive fabric displays: imported cotton prints in a riot of colors, *wax, bazin,* great lengths of cloth from Ghana. The principals arrive early every morning in their cars, lately luxurious ones. In fact, the fashion, due to German influence, was for Mercedes Benz sedans, the source of the women's sobriquet "Nana Benz."

Thus at sunrise a fascinating ballet takes place at the marketplace, where these important women, often impressively proportioned, have themselves dropped off in high style, creating the most splendid traffic jams. Often illiterate or little schooled, few understood until recently why their daughters would want to burden themselves with a secondary education that would earn them a pauper's salary rather than emulate their mothers. Yet since the mothers have the means to pay for such an education for their daughters, there is a fairly high rate of disaffection with trade among younger women. In 1977 only 18 percent of wholesalers' daughters were still in the profession. Three-fourths instead had salaried jobs, for example, as office workers, midwives, teachers, and secretaries. Some went back into Western-style business, but generally their role was filled by village girls who came to the city to be the wholesalers' assistants.

Despite their lack of education, those businesswomen who have been in the trade have long been able to get credit, sometimes in quite significant amounts, from local banks that knew they were a good risk. The amount of purchases declared by the wholesalers, far less than the reality, in 1980 was 12 billion CFA francs. This amount is concentrated in the hands of a very small number of women. Three of them do one-third of all the business and a mere 19 do three-fourths, a tiny minority given the 8,000 wholesalers counted in Lomé in 1976. These are a truly privileged class. The complete absence of price controls and of ancillary costs of doing business and the tiny taxes they pay contribute to their profits. At a political level, under colonialism and during independence, the *nana benz,* aware of their importance and their resources, were very combative about defending their privileged position.

Dakar matrons have also gained real commercial power. The trade in gold, the metal valued by lower-caste Senegalese jewelers, is renowned throughout the continent and much practiced along the pilgrimage route to Mecca—the Moors preferring to work silver, an old Arab tradition. These large women are a sight to behold, covered in jewelry, their mouths full of gold, as they move through airports in their loose white embroidered boubous, from which emerge a quantity of boxes in all sizes crammed with the most diverse merchandise. Palaver and negotiations ease their navigation through customs.

Women throughout the country are equally involved in the drying and distribution of fish, caught by men. These wholesale and cash-and-carry businesswomen hire drivers and wobbly pick-up trucks from the most productive beaches—Kayar, Mbour (a major Senegalese fish-drying center), and Soumbedioune in Dakar—to ensure distribution to even the tinest interior market. Before planes and trucks, the railroad transformed these trade networks, and the women of the informal sector benefited.

The first businesswomen to take advantage of the possibilities offered by the Dakar-Niger railroad did so around World War I; the first locomotive entered Bamako (Mali) in 1904. Today, two international express trains theoretically make the trip each week. Between September and March (the dry season, good for business), 70 percent of the passengers are businesswomen, about 420 women per trip. High-level Senegalese merchant women favor the express trains because they are less uncomfortable. The daily train from Bamako to Kayes is the local market train, but the crowd of female small merchants mostly works the mixed cargo and passenger train platforms twice a week at no charge and is tolerated by the railroad authorities. The Malian wholesalers of market garden produce and fruit and of wood (on the return trip) take the cargo train.[12] Railroads have this effect everywhere, for example, along the Brazzaville–Pointe Noire railway for supplies going back and forth between Brazzaville and Kinshasa and the railway from Abidjan to the great interior market of Bouaké and from there to Bobo Dioulasso and Ouagadougou. The sight of hordes of market women descending upon the train's passengers as it pulls into the station to sell their handicrafts and locally produced foods is a familiar one, and this is only the most visible node of a very extensive network.

Not all women in these coastal and river-dwelling societies go into business—far from it. Often the women who have taken over the market are specialists. Women from the Ivoirian seaboard feel that business has little to recommend it. In Abidjan, almost all market trading is done by foreigners. Togolese Ewe and Dahomeyan Fon women, Ghanaian Akan women, and Nigerian Yoruba women are in control here. The city authorities have tried to give Ivoirian women priority in the marketplace, but they usually ended up renting or selling their rights to foreigners.[13] These differences derive from different cultural heritages and are reinforced by a petite bourgeois mentality left by colonialism.

Businesswomen in Central Africa

Central African societies tend to be sexist; from Kenya to Namibia we find much the same pattern. One begins to think that women's timid and late entry into the world of paid work is the product of colonialism's legacy of misogyny and Victorian puritanism, hostile to women's emancipation in the city. Currently, with few exceptions, only Zairean women, and only quite recently, seem to escape the pattern.

Timid Beginnings

Under colonialism, everything seemed to have militated against women's amassing any personal savings. Even in the Zambian Copperbelt, where women had gone with their mining husbands, very few women had paid work before the late 1930s. During the 1950s some women started gardening, given that men were no longer paid partially in kind. They gathered mushrooms and honey, and some sold their harvest to their neighbors or in the market. Others did the same with firewood and beer, and then came prostitution, quite ill-accepted by Africans.[14] In 1954 about one-fifth of the merchants in the great market of Luburma (the oldest one in Lusaka) were women offering vegetables and fruit in season and cooked dishes, most of them only occasionally. In 1959 about one-third were women. Business-women worked from home, the street and marketplace being the domain of foreigners. This paid work was almost as despised as prostitution;[15] it was thus a survival strategy mainly employed by the poorest women.

In the Belgian Congo, it was the Great Depression that impelled city women to turn to paid work. More mobile than their husbands and with better connections with rural areas, Bateke women began selling staple foods: raw and prepared cassava, cassava leaf, palm oil, palm wine, and smoked fish. A married women's paid work was related to her husband's: sailors' and fishermen's wives sold fish to nearby areas; wives of low-level civil servants and office workers instead tended to have home-based busi-nesses to meet neighborhood needs. Some places specialized. Lokele women of Kingabwa sold their pottery door-to-door, and then trading began and re-quired traveling greater distances to various towns outside the capital. Teke women peddled mainly along both sides of the river, between Leopoldville (now Kinshasa) and the Poto-Poto and Kongo neighborhoods on the French Congo side. Balari women from Brazzaville were invited by the Leopoldville local authorities in the 1940s to come and work market gardens in a reserved area in the northern, African side of the city. After the opening of the Congo-Océan railroad in 1934 and especially after independence, women began going directly to the port of Pointe Noire to buy imported supplies: lengths of cloth, blouses, and fabric of all sorts. On Stanley Pool, trade traveled by pirogue.[16] In Kisangani in the early 1950s, ex-prostitutes, usually Nupe women, retired and used their savings to open shops. But most business was in the hands of foreign men, usually Greek or Portuguese and now Senegalese.

The Informal-Sector Business Boom

In both Brazzaville and Kinshasa, women began to enter the informal sector in the food distribution trades, and supplying fish and market garden pro-duce was soon entirely in their hands.[17] This shift had accelerated with inde-pendence, increasing urbanization, and the growing crisis of capitalism.

From the mid–1960s to the mid-1970s, Lusaka doubled in size, from 250,000 to 500,000. Men, whether miners, civil servants, or salaried workers, lost their jobs and saw their resources dwindle. Education and knowledge of English or French, two of their main advantages, were suddenly less impor-tant for success. But many women carved out a niche for themselves within the informal sector and escaped the only paid work open to them under colonialism, prostitution. A license to sell in the market was almost as sought-after as a housekeeping job in a public institution, and in any case these jobs were almost entirely men's domain. In Addis Ababa in the 1960s, 60 percent of the street vendors were women.[18] But competition was fierce, and door-to-door peddling, illegal and at best tolerated, brought those who did it much vexation—fines, arrests, and bullying.

In eastern and central Africa, things began more slowly for women. Kikuyu and sometimes Luo women now go daily for supplies to wholesale markets on the cities' outskirts, and today they run the markets of Nairobi, where selling food and cooked dishes has always been their domain.[19] But in Harare, where colonial segregation lasted until 1980, there were in 1969 still more than two men for every woman in the market, and, as elsewhere, most women were in informal-sector business. According to a 1980 survey, half of Harare women had no profession, only 13 percent were salaried, and more than a third had small businesses of their own selling vegetables, poultry, or knitted or crocheted goods that they had made. The pace of women's entry into the paid workforce was slower in Tanzania, perhaps because of Islam. In Dar es Salaam in 1985, out of 3,000 food vendors only 100 were women.[20] Similarly, in Windhoek (Namibia) in the early 1980s, a scant third of the women had professions, compared with 82 percent of the men, and the women usually worked in the informal sector. Men sold newspapers, carved wood, or moonlighted as mechanics and cab drivers; women ran clandestine bars and small food and cooked-meal businesses or made baskets and dolls.[21] All were working to survive.

In Zaire, women quickly took up paid work after the violence of 1960–1964 which left many without men and responsible for children. Zaire-anization opened public-sector jobs to a certain percentage of men and eliminated foreign competition. In the cities, runaway inflation made women's role in family survival critical. Given their limited skills and education, they had no choice but to turn to small trading. Today more and more Zairean women with diplomas are leaving their offices to go into business. In 1980 nine of Kisangani's main wholesale traders out of thirty-two were women. They also owned 21 of the 113 cash-and-carry and retail businesses and occupied almost all the stalls at the market. These women earned more than their husbands and were free from their control. In 1962 a new law allowed a wife to open a business *unless her husband forbade it.* An earlier law based on Belgian legislation had required the husband's agreement. Yet her husband's authorization is still required for a woman to open a bank account or buy a license, and the new family laws are a step backward, giving husbands the right to manage their wives' assets. This explains women's interest in the informal sector as a way to ensure their independence. Six of eleven large-scale businesswomen interviewed in 1979 had obtained their start-up capital from a small business, one from her salary as a teacher, another from credit, and another from her work as a prostitute; only two had borrowed from their husbands. Many of these women had chosen not to marry or to marry only after building up personal capital that they stoutly protected. Many women had married foreigners, Greek or African, who could facilitate certain transactions for them. Family-run businesses were common; a mother, sister, or daughters ran the shop while the entrepreneur traveled to find or sell the merchandise.

Women started out, as usual, with food businesses in 1965. Half of the largest import businesses owned by women (five) in Kisangani specialize in foodstuffs from down the river: fish, rice, and beans. The women obtain supplies from upper Zaire and in return send up cloth and even radios. As in Lomé, wholesaling *wax* nets the largest profits.[22] In 1979, just before the currency was devalued and changed (which has made all numbers meaningless), there was rumor of several women who were millionaires and more who were very wealthy.[23] The election in 1980 of a woman to the regional committee of the Kisangani Chamber of Commerce was further demonstration of women's professional success. A women's branch of the Lions' Club was founded in Kisangani in 1979, with several businesswomen as members alongside the wives of male Lions' Club members.

The relative wealth of some women should not make us forget the masses of small-scale market women who are not counted in the surveys. Most are not accounted for because they do not buy licenses and are wary of banks. Their lack of confidence means that they move money within internal networks such as the tontines, involving voluntary contributions paid to trustworthy women who are both lenders and investors. The Association des Femmes Commerçantes (Businesswomen's Association—AFCO), founded in 1972, has certainly not organized the trade. Its president, an ex-teacher forced by the violence to resort to prostitution to ensure her family's survival, uses her position to exploit small-scale wholesalers rather than protect them. As with the women of Lomé, we see the elevation of a small, well-off businesswomen's bourgeoisie that attempts to profit from its social and professional advantages within the current general societal breakdown. Most other women in business are barely staying alive. Their ranks swell not because of increasing emancipation but because women's liberation is paralyzed. What we are rather seeing is a reflection of hidden but dizzyingly high unemployment.[24]

The Special Case of the Cloistered Hausa Wives

Until recently, only Hausa women close to power—women of the court and those of the aristocracy, surrounded by servants and slaves who could move about on their behalf—lived in seclusion (purdah) in northern Nigeria. Progressively, Muslim fundamentalism imposed seclusion on all middle-class women without affecting the small number of liberated women who worked in the formal sector (who in any case had nothing to say in the matter). That these cloistered women are able to do paid work is remarkable. In the 1970s, of a group of seventy women in two neighborhoods in Kano married to men in the most diverse jobs—salaried employees, businessmen, artisans, drivers, bakers, *malams*[25]—only one did not live in purdah, quite simply because she was too poor to do so.[26] Traditionally, or at least since Islam has become more rigid, men were responsible for domestic expenses. Women—free women at least—were reputedly unable to earn wages. It is significant, however, that, in contrast to other parts of Africa, women themselves contribute a large part of their dowries. The dowry is usually their trousseau, household linens, and enameled or copper vessels of exceptional size and sometimes numbering several dozen.

Unlike most African markets, the Kano marketplace—the largest in Kurmi—is dominated by men. The largest vendors sell cement, cattle, or cloth; others sell grain, manufactured goods, and kola nuts or are butchers, tailors, and leatherworkers. Only in the new market outside, in Sabon Gari, are women present, but they are foreigners, Yoruba or Diula. Despite their apparent reserve, Kano women participate in business and, just as do other women, for cash. Because men are not supposed to control domestic life and marriage partners have separate accounts, Hausa women enjoy great autonomy as long as they respect purdah. In theory, their sphere is domestic life, and it is men's job to keep the house supplied with firewood, sacks of grain, and the money for the daily purchases that children and servants go out to make. Servants are either Koranic students supporting themselves and paying their *malams* or poor widowed or divorced girls from the countryside. Women take turns cooking and often buy dishes prepared by neighbor women. They make a living from their work and keep their profits.

These small profits, added to the proceeds from investments from their dowries, possible gifts from their husbands, and their savings in tontines[27] that they organize among themselves allow them to start businesses in sewing, embroidery, hairdressing, or even moneylending. The money they earn in this way is their own, and goes for nonessentials such as presents for their families, clothing, cosmetics, and jewelry for themselves and their children. But most of it is used for the bride-price demanded of their sons and for their daughters' trousseaus. Despite the Muslim law whereby boys inherit twice what their sisters do, trousseaus belong exclusively to women. Young girls put all their savings into them, and women continually add to them both to protect themselves in case of widowhood or repudiation or to pass on to their daughters. These money-making activities, almost entirely linked to matrimony, help give Hausa wives room to maneuver and even freedom despite their apparently total submissiveness. For the past few years, economic crisis and men's increasing unemployment make such supplemental activities critically important to the household's daily survival. Beyond their other activities, the women of Kaduna devote an average of seventeen to twenty-five hours per week to paid work, which in 1985 almost three-fourths used to buy food, wood, and clothing for their children.[28] Astonishingly, they manage all this in purdah. We are starting to see the layering of West African women's business practices and traditions over a strongly, even forcefully Muslim culture.

Since slavery no longer exists and many households cannot afford servants, these female activities depend heavily on the help of children, girls more than boys even though the latter remain with their mothers up until about age twelve. In 1976 the government imposed obligatory primary school attendance in the northern part of the country, and in a year the number of students had doubled. It is now commonplace for poor families to send children out to do errands before school or late in the evening after Koranic school. More and more, children are being given work to do, like preparing cakes or making toys from what they can find to sell to their peers. Ironically, the increase of women's work has stimulated the resumption of work by children.

10

Domestic Service

Since the 1930s work in service to the white settlers has become feminized. Regarding urban migration, we have seen how the colonizers sought men for all household work: cooking, washing, ironing, gardening, guarding property, child care, even infant care. For breastfeeding, wet nurses had long existed in the countries that colonization reached first, such as the Cape. Here, since at least the eighteenth century, and as in the American colonies, white ladies deemed breastfeeding too great a risk to their beauty and even unsuitable.

But there came a point, different in different places, where the work demanded of men opened up less well-paid and thus more despised jobs for women. Early on, working for whites in their homes was both a sign of prestige and a salaried job reserved for men. African men would do domestic work in this setting that would have been considered degrading in their own households. Little by little, called to more interesting or better-paid work (mining, office work, industrial labor), they left domestic work to women. This shift started between the World Wars in South Africa. In Lourenço Marques it happened around World War II because so many men were recruited for work in the mines of the Rand. It also happened early on in French Equatorial Africa with the assistance of loose social mores, women being thought of in terms of their use value—a close analogy to slavery. "Housekeepers" became especially common in Gabon with the arrival of unmarried colonial personnel. The later arrival of their wives tended to masculinize the profession, which was realigned along traditional West African lines, but the shift is far from complete.

Domestic Service in South Africa: A New Kind of Bondage?

South Africa is a case unto itself. In Johannesburg and the key industrial port cities especially, men were in demand for the mines and factories and left women the housework that had so long been a part of service to the whites. Yet in Johannesburg in 1896 most domestics were colored or white (about 4,000 compared with only 3,000 black, almost all men except for a few hundred wet nurses).[1]

Maids were in large part skilled white women who were recent immigrants. They did the ironing or were Irish chambermaids or German cooks. Rarely was any Afrikaner woman, even a poor one, to be found, for they hated to leave their families. Maids were usually under the supervision of a white governess. Housework by blacks was mainly confined to the white proletarian families of miners or factory workers. Black women began to be employed only slowly. Yet Xhosa maids working for Boer farmers are noted as early as around 1777. After slavery, this work began to represent the possibility of independence to young Xhosa women. Thus we know of Hena, the daughter of an important chief who fled to the colony to escape a polygamous marriage and found work with a missionary family in Lovedale.[2] The employment of Africans, far from exceptional on farms or in villages, was noted in Johannesburg for the first time during the depression of 1906–1907, when African girls came to the city to escape rural poverty. Agencies seized the opportunity to do new business and announced the arrival of young Zulu servants recruited for year-long contracts. In 1908 the Anglican mission opened a little housework training school for African women and was quickly imitated by other churches.

In 1917 there was an attempt to promote a "housekeeper's certificate," which supposedly guaranteed the quality of a black maid, who would then only need supervision by colored or white help.[3] This initiative met with scant success, in part because the young women demanded wages similar to the men's and in part because white wives, fearing their husbands' infidelity, spread word that the young women were loose. They preferred children as maids, preferably little boys, and white maids, increasingly threatened by their low-cost competition (50 to 90 shillings compared with £2–5 per month), blocked this as much as they could as soon as things picked up again after the crisis of 1921–1922. Racist prejudices took care of the rest, particularly concerning wet nurses. Notably in the Witwatersrand press it was claimed that a child raised too close to his black nurse risked being imprinted with an inferior culture. The risk to the child must have seemed less with a man.

Galloping racism reinforced hierarchy within the household's servants and loaded black maids down with chores at the pleasure of their white peers or superiors. Despite all this, promiscuity among the people brought about intimate relations, usually concealed by an extremely puritanical society. We know only about affairs that came to trial because of masters' complaints. A white manservant's affair with a black maid might earn the man a reprimand or firing, but the reverse brought prison and whipping to the guilty black man. Children born of such a union were clearly problematic, the more so if the mother was white. The black mother's only recourse was to go back to the informal sector.

The difference in treatment and the myth of the black peril that periodically reappeared among masters of houses, with accusations of poisoning, fire setting, or other misdeeds, provoked well-organized but highly clandestine retaliatory, thieving groups of black servants, who were deprived of any formal professional protection. The most famous was the Amalaita gang, on the eve of World War I, composed of groups of around fifty members, including a fairly large number of girls. Members were maids of about fifteen recruited from among the ranks of the worst-paid and the unemployed. They took their revenge especially in petite-bourgeois and white proletarian neighborhoods. They had a leader, managers, and a uniform and met after nightfall at the end of their long workday. The gang came to light when it attacked a woman alone in her house one April night in 1912. The girls and most of the boys stood watch while three of them raped her, acting, one of the girls said, on the complaint of a mistreated manservant. This greatly exacerbated white society's antiblack mania.[4]

With the beginning of World War II, the poor white classes vanished, and the need for a black workforce in the mines and factories made domestic work the province of women. Yet the percentage of colored people remained relatively high in the Cape colony, where settlers of British origin, who had long preferred white servants, replaced them with the colonial model of colored ones, in contrast to the Boers, who preferred black servants, a souvenir from slavery.

A few figures illuminate the evolution of domestic work from the first quarter of the nineteenth century onward. In the Cape, there were, in 1828, 13,000 female slaves compared with 18,000 male. In 1834, at emancipation, 15,000 slaves were domestics. The great famine of 1856[5] caused considerable migration, and half a century later, after the mining boom of 1891, there were three male domestics for every woman. The number of men kept increasing. In the colony it more than doubled between 1911 and 1921, from 12,000 to a little over 25,000. In 1936, although 80 percent of African working women were domestics, there were in Cape Town one-third more men than women. The situation was quite different in the other cities of the province. In Port Elisabeth and East London, there were four to five times as many women as men.

In all of South Africa,[6] men in 1910 were 45 percent of all domestics, but only one domestic in twenty was white. The shift in male and female populations varied from one colony to another, according to the different rates of proletarianization, urbanization, and migration by gender.

In the Orange Free State, black female servants became far more numerous early on and increased proportionately, with the numbers of men dropping by half between 1911 and 1921.

Natal and Transvaal continued to seek male servants, preferably white ones.[7] The shift to women took place late despite tenacious attachment to traditional family structures wherein African husbands and fathers opposed salaried female work, and the number of black female domestics roughly doubled between 1911 and 1921. Despite this shift, before World War I there were still three times as many black men as women servants in Durban and a quarter more in Pretoria. Johannesburg, in contrast, had male and female domestics in equal numbers. The diamond center Kimberley recruited mostly male servants.[8]

By 1970 the shift was complete. One domestic in 400 was white, 88 percent were black, and among these 88 percent were women, in this profession that employed only one-third of African working women. There were 800,000 black domestics. In a little over half a century, African women had gone from less than one-third to more than three-quarters of the total servant workforce.[9]

Domestic working conditions remain atrocious. Nationalist laws of 1953 and 1956 said that domestics were not part of the working classes, preventing their union-type organizations from being recognized and limiting their ability to act. Despite some calls for change during the 1970s, the 1981 work law reforms did not alleviate the situation. By the end of apartheid there was still no minimum wage or health or any other benefits. In addition, women married under community-property laws are considered minors by South African law; most female domestics cannot even sue in their own names.

A 1980 survey in Grahamstown reveals a David Copperfield situation for maids, who were asked to perform all sorts of tasks.[10] Where a domestic was employed by whites—but nothing indicates her situation is better than anyone else's—she worked some eighty hours a week, and most of these women were also married with children. Some traveled several hours in order to be at their employers' homes from seven in the morning until seven-thirty at night. Others lived in, but if they were married, at least in theory their husbands did not have the right to visit them. If their children had not been sent to live in the Bantustans, mothers could visit them only for a few hours on Sunday afternoons, cut shorter by the travel time required to reach them. Vacations were essentially nonexistent. The women's only amusement was to chat with other employees in the neighborhood when their employers were away. Salaries were minimal, an average of 24 rands per month, reaching as low as 4 rands to start and not above 60 rands at best.[11] Many of these women called themselves slaves. Despite these painful conditions, household employees stayed in their jobs for lack of other options; their mobility was very limited. Most had been with the same employer for five to twenty-five years. The total absence of social legislation made domestic work especially vulnerable, despite a small attempt by the Domestic Workers and Employers

Project in 1970 to help household employees and even encourage them to organize.

Domestic Service in Tropical Africa:
Competition from Men

In tropical Africa, the domestics in a colonial house were abundant and highly specialized (if one was a washerman, one remained one, and the same held for a cook or a watchman), but the number of whites was always very small. Jobs were reserved for a limited and thus relatively privileged group of "boys." Less well known but gradually developing with urbanization and colonization among the urban middle classes is domestic service in African households. Its most visible element, associated with the increasing autonomy of an elite, acculturated bourgeoisie, was the imitation of white settlers by employing one or several boys, most often to the exclusion of women.

From "Boy" to Ayah

In Abidjan, Ivoirians still prefer to use Mossi immigrant workers from Burkina Faso, who supposedly work harder and more cheaply than one of their male compatriots and even more so than one of their female compatriots. In Dakar, bourgeois Plateau families (once French, today Senegalese) have developed the habit in the past ten years of hiring a woman rather than a "boy." Many of these women are from the south. Young Diola girls from Casamance, between fourteen and twenty-five, leave their villages during the dry season to work as domestics in the city, usually seasonally. During their stay in town, they usually live with a relative, often male, who is already working in the city. Six to eight years later, they return permanently to their village to marry. Young women's migration also plays a more and more important role in the survival of the countrysides.[12] A film by Sembene Ousmane, *La Noire de . . .* (The Black Girl of . . .) is a protest against the exploitation of these young women by white colonial families, who might think nothing of moving servants to European cities for several months of colonial holidays—servants who could be loaded down with work at will and traumatized by their ignorance of a language and country they might have dreamed of visiting.

In Zambia, ads for workers still reveal the degree to which male servants are preferred. The tradition is an old one. In the 1930s, except for work in the mines, which began around the end of the 1920s, there were already more men employed in domestic service (around 10,000) than as agricultural workers. In Lusaka, a small administrative center, domestic work was an important part of the job inventory (about 17.5 percent in 1946, 22.6 percent in

1956). Situations were even more sought after because the employer provided lodging and because employees were only legally accepted in the city on this condition. It is estimated that the number of male domestics rose to around 33,000 between 1951 and 1957. The number of women increased from 250 to 800.[13] White settlers' houses, which commonly used a half-dozen employees, maintained quarters for them in a corner of the property as they had for slaves in an earlier era. The housing was substandard and most often did not have hot or even cold water or electricity. Families were at best tolerated. Women continued to be officially ignored in the city, where for whites they existed only insofar as their men and their sexuality were concerned. Where hired, they were rarely given lodging because they were assumed to be living under a man's roof. During the 1930s the city seriously considered for this reason creating "bachelor hotels" for girls trained by the missionary schools to serve in homes.

Change after independence was slow. The survey cited above in 1984 for all of Zambia found 100,000 household employees in the strictest sense of the term—excluding informal family help. This was twice as many people as worked in the mines (53,700). One-fourth of these household employees were women caring exclusively for small children. Because white women preferred to use "nurse boys" for their children, their employees were almost all Zambian, and salaries were extremely low. Regulation of the sector was pretty much out of the question. One-third of the women were married (as compared with two-thirds of men) and often condemned to very long daily commutes; half were relatively independent older women, divorced or widowed, and generally the best-paid and most highly valued of the group; and the rest were young unmarried women who had left school or just arrived from the bush. If they were not housed they had to find sheds to live in in the city and were paid poverty-level salaries by African families. As soon as their first babies were born these families turned to young unpaid female relatives from the village. As these families grew they hired additional female workers who were poorly paid. Rapid turnover of servants was the rule until the last child reached school age, and then many Zambian families turned with relief to male domestics. This devaluation of female labor, always paid worse than male, reflects deep, ancient convictions that it is hardly proper for a girl to work outside her own family and that women are always more or less going to be supported by their relatives. Thus we can better understand the frequent mobility of young women, whose first concern must be to find the man who is supposed to protect them. This also explains the greater availability of older women, who are somewhat removed from these social pressures. The hope once cherished by these women of buying little plots of land or tiny houses for their retirement with their parting gifts from settlers' families after years of good and loyal service is fading. It is harder and harder for a single woman to live without occasional or regular recourse to prostitution.

From Salaried Work to Traffic in Little Girls

In a society in which most people's incomes do not permit them to hire salaried workers, invisible domestic work has become the rule. It is sustained by rural relatives who dream of finding the work or the promotion that do not exist in the village. Here we see again all the traditional characteristics of female labor. The most typical case was that of migrant workers, young salaried unmarried men traditionally unused to doing domestic work, who went to the city with a little girl or young woman from their families to help them in their households. Everywhere that segregation did not prevent it, urban families, mostly polygamous, became the place little sisters and other poor female relatives went in the hope of a basic education in the city. Domestic work was the repayment for the service provided by the host family.

We know little about the development of this assuredly ancient practice during the twentieth century. It certainly spread after World War II and even more following the independences. It became common in cities such as Accra, Lomé, and Ouagadougou and in the southern Nigerian cities. Since village educational and sanitary conditions were often terrible, parents felt that their daughters would be better cared for and educated in the city. More and more, however, with the expansion of informal labor by city women, the girls might obtain an apprenticeship, particularly in trade or handicrafts, and even save a little money.

The result was clearly an increase in child labor. Little girls in particular were used to back up market women in their work or watch children while their mothers worked outside the home. A recent demographic survey in a petite-bourgeois Abidjan neighborhood where husbands were office workers or clerks had surprising results for the age-groups from ten to fifteen: Households had many more girls than boys. Sociological study revealed that they were invisible domestic labor. This took on disquieting proportions in cities such as Segou (Mali), Ouagadougou, and Bobo Dioulasso (Burkina Faso), where little girls, often of no more than nine or ten, were exploited for all kinds of domestic labor. These little girls were Dagara in Ouagadougou and Dogon (from Mali) in Bobo Dioulasso.[14] They arrived in groups, led by adults who said that they were their relatives, but the phenomenon begins to suggest organized trafficking. And the little girls—or, rather, their parents—had agreed to this. School, which no longer guaranteed employment, had become worthless: Better that the girls should be sold to support a family and set aside a little money for their trousseau. But most of the time, their money was used for their brothers' marriages.

These domestic work conditions recall the European nineteenth century, when raw country girls hardened to work were used without any limits on their hours, social protections, or control and with little or no remuneration. Although many wealthy families did of course provide poor rural relatives real assistance and held up their end of the bargain by getting the girls to school, often this was not true of working-class families and especially of illiterate ones. These abuses in their own way come close to the ones that black adult domestics working for South African whites endure.

11

⚡

Prostitution: From "Free" Women to Women with AIDS

The particular nature of prostitution in Africa today derives to some degree from traditional social practices. For example, in Cameroon it was usually considered indecent to have sex before marriage. This was considered a grave injury to the family of the young woman who was to be given in marriage, and the guilty young man received a heavy penalty. But married women apparently enjoyed the right to their bodies. Thus among the Bassa in cases of adultery, the lover owed the husband only a chicken in recompense, which both formalized his liaison and recognized the wrong done by this tacit polyandry. Among the Ewondo things went even farther. A greedy, polygamous man who could not satisfy the needs of his many wives (acquired for their productive capacity) profited in what seems to have been the most normal way in the world from their sexual adventures. He could even practice *mvié* (a three-way commitment) by renting his wife temporarily to the lover she was so taken with. This was basically service purchased at a rate set by the owner. Among the Duala women were rather routinely sold or given to brothers, male relatives, friends, and clients without concern for the women's opinion. The Fulbe of northern Cameroon, who assimilated aspects of Hausa culture into their own, had no opposition to prostitution in principle. It was ironically the mountain-living northern tribes, the Mofue and Mafa, neither Islamic nor Christian, who were hardest on adulterous women. The young woman enjoyed exceptional freedom of choice in her marriage, including the freedom to reject the suitor proposed by her parents and to go to live without further ado with her heart's desire. But if she betrayed him, she risked stoning.[1]

Since marriage made them adults, wives who decided to enjoy their independence were able to make changes in their situations, taking advantage of the new conditions created by the whites' arrival.

Origins

Strictly speaking, prostitution existed from the beginning of the colonial period, if not earlier. It was noteworthy in such areas as the railroad work sites, the mining compounds, and wherever else a large group of young adult male workers were concentrated. Only recently, however, has it become many urban women's primary profession, and only recently (except in southern Africa) has it been "modernized," with Western-style pimps, and organized networks, and become a survival strategy for many families reduced to poverty.

Prostitution arose from a young woman's own initiative, and she was her own boss. In a way these women could be considered entrepreneurs within petty merchant capitalism, selling their own services—which included sex of course but also a whole series of other household tasks such as preparing meals, serving beer (using their own beer, clandestinely brewed), laundry, ironing, and providing relaxation for their clients, who could not afford regular domestic help. All these prostitutes were self-employed, and thus it was difficult for colonizers to distinguish between *independent* and *free* women, the latter expression, being pejorative, revealing prejudices of the time regarding women's condition.

In tropical Africa, an unusual variant was introduced by the Europeans. We would have to call them "mistresses," although in the case of the *signares* of Senegal and the colored ladies of Luanda they were actually indispensable, often formidable, associates in frequently prospering businesses connected with the slave trade. The term "mistress" is more accurately applied to the companions chosen by male colonial personnel in the early days of African conquest: military men, sailors, and colonial officers who spent several years in one place in an era when European wives seldom came to Africa. This is how we can understand the fashion of *ménagères* ("housekeepers" and common-law second wives) in Equatorial Africa and the *moussos* of French Sudan (now Mali). "To take a *mousso*" meant to keep a native woman and was a practice accepted and even recommended by military doctors, who saw it as a kind of health insurance. These African women were to "amuse, care for, dispel boredom and keep the European man from turning to alcoholism and the sexual depravities unfortunately so common in hot climates."[2] They were above all to be beautiful and free-spirited. Young Peul women were particularly sought after. At the time of the conquest it was common for European or African soldiers to get as a bonus (to the great chagrin of the missionaries) up to two or three captive women, plus several slaves to help them keep house. Of their unions were born sufficient numbers of colored children that the White Sisters in 1898 opened an orphanage for them in Segou, an example later followed in Côte d'Ivoire. This practice did not last, at least not so openly. The first white wives arrived in the early twentieth century and quickly put things to rights. Yet the custom continued in the bush, even after independence, and sometimes even among the young French men who came to do voluntary national service in the countryside in the name of international cooperation.[3]

Miners and Prostitutes: South Africa

Native prostitution was much more common and flourished where colonialism required an almost exclusively male workforce and created a market for sex. The first region where this was true was obviously South Africa, where the mining revolution took place as early as the last quarter of the nineteenth century. In 1896 there were 25,000 white men in Johannesburg for 14,000 white women but only 1,200 black women for almost 40,000 black men, migrant minors hired on temporary contracts.[4] The ironic result was that in the 1890s and for a long while later, white prostitution by women who had recently immigrated was much more common than prostitution by African women, even colored women who were South African by birth. Almost 10 percent of white women over fifteen found themselves under the control of some two hundred to three hundred pimps, the result of a Western-style underworld of English, German, and Australian immigrants especially. In the great mining city of the interior, prostitution was mainly a Western import via the Cape or for a small group of Asians via Durban in Natal. The women worked the hundreds of bars and flophouses surrounding the mining cities. By the late nineteenth century, there were 133 houses of prostitution in the city itself of Johannesburg, with almost four hundred women working in them.[5] Prostitution in South Africa soon took on a Western look, with private bordellos whose downtown location turned out to be profitable to a number of industrialists and banks. Charles Dunnel Rudd, a mining magnate and an associate of Cecil Rhodes, apparently owned at least three, as did the Banque Française de l'Afrique du Sud.

Things changed, however, during the first decade of the twentieth century. During 1907 and 1908 the police used a near-rebellion by prostitutes to justify wholesale deportations of women and their "foreign" (i.e., not born in South Africa) protectors, which destabilized the wild downtown neighborhood of Frenchfontein. In the same period, the failure of the final Zulu rebellion in Natal, drought, and the spread of poverty attracted a growing number of African peasant women to the city. They quickly discovered that housekeeping, the only urban trade they were skilled for, had been taken over a good ten years earlier by men. What remained to them were clandestine activities such as beer brewing and occasional prostitution. Around 1910, police counted some two hundred to three hundred regular black prostitutes, most working in the poorest neighborhoods, where workers' poverty might make them forget their segregationist impulses. Traffic in women by organized pimping networks, an investment of dirty money, became unprofitable. The police and churches closed their eyes to what was of less and less concern to them because marriages among white gold-mine workers were rapidly increasing.[6] As prostitution became more Africanized, it became increasingly informal. From that point on, its development is unknown, because it has gone unstudied.

Nairobi's Female "Entrepreneurs"

In Nairobi, prostitution appeared in the very beginning of the century in the railroad work camps. As elsewhere, it was linked to two apparently independent factors: the large number of male workers and the housing crisis. Of course, it began with the prostitution of poor women who accosted their clients in the streets and were pressed into service as they were everywhere, but in the 1920s one of oldest forms of prostitution took a new twist. Called *malaya* (a Swahili word for this activity), it was a fairly typical African institution that developed in different ways.

The precarious, poverty-stricken neighborhood of Pangani was the heart of it in Nairobi until the authorities destroyed it and the Pumwani neighborhood replaced it in the 1930s. *Malaya* was an arrangement whereby independent and discreet women rented and even bought rooms or shanties to receive men and act out married life, treating and caring for their clients like husbands. What was unique about this was that the women were their own bosses, most having broken off any connections with their rural families. Their profits were significant, higher than average for the neighborhood, and gave them some social status. A recent survey among women who came to the city before 1920 shows that in 1932 they had owned 42 percent of the houses in Pangani, and about ten years later they owned 41 percent of the houses in Pumwani. Some even owned several houses and had capital invested outside—but not in their villages, for they had turned their backs on rural enslavement of women. In some cases, they had also invested in businesses; some had commercial licenses for shops they ran or had someone else run for them. Yet we should not exaggerate their success. Although one-third of 132 women who owned the property they lived in were relatively well-off older women, only 4 percent of renters were old women. The others could not afford to rent, and more than half were childless and survived only on a little illegal work or public charity.[7] Yet despite the colonial administration's hostility to the urban informal sector and missionaries' obvious puritanism, Islam's relative tolerance allowed many women who had broken with their families of origin to recreate a "family spirit" in the city thanks to their conversion to Islam. They were accepted in neighborhood associations and esteemed because of their social standing and their possible generosity. They enjoyed a guarantee, essential to them, that they would be buried by their new religious community, since they would no longer be buried with their ancestors.

The *malaya* of Pumwani were relatively protected because the colonial administration tolerated them. In the rest of the city, however, prostitution was a crime and took two forms. The most ancient and poorest were the *watembezi*, or walking prostitutes, who solicited in the streets. They changed their system when at the end of the 1930s they realized they could make more money in much less time through the *malaya* system. They became *wazi-wazi*, who took clients to the room of a hotel for sex charged in quarter-hour increments. *Wazi-wazi* could recruit customers right from their own homes, even in front of their own doors, like the women in the windows of Amsterdam. Their shameless attitude brought them harassment from the colonial administration and shocked prostitution's old hands, who were not in favor of public hawking of wares. Despite it all, the trade brought a certain wealth to the most enterprising, although most continued to live in poverty because, ironically, these stubborn women were far *less* independent than the *malaya*. Unlike them, they had not broken with their families. On the contrary, as good daughters and wives they had gone into exile in the city to help their rural households survive and pay taxes and debts incurred during the drought and to amass the necessary bride-prices for their brothers' marriages.

Nairobi prostitutes were renowned for their high level of organization. They created associations and unions, and refused to be ordered around by anyone. From 1945 on, they fought particularly hard against the combined strength of various hostile political and social forces, among them the segregationist colonial administration, opposed to uncontrolled migration, tribal associations born of rural conservatism, such as the Luo, which pursued and sought to bring back the young women who had fled their traditional environment to live their lives, and even Mau-Mau troops, who between 1950 and 1955 asked their members to make their common-law marriages official. Prostitutes' self-reliance was encouraged by the venereal diseases massively brought into the city by World War I, causing a high incidence of sterility. Sterility made their work easier, without its being clear whether they were prostitutes because they were sterile (and thus rejected for marriage) or were sterile because of venereal infection. Considering the importance of procreation in African thinking, their sterility reinforced their independence. The women adapted and practiced the commonly rural custom of "woman-to-woman marriage," which allowed them to pass their often considerable assets on to another woman's child, adopted under this custom.

Prostitution in Islamic Milieus

"Free women" appeared in Nairobi sooner than elsewhere but were far from the exception during the colonial era. Their form of prostitution was fairly characteristic of the Islamic areas' strongly hierarchized societies, both in the east among the Swahili and in the west among the Hausa. These were "young women from good families," as they say in Europe, who found this their only means to win emancipation. Such was the case in Atu on the archipelago of Lamu, off the northern coast of Kenya. Here wealth came from the slave and ivory trades, run almost entirely by men. Retail trade was run by Indians, and wives were relegated to the domestic sphere because the fields were worked by their slaves. The abolition of the slave trade by the British in 1873 and of slavery in 1907 impoverished the island. Women, often divorced or repudiated, tried their luck in the growing port city of Mombasa, where prostitution allowed them to build houses for themselves back in their villages and even to help their female relatives financially so that they could imitate them. Partially freed from male control, the women were also able to break off marriages they disliked. Around 1975 almost two-thirds of migrant women, all divorced, were prostitutes in Mombasa but had not broken with their families.[8] These women felt that they might return to married life later or intermittently, under better conditions, because prostitution did not make them outcasts and in no way prohibited their remarrying. On the contrary: the woman, having gained greater economic weight than the man, owned her own house, lived there with her children, and any future partner would come to live with her there if she remarried. If they divorced, he left to return to his mother's house.

The situation is even more surprising in Hausa cities, where the prostitution of young "liberated" women who have fled the rural yoke is integrated into a culture in which women are commonly secluded. A visitor can travel throughout the city all day long without seeing a woman, except for a few high-level administrative workers and elite women. Although more and more educated women do manage to avoid seclusion, the custom affects working-class women more and more. Yet as early as 1932, Margery Perham observed a line of French-speaking immigrants waiting to be circumcised so that they could visit the Muslim prostitutes of the city.[9]

In effect, the young Hausa women's situation is very close to the *malaya:* they are *karuwai,* or courtesans. They live cloistered together, and wait to be courted by clients who do not necessarily visit them for sex, at least the first time. Instead, clients obtain what they desire only following certain gift-giving and politeness rituals. The strangest thing is that the *karuwai* are proud of thus respecting the customs of modesty and seclusion demanded of women within a system at least officially quite distinct from houses of prostitution. These young women are usually about twelve, the youngest barely ten, and the oldest twenty-four. Almost all have already been married and thus, to the Hausa, are adults. Not all necessarily wanted to become *karuwai,* and not all have broken with their families of origin. For example, a girl might come to the city with a male relative or husband and later want to escape his control or start out fleeing a condition or rural marriage that she disliked. Parents start by looking for her but soon let her behave as she likes because her escape has already dishonored her. Often, the family will later choose to renew contact with her in order to exploit her; her earnings provide them a certain social standing. Some of these women remarry and then divorce, shifting from one social status to another according to circumstance. One-fifth also do another occasional or regular job as craftswomen or waitresses. Some, thanks to their friends, are able to find work in a modern sector of the economy. Others acquire real status as businesswomen. The wealthiest, thanks to their contacts, get jobs with the government. In 1973, they owned 71 out of the 123 houses in Katsina lived in by *karuwai.*

The *karuwai* have long enjoyed a good reputation. Liberated, innovative women, they were said to be the most intelligent and often the best educated of Hausa women. Their mobility also allowed them, after World War II, to accompany the bravest men in the Hausa diaspora's attempts to conquer the southern part of the country. They have official representation in Ibadan. Starting in the 1950s, they organized politically into distinct branches within the two primary parties of the South, the Nigerian Council of Nigeria and the Cameroons (NCNC) and the Action Group. Their freedom of movement allowed them to play a political role forbidden to wives, notably by registering on electoral rosters and voting.[10]

But they have since become much more working-class, and with their increasing poverty their situation has deteriorated. Since the early 1970s, drought has propelled more and more young rural women to the cities for survival. Many are foreigners and practice Western-style prostitution, like the *wazi-wazi* of Nairobi, in flophouses or by soliciting in their doorways or even against the front wall of their homes. These women are known as the "how-much-you-go-pay?"[11] Two-thirds of the five hundred *karuwai* in Katsina in 1973 were poor girls who had left their villages with little or no schooling. This work of theirs was indeed the only thing that gave them financial independence, even more so because half had no children. Their sterility was doubtless due to venereal disease. Unlike many other countries, the government has never sought to tax their work. The difficulties of their lives, however, and the extremities of their situation exposed them to frequent problems and even danger. During the worst years of the drought, expiatory measures to bring on rain targeted them directly as sacrificial lambs. To expel them from Sokoto and then other Hausa areas, they were required to marry or leave. In two weeks, half the *karuwai* of Katsina had done so. Some fled or hid with married women friends; their relative freedom and childlessness had helped them to make many friendships and to be very serviceable to other women. This behavior clearly shows the flexibility of their position and their solidarity as a group.

Free Women in the Cities of Central Africa

Courtesans are not limited to Islamic countries. In the 1950s in Kisangani or Kinshasa, some divorced and widowed women spent their youth working as prostitutes so that they could open shops or draw upon their investments as they aged.[12] Others at a higher level were independent mistresses to wealthy Africans or were real courtesans, changing their partners quite infrequently.[13] They were called *vedettes* (stars) in contrast to *chambres d'hotel* (hotel rooms), Western-style prostitutes who worked the bars and hotels.

On the eve of independence there were apparently more than 4,000 "free women" in Kinshasa. The *vedettes* (also called *basi ya kilo* in Lingala because they were the only ones who could afford to buy meat by the kilo) were well-off. They were more free, more elegant, and even more cultivated than wives because they were not, like wives, held to a modest and reserved demeanor. They could dance, joke, and laugh with men, who were happy to take them out to or meet them in public places. They were sought after by celebrities and even by Europeans.

Strictly speaking, these women cannot be bought. Their remuneration takes different forms—everything necessary for a good life, material security, but also professional or social advancement or simply well-being (or better-being). They find it appropriate to be given expensive gifts. They "borrow" to buy a house or a business and there is no question of repayment. They choose their suitors by financial capacity and calmly reject those they consider beneath their needs and pretensions. Urban young women in the Congo, proud of having purchased their independence with their bodies, have in fact invented a new slogan proclaiming their own kind of informal polyandry: "*Chic, chèque et choc*" (Looks, Checkbook, Heartthrob). This means that a woman has three men in her life, one she goes out with, one who writes the checks she needs to buy supplies and clothing and to have her hair done, and one she is in love with.

Is their existence linked only to a kind of women's liberation and the excesses of modern consumer culture, or does it have traditional roots? We find similar women in the past in the courts of the great chiefs: slaves, concubines, even, in the ancient interlacustrine states, the courtesans of Rwanda or Bunyoro.[14] But the *vedettes* have acquired quite a modern independence. Their problem remains survival as they age. As elsewhere, they try to ensure their future well-being by buying houses, shops, or gifts for their families—especially their nephews, since, as we have seen, most have few or no children. The more highly educated probably practice birth control, and, as everywhere, many fall victim to venereal disease. Today, in addition, many are condemned by AIDS.

Having left the traditional family mold, they have organized themselves into multiethnic groups. Before independence, some large companies had promotional fanclubs such as the Friends of Polar or the Friends of Primus (both beers). Male members received a hat with the company's logo on it, and women, for their promise to remain faithful to this or that bar owned by the brewery, could drink free. Similar groups formed around dance bands, where women were the "groupies." These groups of "free women" were even more successful because they were the only women's groups not to be controlled by Belgians through social agencies or by the Catholic church. After independence they became more diverse and most now are of modest size. The group chooses a name such as the Etoiles (Stars) or the Élégantes de Léo (Leo [poldville]'s Elegant Ladies). Sometimes they designate a man to arbitrate their conflicts. He is often a bar owner, married or not, renowned for his wealth but also for his impartiality, and not a potential pimp. The association plays both a protective and a social role. It is supposed to train women new to city life and to spread fashions but also to guarantee some mutual aid and defend its members' interests. Thus these kinds of prostitutes' associations are common in the city. They also occurred in the *Brazzavilles noires*,[15] the black sectors of Brazzaville, the capital of Congo, across the Congo River from Zaire.

Many of these women have other jobs in small trades or even salaried professions. The latter have the most respect, being properly speaking the freest, because their survival does not, or at least did not until very recently, depend on prostitution. Their clients provide them both contacts and the possibility of living beyond their means, with a pronounced taste for expensive clothes, new hairstyles, and beauty products.

We find a similar professional hierarchy in Kigali, the capital of Rwanda. At the bottom are the women who worked the small neighborhood bars, frequented by neighborhood people, and at the top are the "Kiyoru women," named after the city's luxury restaurant, the aristocrats of their trade.[16] The former have more choices; they can get hired for regular work, with the triple advantage of stable monthly revenues, a regular clientele, and the bar owner's protection, or they can go from bar to bar. They are free to choose their own hours and clients but have no security. Women sometimes combine the two kinds according to their needs and availability, though competition between the two groups results in rivalries.

The "Second Office": Semiprostitution

Since independence, in Kinshasa, Kigali, and many other cities, having a "second office" (or even a "third office") has become more common among the bourgeoisie, mainly civil servants and businessmen. This is a kind of modern polygamy, perverse because it is unofficial.[17] The rules are about the same as for *malaya* in Nairobi: an independent woman receives a man in her home, prepares food, offers beer. Her home, of course, is a relaxing, welcoming place for men who appreciate the chance to come there to chat and eat. With luck the woman can become the "office" of a politician or a high-level official. She may have other male friends, but usually this is in spite of the first. The great difference between this and marriage is the absence of a bride-price and, in Christian society, the clandestine nature of the liaison. Unexpectedly, the result is an accelerated cultural syncretism in urban areas, because the man naturally seeks his second office from outside his usual, recognized familial or ethnic circle. This system is becoming increasingly structured. The new couple has children, the "in-laws" demand recognition, and gifts and financial advantages are due them.

If we exclude countries such as Zambia or the Islamic Sahel, where colonial puritanism reinforced traditional beliefs, prostitution is far from having earned its practitioners the disapproval customary in Western countries, no doubt because of the very solid sexual autonomy that has protected women for so long from pimping by men. Women keep their options open to marry despite their ambivalence toward marriage, which they still desire as a guarantee of social status and protection but within which they are intolerant of partners whom they deem flighty, lazy, and incapable of meeting the needs of a family and children.

This semiprostitution[18] is growing in the city, especially among the middle classes, whereas full-time prostitutes tend to come from the villages. Prostitution is an unofficial second job whose revenues may start out small but quickly become indispensable. It is practiced in different ways. There is streetwalking (in Yaoundé called an "evening walk"), wherein women walk up and down the streets downtown without necessarily approaching men or even actively seeking them out. They know that the harder they are to get, the more expensive the gifts they receive will be. There are also "work sites," more like houses of prostitution but in which the owner charges the woman only for rental of the room. These are commercial establishments in which the waitresses may also work as prostitutes in a room at the client's disposal. These various practices are the province of both genders; there is also and increasingly male as well as female prostitution. This is a clear indication of the crisis of traditional family structures: In the city, individuals discover that they no longer need the community to survive. Traditional criteria are replaced by a new hierarchy of values whose adoption reveals the degree of assimilation to "modernity." Western attitudes and access to an ostentatious kind of consumption are its main symbols. Looks become essential; the prostitute parades around when she goes back to her village, and the city woman tries to outshine her schoolmates or office colleagues.

The Modern Traffic in Women

We must not overembellish liberated African prostitution, though it may be more relaxed than Western-style prostitution. In a society where marriage remains the only recognized condition for a woman, free women are subject to all sorts of mistreatment: The man who takes her as a partner has no respect for her because he has not paid the bride-price required by custom. Properly speaking, she is worthless. In many societies, she is no longer marriageable. In addition, as soon as she gets pregnant she loses her livelihood, because, as they say in Zaire, "A man doesn't mount another man's pregnancy." The woman loses respect for herself and becomes "like a garden without a fence, . . . a back-room missus."[19]

Prostitution has two common sordid aspects characteristic of the sex trade in places where young, isolated workers congregate. Thus western African ports were early on (as in South Africa) significant prostitution markets. In Nigeria, prostitution started earlier than elsewhere. As early as the beginning of the 1930s the little town of Opobo, in the coastal province of Calabar, was already a recruitment center; at least sixty women there lived off prostitution. In 1940 many prostitutes working in the Gold Coast came from this region. But prostitution was a particular specialty of the Obubra of the Cross River Basin. Starting in the 1920s, between 15 percent and 30 percent of women there went to become prostitutes in Nigerian ports (Lagos, Calabar, Port Harcourt), in Cameroon and Fernando Po (Equatorial Guinea), and in the Gold Coast. In this country there were more than five hundred Obubra prostitutes in the 1940s; 80 percent worked in Accra and the rest in Sekondi or Kumasi, in the interior.

Why did this region play such a primary role in furnishing prostitutes? It was conquered and occupied by the British relatively early, between 1888 and 1909. Forced labor ravaged the people, condemning men to exile and causing a significant surplus of women that the soldiery took advantage of. A factory opened in Ediba, which caused an influx of businessmen from the coast, who began buying local concubines. Ediba women were the first to go to the main market city, Bansara, to work and thence to the coast. This is how the custom began, and it developed even more because except in the cocoa-producing areas the region offered women no alternatives except work in the palm plantations. In 1939 the average income of a household was barely £2 a year, in contrast to £12 elsewhere. Prostitutes were, in the phrase of one colonial officer, "itinerant gold mines," to the point that when villages in this area wanted post offices accorded them it was attributed to their desire to keep in contact with these expatriate prostitutes. In 1942, postal money orders rose to £7,000, twice the amount of official public revenue from the district![20] These women had set themselves to earning money for their families who had remained in the villages to live on and allow them to build "hard" (i.e., cement) houses.

Sometimes this market trafficked in little girls kidnapped and then exported to Gold Coast ports. Trafficking was made easier because in cases of divorce, which were common because of women's independence, the children depended not on the father but on the mother's brother, who might have few scruples about hiding their sale as a kind of pseudo-marriage and justifying a supposed bride-price.

This is real trafficking, with the accompanying network of contacts (generally former prostitutes), merchants, and moneylenders. In contrast to Europe, it was organized by women, at least as concerned adult prostitutes. Women organized the trips, provided information during the journey, and, once they arrived, settled them in a friendly neighborhood where they would all live together in the same house. They soon began hiring young men, usually related, with enough education to keep the accounts and to serve as housekeepers and defenders as needed. Lack of safety made these young men numerous, although the women did manage for a long time to keep the men in their service rather than the other way around.

Thus pimping first appeared only a few years ago. "Free women" are less and less free as prostitution grows in today's cities, mostly controlled by women such as the *mamies* of Ghana or the *matrones* of Abidjan. This is a new kind of slave trade. Parents in poor outlying areas of Nigeria, Ghana, Burkina Faso, or even northern Côte d'Ivoire sell their daughters in claimed or simulated marriage and do not ask too many questions once the bride-price has been paid. The "fiancés" and "husbands" are nothing other than an army of "nephews," young unemployed men and delinquents from the big city charged with finding and transporting their human merchandise to the flophouses where they will be put to work. We are far from yesterday's free woman here. The increasing danger of the metropolitan areas has encouraged the recent appearance of African pimps, who until recently were all white.[21]

This enormous industry is on a tragic path: Around 1990, at least 80 percent of Nairobi prostitutes were sero-positive for AIDS. Today it is likely that almost all are infected, as it assuredly is in Kinshasa, Douala, Abidjan, and elsewhere. Not only will these women die of it but, having lost their livelihood, they will descend into poverty first.

12

Women and Factory Work

Women were seldom employed in colonial industries. The colonizers' rationale for this was based both on tradition (which forbade women's leaving their villages) and on their belief in women's inability to understand things modern because of lack of instruction or perhaps intelligence—hardly convincing but effective, because the result was that with few exceptions, the idea of women's having salaried jobs was not accepted. Western cultural traditions made white powers look to men, who were, it is true, more available. They no longer had the right to make war or hunt, whereas women remained responsible for most food production and subsistence-level business and seldom had the chance to enter the modern workforce. This division of labor by gender arose neither from chance nor from fatalism but from the most profitable symbiosis both for salaried African men and for their urban employers. Men brought back cash, and the women helped ensure the group's survival. This system allowed the men to be paid lower salaries.

Women's labor power was not used in the earliest phase of colonialism except in little-known cases of thinly disguised slavery—for example, the hundred or so young Christian women in a Ségou workshop, "bought back" by the Sisters to convert them but used in the 1930s as factory weavers under conditions that disregarded child labor laws entirely. This case is perhaps an extreme one but certainly explains why the first strikes there were launched in 1946–1947 by girls from ten to twelve years of age.[1]

The African mind-set hardly allowed women the freedom of movement needed for work in a factory. Almost everywhere, women workers were despised. Usually young and divorced or unmarried, they often sought regular salaries because they were responsible for one or several children. Among men, the financial autonomy of their wives in the factory was ill-accepted: it meant that a woman was "lost," suspected of using her economic indepen-

129

dence to satisfy "immoral" appetites. Confusing cause and effect, public opinion claimed that women worked in factories not to escape life as a prostitute or concubine but to achieve sexual freedom.[2] Work of this kind supposedly led straight to libertinage: "Women who work in the factory are no good for a husband. They might earn money and give it to a lover. They might make children, but they are really not committed. They do as they please because they have money from the company."[3]

A Small Number of Female Factory Workers

This mental block on the part of both Western employers and Africans meant that at independence female factory workers numbered close to zero except in South Africa. "In Africa, the modern sector is in fact the preserve of men," it was noted in 1970.[4] This remains true, although ten years later female salaried workers had advanced significantly. Women remained not even one-fourth of salaried employees, and the percentage in industry seldom reached 10 percent.[5] Enclaves within South Africa, especially Swaziland, were an exception because of the absence of men, who were attracted by less impecunious contracts to the mines and factories of South Africa.

Yet women were sometimes more apt and often better trained for manual labor than men. Administrators in Equatorial Africa officially demanded men for "services," work "in the general interest," such as clearing trails and building public buildings but were well aware that the men would send their wives and slaves in their places. Some colonial officers went directly to collect the women in the villages, although nothing was said overtly.[6]

This same kind of tolerance was practiced on Tanganyikan (now Tanzanian) plantations. From the time of the Swahilis, slaves, both men and women, were the bulk of the workforce in sisal cultivation, and were replaced often, because their mortality was 22–30 percent per year. The Germans and then the British replaced them with young, often unmarried, migrant adults recruited for two-year contracts, usually Ngoni;[7] some workers, especially the Makonde in northern Mozambique, started coming as whole families, and plantation owners certainly did not refuse to hire their wives, reportedly hard workers. The British began to worry when, in the beginning of the 1930s, there was question of ratifying the International Labor Organization's convention seeking to regulate women's labor, among others. Although local authorities confirmed that the question need not even be asked, protests were raised in 1938 when the rule against women's working at night went into effect. But we must recognize that this officially applied to only a tiny minority. In 1951, Tanzanian women were only 5 percent of salaried workers, even though 80 percent were agricultural workers compared with only 47 percent of men.[8] This local survey is probably indicative of the situation in all of sub-Saharan Africa.

The South African Case

Until the 1960s, in South Africa as elsewhere, the female proletarian class was little developed and even less so among African women. The mines traditionally used only men as they did in Europe. Industry was limited in the 1920s and mostly employed white or colored men. Sex stereotypes, racial discrimination, and legal rigidity, restrictive in matters of apprenticeship, forbade women and especially black women to claim decently paid semi-skilled jobs. At best a cottage weaving industry was attempted, without success and under the most shocking conditions of exploitation. In total, around 1917, some 6,000 female workers were counted in the Cape colony, two-thirds under nineteen, and almost all white, with a few colored women. White women factory workers, mostly in the textile industry, though better paid than an African male worker, cost employers much less than white male workers. Their numbers increased with the South African industrial boom of the 1930s, which was especially centered in the Cape. They continued to be employed in the textile industry but also entered the leather and book industries. The bulk of them were colored; Asian workers were more rare and sought after, but African women continued to be practically excluded. A law of 1930 gave local authorities the right to expel women who could not prove residency from certain cities, which contributed to keeping black women in domestic service, which had been abandoned by white and colored women, and which came with housing.[9] The best they could hope for was to become waitresses or seamstresses.

Change began with World War II. Once the problem of poor whites was resolved, the gaps left by white female factory workers who now preferred office work, retail sales, or waitressing had to be filled. African women leapt into this gap, helping to meet needs connected with intensified production during the war. Faced with working-class penury, some industrialists, for example, in the shoemaking and wool industries of the western Cape (in Port Elizabeth or Uitenhage), began to think about hiring black women. Although they were paid a third less than men, these jobs meant regular work for them that was less exhausting and better paid than domestic work.[10] In Transvaal, colored women now constituted but one-fourth of female workers; they began going to work younger, between fifteen and twenty-five, and half of them stopped when they married. African women instead found factory work more compatible with their family responsibilities. They entered the factory as adults, half of them between twenty-five and thirty-four, or else when they became widows, and often after having begun their working lives as domestics.[11]

Women's entry into the industrial sector gave them a freedom of movement up until then unknown. Female workers, generally a little better educated, were less subservient here than in domestic service and earned more.

In the Cape they tended to be from the more established black families and to be daughters rather than wives of teachers, agents, or pastors. They earned a certain autonomy in the factories not only in urban society but also in their private lives. Divorce increased. Connections with their rural families grew distant, and as financially independent women they learned to do without men's help in assuming their family responsibilities.[12] They were a small, homogeneous group, energetic and militant, first in the garment industry and then in the food industry, combining a relatively privileged place in black society with a class consciousness marked by marxism. In the 1940s and 1950s, before apartheid made it impossible, their union activities were known for being mixed, drawing together women of all colors.

Urban female salaried workers greatly encouraged independent womanhood. This is why the nationalist government in 1952 took drastic measures to press them back, imposing on them passes that were needed to establish residency as it already had on men.[13]

The turning point came after 1960, when wives' salaries became indispensable to maintaining a certain lifestyle and single women had no choice but to work for a salary. Apartheid took care of the rest; the government gave regular women residents of the city an advantage over immigrant workers. As for other women, many were among the 3.5 million deported between 1960 and 1983 to Bantustans.

Starting in the 1970s, the combined pressures of urban social movements and international opinion forced the state to remedy the destitution of at least some of the "homelands." The beginnings of economic depression also caused industrialists to reduce their production costs and move. A series of industries that had employed much of the labor force—first of all, the textile industry, light electrical assembly, and chemically polluting industries—moved to the Bantustans. As in Swaziland and Lesotho, which were deserted by men, a great number of women were hired on-site both because there were so many of them and because they were more likely to accept famine-level salaries without flinching.[14] Between 1969 and 1981 the number of African women working in salaried jobs quadrupled, and among women factory workers, the percentage of African women went from 30 percent to more than 42 percent.[15] At the same time, repression cracked down on the militants who had been so active in the South African Congress of Trade Unions (SACTU). Ray Alexander went to Zambia in exile, Bettie du Toit went to Ghana, and others such as Mary Mafeking, Frances Baard, Mary Moodley, and Liz Abraham were arrested, banished, or exiled to distant Bantustans.[16] Unionism hid under a call for social change that was not without ambiguity—measures called for in the name of "women" (with no specifics), cautiously ignoring the racial discrimination from which all nonwhites suffered.[17] Black women's work in industry is now a reality in South Africa. Despite their energetic participation in the renewed fight against apartheid, however, the general political debate seems to have overlooked the question of working women.

Women Factory Workers: Loose Women?

In tropical and South Africa, a female proletariat arose in the 1960s but on a large scale only with independence. It was not until 1957 in Tanganyika that the colonial state finally decided to guarantee a minimum wage that began by establishing a lower wage for women.[18] The Tanzanian state stopped this discrimination, officially at least, in 1962. The percentage of independent women (divorced, widowed, or other) who migrated to Dar es Salaam went from 13 percent in 1950 to 33 percent twenty years later, and most were sixteen to twenty-four. They were the majority of women recruited to the factory.[19] The same was true in 1965 in Kinshasa's largest textile mill. Women workers were much more rooted in the city there, much younger on average than the men, and had a lower level of education, although in the preceding ten years the educational gap had closed somewhat.[20]

Tanzanian working women were held back by their low educational level; recruitment was usually confined to persons who had at least been to elementary school, which still meant just a third of girls.[21] Yet they are no longer exceptional. Wherever there is need for a large low-skilled workforce, women are preferred; for example, in the Tanita peanut factory, three-fourths of the workers are women,[22] and in a particularly archaic factory manufacturing a pyrethrum-based antimosquito product women, "hard workers, patient, and not difficult," are preferred.[23] But the use of women declines with increasing mechanization, and companies continue to doubt women's competence and especially their diligence. The Tanzanian Kibo match factory, which employed 90 percent women before 1969, reduced its female workers to 30 percent and then to 20 percent in 1975 despite doubling its total workforce. The change was even more radical at the Moschi coffee factory, where automation begun in 1972 resulted in all eight hundred female workers' being fired.

Employers especially fear pregnancy in their women workers. The Tanzanian law of 1975, designed to protect women by guaranteeing them paid maternity leave of twelve weeks every three years, has sometimes perversely had the opposite effect, with companies putting an immediate stop to female hiring.

Women working in factories are usually heads of single-parent families: 79 of the Kinshasan women workers already cited had lived with 198 men during the past thirty-six months, by their own estimates. Salaried work seemed to them the answer to a marriage situation that was both fragile and uncertain. But women with children know how to cope as they do everywhere in the world. Their own proletarianization often implies a female subproletariat whom they depend on. In Tanzania, 40 percent of them have their children kept by their families, generally by a grandmother; 30 percent pay a salaried woman or *ayah;*[24] 20 percent bring a younger female relative from the village who is officially a domestic, 5 percent use their own parents, and the remaining 5 percent coordinate with female neighbors. In other words, even though the small salary they receive and the disrespect they are held in leaves them with no illusions about their active participation in the operation of a factory where they endure their work "as a flag obeys the wind,"[25] their absenteeism and incompetence are above all a pretext if not a prejudice rooted in a half-century of male colonization. Otherwise, how can we understand, even allowing for enduring cultural differences, why these illiterate working women should be so prized in Asia for their ability and docility while being rejected in Africa for their incompetence and disorderly conduct?

Making Less Money Than in the Informal Sector

In western Africa, where women have always been a part of working life, the relative absence of female factory workers is even more surprising. This is not entirely attributable to Europeans' bad faith. The case of Nigeria, which has several solid automotive, tobacco, textile, and food factories around big cities like Lagos, Ibadan, Kano, and Port Harcourt, might suggest that women do not *want* to become factory workers because they know it is not in their interest.[26] Why would only men go from the informal sector to industry of their own free will, whereas nothing in Yoruba tradition keeps women from working outside their homes and doing paid work? True, women are seldom recruited by multinationals, and those who work in industry do so in small, backward businesses, as in Tanzania, which seek low-skilled workers and pay particularly poorly. But this is not always the case.

The case of the Odu textile mill allows us to understand women's motives. This factory was established in 1966 in the current province of Ondo in Nigeria, a region where hand weaving was an ancient craft. The local chief, educated and "modern," wanted to create jobs locally. But in 1972 the factory employed only 62 women compared with 1,300 men. The percentage of "independent women" working in Nigeria was the same as in Tanzania, 63 percent. Was this chance, in two countries so different from each other? The workers were young—70 percent of men and 95 percent of women were under thirty—but there the similarity stopped, because in Odu all had a satisfactory level of education.[27] For one-fifth this was their first job. The others (15 percent of men and almost 40 percent of the women) came from another occupational sector, either teachers or clerks, or traders having a hard time. Some had come from Lagos, where the cost of living was high; they had changed jobs because their salaries had been too low or too irregularly paid. A very few women came from the informal sector (surprising for Yoruba), no doubt because they were unmarried and it is generally the husband who provides the small amount of capital used to start a small business.

Considering this relatively exceptional cultural level for workers, one might expect these women to have held semiresponsible posts, but this was hardly the case. They had been hired to prepare cotton thread for the looms, an easy, repetitive job that required no excessive physical labor, and they could do it while sitting and talking. But they knew that the company would give them no promotions or salary increases for fear of having to give them more during any future maternity leaves. So for them it was just a temporary job, useful only for earning the minimum they needed to start an informal-sector business in which with a little luck they could do much better. Men, in contrast, had ambitions to become independent craftsman, which required some advancement. Thus although men and women were equally qualified in this company and had the same goals, their attitudes toward the job were radically different.

We should not forget about African male sexism, particularly but not exclusively in Muslim countries. Among the Hausa of northern Nigeria a man, more so than elsewhere, will not accept being supervised by a woman. In Zaria, for example, a little electricity-generating factory founded in 1976 employs 350 people, one-third women. They are remarkably well treated and in theory enjoy the same rights as the men. They have equal pay for equal qualifications and seniority, and their jobs are guaranteed. The only difference one might observe is that only women are required to sweep the workshops, because the men refuse: "They don't know how, it's not their role." Yet in 1983 a revealing thing happened when a group of workers were to be selected for additional training in preparation for promotion. No woman was considered by management for the training, although the numbers of candidates of each sex were about equal. The women protested but found support neither among the foremen nor among the male workers.[28]

Except in South Africa, the number of African women factory workers remains remarkably low. Their situation has been little studied, as though they did not exist.

13

Women and Poverty: The Future of Female Informal-Sector Employment

Since independence and especially with the cycle of droughts that began in 1973, there has been an increasing flow of poverty-stricken young women from places such as Uganda, Rwanda, and Zaire to big cities such as Nairobi, Kampala, and Kinshasa. This is human evidence of the terrible condition of the countryside. Far from having been rejected by their families, these young immigrants have instead been sent by their families to the city for several years to earn the meager funds they need to revitalize their dying villages. More and more it is question of keeping the family group alive, in the city and the country.

Today more than ever, city life is in women's hands. The lack of regular jobs in industry and in the service sector, accentuated by the economic crisis and uncontrolled population growth, causes a considerable increase in informal-sector work in cities like those cited, where almost 70 percent of inhabitants are under twenty-five. What in the early days of independence was merely supplemental support has become households' very livelihoods. Men's salaries are now utterly insufficient, and the number of unemployed young people continues to increase.

Female Poverty

Socially marginal in the extreme, in the cities in disproportionate numbers in relation to their work, increasing numbers of women—widows, unmarried mothers, orphaned girls—are excluded from any regular work. Gradually, all that is left to them is prostitution, actually a disguised form of begging. The schoolgirl sells herself for a few treats, the college student sleeps with her teachers for a few more points, the employee becomes the boss's mistress to keep her job, the market woman compensates for mediocre sales by going out with some of her clients, the partner or wife of a polygamous man takes other lovers to make up for his insufficient income, and especially young rural women, driven from their villages by poverty, fall prey to the prostitution that is commonplace in many large African cities—Addis Ababa, Abidjan, Kisangani, and Accra.

Their lot is the more desperate in that they come from extremely misogynous cultures like those of central Africa or hierarchical societies with slaving pasts that lead families to treat their daughters as merchandise—selling them to traffickers who market them in the city as domestics or bar girls, or exploiting them to earn a little extra at three important stages of their lives: when their pregnant daughter points out the guilty party and they can try to get reparations in hard cash, when the baby arrives and the family can again seek damages or at least impose marriage, accompanied by a bride-price, and when, some months later, if the newborn dies, they have a new opportunity for ransom. Prostituted or not, the daughter's life is reduced to its economic value. A widow is no better off: tossed out like damaged goods, she can either return to her family or sell herself. This is the kind of choice that can land her in the cities of Zaire.[1]

Yet prostitution is not a woman's *only* recourse but is sometimes combined with other survival strategies, more and more commonly microenterprises.

The Female Informal Sector and Urban Survival

At first glance, women seem to be going about their modest trading activities in front of their own homes, in tiny neighborhood squares, or in the marketplace and to be working in order to satisfy their need for pocket money, amusements for their children, clothing, or jewelry. But this stereotypic view does not withstand closer scrutiny: The husband's reduced or nonexistent income has changed the purpose of women's work both among working-class women and among most office employees. It is clear that in the cities paid work is essential to women's daily bread. Little by little, women have gained a toehold everywhere. Their frequent illiteracy often requires them to work clandestinely, and this keeps their profits from being eaten up by taxes and licenses. Very severe competition and their not expecting to be paid by the hour helps to content them with the tiny profit margins that make their services competitive compared with expensive goods bought in the formal sector or with imports. Cooked dishes bought on the sidewalk are less expensive than in the cafeteria; locally produced goods and contraband sold illegally are cheaper than in the local supermarket; and the domestic work of a young female relative or little girl comes more cheaply than that of a salaried houseboy.

Food, clothing, and a panoply of basic services are now provided mostly by women, especially in impoverished megalopolises such as Kinshasa and Abidjan. Here is our explanation for the "abnormally" large number of women in a capital such as Addis Ababa, and it is true even of smaller cities such as the Zambian Copperbelt towns and Saint-Louis du Sénégal, which have lost their administrative, manufacturing, and even mining jobs (or never had many to begin with) and today are losing economic momentum.

In Saint-Louis, for example, women have not only taken over supply distribution but also increasingly the production side. The town, which has one of the largest female populations in Africa, counted at least 70,000 women (out of 130,000 inhabitants) in 1985, of whom almost half were of working age. Of this group, at least half were doing income-generating work and making small and precarious incomes that were still vital in a city where there were not many options. Despite its four high schools and its new university, most jobseekers go to distant Dakar. Women are a majority of domestic workers and also specialize in everyday handicrafts production. Truth be told, women support the city's population. Ironically, they are less a part of food production. They are content to buy fish from the fishermen and to help male gardeners water, tend, or harvest market garden produce, which they then sell at market or in neighborhoods. They are, however, a large part of the manufacturing sector, working as dyers, seamstresses, and producers of dried fish. Very few (22 dry cleaners and 6 seamstresses) are registered with the Chamber of Trades, and none votes in the Chamber of Commerce. Yet the women dyers' cooperative has 109 members (out of at least 250 dyers) and the dried fish producers' cooperative has 320 female members (out of 1,500).

Once reserved for lower-caste women, these professions recently opened up both out of necessity and because of technological advances, for example, in the use of chemicals for dying instead of indigo or kola nut, which required real knowledge. We must add about 100 seamstresses as well, 100 or so women restauranteurs, even more women renting rooms (since boarding schools closed in 1980 for lack of money), and innumerable improvised makers of cooked dishes for sale in the marketplaces, streets, or school entrances.[2] Many are surrounded by apprentices from the numbers of young women who have left area schools. For very low wages they keep their employer alive and ensure their own survival by buying the right to use their work tools for their own benefit (a sewing machine, for example), selling lower-quality products to a less-moneyed clientele.

Clienteles can be scarce, except for those buying fish, and then one has to sell it all over the region, along the river or in Dakar, even on the other side of the river in Mauritania, and in the English-speaking ports to the south. Every craftswoman is surrounded by young vendors who will walk her merchandise around for sale and on credit. The finest women dyers, specializing in the dark indigo dye highly prized by Mauritanian women, sell it on the Mauritanian side of the river. Other women merchants buy contraband of various kinds in Rosso (Mauritania). Profits come with risks but are relatively high. Women are also important in distribution. Since the 1970s, about thirty wholesalers and over a hundred retailers monopolize the food market, having stolen from men what was once their exclusive province—hats, dresses, shoes, and some dry goods like sugar, coffee, tinned milk, oil, and rice. Still outside their control are butchered meats, hardware, and audio and visual equipment—anything requiring sitting on expensive stock or credit beyond their financial reserves.

All indicators lead us to believe that this is spreading throughout Africa, and particularly in the cities. How else can we understand how so many poor people survive, often enormously in the majority in urban areas, when formal supply networks have disappeared and only the wealthiest can enjoy the fruits of the shamelessly bold parallel market? Today's large cities survive on female labor, tireless and meagerly paid; a tiny percentage of women actually "make it."

But everyone uses these informal networks. For example, parents in Dakar can send an allowance (in two days and in cash) to their children at school in France—not through formal banking mechanisms (which are increasingly unsafe and slow) but by going to the Sandaga market at the city's center where more money than one might guess is moving around. Not all informal networks necessarily involve women, but more and more some women do hold important positions within such systems. They are part of the little-understood social forces that may in years to come overturn the nation's economic assumptions and domestic politics.

Queen mother brass head, Benin City, early fifteenth century. Museum fuer Voelkerkunde, Staatliche Museen, Berlin, Germany. Photo courtesy of Bridgeman/Art Resource, New York.

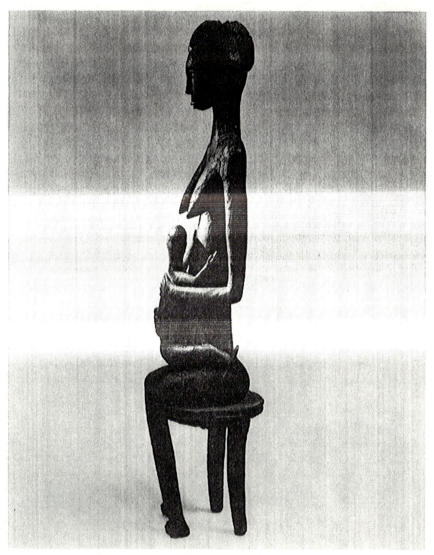

Mother and child statue, Bambara, Mali. Photo by Jerry L. Thompson, courtesy of the Walt Disney-Tishman Collection of African Art.

Women and apartheid in Johannesburg, 1977. Photo courtesy of the author.

Women selling crafts at the pier, Ganvie, Benin. Photo courtesy of the author.

Women at Ganvie, Benin: A water-village on the lagoon. Photos courtesy of the author.

A Christian cult at Dissin, Burkina Faso. Photo courtesy of the author.

Anyi chief's wives attending yam festival at Asouba, Côte d'Ivoire. Photo courtesy of the author.

Rice harvest in Casamance (South Senegal). Photo courtesy of the author.

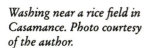

Washing near a rice field in Casamance. Photo courtesy of the author.

The first wife of a Senegalese civil servant, Dakar. Photo courtesy of the author.

A girl in Kaolack selling peanuts. Photo courtesy of the author.

Chad marketplace, Djamena. Photo courtesy of the author.

Market women offering their produce at a railway station, Côte d'Ivoire. Photo courtesy of the author.

Cartoon from Na Zona da Frelimo.

Poster from Na Zona da Frelimo.

Portrait of a couple, Bamako, Mali, 1950s. Photographer unknown. Photo courtesy of the Museum of African Art, from Africa Explores: 20th Century African Art. *Collection of Susan Vogel.*

PART FOUR

Women and Modern Life

14

Women and School

About girls' education in traditional society I will say no more than has already been sketched. Little girls were raised by their mothers, aunts, and sisters in their image. Their place and role in society varied; their initiation and religious practices differed according to where they were and in what era. This essay is not an anthropological study; our problem is instead to understand, given the heritage that we now have some sense of, what changed with colonization. We might have guessed that women were not the favorites of colonial schools, both because of their inheritance from their own cultures and because of that imported by the colonizers.

Congolese Conformism

The Belgian Congo is a caricature of excess. In British-colonized countries, the influence of the Protestant Reformation favored individuals' advancement and mitigated at least some of the period's conventionality. The principles of equality emerging from the French Revolution and the tendency toward assimilation in the Portuguese-colonized countries had the same effect. None of these advantages were obtained in the Belgian Congo, where at independence there was one female high-school graduate—Sophie Kanza, daughter of the mayor of Leopoldville, who had graduated from Sacred Heart High School in June 1961.

The colonial authorities tried as they might to blame families for rejecting modern schools for their daughters. It is true that in the early days of colonization parents were wary of their daughters' conversion, which went along with school attendance. They most feared that the young woman would draw support from her new religion to avoid the traditional marriage prepared for her years earlier, in which there had been no question of consulting her. If she did avoid it, the bride-price would have to be repaid, since it was generally paid in advance in central Africa.[1] Belgian conservativism in matters of female education did not help matters. Catholic missionaries were in charge of almost all the schools;[2] most came from Flanders and were very conservative, very rural, and hardly interested in girls' emancipation. Thus a double discrimination against girls arose, one a product of traditional local cultures and the other of Western culture.

Missionaries' Prejudices

What we might call Christian patriarchy sought to achieve Christianization without Westernization, always the missionaries' key contradiction. They thought they could avoid the ill effects of an overly broad-minded education and subversive ideas by emphasizing biblical teachings and Christian practices. But in fighting customs that they felt conflicted with religion, such as polygamy, traditional ritual, and early sexual relations, they brought about a radical shift in women's lifestyle; they turned African women into wives on the Western model, at the same time trying to preserve the "good" traditions that would combat peasant women's paganism and city women's debauchery.

Missionary ideology emphasized the differences between the sexes and male superiority. All authority came from God through the image of the father upheld by the mission. Monks and priests served as model patriarchs, creating farming businesses and distributing food along with the good word. Neither boys nor girls were intended to assimilate with whites, but the Christian way called for the father to dominate his children and the family head to dominate the private farm. Men were encouraged to cultivate for colonial export. Missionaries would have liked them to subsistence-farm as well, considering it indecent for women to work outdoors. Therefore they distributed seeds to the men and provided them agricultural training and the rudiments of management while complaining about their laziness. The girls, educated by nuns, were supposed to develop the qualities of docility and sweetness and to practice housekeeping. The goal here was to make them good mothers, prepared to remain in the home and instill Christian values in their children.

Therefore, education could not be the same for both sexes. Rules regarding access to school, the subjects taught, which language was used, and, ultimately, the numbers of each sex who attended school all differed according to gender. The evolution of colonial ideology can be read in its progress in teaching boys, with the twofold goal of creating assistant religious officials (priests and pastors) and giving them training that colonialism could use. But girls' training hardly evolved at all; its goal remained inculcating the Christian morality essential to their role as wives and mothers.

A Domestic Program

In the Belgian Congo, neither the laws of 1890 or 1892 nor the concordat (an agreement signed into law with the Vatican) of 1906 mention girls' education. Even so, some schools emerged at the end of the nineteenth century that taught boys farming, woodworking, ironworking, and bricklaying and made girls good wives who knew the basics of washing, cooking, and sewing, all European-style.

The minority Protestants were more innovative; their schools taught the sexes together and required Bible-reading, seeking to create girls who would be agents of conversion. The Catholics kept the sexes segregated and taught girls only religion. Reading and writing, which boys began to demand along with a little geography, were considered hazardous to girls' mental health and likely to distract them from their domestic duties. As a result, in 1906, girls made up only 15 percent of 48,000 schoolchildren.

The education code (not promulgated until 1929) maintained that "the domestic education of women is an important factor for the elevation of the race and the development of its needs." This set the model whereby only village elementary schools (which covered the first two years) could teach the sexes together, and even then the only manual labor taught girls was a little gardening. Actual primary school separated the sexes for three years and was sometimes followed by a professional school, also sex-segregated, which lasted from one to three years. Only boys could choose to take French, useful to would-be administrative agents. They were expected to become instructors, craftsmen, agents, and animal husbandry farmers knowledgeable in irrigation, horticulture, plantation agriculture, and animal husbandry. Girls could choose between being housewives or primary schoolteachers or train in social centers for married women as household aides to European families. (This latter was rare, because most domestics were men.) Girls learned to make Belgian-style soup (important in the old Belgian colonies), cheese, and butter, to improve their pottery, and to make mats. The gap in educational level between the genders widened. On the eve of World War II, out of some 10 million inhabitants, half of the boys (several hundred thousand) had some education. In 1958 there were 1.5 million children in school, but almost all of them were in primary school. Yet only 20,000 in the schools were girls. Missionaries ran several novitiates but only twenty-four small professional schools designed to "occupy" girls between the end of primary school and marriage at fourteen to sixteen: nine women teachers' schools, twelve housekeeping and farming schools, and three health schools that trained about a hundred nurses' aides per year.

One step was taken only after the war. The education code of 1948 for the first time gave boys the chance to go to secondary school for six years, and this encouraged new public primary and secondary schools to develop alongside the religious ones. Yet progress was slow. The Catholic University of Lovanium, created in Leopoldville for the white settlers, had only one black student in 1954 and only six black graduates by independence.

The philosophy behind girls' training remained practical in focus. The education code merely stated that the government "would have liked" to develop girls' education at the same rate as boys' but placed the blame for the status quo on traditional society—the "atavistic servitude" of the female condition—and on women's "generally lesser" intellectual receptivity. Last, it blamed Congolese families for opposition to their daughters' education.[3] These daughters could attend to the first three years of secondary school but until the mid-1960s could not go to the three latter years optional for boys, where classes were in French. Yet for the first time girls could learn French in "ordinary" primary schools, where "simple and practical" subjects were taught in local languages. In theory, they were allowed to enter the university, but at independence there were no female university students. Some innovation was shown in the creation of a few less narrow professional schools, but these continued to offer courses in "women's trades"; in 1960 there were seven of them, specializing in clothing, dressmaking, hats, and textiles. A Belgian mission sent by the new liberal-socialist coalition government (not Catholic for the first time) in 1954 sharply criticized the training given girls, arguing that not even housekeeping was taught correctly.

Belgian missionaries were not the only ones to promote such distorted forms of education. The White Sisters did no better in Segou with their Malian girl charges when in 1922, to finance their mission's work, they organized the workshop for weaving fine woolens described above. Under cover of apprenticeship, the little Christians were put to work. As early as three or four, they sorted wool. Soon the young workers who had been placed at the nuns's disposal by local chiefs (by order of the administration) numbered a hundred. International recognition came with a gold medal at the Decorative Arts Exhibition in Paris in 1926 and again in 1931 at the International Colonial Exhibition, where six little Malian girls were sent to weave for the spectators in Vincennes (France). Photos from the period clearly show how the children were used. So many orders came in in 1930 that Bamako's new bishop repealed the requirement that little Christian girls of the city go to school: "Girls who do not go will go to the workroom," the sisters said. Orphans given to the mission's care received no education at all but were put to work at five or six. The Sisters, hardly better treated by the Fathers, did not feel this life of continual labor unusual for little girls. Only Christian boys had to go to school until the age of twelve.[4]

Thrown into the Informal Sector

The educational imbalance, one of the greatest in any colonial situation, increased. When Congo became independent there were only 20 percent of girls in primary school (out of 1.6 million students) and only 4 percent in secondary school.[5] Barely one-fifth of the 2 million school-aged girls (five to nineteen) went to school.[6] The result was that, even in big cities, most women could not speak French. In Stanleyville (Kisangani) in the 1950s, fewer than 5 percent of women held salaried jobs, only 15 percent had gone to school, and few women had visited the city's downtown, the whites' sector. Yet women's condition in the city was still better than in the villages, because in Kisangani one-third of the school-aged girls did go to school compared with half of the boys.

Few girls could imagine themselves having jobs in colonial society. The clergy were still their likeliest employers. Several thousand women worked in missions, and there were 745 African nuns. But there were still only 15 nurses compared with 485 midwives,[7] and the situation hardly changed during the early years of independence. Around 1970 there were officially only 70 salaried women employees (almost all nurses or teachers) in Lubumbashi out of 6,600 women working for pay. In contrast to Senegal, there were no women doctors in Zaire in this period (compared with 300 Zairean male doctors), although several hundred male medical assistants had been sent to Europe for additional training. Eighty years of education had produced only a few hundred nurses and teachers, a few dozen women directors of health centers and housekeeping schools, and one assistant teacher at the university.

Blaming this entirely on "tradition" would be too easy. The truth is that the two notions of female dependence, the African and the European, each as limiting as the other, reinforced gender inequality. What is less well-known is the impact this kind of training may have had on the minds of young Zairean women, standing in the doorway to the modern world but denied the key in the name of the morals they had been taught. This is at least part of the reason "free girls" today are still waiting for a slice of the pie they have been forbidden to taste or even to want but making no effort on their own. African women have been sinned against by omission. The concerted effort to exclude them has put even more distance between them and men, especially those known as *evalués,* participants in modern Western-style African society.

Men have often been unable to resist family pressures requiring them to marry a girl from their village or at least one living "traditionally," but everything has encouraged them to look for something different. This explains the success in cities of independent women. These women are the only ones who have managed to free themselves in their own way from this double yoke, but men are able to see them only as mistresses.[8] Thus the vicious circle is closed: the girl, trained to be obedient and submissive, rebels against the rough traditional limitations imposed on her and against the inferiority of her modern condition. She escapes it all, but at the cost of remaining outside social norms and mores. She has no recourse other than the informal sector, whence the confusion between her being "free" and her being "easy."

South African Conformism

In South Africa, in contrast, more African girls were educated early on than boys, at least in primary school. Equality in numbers between the two sexes, achieved in the Cape colony in the midnineteenth century, persists today. In the early 1980s there were 1.6 million African children of each sex in South African schools.[9] The reasons for this are complex and derive from enduring African customs and beliefs with regard to boys, girls representing the weak link in the chain. The reasoning most often advanced is that predominantly pastoral societies needed very young boys to guard the herds, a male privilege, and this tendency was reinforced by migrant mine work, a sign of entry into the modern economy that required no particular educational level. Girls (or their mothers, the old society's veritable beasts of burden) were felt to be probably more receptive to Christian teaching. Missionaries were very active in South Africa beginning in the eighteenth century and paid particular attention to girls, whom they wanted to turn into vectors of Christian domestic values. Ultimately, particularly in the twentieth century, girls could hardly hope to become anything other than housewives (which was the expectation of the training they received) and so might hope to increase their market value (expressed in a higher bride-price) by gaining skills. For all the above reasons, the number of educated girls at the elementary level was from the start at least equal to the number of boys.

Retrogressive Education

South African girls' education had at least one thing in common with education in the Belgian Congo: it was and remains backward. The Protestant missionaries of South Africa and particularly the Boer Puritans considered African women inferior beings, but all things being equal white women were hardly thought of any better. The domestic ideal predominated, since the missionaries' influence, buttressed by Victorian ideology that kept women at home, spread much earlier than in the rest of Africa. The influence of nineteenth-century Protestant missionaries on the Xhosa of the Cape's eastern borders was considerable. Here, in the twentieth century, more than anywhere else in Africa, domesticity was advanced as the only possible option for girls.

This makes girls sound privileged,[10] but that is a numerical illusion. Qualitatively, it is quite the opposite; in 1955 the total number of African women in the last two years of secondary school was only 432. Inequality was flagrant even among whites, with many girls leaving secondary school before their certificate while boys finish their last year and may go on to the university. Higher education was popular among white males but attracted few girls. In 1970, with about equal opportunity, there was only one girl for every two boys who received her B.A., one out of five who got her Master's, and only one in ten who reached the Ph.D.[11] Girls' inferiority was only the exaggeration of what was common in the West; that same year, girls made up only 30 percent of British undergraduates and 16 percent of graduate students, and women were only 9 percent of teaching personnel.

The figures are much lower for black women. Girls stop attending in the middle of secondary school, but there are still more girls than boys at the end of junior high school; 70 percent of girls fail the junior certificate compared with 42 percent of boys. Only one girl for every two boys completes her education, and only 3 percent earn the right to enroll at the university, four times fewer than boys.[12] School attendance is not obligatory for Africans, and in 1970 23 percent of women in the cities and 60 percent of peasant women had never been to school. Shula Marks tells us the sad story of a poor orphaned girl in Transkei, Lily Moya. Born in 1933 to a family of Christianized peasants on the eastern Cape, she was a gifted child and completed school at fifteen, the only girl in a class of boys where the youngest was six years older than she. In the mid-1950s she dreamed of going to the university. Despite the well-intentioned but clumsy help of Mabel Atkinson, a Scottish Fabianist teacher who was able to get her into a school in Durban, Lily could not withstand the tensions in her situation and became seriously mentally ill for the rest of her life.[13]

Not everything can be blamed on apartheid, although it has been legally recognized in South Africa since 1865 that the cost of educating a white child is greater than for a black child. The black child receives elementary and professional training, according to the Education Act. But the dominant ideology gets passed down from generation to generation among both blacks and whites. It teaches fear of pregnancy for school-aged girls—a real fear, because almost 40 percent of girls who left school in 1976 had to leave for that reason.[14] Too, parents believe that boys are smarter, that education is more important for them, and that women belong in the home.

The Absence of Vocational Training

The content of this training is of course just what we would expect, given such prejudices against girls. Girls' vocational training excludes or deemphasizes the sciences. Their only vocational options have remained the same for over a century—as domestics, teachers, and housekeepers. In 1977 there were only twenty-two vocational schools for African women, five in Transkei, all oriented toward "female" careers such as sewing and housework. Progress has been slow since the nineteenth century. Then, on the contrary, some schools appeared pioneers in the field, no doubt because it was so easy to recruit girls. Lovedale, for example, one of the very few mixed institutions (for both Europeans and Africans), created in 1838,[15] had more girl students than boys from the start, ninety-four compared with thirty-eight. Lovedale girls were not taught math and classical languages at first, but in 1868 Lovedale opened a boarding school that gave young African women their first chance to pursue advanced studies (although until 1922 they were focused on subjects traditionally female).[16] In 1879, however, Lovedale girls applied to enter the University of the Cape for the first time, and four were admitted. Twelve years later the city was shocked to learn that a "Bantu girl" had been first in mathematics at the university. The number of young African women at Lovedale did not increase much. In 1939 the level of girls' training had dropped instead; twenty girls received the junior certificate compared with fifty-three boys, and only one girl and thirty-two boys received their certificates of completion of studies.

Since 1856 Lovedale boys had learned trades as masons, carpenters, blacksmiths, mechanics, ironworkers, and printers, but it was only in 1871 that the first female trade-school section was formed to train seamstresses and maids. More than 15 percent of the girls who came through Lovedale had careers in service to the whites, most often at the Lovedale mission itself. At the other end of the scale, the *African Yearly Register,* a kind of *Who's Who* of upper-crust black South African society, between the wars mentioned 29 women considered prominent compared with 325 men. These women, truly exceptional for their time, had mostly come from Lovedale.

Significantly, the cost of providing vocational training was legally estimated in 1863 as £10 per year for a girl and £15 for a boy. Boys had a trial year followed by two to four years of apprenticeship, whereas a girl had only three trial months plus one to two years of housekeeping training. Things were the same at St. Matthew's, the main Anglican school in Ciskei and one of the three best for Africans, along with Lovedale and Healdtown (the latter run by Methodists in the eastern Cape).[17] Until 1927 it provided primary education and trained housekeeping teachers. Between 1895 and 1959 it produced over five hundred teachers; the women of the group were mainly intended to teach the youngest classes and ultimately taught all of them.

We should not be surprised if, under these conditions, the first African nurse did not graduate from Lovedale until 1907. Only in 1938 were female candidates allowed to apply regularly for the South African Medical Council Certificate. This was after more than a century of colonization, with the double handicap of racism and sexism. For a long time, only a "hospital certificate" was available at St. Matthew's. Although today there are almost as many black nurses as white ones, the black nurses are used to care for the almost five times as many blacks.

A Late Start

Even though the South African case approaches caricature, until very recently women have rarely had the chance to pursue "modern" careers in

Muslim countries as well. For a long period in the Sahel, boys hardly went to school and girls did not go at all.

Education for Daughters of the Bourgeoisie Only

In Senegal, boys' schooling was encouraged by the creole cultural heritage of the people of Saint-Louis and their desire to assimilate, encouraged because French nationality had been given to those born in the "four communes."[18] Only girls from educated, usually Christian families could do the same. A 1975 study revealed that in a sample of one hundred women who had been to school, the encouragement to study had come mainly from their fathers, sometimes from both their parents, but almost never from their mothers alone unless they were widows (15 percent). The same is true in Guinea or Tanzania. In contrast to the case for boys, a girl will go to school only if her father is literate.[19] In Guinea, fathers of schoolboys were ten times more likely to be illiterate than fathers of schoolgirls.[20] And whether the daughter was educated or not, the notion persisted that education was less important for girls because they were less intelligent. This belief was often shared by the girls themselves, who pointed to their lower grades, due mainly in fact to the time taken away by domestic labor, for which boys had little responsibility.

In Senegal, the father of a girl going to school was usually working for the French, and it was he who paid her school fees. Mothers who had gone to school before the early 1930s were rare, and those who had had salaried jobs could be counted on the fingers of one hand. The female section of the medical school opened only in 1922, and the Rufisque normal school in 1938. Seven mothers and only two grandmothers (paternal ones) in the survey had themselves been midwives or teachers.[21] More than one-fourth of fathers, however, had been to French West Africa's single undergraduate school, the old "school for chiefs' sons"), which became the Ecole Normale Supérieure William Ponty, seedbed of the future West African elite. One-third of them came from Saint-Louis and one-third from Dakar. These privileged students made up only 5 percent of educated boys before 1930.

The influence of Islam explains why attendance at mission schools was much rarer than in the Belgian colonies. Muslim families did not accept the notion of sending their children to Christian schools, so most girls attended public school. Before independence it was inconceivable in Senegal as it was in the Belgian Congo that an African woman would take her high-school exit exams; teachers were the first to discourage it. Therefore it was not surprising that these young women saw access to a "modern" job as a kind of liberation and emphasized their own daughters' education even more than a good trade or (third in importance) a good marriage.

Generally, and in contrast to southern Africa, girls likely to go to school were of a much higher social class and more cultivated than boys. This was true even in the Gold Coast, the tropical colony where, except for Freetown in Sierra Leone and Monrovia in Liberia, education was most highly developed. At independence barely one-third of girls had gone to primary school. Despite Ghana's socialist government, the percentage hardly increased in the early years of independence and went up to only 41 percent twelve years later out of a total that had almost doubled to 1 million students. In 1973 only 10 percent of students at the university were female, and there were five times as many unemployed women as men.[22]

In Lagos, Nigeria, progress lagged as well, despite the efforts of Oyinkan Morenike Abayomi, daughter of the first Nigerian awarded a peerage by the crown,[23] as the founder of the magazine *Nigerian Pioneer.* On her return from Britain, where she had received her degree in the 1920s, she began promoting the education of girls who were not of the privileged elite as she was. To raise funds, she founded the British West African Educated Girls' Club (soon rebaptized the Ladies' Progressive Club) in 1927 and obtained the support of the local government on the condition that she demonstrate that her project benefited the people of Lagos. The result was the creation in the same year of Queen's College, the first—and until the 1950s the only—secondary school for girls. But in this school, overtly acknowledged to be reserved for the privileged class, the only subjects taught were needlework, home management, and singing. Mathematics and a foreign language were offered only by specific parental request. In the early 1950s the number of high school girls in Nigeria remained ridiculously low.[24] In 1942 there were just 1,500 girls out of 11,500 students in Nigeria's forty-three registered secondary schools, out of a total population close to 50 million, and the number remained unchanged a decade later.

Neither in Lagos, the Gold Coast, or Saint-Louis do we find anything like what girls had in Sierra Leone, where thanks to creolized society (which was integral to Freetown when it was founded) Freetown earned its sobriquet of "the Athens of West Africa."[25] Here as elsewhere, the missionary schools of course propagated the same moral and spiritual values of Christianity, imposing Western history, sciences, and arts on boys to make them good vectors for conversion; boys also received practical training in agriculture and crafts. Following the model of the British public schools, a few elitist public schools served the gentrification of the creole elite. The first university college, Fourah Bay, was created in 1877. Following the British model, education was not free. Knowledge was earned not only by personal merit but with the help of all one's relatives, to whom the students would become debtors. Puritanical and African values combined to reinforce the idea that those who succeeded had to reimburse their investors.

Girls as usual were taught needlework and the domestic arts. Yet Protestantism developed in everyone the literacy necessary to read the Bible, and some bourgeois girls went farther. Such was the case of Adelaide Smith, a young métis girl of Fanti, Mandingo, Maroon,[26] and English origin (an ethnic mix typical of Sierra Leonean creolization). Her father raised her in England. When he died in 1897, she returned to Freetown, and after a difficult adaptation she moved to the Gold Coast in 1903, where she married a creole lawyer, Caseley Hayford. After her divorce in 1914, she returned to Sierra Leone and fought for girls' advancement, seeking an education for them similar to boys'. Putting her ideas into practice, in 1923 she created a girls' technical and industrial school that lasted as well as it could until 1940 despite recruitment difficulties. She also fought for women's franchise, won in Freetown as early as 1930.[27] At this time the government gave several scholarships that allowed girls to pursue their studies in England. Lady Abayomi, when she founded the Nigerian Women's party, called for this privilege in Nigeria in 1944.[28]

The Turning Point of the 1950s

The education of young girls, with few exceptions, was not taken seriously until the second half of the twentieth century. Starting in the 1950s, elementary education began to spread, though not without difficulty. In Nigeria, for example, a public primary education system was introduced in 1955–1957 in the southern provinces and was theoretically free, but it became impossible to maintain, and in 1958 the eastern regional authorities brought back a system of payment wherein the cost increased with grade level.[29]

Igbo women traditionally paid for their children's education, and free schools had allowed many of them to send their children to school for the first time. In this region, which converted to Catholicism at the beginning of the century, people have long understood that social advancement came through Western-style education. The ending of free schools was a tremendous shock, and protest demonstrations began in February 1958, three weeks after the measure was announced. Hundreds of women came from the poor neighborhoods of Port Harcourt to the city's offices and were dispersed with tear gas. The city's schools were closed. But over the course of weeks and months that followed, demonstrations increased in the provinces, in Aba, Owerri, and other towns. A train was stopped by a thousand women in Agbani, where the minister of education tried to negotiate with them.

This movement mainly involved villages and the poorest urban neighborhoods. The Onitsha Market Women's Association, for example, which could afford to pay, was indifferent to the issue. But women in the movement, more worried about education than about politics in general or about Nnamdi Azikiwe's self-governance experiment in particular, did not hesitate to shout slogans calling for the return of whites to power, to counter what seemed to them men's carelessness. Despite the declaration of a state of emergency, the government ended up giving in to some degree and stopped demanding payment of fees for the first four grades, allowing local authorities to decide whether they could allow free schooling. The result was that at least 100,000 children were again deprived of schooling and 2,500 teachers lost their jobs.

Women who were a little better off had been particularly active in earlier years (1956–1957) against the government's attempt to make schools secular. These women started a veritable "school war," creating the Catholic Eastern Women's Association (CEWA), which provoked several mass demonstrations that gathered several thousand women in support of free schools. "In contrast to our men who seek compromise, hesitate and vacillate, our women have decided to persevere and obtain for their children the education of their choice," wrote the local Catholic paper, the *Leader,* on February 9, 1957.

Because of this pressure, the proportion of girls going to school (which had been almost zero) increased much more than that of boys, but it should be emphasized that this was more pronounced before than after independence. It seemed as though the colonial administration was really trying to bridge the gap between girls' and boys' schooling. Between 1950 and 1980, the total number of children in school doubled and in certain areas even quadrupled, especially among boys.

Inequality remained high in the Muslim north. In 1968, in Kano, a city of about 1 million, there were still barely 50,000 children in Western-style primary school, 27 percent of whom were girls. Almost ten years later, in 1976, the total figure had more than tripled to 160,000 children, but the percentage of girls had dropped below 25 percent. Following a serious education promotion campaign, the figure doubled again in one year to more than 340,000 children in 1977, but the percentage of girls remained virtually unchanged.[30]

Like Angola and Guinea, socialist Benin made serious efforts against social conservatism.[31] In Guinea, Sékou Touré worked especially hard at the beginning of his tenure. The proportion of girls in school went from one in four in 1959 to one in two in 1966, with, of course, more noticeable improvement in the city.[32] This was slowed in the 1970s by the general deterioration in education, although Touré's mandate requiring the use of native languages may have favored girls' education because they knew little or no French. Ironically, in southern Africa (Botswana, Lesotho, Malawi, and Swaziland) the schooling rate for girls, approaching the South African model, reached a maximum. In these very pastoral countries, men continued to rely on animal herding or migrant work in the mines, but the market value of girls rose with their educational level. This explains the anomaly of the early 1960s in these very poor countries, whereby numbers of boys and girls in elementary school were almost identical. The outcome was a deep sense of frustration among girls not allowed to enter the workforce for which their training had prepared them. They were required instead to remain on infertile lands or find underpaid city jobs beneath their abilities, ranging from domestic work to prostitution.

In the rest of Africa, schooling rates were generally 15–30 percent higher for boys. In 1980, 99 percent of boys but 35 percent of girls were in primary school in Togo and 83 percent of boys but 37 percent of girls in Guinea-Bissau. In South Africa, where the rate fell in 1950 to 49 percent of girls compared with 73 percent of boys, girls had thirty years later caught up with boys but only because schooling had not increased for the latter (73 percent overall).[33] Girls also repeated grades more often and were more quickly discouraged than boys. On average, less than one-quarter of girls aged twelve to seventeen attend high school compared with more than one-third for boys, and female students make up only 15 percent of the age-group from eighteen to twenty-three. The early age at marriage in Islamic areas and of pregnancy in central and southern Africa is a major handicap to girls pursuing higher education.

Thus in 1980 almost three-fourths of African women still could not read, and everywhere except in Lesotho the number of illiterate women was higher than that of men, sometimes much higher—on the order of two-thirds in the Congo, Tanzania, Zaire, Uganda, and Libya.[34] The case of tiny Lesotho seems all the more remarkable, with its 85 percent of girls educated, ahead of 81 percent in Swaziland, 79 percent in Botswana, 69 percent in Zimbabwe, and 68 percent in Kenya. Elsewhere in tropical Africa—Tanzania, Cameroon, Togo, and Madagascar—at best little more than half of the girls were attending primary school by 1980.

Factors Underlying Variation in Educational Levels

It is difficult to ascertain the reasons for variance in each country. Curiously, development level (per capita gross national product), religion (animism, Christianity, or Islam) and even ideology (conservative, moderate, or socialist) seem without exception to have little effect. Level of urbanization, the value traditionally attached to women's rural work, and colonial history are, however, significant, as is the choice of a gender-segregated school. Girls go to school in the city more than in the country, and gender-segregated schools, though these perpetuate girls' educational inferiority, favor their attendance quantitatively both in strongly Catholic missionary countries (Belgian and Portuguese) and in Muslim areas, where the number of girls going to school is on the rise.

Ultimately, it is not as one might have thought—that in predominantly Islamic and in very poor areas girls' education is least likely. Educational discrimination is most marked where a strong animist tradition of women's work and a Catholic, French-speaking colonial heritage are found together. Zaire, Togo, Côte d'Ivoire, and the Central African Republic are the nations where the increase in numbers of girls going to school remains least. We must, however, set aside the southern African countries cited earlier, which are seeing great advances in this domain. Traditional conservatism also holds sway in Guinea-Bissau, despite the key role played by women during the independence struggle; only 3 percent of girls were attending school in 1950 and still barely more than a third in 1980.

The Protestant tradition seems to have been less hostile to girls' education. Still, those who understood that social advancement for girls as well as for boys took place through schooling were rare. One exception was a Duala cocoa plantation owner who, when his elder son died prematurely, sent the next child, who happened to be a girl, to Berlin to complete her secondary studies. She was only the second woman to leave the country. When World War I was declared, she was forced to return home before taking her high-school exit examinations.

This girl became Madame Diop, born a Cameroonian when Cameroon was under German rule, mother-in-law of the founder of the Présence Africaine publishing house and mother of the poet David Diop.[35] As a young woman she had been engaged to the secretary of the Duala chief Manga Bel. Accused of negotiating with the French, he was hung with the chief by the Germans in 1915. After a brief marriage to Cameroonian, she married a Senegalese man from Dakar, who thus had French nationality, and in this capacity was named administrator in Cameroon as a replacement for the white officials who had gone off to the front. She was an exceptionally well-educated woman for the era and exceptionally intelligent. As she wittily related, "We were married [around 1918–1920] in the church to please my father, in the mosque for my husband's family, and at city hall for ourselves." Luckily, it was the civil ceremony that enabled her to keep her children after her husband died in the mid-1930s, contrary to her Senegalese in-laws' intentions (according to Muslim law) of sending her back to her father in Cameroon and keeping her children, the youngest of whom was three at the time.

Apart from this example, and although a very small number of women (almost all from West Africa) were part of an elite between the World Wars, we must beware of a Eurocentric belief that would link education to women's emancipation. Of course, success in school allowed a tiny minority of girls to claim high-level positions. We have examples today of women serving as directors of national archives, teachers at the university, elected officials, ambassadors, and even ministers (in Burkina Faso, Ghana, Mali, Senegal, Tanzania, and Zimbabwe, for example). In Rwanda and Burundi (despite both being very Catholic countries) two women became prime ministers; Rwanda's prime minister Agathe Uwilingi Yamana, the mother of five children, was assassinated in 1994.

Yet ironically, the level of education, because it allowed girls less than boys to claim skilled jobs, risked their rejection not only economically but socially. A girl leaving school today can hope to become a nurse or teacher, a hairdresser or a flight attendant, but she can also become a wife and mother who likes her femininity Western-style. Rather than providing her with independence like her mother, who may have been illiterate but was a competent, working market woman, today's woman will often use her intellectual "worth" to seek a high-level man who will marry her, keep her, or help her get the secretarial or salaried post that her gender often keeps her from getting on her own.

Most young middle-class women in the city have jobs, because the household budget requires it, and, thanks to one or more female servants, informal or salaried, no housework responsibilities. In 1983, when thousands of Ghanaians were being expelled from Nigeria, bourgeois Nigerian market women and lower-level women managers reacted the most strongly, complaining bitterly about the loss of their servants.[36] The most highly prized job for an educated girl is a secretarial one. These jobs had been filled by men, who had the necessary training. In South Africa, in contrast, the secretarial trade remains nearly the monopoly of white women (only 2 percent of black South African women working in 1975 held office jobs). In Kenya in 1976 the salary of a secretary was five times higher on the average than that of a woman factory worker, though high-school teachers earned only three times more.[37] Other women had jobs as primary-school teachers or nurses with miserable salaries, almost always less by a third than those of similarly qualified men. Many of these women had to resort to informal work, given the yawning gap between their aspirations and the possibilities the job market offered them.

After independence in Uganda, for example, the job market was virtually stagnant for ten years despite a very marked increase in the total number of primary-school students and an effort to push girls to attend secondary school. Girls in particular lacked job options, except for nursing (75 percent), teaching (30 percent), or work in public administration (27 percent).[38] One study of girls in secondary school (part of their country's intellectual elite) in 1967[39] revealed that only 2 percent of them planned to seek refuge in marriage if they failed their exams. We can guess from their responses the immense bitterness of these young women, who of course would find no place in the labor market. Even rarer are the women who go on in their studies to become judges, doctors, and lawyers. Many owe this to a creolized family background that supplied them with Western cultural standards.

Female Conservatism

Women's groups often reflect the narrow-mindedness and elitism of many of their members, most of whom have jobs. Certainly, in a country such as Nigeria, women's associations have played an important liberatory role.[40] But many of them have shown themselves to be quite conventional. The Kenyan women's association Maendeleo ya Wanawake is typical. It has branches throughout the country, in both rural and urban areas, and officially promotes women's development. In fact, it is mainly made up of bourgeois women who work in the public sector, the liberal professions, or business and who are often connected by marriage or birth with influential men. Their style, characteristic of English-speaking countries, is to organize fashion or craft shows, hold receptions, and do charitable work. The model to follow remains that of European bourgeois ladies; to their way of thinking, men should call them "memsahib," the Indian term of respect used to greet white women.[41] These urban elite women are clearly very far from rural and proletarian women, about whom they hold astonishingly antifeminist views. They remind one of the words of Aoua Keita, a woman who in the 1950s had been a great political militant with the Rassemblement Démocratique Africain (African Democratic Assembly). This Malian midwife, who became the first woman in a French-speaking country to be elected a member of her nation's parliament, still recommended that women stay at home and above all care for their household and children.[42]

The Federation of Gambian Women, a coalition of several organizations (the main one made up of alumnae of the capital's secondary schools), has adopted a similar attitude. It is by definition elitist in a country where in 1976 only 27 percent of children (and even fewer girls) from five to fourteen were attending school. And in a 90 percent Muslim country, all of its leaders are Christian.

A national organization of Tanzanian women calls for women's civil rights and tries to encourage girls' education and to promote their attempts to create microenterprises. Yet during the 1980s it remained very conformist, reminding women of their "domestic duties" by organizing sewing, knitting, and cooking classes and supporting the government's struggle against the "provocative" wearing of miniskirts. In other words, aside from the remarkable exception of the Association Internationale des Femmes Africaines, which took vigorous stands regarding emancipation, birth control, and other issues, the existence of women's groups in Africa reveals less emerging consciousness of a liberation struggle than an attempt to adopt the conventions and prejudices of a middle class struggling to preserve its privileges.

Yet, just as they were in Algeria, women have often been at the forefront of resistance and armed struggle against the colonial powers. Ironically, after the explosion of the 1950s and 1960s women have sometimes had to go back to where they started in states that became independent. The Nigerian case analyzed in the following chapter is an excellent example.

15

Ӿ

Women and Politics: Resistance and Action in West Africa

We know little about women's role at the end of the nineteenth century during the period of resistance to the colonial conquests except for the special case of the female warriors' devotion unto death to King Behanzin of Abomey. During the colonial period and even beyond, women's resistance was directly connected with their economic power. West African women, especially market women, and South African urban women defended the rights that were being swept away by the colonizers, persevering in a way that often made them stronger than the colonial officers in their obstinacy, level of organization, and courage. Though it may not have been their original goal, these women in effect played a political role. They deliberately entered politics as such only late in the game, however, probably because it had always been reserved for men. It became even more men's arena under colonialism because only men were allowed to make their voices heard and in some cases even to vote. In western Africa, particularly in the English-speaking areas, indirect rule caused the colonizers to institute certain reforms earlier than elsewhere. Except in Freetown, where well-to-do women obtained the vote in 1930, however, almost no kind of political life for women began before the 1950s—not much later than in France, where women could not vote until 1945. Change was abrupt and somewhat unexpected in French West Africa, where suffrage, which had been very narrow was expanded in 1952 to include mothers of two children. Because almost all women were at twenty-one (the age of majority in that era) married mothers, women's votes gained particular importance because for a brief time there were more women voting than men, universal suffrage not having been instituted until 1956.

In the rest of Africa, women's autonomous presence made itself known even later because of the strong combined pressures of traditional practices, lack of schooling, and conformity to Western values. Peasant women living in traditional systems had a hard time escaping their subjugation. They did have demonstrations, however, and always for the same reason: threat to their survival by men's authority and the demands of power. These revolts presupposed some degree of economic autonomy: Market women were the first to organize a group claiming their rights, as they were the first to be able to accrue personal savings. The movements' chronology closely parallels the chronology of women's trade, starting with the early years of colonization in areas where market women have long existed, such as the western coast of Africa, and only a few decades ago in some areas of central Africa. This was the case in the Congo Basin and, more spectacularly, in the Portuguese colonies, Zimbabwe, and Namibia.

There is nothing surprising in the fact that women's first and strongest demonstrations, always to protect their survival strategies, took place in Nigeria and South Africa.

A Difficult Encounter Between
Market Women and the Elite

In southern Nigeria and, more generally, in the countryside around the Bight of Benin, women rebelled in more or less the same way regardless of their lifestyle or ethnic group (rural Igbo, urban Yoruba, or Ewe). The ways in which the women organized were similar throughout the coastal area, where news spread quickly because most of them were in business or were teachers: businesswomen's frequent travels kept them informed about what was happening elsewhere, and teachers' letter writing and the press kept their group informed. The Igbo "women's war" against the tax brought in women from the markets of Lagos, of whom at least one-sixth were Igbo.[1] The Yoruba network handled the rest. But the number of educated women remained quite small. Most were relatives and daughters or wives of high-placed men, intellectuals or political men of the colony, whose own numbers were limited. Mrs. Funmilayo Anikulapo-Kuti, a socialist and the founder of the Ladies' Club of Abeokuta, knew and in fact criticized Mrs. Oyinkan Morenike Abayomi, a reformer with a similar group in Lagos.

Most militant women lived from their trade in the markets, places where people regularly gathered. They obviously rejected the supplementary contributions that the always hard-pressed colonial administration tried to extort from them in the form of head taxes, licenses, market taxes, fees for water rights, or price controls. But what these women were actually re-belling against was the destruction of the old order, which had guaranteed them a certain autonomy. They had been used to managing their own affairs without meddling from men, African or white. Men's effort to end their au-tonomy in the name of foreign principles propagated by missionaries—that women should stay at home, submit to the will of the colonial officials and their husbands, and essentially renounce their economic and social privi-leges—was intolerable. To their sense of deprivation was added the loss of real advantages. These women of the coastal societies who ran the markets (known as *alaga*) saw themselves being stripped of all their representation. Educated women of Christian creole origin of course translated their unease into language inspired by Anglo-Saxon feminist movements: the right to vote and to run for office. The meeting between working-class and bour-geois women was smooth: paying the tax was an incomprehensible new de-mand and in any case was incompatible with the concomitant deprivation of the right to representation. The tax became tolerable only when accompa-nied by recognition of women's civil status, which meant responsibilities, true, but rights as well.

These women, much more obstinate than their men and quicker to use any weapon, traditional or modern, demonstrated a remarkable capacity for struggle despite their general illiteracy. They were able to stir interest in their cause and even pay literate men, accountants, lawyers, and urban professional men, who were plentiful in Nigeria between the wars. With these women there was no negotiating, no possibility of compromise. They simply argued with the authorities until they won. Wole Soyinka has described one of their demonstrations in the autobiographical *Ake: The Years of Childhood.* The Europeans, with their principles and Victorian morals, were lost. They could level the men with armed struggle and diplomacy, tossing shreds of power to the traditional chiefs. The chiefs were content or able to exploit them to their own advantage with the new means afforded them by indirect rule. But with women there could be no half measures. In most cases the women won, at least temporarily. The colonial authorities were disarmed and could no longer resort to force. To massacre women would have caused a scandal. Women quickly understood this and, strong in their relative impunity, used it to their advantage. Where else do we find these repeated, massive demonstrations, which over the course of months, even years, pulled several thousand women together to support each other so energetically? The suffragettes of the Anglo-Saxon tradition were influential too, of course, at least among edu-cated women, in Nigeria and South Africa, although we find similar women's resistance movements in French-speaking areas—Togo and even Côte d'Ivoire. Perhaps it is the lack of research elsewhere that makes the stubborn resistance of Nigerian and South African women appear extraordinary.

The Struggle Against the Tax

The most spectacular, because most unexpected, episode was the movement of the Igbo peasant women, furious to see themselves excluded from the local collective way of life, up to this point run by consensus and balance between diverse groups of lineages, women, and villages, by the forced introduction of warrant chiefs. The administrative chiefdoms created out of whole cloth by the British authorities recognized only male power. The women were not fooled. They already had strong internal cohesion, and they responded with a mass strategy.

Women's associations arose from the patrilineal exogamous system, which made married women by definition outsiders in their husbands' villages. They developed the habit of meeting together to combat their relative isolation. Their "foreign" origins gave them recognized authority as arbiters in the villages' internal conflicts, and in fact they were usually less involved than their husbands in the sometimes age-old histories of local kinship quarrels. They legislated among themselves and might intervene as a group against the men, for example, if one of them beat his wife or mistreated her. At the same time, their belonging to the married women's association of their village of origin placed them at the center of an information and communication network extending between villages, which was important in a politically decentralized society. These associations, which were based on both kinship connections and trade relationships, gave the region's women the remarkable cohesion they had drawn on thoughout their history. This authority of theirs was reinforced by their privileged role in food cultivation: They were the ones who grew taro root, a local staple. As of World War I they began to be the primary growers of cassava and palm-oil producers. Craftwork was less widespread than among the Yoruba, but they still controlled the village craft market. This too meant the opportunity to circulate and foster exchange between neighboring groups.

Colonial intervention threatened this well-organized structure.[2] The introduction of money, which the women had seldom had access to, devalued the cowry shells that they had used for their small-scale transactions, and the introduction of taxation was the straw that broke the camel's back.

The first alert took place in 1925 in the port of Calabar, where the British had tried to impose a license on market women. Their rebellion spread from Calabar toward the interior in an eminently religious form that the colonial officials little understood but opposed as a direct revolt against their authority. The demonstrations, led largely by old women, called first for restoration of traditional morals and customs. This movement, called Nwaobiala (the name of a dance performed by the demonstrations), claimed that it was transmitting a message received from the spirit Chineke. The message went from group to group toward the north of the country via the chiefs, who each in turn made the link to four other chiefs. When all the chiefs had been informed, they were to gather in Okigwe to receive Chineke's answer. Most of them bent to the women's will despite the British administration's opposition. The message took various forms, but the gist remained this: abandon the new money customs to return to cowries, especially for marriage payments, which the circulation of British money was making prohibitive; let the women set prices in the marketplaces as they had before and even sometimes refuse to grow the newly introduced cassava; demand that paved roads be removed and the old paths restored; send the Christians back or at least ensure that Christians, animists, free people, and slaves married only among themselves; stop requiring young women to cover their nakedness before marriage; halt prostitution but at the same time abandon trials before native courts of married women accused of adultery—in essence, return to precolonial customs, rejecting the foreign innovations of which women felt they were the primary victims.

There were many disturbances and some violence. Women blocked roads, set fire to markets, took their children out of school, and assailed the local courts with their complaints. The government sent in troops to restore order but avoided direct confrontation, pretending to see all this as merely a traditional Igbo religious purification ritual. In fact, this was the form the movement took in Owerri, where at least a thousand women participated in ritual sacrifices that they had asked the traditional priests to make and wanted to force the Christians to make as well. The disturbances lasted from October to December 1925 and eventually died down of themselves. Because nothing was resolved, however, they started up again at the first opportunity.

What detonated the next round of demonstrations was the inauguration of the tax, which was introduced in 1927 and 1928 in the five southern provinces. The prospect of a census persuaded women that taxes would be imposed on everyone, although they were supposed to affect only men. This time the women directly attacked the warrant chiefs and native courts created by the colonial administration. After some disturbances in 1928, the real "women's war" (*ogu umunwanye*), called the Aba revolts by the authorities (Aba being one of the main towns involved), exploded the next year. The fear of general taxation, intensified here and there by the ineptitude of certain local civil servants, transformed what had been isolated demonstrations into an organized movement. The signal was the October 1929 order of the chief of the district under warrant chief Okugo of Oloko to begin a census of the men, women, and cattle in his district. Knowing how unpopular this measure would be, Okugo foisted the task on a mission schoolmaster. One of the women accused the schoolmaster of having started something that had caused the death of her daughter-in-law, who had been pregnant and thus doubly vulnerable.[3]

Believing that this census foreshadowed imminent taxation, the women alerted the women of neighboring regions, who in turn sent messengers to more distant villages. Women began to flow into Oloko on November 25, and on December 4, in an effort to calm things down, Okugo was sentenced to several days in prison for having used violence against women demonstrators who had entered his house. A further attempt was made to quiet the women on December 22 by giving them Okugo's cap, the emblem of his authority. Encouraged by this early success, the movement continued to spread. By year's end ten native council courts had been sacked and others damaged, houses of high-placed men attacked, and foreign trading posts pillaged. On the other side, fifty-five women had been killed, twenty-nine in Opobo on December 16. Order was reestablished only in January 1930.

The inquests and trials that followed demonstrate the extent of the movement: some women were animists, others Christian, some relatives of or close to men in important positions and others from the most anonymous backgrounds, and often leaders of women's associations. Only a few women had been to school, among them Janet Okala, Owerrinta's first baker (nicknamed "Mama Bread"), and Miss Mary Okezie, a teacher at the Umoacha mission school, who wrote up the complaints of the women from Aba. This diversity is evidence of Igbo women's solidarity in defending not only their economic autonomy but also their political and cultural identity. The movement's leftover religious overtones, so strong in 1925, had disappeared by 1929.

Convinced that it was the warrant chiefs imposed on them who were responsible rather than the distant British authorities, the women demonstrated against them. The disturbances continued until they had been assured that they would not have to pay taxes. They did not see the inquests as directed against them but rather seized the opportunity to settle accounts with these much-hated warrant chiefs, and some of them were indeed deposed. They called on the colonial authorities to keep their agreements and protect them against oppression by the local chiefs so that their relations with the government might be as cordial as those with the missionaries. One petition went so far as to ask that there be a white man in every native court "because our black men are too wicked." Sometimes the tone they took shows real feminist awareness, for example, in the question asked by an Oloko woman—"Don't you agree that the world depends upon women—that it is the women who multiply the population of the world?"—or the signature at the end of a letter written by Miss Okezie, "The Women, Owerri Road, Aba."[4]

The commission's report, published in July 1930, went so far as to compare this movement to that of the British suffragettes. The message was heard, and starting on this date the authorities introduced a few women into the native courts, until then made up of men. This decision put a stop to rumors spread by the colonial officials—overwhelmed by events and hardly prepared for the notion that they were a result of women's own initiative—attributing the disturbances to unofficial, indirect maneuvers by men. The men had in fact taken no such action, knowing from experience dating to the conquest that there was no point in rising up openly against the new powers. In addition, men did not enjoy an interregional associational network like that of their wives that could draw together even the cowards and laggards. The colonial authorities did not forget their experience, mainly because the resistance to taxation was long-lasting.

After 1930 the head of the family (normally a man) was taxed for the whole household, but this remained ill-accepted. In 1938, over more than a thousand square kilometers in Owerri province, men and women rebelled. Fifty-five men and three women were arrested, and for a week and a half there were meetings bringing together over five hundred women each time. The women complained about their men's poverty, the expense the tax represented for them, and how wise it would be to give women, not just the chief and his assistants, responsibility for collecting the tax. There was no next chapter to this episode.

Not until after the war was taxation timidly imposed on women's incomes.[5] The measure again caused an outcry among the women of Onitsha and Aba, the main trading centers. Over a thousand market women organized a protest march. After several had been arrested, they launched the Aba Women's Association, a vote of defiance against Mrs. J. N. Egbutchay, chair of the local branch of the Nigerian Council of Nigeria and the Cameroons women's group, accused of compromising with the government. The Onitsha women's association threatened to support an independent candidate in the next regional elections; the following year, the finance law was amended.[6]

Women's political influence was thus very real, but they were still far from an understanding of the state. Concerned with their daily needs, they defended their right to survive and still had no sense of a "social contract." The tax wronged them; they would not let this idea go, and it only became more rigid over the years.[7] These Nigerian women were not yet ready to defend the beliefs of their Anglo-Saxon sisters, who accepted equality before taxes as part of gender equality. They believed instead in the specificity of women, whose interests should be protected and who, given their particular place in society, should be relieved of the burdens that weighed on men.

This is the basis of today's informal sector—all the economic activities, usually of women, that reject any kind of political control, whether it be by a colonial government or by the modern independent state.

Taxation in the Marketplace: Lagos Women's Struggle

The great port of Lagos has long been the center for Nigerian political thought and action. Women have played an undeniable role, although relations between the market women and the elite have been difficult and ambiguous except during the key period of the 1940s and 1950s, the demise of colonialism.

Lagos market women organized very early on. At the start of the 1920s, the authorities counted about twenty-six markets, each with its own *alaga* responsible for it and designated by consensus. The precise date of birth of the Lagos Market Women's Association is unknown, but the group was thriving by the mid-1920s. Unions also organized in sections or by speciality. The Alakoro Women's Union was registered in 1938, the women sellers of the Faji market in 1939, and the *gari* sellers in 1940. Supposedly, the movement was started by a man, the nationalist Herbert Macaulay, who founded the Nigerian National Democratic party (NNDP) in 1923, an ally of the traditional chiefdoms. It is true that between the wars market women demonstrated loyalty without fail to the customary chiefs and marched with the NNDP, unhesitatingly seeking Macaulay's aid when they needed to. Around 1925, about 1,000 women belonged to the NNDP, but the two organizations remained fundamentally distinct. The women had been demonstrating their capacity for action for a while; as early as 1908 they had mobilized occasionally but effectively behind the traditional authorities for water rights. Water taxation threatened them directly, because carrying water was what allowed many of them to earn a living. At the *oba*'s call they would close the markets and shops and 15,000 would go to demonstrate in front of the colonial administrative building.

At the origin of this movement was Mrs. Alimotou Pelewura, an assertive Muslim Yoruba woman born in Lagos, who became Macaulay's close friend. Aware of the aura surrounding her, Mrs. Pelewura once proudly began a speech in a 1943 meeting in Abeokuta, "I am she who is called Pelewura."[8] She had succeeded her mother as a small fish merchant in 1900 and developed her business to the point that she owned a flotilla of pirogues, employed her own fishermen, and had built her own fish shed. Already in 1910 the chief of Lagos esteemed her an important person. In the early 1920s she became *alaga* of the Araromi market, the biggest meat market in the city. Although she was illiterate, she was able to organize her association just as she did her market. She asked women to contribute three pence per week to a common fund that would allow them to hire two secretaries (generally boys, because women rarely knew how to write) and, if necessary, lawyers to defend their interests. As was true everywhere, what set them off was the threat of a tax. Burned by the Igbo women's scalding resistance, the colonial government waited to launch the tax until 1932, when it faced a deficit because of the Great Depression. The reaction was so violent that the government retreated and waited until the war to try again.

In 1932 Pelewura was named to the customary committee of the *ilu* of Lagos,[9] where she became spokeswoman for the eighty-four representatives (all women) of the city's markets. Then she joined the executive committee of a new party, the Nigerian Union of Young Democrats (NUYD), which planned to create a women's branch. Another, more radical new party, the Nigerian Youth Movement (NYM), also recruited a large number of market women when it began in 1938.

When the war came, the government tried to introduce a per capita tax on women and an income tax for those who earned £50 a year or more. The government also began to requisition food and place price controls on it (called the "Pullen controls" after the official charged with implementing the measure), because mobilizing over 110,000 men as it was doing would have an impact on agriculture.

The women reacted vigorously. First, among the illiterate women, there was a petition signed with their thumbprints; then the markets were closed and there was a march to the government buildings and then a vast meeting of several thousand. The Pullen Plan, which deprived the women of any flexibility in their transactions, was a direct attack on their livelihood. Buchi Emecheta's novel *The Joys of Motherhood* gives a good sense of the difficulties that market women endured during this war in Lagos, where an active parallel market developed. The government tried to gather up its own food and to impose prices for goods that were often below market price so that it could resupply its own often poorly stocked offices. Women organized in resistance and blocked the official *gari* trucks on the roads. A whole series of satirical songs expressed their feelings:

> *Strange things are happening in Lagos.*
> *Europeans now sell pepper,*
> *Europeans now sell palm oil,*
> *Europeans now sell yam,*
> *Though they cannot find their way to Idogo*
> *And yet Falolu is still in his palace and alive*
> *Europeans were not wont to sell melon seeds.*[10]

To defend those of their number who had been imprisoned or heavily fined, they created more petitions and called on experienced jurists and nationalist militants such as Macaulay and his son. The authorities realized that they were powerless in the face of the women's obstinate refusal to negotiate. The traditional elites avoided taking a position because they felt incapable of influencing Pelewura. Despairing, Pullen tried to buy her by offering to bring her into *gari* sales in the city. She answered him haughtily that if he offered her £100 a month she would never help to "break and starve the country where she was born." Finally, the government gave in on the income tax, raising its floor to £100 in annual income, which made it difficult for women to plead inability to pay.

Women's pugnacity came to a head with a thirty-seven-day general strike led by the militant unionist Michael Imodou. Market women organized in support of the strikers, selling them food at low prices and distributing some to them free. Whether because of their efforts or because of the war's end, in August 1945 price controls were abolished, and the women could consider this a victory. Between 1953 and 1956 they were still mobilizing against the Slum Clearance and Resettlement Plan. But after Macaulay's death in 1946, they lost some autonomy as some joined the new nationalist parties, some Nnamdi Azikiwe's National Council of Nigeria and the Cameroons, and some the Lagos section of the Action Group. The military coup in 1966 silenced them.

There were few connections here between working-class market women and educated elite women. The only exception was the period during the war, when the Women's League (which succeeded the very Victorian Lagos Ladies' League in 1923) supported the *gari* war by petition. Up to that point, educated women had concerned themselves with calls for improved social conditions, for example, the creation of a maternity hospital. The colonial administration responded by telling them that what they were asking for was a "medical luxury."[11]

After the war, the elite women tried to organize but on a different basis from the market women. Their new head, Oyinkan Morenike Abayomi, was, as we have seen, concerned with girls' education. Abayomi's thinking in this era was the same as that of Mrs. Funmilayo Anikulapo-Kuti in Abeokuta or that of Constance Cummings-Jones, elected member of the Freetown city council from 1933 to 1942: that women were the great losers of the colonial regime, except in Sierra Leone lacking the right to vote and even less the right to run for office. This political struggle was uppermost in Abayomi's mind when she founded the Nigerian Women's party. The party put a certain distance between itself and the market women, whose objectives were more concrete and who certainly did not give these upper-middle-class women the right to speak for them. Even though the *yalode* (market chief) of Lagos, Mrs. Rabiatu Alaso Oke, a major Muslim woman fabric wholesaler, was named vice president of the party, the division remained.

Unlike the Lagos Market Women's Association, which had more than 8,000 members, the Nigerian Women's party's membership hovered between 500 and 2,000 members.[12] This modest figure was enough to make Abayomi the first woman to be named to the city council. The Women's party was not a political party as we understand it. It basically attempted to give "the whole of the people the rights of British citizens through constitutional means," especially women, who were recognizing the backwardness of their condition compared with that of women elsewhere in the world.[13] In 1950, although the party for the first time ran five candidates in the city council elections, none was elected.[14] Abayomi and many of her friends, all Yoruba women from Lagos, eventually decided to rejoin the Action Group.

The Egba Women's Political Alliance

In contrast to what happened in Lagos, where working-class women depended on the traditional chiefs, the Egba women of Abeokuta opposed the chiefs as their primary exploiters. Egba women were used to certain rights in the public domain. They participated in political discussion, had representation on official bodies, and enjoyed individual inheritance rights. They were exasperated by the customary chiefs' blind obedience to British authority, ignoring women's traditional rights.

From the start, their movement had a political side to it. At the end of the 1940s the Abeokuta Women's Union (or AWU, later to become part of the Nigerian Women's Union), sustained by their political sense and the tenacity of their leader, Mrs. Funmilayo Anikulapo-Kuti, managed to unseat Ademola, the city's *alaka*, in effect the head of one of Nigeria's major cities. As among the Igbo, their opposition focused on a local representative of British power rather than on British power itself.

Born in 1900, Mrs. Anikulapo-Kuti, known as Beere, was the daughter of a seamstress and a small planter whose father had been an emancipated, baptized returned slave from Sierra Leone.[15] Her conversion meant that she had gone to Western-style school and then to the Abeokuta Anglican high school before going to England from 1919 to 1923. There she discovered socialism and anticolonialism. When she returned to take over direction of Abeokuta's girls' school, she also started refusing to use her Christian name, Frances, and her husband's European surname, Ransome.[16] She also attempted to speak Yoruba rather than English even in her dealings with the colonial authorities. Her contribution was understanding the need for unity between elite women and the vigorous societal stratum constituted by the market women, whom she had come to know by organizing a night school for them.[17] In 1942 she created the Abeokuta Ladies' Club, which in 1945 defended the market women when the government began taking their rice from them without compensation. Her calls to the press got the rice controls lifted. If we are to believe the childhood memories of her nephew, Wole Soyinka, eleven years old at the time, this was when women's massive demonstrations against taxation and against Abeokuta's *alake* and his *ogboni* (dignitaries of military origin) began.[18] Losing control, the young British district officer assigned to the city doorway of the *alake*'s palace ordered Beere and the others to "shut up, you women." In a reply that has become legendary in Abeokuta as a "linguistic knockout," Beere said with exquisite firmness, "You may have been born, but you were not bred. Would you speak to your mother like that?"[19]

A lively period of demonstrations followed whose effect was to have the inept officer recalled and which proved the beginning of the end for the *alake.* To the tune of the old songs, eminently respectful, the women sang new words that they had invented. Women of all faiths—Christian, Muslim, and animist—took to the streets to shake up any *obgoni* who happened to cross their path, singing:

> *Hail, king of hunchbacks,*
> *Ademola has carried trouble,*
> *Son of beast who inherits okra,*
> *Child of intrigue who takes the soup-pot,*
> *Hail, father of beasts*
> *Hail, king of wood daemons.*[20]

Strong from this success and wanting to attack the *alake,* who was suspected of using goods he had requisitioned for his own personal ends, in 1946 the club became a less elitist group, the Abeokuta Women's Union, whose slogan was Unity, Cooperation, Autonomy, and Democracy. The AWU enjoyed an alliance with the city's women's associations, Christian, business, and ethnic. An executive committee was organized that tried to keep educated women and often illiterate businesswomen, including several market representatives, on the same footing. Soon there were 20,000 members, more than three times the membership of the Lagos Market Women's Association at any point. These activists were then able to mobilize 80,000 to 100,000 women.

As among the Igbo, indirect rule had lost Egba women some of their rights, including the right of representation in councils by the *yalode* or female head of the market. It was not that the British had explicitly excluded women; they had simply never even imagined that women might have a public role to play. When they ordered the local authorities of Abeokuta and Ijebu provinces to find financial resources, they allowed the *obgonis* to impose a fairly heavy tax on men as on women, something that had already provoked serious rebellion in 1918. In contrast to the rest of Nigeria, this region had a cash economy wherein the activities of market women were obvious. Women began to feel that this measure weighed more heavily on them than on men; they were to be taxed starting at age fifteen rather than at seventeen as were the men, whether or not they were married. The measure implicitly recognized their economic position.

Ademola II, Abeokuta's new *alake,* and the first to have had a European-style education, came to power in 1920. He took advantage of his position and British support to steal lands and embezzle taxes. As early as 1938 a violent protest took place in front of his palace. Anger mounted during World War II when he took advantage of colonial orders to increase requisitions. Women were his first targets, because they brought chickens, yams, *gari,* and rice into the city. All the *alake* had to do was to set up a few roadblocks in order to confiscate a large part of their wares, offering the justification that "no one should eat as long as the soldiers have not been fed." Women, paying both their own taxes and, through their work, some of their husbands' taxes, were providing at least half the district's revenues. They became more and more impatient not only with the ill-treatment to make them pay that they endured but also with the fact that, despite the obligations imposed on them, they had neither the right to vote nor any representation—merely the right to complain of having been beaten and bullied.

Kuti, convinced that women had suffered more than men from colonization, planned a "modern" political action calling for the right to vote and representation in local courts. From 1946 on, under her direction, the AWU became a resolutely feminist pressure group. It launched a protest campaign against taxation of women and price controls in the markets with the slogan "No taxation without representation." Things started in June 1946 with a petition. Not only did they receive no response but in October the *alake* decided to increase the taxation of women. Thousands of women came to demonstrate in front of the palace. The *alake* answered that he would receive them only individually, because they had "no group business," no economic interest as a whole. Therefore more individual AWU women went on trial for refusing to pay the tax, and others launched an audit of the accounts of the Native Authority System. The AWU ran more and more petitions and press campaigns, in short, using every modern means available to activists. Kuti herself refused to pay the tax and was imprisoned. In 1947, the movement entered a more radical phase with increasing sit-ins, demonstrations, and market closures. Kuti accompanied a delegation of the NCNC to London, where she informed British unions and the crown of what was happening. She became a well-known figure to the British press and public, had articles published in the *Daily Worker*, and was even invited by the mayor of Manchester to speak on the condition of women in her country.

Back home, the union's actions were very much in keeping with women's traditional customs, notably including songs underscoring women's superiority and making fun of men's weakness that publicly denounced an unacceptable *oba*. As they marched, the women sang, "This *oro* festival [demonstration] has no regard for men/This *oro* could carry men away even from their rooms" or even "Ademola Ojibosho/Big man with a big ulcer/Your behaviour is deplorable/Alake is a thief/Council members thieves."[21]

A new mass demonstration took place on November 29 and 30, 1947, and pulled in more than 10,000 women. It was repeated ten days later. The *alake* had bought several months' time by promising to name women to responsible positions and then dividing in order to conquer by trying to keep Kuti out of the negotiations. In April 1948 she refused again to pay her taxes. This time the whole community reacted; on December 20 the men finally broke their silence. They organized a meeting in which they affirmed their desire to support the women in the name of happiness, freedom from oppression, and peace in Egba country. All the southern regions then settled down to wait for the government to give in. It held out only until January 3, 1949, when the *alake* abdicated, the tax on women was abolished (whereas the one on men was increased), and four women, one of them Kuti, were named to the new interim council. It had taken the women nearly three years of essentially continuous struggle to win.[22] In contrast to the Igbo women, they had not resorted to violence but won by virtue of their cohesion, organization, and determination.

Despite the loss of its main reason for mobilizing (taxation), the AWU continued to act as a pressure group every time the interests of Egba women were endangered. In 1952 actions began again when there was again question of taxing water (at three shillings per woman per year) to finance a new water-supply system. Women had been exempt from water taxation since 1948. Demonstrations, while not reaching the same size, occurred sporadically until this unpopular tax was repealed in 1960. There were other disturbances in 1952, when the administration tried to oppose the women holding their annual demonstration to celebrate the anniversary of the overthrow of Ademola. The police drove them back with tear gas and arrested fifty or so women. Kuti managed to have the incident discussed by the British Parliament.

Strengthened by its accomplishments, the AWU decided to expand to a transregional, transethnic structure and became the Nigerian Women's Union. Sections were created in many areas, including Kano to the north. Many of its members joined in the struggle for independence with the Action Group or the NCNC (to which Kuti had belonged until 1959). The union was more reformist than revolutionary and often drew on arguments deriving from British democracy. The movement did not ultimately take sides, and its later history shows that women stepped away somewhat from political struggle.

Female Pressure Groups and Political Parties After the War

In the early days of colonization, women's solidarity owed much to sex segregation. Accustomed to living among themselves and meeting their own needs, women quite naturally gathered in action as they did in work and celebration. Colonialism shattered their unity. Social distances increased; in the creolized bourgeois class, educated women, who were often teachers, adopted their husbands' concerns. Peasant women, in contrast, found themselves marginalized and rejected in the informal sector by colonial paternalism that exacerbated traditional male-supremacist leanings. At least three layers of female society could be observed, each with its own reactions: educated women; wealthy market women, more or less illiterate; and working-class women, both illiterate and poor. Only the first two groups, in very

Ghanaian independence in 1956, the Congress People's party (into which Kwame Nkrumah had integrated the National Council of Ghanaian Women) had ten seats reserved for women in parliament.

Modern Bourgeois Women: The Ladies of Freetown

In Sierra Leone, the gap between creole women, raised in highly Victorian fashion since the nineteenth century, and working-class market women—hairdressers, washerwomen, and seamstresses—was enormous. The latter group remained similar to the Temne and Mende women from the countryside who held important roles because they could sit on their municipal "headmen's" councils or urban chiefs' councils established within the British protectorate.

Adelaide Caseley Hayford was the first Sierra Leonean feminist.[31] In 1915 she gave a public lecture on "the rights of women and Christian marriage." In 1918, the National Congress of British West Africa, whose president was Adelaide's husband, suggested organizing women to join the struggle that elite educated men had begun for the right to participate in the colonial government. Wives and female relatives were asked to help solicit financial assistance for the organization. The Sierra Leonean example was followed in Bathurst (the Gambia) starting in 1926. The press praised this "army of effective, though silent workers"[32] made up mainly of private societies whose focus was normally music or dance, parish organizations, and charitable societies.

Starting in 1930, when wealthy women received the right to vote,[33] several women students in Britain joined militant organizations in London or at home, especially the League of Coloured People (LCP). They were often part of the movement of the suffragette and journalist Sylvia Pankhurst, who was very active on Ethiopian issues, for example, supporting Princess Tsahai in London in this regard. Some, like Constance Horton (later Mrs. Cummings-Jones, cousin of Mabel Dove), were elected to the city's executive council.

The first political movement to recruit women was the West African Youth League, founded by the Sierra Leonean marxist journalist I.T.A. Wallace-Johnson first in the Gold Coast in 1934 and then in his own country four years later. Five women sat on its first central committee. Four were teachers and the fifth in business; one was a graduate of Howard University in Washington, D.C. In 1938, Cummings-Jones not only was the first woman elected to the municipal council of an African city but came in first in votes. That same year, a woman graduated for the first time from the national university, Fourah Bay College. In 1943 the first two African women judges—both Sierra Leonean—were named, one to Freetown, one to Lagos.

Cummings-Jones worked largely with the market women and actively participated in the fight for self-determination. The result was that soon after the war (which had greatly increased the number of women workers) two working women's unions were born: the Sierra Leone Market Women's Union and the Washerwomen's Union.

The Sierra Leone Women's Movement emerged on the political scene in 1951. As elsewhere, it soon became enslaved to the reigning parties. Although four women led a strong campaign in the elections of 1957, two within the colony of Freetown and two within the protectorate (i.e., everywhere else), none was elected. Yet Cummings-Jones certainly had been elected and hoped for the portfolio of minister of social welfare. She was rejected, however, by her male peers, and attempts were made to keep her out by having her husband named ambassador to Liberia. She finally gave up when she became aware that her life was in danger.

Ironically, a female chief, Mrs. Gulama, was the only woman elected to one of a dozen seats reserved for the native authorities and named a minister but not given a portfolio. In 1960 it was again a woman chief, Nancy Koromah, who was elected headman of the Freetown Mende. Her role was significant because it meant reconciling the opinions of the city's nine Mende sections and presiding over the headmen's council. Her election victory was a political awakening for all the women in Freetown, educated or illiterate, Christian or Muslim, in salaried, informal-sector, or liberal professions. In 1964 Koromah was elected to the city council at a time when the new head of the women's section of the National Congress was for the first time a Krio who did not come from the elite classes. Instead, this new chair was a young socialist, educated in London and the Eastern-bloc countries. Yet after independence, male ambition won out again, and women found themselves relegated to the domestic sphere.

The Sierra Leone Women's Movement had one rare quality: politicized women were so rare that they had no choice but to organize across regional and ethnic barriers. In the 1950s their movement, which mobilized supporters of all social classes, was a real crucible for the awakening of Sierra Leonean national consciousness.

Political Awakening in French-Speaking Africa

In French-speaking Africa, things were not nearly so far along, for French-speakers were necessarily less affected by Anglo-Saxon-style feminism.

The Market Women of Lomé

In Lomé (Togo), the same types of political action can be found among Ewe women as are found among Nigerian or Ghanaian market women, but they are less well known. The essential role of Loméan businesswomen, especially the "Nana Benz," has been underrated. Usually for economic reasons, these women had long had to demonstrate their ability to organize against the state. As early as 1933 they played an important role in a popular movement that they largely sustained, all but impelling the men to act. Because of budgetary crises during the Great Depresssion, what was at stake was the threat of licensing of market stalls and income taxation that would have hurt women the most. Their agitation rapidly spread. The militant leaders found guilty were the Duawo, members of a youth group begun in 1931. The head of the council of officials did not hide his sympathies with the demonstrators, and two alleged leaders—both men—were arrested January 24. Reaction was swift: that night and the next day crowds descended on the streets, and there were so many women among them that the whole demonstration was attributed to them without their role's having been clear to the administration or even examined. It might well be supposed, considering the market women's importance at the time, that their organizing was the motor for this action, as it had been a few years earlier among the Igbo and in Lagos.[34]

What is certain is that, in their way, today the major market women of Lomé still "own" the city. Their resistance against President Gnassingbé Eyadema's power is stubborn, and his death squads would certainly have had an easier time of it without them. The long general strike that paralyzed the nation for several months in 1992–1993 is greatly in their debt. But this matter has never been studied in depth. The role of women has always been important to social movements, especially during strikes, because of women's function as suppliers of material needs. It is women who feed the strikers and through their informal-sector work may even help replace wages lost from days unworked. The level of survival was so low that men could not without their help have maintained the pressure exerted by their refusal to work.

The best example is still the early miners' strikes in the Zambian Copperbelt in 1935.[35] In his superb novel *God's Bits of Wood*, where he retells the story of the great Senegalese railwaymen's strike of 1947–1948, Sembène Ousmane paints women's militant role gloriously, even mythically. The story is much embellished in the novel but still contains an element of truth.

The Abidjan March

At the close of the 1940s, Abidjan women's militant explosion was a significant landmark, because it occurred within a female population much less active than its Yoruba, Akan, or Ewe sisters. These women deserve even more credit because they were only barely tolerated by the men of the Ivoirian independence party, the Parti Démocratique de la Côte d'Ivoire–Rassemblement Démocratique Africain (PDCI-RDA). Some women had begun organizing almost as early as the men in 1949, starting a women's section of the party. They set up an office with a leading party member attached to it.

These women activists traveled throughout the country to awaken women and call them to organize. They planned to hold a congress and, more important, to begin a massive literacy campaign immediately, but faced with both global colonialism and repressive harassment by the Ivoirian administration, their activities remained very limited.

Violent disturbances broke out in February 1949. The administration took advantage of them and struck hard, arresting thirty-two male activists in the PDCI-RDA, eight of whom were its main leaders. Civil servants suspected of being sympathetic were transferred. With the men so quickly eliminated, the women organized under the leadership of Marguerite Sacoum, the first secretary of the RDA Women's Committee. Galvanized because several among them were wives of prisoners, she and her friends pushed the reluctant male activists to act. They were politically prepared; they went through city neighborhoods and villages to raise the consciousness of their female neighbors and incite them to organize as the men had against colonial despotism. Their cleverest idea was to use the *adjanou,* a ritual that Akan women practiced in cases of grave threat (usually of war) to turn aside bad luck. Armed with old rifles, sticks, and huge pestles, they spread through the village, punctuating their chants by striking their weapons on the ground. At night they rubbed their bodies with white clay and took turns marching naked until dawn. The leaders in turn took the ritual to Abidjan working-class neighborhoods to "save the party," despite men's fears of seeing the demonstrations degenerate.

The spark was the arrest in August 1949 of Marcelline Sibo, a market woman and leader of the Agni women activists. A first march on Abidjan's central police station called for her release. Then thirty little buses and trucks loaded down with women tried to get to the Grand-Bassam court (about ninety miles away), where Mrs. Sibo had been taken. They were stopped by the police but still managed to win her freedom. The success of this enterprise spurred them to action.

All the party's efforts at negotiation had failed. It was again a woman, Anne-Marie Raggi, secretary of the women's subsection in the Grand-Bassam neighborhood, who suggested boycotting imported products, a suggestion that was enthusiastically adopted. Devotedly observed by all, it spread countrywide in the second half of December. The prisoners themselves had begun a hunger strike on December 12. Until this point the women had been waiting for the party's green light to take action. But as they saw that nothing was happening, they again took the initiative and marched on the Grand-Bassam prison, prepared to take it by storm. When the police blocked the bus route, they took off on foot, breaking up into small groups in order to get past the roadblocks placed in their path. The demonstration was of considerable size and lasted three days, from December 22 to 24, mobilizing between 2,000 and 4,000 people, mostly illiterate women led by a few educated women referred to as "women agents" (*femmes-commis*). The goal of the first day's march was to demand an audience with the attorney general. Receiving no answer, they camped overnight on the spot and continued their wait the next day while the mass of women grew. On the third day they attacked and were dispersed with clubs, tear gas, and hoses. Several women were wounded and four arrested.[36] Disappointed, these women who had refused to give up finally had to accept the party president's injunctions and go home and await the end of the trial that would free the prisoners.

Despite this near-failure, the movement was a real first in French-speaking Africa. The administration had not seen its like since Lomé's prewar days. For Ivoirian women, although they were acting in their capacity as wives and mothers, it was their first autonomous political demonstration. Unfortunately, except for a few individual accounts, we know very little else about this movement.

The Militant Aoua Keita

Truly militant women were rare, but Aoua Keita was one. Born into an aristocratic Sudanese family that claimed descent from Sundiata, the founder of the Malian empire in the thirteenth century,[37] she was raised by her mother in her father's compound, surrounded by his co-wives and slaves. In 1923 her father, who had fought in World War I and was already elderly when she was born after his return, sent her to the first girls' school in Bamako against her mother's will. He was not particularly feminist; he simply felt that since this particular wife (much younger than he was) had no sons, one of her daughters should be able to take care of her after his death. Little Aoua, academically gifted, did not disappoint him. She was always one of the best students, and in 1931, in Dakar, she obtained her diploma in midwifery, the only training offered girls at the time.

Her first job was in Gao on the river, a completely obscure posting where, as the only emancipated young woman around, she met with what she later described as "wild success."[38] She got a maternity hospital built. She entered a typical marriage, arranged by her father, with a young doctor named Diawara who came to join her in her posting. He was another rare assimilated person who held French nationality and voted at a time when no women had the right to do so. Politically aware and educated, as a young woman she read the newspapers and, thanks to her husband, entered politics. They joined the professional association of health workers and participated in its first large strike, which lasted three months in 1945. The next year they joined the Union Soudanaise du Rassemblement Démocratique Africain (USRDA, Sudanese Union of the African Democratic Movement). Aoua, in her husband's shadow, began to organize in secret discussions with other midwives, having been reproached by the husband of a less tolerant neighbor with "Politics is men's business and not yours."

She entered politics because she became sterile after an operation. In 1949, her mother-in-law required her son—who was at the time opposed to polygamy—to divorce.[39] Aoua, in midlife, was now an independent woman. "We have created an adventuress," cried her astonished father and her despairing mother, the latter very traditionally minded. She went alone from posting to posting, often given punitive assignments because the administration greatly disliked the political activities that were facilitated by constant contact with her patients and their families. She was an intelligent, impassioned activist who tirelessly explained to women what was at stake and rallied them to her cause.[40]

She was a rouser of minds and spirits. Almost the only literate woman in an illiterate majority, she played an extraordinary role in Gao when she returned there after fifteen years, managing with the other women to organize against repression that threatened to influence the legislative elections of 1951. She thumbed her nose at the administration, which was completely unable to stop her. The depth of these women's conviction can be measured by recalling the fact that in this highly Muslim region women in principle did not leave their homes except at nightfall. A few days before the elections, all the Sudanese civil servants suspected of being RDA sympathizers were transferred far away. Thanks to her knowledge of the law, Aoua managed to get hold of their voting cards and, using her women's network, to have them delivered to their homes. In order to thwart electoral fraud, on the morning of the vote every woman got to her voting site very early and occupied it, helped by a schoolboy to read for her. Aoua even managed, with fine authority, to obtain the removal of two military officers who had been trying to force their soldiers to cast their votes for the French party by refusing to allow them to enter the voting booth alone. Aoua wrote later, "So then, where were this liberty, this equality, this fraternity? To whom do they apply? My self-esteem as a member of the colony was hurt."[41]

The USRDA's success in the voting district was total. After organizing women, Aoua Keita turned to organizing young people. Transferred in retaliation to Casamance in southern Senegal despite her uncontested professional abilities, she swore from that point on to devote herself to her country: "Henceforth, my life will be devoted to the USRDA. I therefore resolved to do everything to ensure that my party functions properly by participating more in all political and union activities, not only in my country but in all of Africa as well."[42] This resolution led her several years later, after her nomination to office in Bamako, to give up her French nationality. She became a member of the political bureau of the party, assumed leadership of the women's organization that she had created, and in 1955 launched a call to women of what was then French Sudan. In 1959 she was the first woman in French-speaking Africa to be elected to the assembly governing her country,[43] to her mother's terror and not without admonitions by Modibo Keita, the first president of Mali, to the men of his country to accept her.

Aoua was not quite alone; she worked closely with Aissata Sow, the female head of the Sudanese teachers' union, and in 1957 they created the female salaried workers' union of the Sudan together. But she remains an exception because of her intelligence, her determination, and her not being a "normal" African woman—being divorced, independent, and sterile. Her commitment was sincere. A man, astonished at the political pretensions of this woman, once said to her, "Why are you so stubborn? . . . You are nothing but poor women who cannot be council-members . . . and certainly not deputies. Why are you troubling yourselves for nothing?" She replied, "We are mature enough to know what we are doing. We do not seek to become council-members, nor deputies, but to become free as the wind."[44]

Aoua Keita essentially worked for and with women with eminently feminine means, both in her profession as midwife and in her talents as a seamstress, and never gave up her femininity, calling on women to take care of their looks as well as their economic autonomy. She recognized that the primary obstacle to women's political awakening was their husbands' opposition and in 1958 was impressed by Sékou Touré's militant feminism and that of Guinean women. Once a deputy, she worked enthusiastically for marriage law reforms.[45] Yet her conservative view of women's role was surprising. As a woman of the land, if not the bush, she was critical of modern city women who took on the futile, bourgeois lifestyle of house-bound women. In her speeches and her book, she calls on women to remain faithful to tradition and to take care in "all qualities that are the pride of the mistress of the house." A woman should first be a good wife, a good housewife, and a good mother, sparing her husband the expense of a maid. She went so far as to make a speech in this vein at the USRDA Congress in 1960, a speech that brought in male members and engendered the hostility of women.

Her political program was in reality rather short-sighted. It stopped with liberation from the colonial yoke, which should of itself bring about women's emancipation. Justly proud of her successes, she ultimately sided with men, who had a hard time admitting success in a woman. She herself did not seem to feel that other women might achieve what she had. Perhaps even though she sought to change society, she had internalized what it taught her: that she was not like other African women.

When her memoirs came out in 1975 and the book received the grand prize for French-speaking black African literature, Aoua Keita entered the ranks of French-speaking heroines of women's liberation. In the following generation her example was followed by a few women who did not have to give up their husbands or children for it. In 1991 Malians of all ages and all social conditions also took to the streets to drive out the dictator Moussa

Traoré. Today, two women are ministers in Alpha Oumar Konaré's government.

Sékou Touré and the Women of Guinea

In the early years of independence, Guinean women's lot was much like that of other women in the world—political activism was not inconceivable but rare. One leader tried, at least at the beginning of his rule, to go farther. Sékou Touré's Parti Démocratique de Guinée (PDG) wrote into its statutes a minimum number of elected women at all levels—local, regional, and national. In the struggle against elitism, loyalty to the party took priority over education, which favored activist women, with their very low educational level. The fight began in 1953, long before independence. By 1968, 27 percent of the seventy-five party deputies elected for five-year terms to the national assembly were women. Women made up 16 percent of regional officials and, even more remarkable, 12 percent of the party's central committee—twice as many as their Soviet or Chinese counterparts.

This attitude was no ruse. In his speeches Touré referred to the two most oppressed groups within Guinean society, peasants and women. He considered the contradiction between men and women one of the fundamentals of society and declared that women were twice exploited, once by colonialism and again by men. Alliance was necessary and complementary: women supported the party and the party emancipated women. In a famous speech made before independence, Sékou Touré did not hesitate to make the women of Guinea his electoral accomplices: "Every morning, every noon and every evening, women should ask their husbands to join the RDA. If they refuse, the women should refuse intercourse with them; the next morning, they will have to join."[46]

He sought women's political support, and women used it to protect themselves from men's going too far, for example, in 1964, when party leaders tried to do away with party women's sections in the villages. The men's argument was that these women's groups sowed discord within families. The women took things in hand so effectively that Touré the following year required the women's sections be reestablished and even reinforced their privileges. These privileges were still very limited—at most, allowing the party's password to be divulged to women, allowing women's education councils to be held in assembly, allowing women to organize party receptions, and including women in "human investment" programs. The most concrete measure was doubtless giving women the right to "verify the effective application of party decisions concerning women."

Women were active during the early years. They reacted more to the difficult 1959–1964 period than men did, daring to demonstrate their displeasure with the disappearance of staple foods and protesting certain points in the 1964 and 1967 educational reforms. Yet women were far from political equality despite the Basari proverb, "Man is the anvil, the child the iron, and the woman the fire," despite Women's Day's being instituted in 1965 as an annual holiday on February 9 to commemorate the killing of the national heroine Mbaliya Camara, according to the official version of the story, during police repression of an RDA demonstration in 1955. (In reality, she was run through with a sword by a provincial chief who could not stand being challenged by a woman.)

Generally, the aim of the Guinean women's organization was to advance the political and social progress of its members—whatever their origin and educational level—by every possible means. The Guinean legal code became very favorable to women and was the most innovative in French-speaking Africa with regard to marriage and divorce.[47] Whether these early efforts have left long-lasting traces remains to be determined; in any case, it was again women, finally exasperated with the government, who organized a decisive demonstration in 1977.

16

Women and Politics: Delay in Zaire

Women of the deep Congo, in contrast to their sisters in West Africa, had a very hard time escaping the double oppression of their role as beasts of burden in traditional rural societies and the narrow conformism of the Belgian Catholic church. Tradition in effect denied them any opportunity for political participation. As everywhere, the enormous burdens that they carried finally led them to react but sometimes not until long after independence.

Peasant Women Discover Insubordination

This is what finally happened among the Temba women of Kivu, a relatively fertile province in eastern Zaire, when regional economic shifts gave peasant women the chance to try their hand at market work. Up until this point, while women were exhausting themselves in the fields men had begun to join the workforce and the money economy. Since the early days of colonialism, men had been called on to produce peanuts and to staff construction sites and had gone on to work in the mines or elsewhere. In order to achieve this end, Belgian colonial officials had restructured the country and given traditional chiefs (*mwami*) more power. Women began to grow cash crops for regional markets. Cassava, introduced between the wars to replace plantains, increased in importance. Women produced and prepared it and began taking it to market on foot, especially when a road was built connecting Kivu with the region's main center, Bukavu. This obsessive cassava production and transportation began to be called *ebutumwa bw'emiogo*, "the cassava tyranny." The women became exasperated when their small trade, as unprofitable as it was exhausting, began to be the target of price-fixing by local potentates. Starting in the 1970s and increasing during the 1980s, local prices dropped because of increases in the costs of imported merchandise. In the 1980s, it took ten baskets of cassava to buy one skirt-cloth that had cost only two baskets a few years before. Ironically, what encouraged the revolt was the government's new decentralization policy, designed to lighten the burden on a state that could not afford to support local development. These women, ignorant and isolated, found it easier to address their direct exploiters, the chiefs invested with discretionary power by the national administration, than a distant "state" that they knew nothing about and could not reach.

As usual, what started the disturbances was a tax on the cassava trade. This cash tax had existed under colonialism but had been abandoned after 1960. It was brought back in the mid-1970s and doubled in April 1982. Then a chief from a village along the six-mile road that the women cassava producers took to the Bulambika market also started charging for the right to pass, supposedly to keep up the bridge. Another 10 percent was taken from them at the entrance to the town. But the bridge fell into ruins, while the chief's wife defied the peasant women by selling the cassava taken from them at a profit in the same marketplace.

The enraged market women were illiterate and therefore went to their priest to ask him to write up their complaint to the chief. The chief started out encouragingly, promising to receive them. After a week or two of delaying tactics he took a less conciliatory tack: Since when did women think they could give orders to men? What was the meaning of this basic breach of custom? Instead of giving in as they usually did, the women met at the parish building and went to the chief's seat to stand up for themselves. This was a small thing—they numbered no more than a hundred—but the phenomenon was surprising because as long as anyone could remember, convention and male power had never been braved with such insolence in this patrilineal, patrilocal area. The women won, and in the next local elections they voted en masse for candidates who would defend them. The tax was suspended, the toll was stopped, and recommendations were made in high places to avoid any other excesses.

Of course, this example is small, but it certainly illustrates both women's condition and the bases for changing it in profoundly rural parts of central Africa. It also gives flavor to an official proclamation made by President Joseph-Desiré Mobutu about women's condition. Without worrying about the contradictions inherent in his speech, he affirmed in two paragraphs, one right after the other, both the equality of men and women (reduced to procreators, *mamas* in Lingala) and women's natural subjugation to the family head: "The integration of woman—we desire it at all levels. We want to recognize the Zairean woman's rights which confer on her the status of equal partner to man. But it remains understood, with all due consideration, that there will always be a boss in every household. And until proof to the contrary, the boss in our land is the one who wears the pants. Our female citizens should also understand this, accept it with a smile, and with revolutionary submissiveness."[1]

Abo: Revolutionary Woman or Tool of the Revolution?

It would be unfair to say that Zaire saw no political awakening by women, but it was slow and rare. The case of Léonie Abo, the companion of Pierre Mulele, is all the more striking in that it shows the degree to which such awakening was exceptional for the time, though limited in scope. Abo became a militant section chief and a courageous fighter. She supported Mulele in his flight to the bush until his execution. Only late and timidly did she understand her role and her strength.

She was born in the Kwilu region, on a palm plantation that belonged to the Compagnie du Kasaï. The daughter of a palm-nut cutter, she was adopted by a village chief. She went to primary school, including three years of boarding school with the nuns, but barely spoke French. Though her background made her a member of the village aristocracy and she had been vaguely converted by her teacher, she was still subject to the harsh customs that govern women's lives in her country—submission to the will of her father and his brothers. Her marriage had been planned by her family more than twenty years before her birth, with prior bride gifts. It was to take place after she left school at twelve. She was able to escape it only because her promised husband had joined the Force Publique, the army disgraced in the region since the terrible repression of 1931. Thanks to the priest, her adoptive father broke the engagement by getting her admitted to the regional school for assistant midwives, a certificate she received in 1959, before she was fourteen. She acquired these vocational skills somewhat by chance. When she returned, without ever having been consulted she was married to another boy, who was jealous and brutal. At seventeen she took her life into her own hands for the first time and sought to divorce him to marry a young orderly. Because her rejected husband filed suit against her, she was sentenced to a month in prison. By this time the revolt was under way, and one of her brothers took her by force to the resistance fighters led by Pierre Mulele. At no point did anyone ask her opinion, not even Mulele when he decided to make her his companion.

Mulele, a young Maoist revolutionary, had very specific ideas about women's emancipation. He gave them classes to teach them equality. They were the first to find this ridiculous, because no woman dared to speak aloud in the presence of men. They had always been taught that decency demanded never addressing a man in public except, at most, to answer him by whispering her message in the ear of an uncle who would speak for her. It was only very slowly that some women in the resistance became more self-assured. Abo was not one of them, and although she was known as first among the women guerrillas, she was not given responsibility for the women's commando. A man of very high moral standards, Mulele forbade his troops to chase women, and pregnant women were expelled from the group. This rule did not keep him from very officially taking a second and then a third wife, once again without Abo's having anything to say about it.

Abo became more self-assured in the second half of her life, after the rebellion was crushed and she went to Brazzaville and then on to Europe.[2] Her story shows a limited understanding and a confused though real developing consciousness of the struggle in which she had so directly participated. Despite the constraints burdening her life and a relatively exceptional degree of education for girls of her generation, the modesty required of women in her country remained with her. She is a witness, moving but a little desperate, to the long road that women have yet to cover before they can assert themselves socially and politically.

17

Women and Politics: The Wars for National Liberation

There would be much to say about the role that southern African minority white women played as suffragettes and factory workers, but this is not the purpose of this book. In the 1940s African women made up almost 70 percent of the women in South Africa and mostly lived in what were still called native reserves, since 1913 set at 13 percent of the nation's lands. Little by little, complex social alliances formed, despite sex, class, and color bars.[1]

South Africa

By way of an outline,[2] white women's struggle took two basic forms: what was most important to women of British origin with a fairly high level of education was the fight for white women's franchise. At the end of the nineteenth century, their standard-bearer was the author Olive Schreiner. Her first novel, published in 1883, called for equality between the sexes. But such women were a tiny minority.

The struggle was different for white women factory workers. In the proletariat, there was a particularly oppressed, exploited, and underpaid group mainly of poor Afrikaners (Dutch in origin) and colored women, half African and half Asian.[3] Many of these women began working in the textile industry between the wars. Their union was characteristically far more interracial than the others at a time when black organizing was practically forbidden; they may all have been aware of their common inferiority as women. The Garment Workers' Union, mainly composed of female factory workers, most of them white, was the champion of interracial union organizing before

1940,[4] but here African women were in a tiny minority. In 1921 only 7 percent of women factory workers were African, and as this industry developed between the wars this percentage decreased.[5] In the early 1920s 50–60 percent of city women were white or colored compared with only 4 percent who were African.[6] This meant there were an average of three African men in the city for every woman and in the Rand almost nine.

The "Prehistory" of Women's Resistance

African women worked mainly on farms or in the city at the most devalued jobs—domestic service and especially informal-sector jobs. With few exceptions, their childhood and youth (in contrast to boys, who became migrants early on) were spent in isolation similar to what Dora Tomana describes. She was a Capetown woman activist with the African National Congress (ANC) in the early 1950s who had grown up in a hamlet about three or four hours' walk from the nearest town. The closest shop was an hour's walk and the nearest source of water almost a mile away. There was of course no paved road, and the mission school had just two classes. Her family, although very poor, felt fortunate to own a plot of land. The same was true among the Zulu, where Phyllis Ntantala was the daughter of the local pastor and later the wife of an activist who was assassinated. (Today she lives in exile in the United States). Tomana certainly benefited from being the first child in a family whose three children were all girls and Ntantala from being attentively educated by her father after her mother died.[7] But although the old women of Phokeng (a tiny town in a Bantustan emptied by men's labor migration) offer us, with their lives and work, a perspective diametrically opposed to the usual assertions about how passive, conservative, and politically apathetic women are, few women indeed grew up in environments that would have made them active resisters.[8] Many of the earliest women were activists because of their husbands, as Phyllis Ntantala herself acknowledges.

The three largest cities in the country, Johannesburg, Durban, and Cape Town, were those in which the numbers of African women were proportionately the lowest. On the Bantustans the opposite was true, especially for women between fifteen and sixty. Yet politics were forged in the cities, and black civil rights struggles developed in the cities. Thus can we understand why women's politicization took a long time to begin.

Before World War II, women's actions were limited and from the start focused on what became the linchpin of their struggle against apartheid: the refusal to carry passes, thus reclaiming their freedom of movement. This was called for by migrant women, and it was the first time that women's claim to rights was based in something other than tribal or traditional custom. It became a rallying cry. The pass war was to South African women what the struggle against income taxation was to West African women. They defended their own special condition—their special right to survive, to take care of their children, and to perform informal work, which went unrecognized by the dominant male society. In fact, in daring and even provocative fashion they used means similar to those used by West African women in revolt: petitions to the highest authorities, massive street demonstrations, energetic singing. They were sometimes bolder than the established male political organizations—the African National Congress, the parties, and the unions—liked.

The ANC was, like European resistance organizations, conceived as a men's movement when it was created in 1912, but because of the women this did not last long. The women initiated their first fight against the pass laws in Orange Free State the following year. Until this point, passes had been required only of men, women being present in such small numbers that they were not even counted in the workforce. The only state that had sought to recognize them was the Orange Free State. This was no coincidence; it was the only state in which the number of African women in the cities was already equal to the number of men. In Bloemfontein, the capital, in 1921 there were 8,588 African women compared with 9,300 men.

In 1912 women started a Native and Coloured Women's Association (though there were very few colored women in Orange) to write protest petitions to the federal government. Getting no answer, they went as a delegation to Capetown. A crisis broke out in June 1913 after several women who had taken a petition to the mayor were arrested in Bloemfontein; six hundred African women marched on city hall, pushing the police aside and noisily demonstrating until the governor agreed to show himself. They then began a passive resistance campaign, as Gandhi had done, by leading Indians in Natal, refusing to pay fines and getting themselves imprisoned as often as they could. For the first time, a white suffragette, I. J. Cross, even wrote an article on the affair, although it had nothing in common with the era's Western-style women's groups, which sought civil rights for women.

Whites rallied around the notion of the "family." African women seemed no threat in the city and incarnated family stability and the safety of children—the era's domestic ideal, in sum. The federal government gave in, the Orange Free State in 1920 had to abandon its claims, and African male activists, though supportive of the action, found themselves a little overwhelmed and learned their lesson. The ANC created a women's section, called the Bantu Women's League, made up of "auxiliary members" without votes.

Other antipass campaigns came in 1913–1914 and then again in Transvaal in 1928, but things went no farther for a time. The leaders were just a few women. Teachers and nurses, they were members of a lower-middle-class population hardly likely to rise up against their fate, enamored of the domestic and family values that were then women's lot. We especially know the name of Charlotte Maxehe, called "the mother of African liberty." She was part of the tiny elite of black women at the turn of the century. Born in 1874 in the Cape colony, she had the exceptional luck to belong to a choir whose tours took her to England and then Canada and the United States, where she attended a segregated university in Ohio. There she discovered the thinking of the great civil rights activist Booker T. Washington and joined the African Methodist Episcopal church, one of the earliest and most important of the independent black churches. The wife of an early ANC activist pastor, she became president of the Bantu Women's League and then the National Council of African Women that succeeded it in 1933. Its actions were limited to the social sphere in an era, it must be noted, when repression made almost any political activity impossible.[9]

After 1930, the Communist party became almost exclusively an African one. From the beginning, it had advocated nondiscrimination in race and sex, though limited by the usual sexist stereotypes. This is where the earliest women activists got their training: Josie Palmer, who remained active until the beginning of the 1950s, when the nationalist party condemned her to silence;[10] Mary Wolton; and Ray Alexander, who played a particularly active role in union women's organizing, was elected to a party political office in 1938, and was also banned in 1953. From this era dated the idea of giving African women the chance to organize politically.

Popular Interventions

World War II created industrial jobs and eliminated the problem of "poor whites." At the same time, inflation and the housing crisis made blacks' condition ever more precarious. Unemployment grew, although the black work-force increased and women massively joined the urban labor force, still mainly as maids or in informal-sector jobs. Conditions were now set for them to claim to have their voices heard independent of parties and the authorized unions.

Without being recognized leaders themselves, women living in township working-class neighborhoods had long expressed the growing discomfort caused by specific practical problems. They first organized to protect the rights they had gained—the right to occupy squatted housing, no other housing being available for their families, the right to circulate freely, the right to brew beer in secret, one of their primary livelihoods—and led a desperate struggle against passes, which were finally imposed on them in 1952 without their ever having stopped campaigning against them.

In 1943 and 1944, many women joined the bus boycotts to protest fare increases, for example, in the township of Alexandra ten miles from Johannesburg. They were noted for their organized resistance to the destruction of squatted neighborhoods. One of the most famous of these movements was the shantytown movement started near Johannesburg in 1944 by James Mpanza and his wife, Julia. The right to housing was firmly defended by the women who marched en masse on Cape Town in 1947 and in Crossroads in the suburbs. In the 1970s they organized an effective women's committee, ready for anything, including physically blocking the bulldozers.[11]

There were many other actions, especially around Cape Town, which had a tradition of residential nonsegregation. It is largely to these women and their stubborn resistance that we owe the gradual lowering of the color bar in working-class neighborhoods, long before its recent official disappearance shortly before the end of apartheid.

Elsewhere, war-driven scarcity brought about the boycott, started by the Food Committee, of overcharging businesspeople throughout the cities, in particular Johannesburg, Cape Town, and Durban. Women were the pillars of this action, as they were usually responsible for their families' subsistence. They organized protest marches and raids against traders accused of hoarding goods to drive up prices, giving them notice to put their hidden reserves on sale immediately. Many women, illiterate as they were, became aware of their strength at this point.

After the war, the end of the crisis in staple items eroded the women's actions, but their like picked up every time poverty threatened, such as in August 1953 in Cape Town, when the government decided to raise the price of bread. This movement caused ANC women activists to think of creating a national women's federation. The turning point came in 1949, when a young militant radical named Ida Mtwana was put at the head of the ANC Women's League, created in 1943. The ANC also changed its president at this time and began a radical program of action against the nationalist party that had just come to power and begun to build the structure of apartheid.[12]

The baton was also taken up by young working women despite their still small numbers. The Garment Workers' Union's interracial views were upset in 1940 by the massive entry of colored women into the textile industry, which white women ill withstood. This interracial heritage was transmitted to the rapidly developing food industry, in particular in the canned food and fruit-juice sectors. In effect, these new jobs, very badly paid and thus very feminized, attracted few white women. The Food and Canning Workers' Union, started in 1941 by Ray Alexander in the western Cape province, gave birth to a union that was interracial and radical right from the start (in fact, it was made up of colored and black workers) and that turned out to be a political training ground for many young militants, among them some destined to become famous: Liz Abraham, Elizabeth Mafeking, and Frances Baard-Rose.[13] These young women with little or no education, hardly politicized to start with and often from very religious families, got their training "in the field" and became formidable leaders. They were especially clever about using their legal nonexistence in their actions. In a 1944 ruling they gloriously won the right to join the legal, duly registered unions of the Industrial Conciliation Act of 1924; it excluded "pass-bearers" but of course not women by name.[14] Their success, which for a time favored women's union organizing, was short-lived. Six years later, passes were legally required of women and their leaders were banished, paralyzing women's union and political activity for twenty years.

Since the war, black women had understood that much of their vulnerability stemmed from a lack of political rights. They began to make the connection between basic economic rights and the right to vote, which had finally been accorded white women.[15] The ANC was the first to welcome them, and in 1943 they were recognized as full-fledged members with the right to vote and participate in all leadership positions. Here again, the great push unifying all these women was their fight against passes.

Passes and the Politicization of Women

With passes, for the first time African women *as women* became the targets of white power. Once considered negligible, they were ejected from the modern urban economic world. Until this point the government had been able to pretend without much trouble that it was keeping them in the countryside doing subsistence work and procreating. The rural crisis ended this myth. Nationalists were urgently required to forbid access to the cities to African women, who were being pushed to migrate in what threatened to become uncontrollable numbers. In 1951, one-fifth of African women already lived in the cities. It was understandable that they responded as a group to this action taken against them, and they did so with remarkable tenacity and energy. It still took twelve years for the government to pass a bill that it had announced as early as 1950 but that was delayed for three years because of women's reactions to it. Its application was extended with difficulty over the course of a decade, and it was only on February 1, 1963, that the government was able to proclaim that all South African women had to own the pamphlet that they had fought against so long. This struggle was mainly what brought them into the political arena.

At the beginning, women's response was twofold. First they organized the various antipass campaigns that continued over the years. Then they assembled in 1954 into a national federation that at one point was distinct from any political affiliation, even though it was supported by political organizations, clandestine or not: the Communist party (prohibited in 1950) and the ANC (banned in 1960). It started in Port Elizabeth, the capital of the eastern Cape province, under the leadership of Ray Alexander, and then spread to the main cities. Sixty-three organizations responded to its very open invitation to hold a national conference, which in April 1964 brought to Johannesburg just over 150 women, mostly black and all city dwellers. The resulting charter confirmed their participation in the struggle for national liberation from white power. The federation's functioning was rough, because increasingly ferocious repression was a serious obstacle to its directors, to communication across the country, and to the organization's financing. The Federation of South African Women still managed to be active in many arenas, especially the fight against the application of laws regarding Bantu education and for restoration of the right to birth control. In 1955 the federation launched plans for a gathering in Pretoria to present women's claims directly to the central government.

This was the opportunity for a rapprochement with women. The nationalists in power, who had been cautious on this hot topic, had effectively resolved to apply the pass law to women by requiring them to obtain passbooks. Despite the police, over 1,000 women managed to meet in the capital. For women from all over the country this was the beginning of an unprecedented antipass campaign. In the first half of 1956 some 50,000 women attended thirty-eight demonstrations in thirty different places, both peaceful presentations of a petition and public burnings of the hated passbooks. Despite arrests, the movement continued to grow in 1956 and 1957.

This was the point when for the first time peasant women joined in, in Zeeruste (western Transvaal), where Bafurutse women, mostly wives of absent migrant workers, had been required to accept the passbook. Their resistance, passive at the start, became violent. The district prisons overflowed, and hundreds of refugee women pushed against the borders of the British protectorate of Bechuanaland (today Botswana). The ANC was not the only instigator. The women also revolted in the name of the rights of the family, of the traditional authorities, and of their husbands, as the administration had made a decision regarding the women without asking their husbands' opinions. Although their motives began rather conservatively, the course of events helped to politicize and radicalize them.

A half-million passes had already been imposed on women, and by the end of 1958 they exceeded a million. The final blows were dealt that year, when the passbook was imposed on nurses, despite resistance that was crushed at Pretoria's hospital in March, and in Johannesburg despite the unexpected vigor of the Sophiatown women's uprising. Almost 2,000 were arrested in October, and many women were deported. The following year in Natal, the women's fight against passes continued, first in the areas around Durban, where the authorities took advantage of the uprising to destroy the enormous squatters' neighborhood called Cato Manor in June 1959. After a demonstration that brought 50,000 women together, the expulsion of thousands of them to the Bantustans only exported their spirit of resistance.

Considering the clandestinity of most of their actions, it is very hard to gain a precise sense of the extent of female activism after 1960, when the Sharpeville shootings began the period of worst repression. Neither the Women's Federation, which managed to survive until 1963, nor the ANC recruited in the Bantustans, and their actions could only be felt in the large cities. What is certain is that with this formidable police undertaking of imposing passes on the women, the women suddenly found themselves affected by the antiapartheid struggle, even though the motivation for most was not political and at first hardly revolutionary.

Very much influenced by the missionaries' message and molded by almost two centuries of teaching in domestic values, South African women were generally pious, usually willing despite their poverty to support their neighborhood religious community and *manyanos* (women's religious associations) financially. In the tyrannical world in which they lived, the church was a safe and therefore reassuring place. Politics, in contrast, was dangerous to them and their children, but they found themselves in a situation in which they had no other choice. We can understand the weight that the political engagement of a man like Bishop Desmond Tutu can take on in such a country, more than anywhere else except Latin America, for similar reasons.

Whatever women's motives, political, military, or more often traditional, they began to resist, always passively, often openly, with such disconcerting courage that they gradually won men's respect in a society ill-prepared to accept women in political roles. Lilian Ngoyi's election to the national executive office of the ANC in 1955 was a sign of this. Another was the decision to make August 9 Women's Day in honor and memory of the massive 1956 demonstration in Pretoria. Finally, in 1959, Albert Lutuli, the ANC president, grasped the consequences and officially confirmed that each position in the organization was open to both men and women and that every nomination or promotion would depend on merit alone.

The antipass struggle was a bitter failure but also a hard political apprenticeship for women. Some years later, their men's rebellion in the savage Durban strikes of 1970 and their children's rebellion in the Soweto uprising of 1976 again left them no choice. In the name of family values, so deeply anchored in the South African mind-set, despite all that had been attempted by the Afrikaners to destroy the cohesion of their black adversaries, they actively, massively joined in resistance to oppression, no doubt more than anywhere else in Africa and in ways that were uniquely theirs: no wonder that Nelson Mandela understood that the ANC would win as soon as women entered the struggle.

Women and War

South Africa is not the only place in which women's political consciousness has been forged by active resistance. Women played an important role in the liberation wars during the Mau-Mau uprising in Kenya, in the Portuguese colonies, and in Zimbabwe and Namibia. These were societies in which women, usually close to the land, were extremely submissive to patriarchal authority. Their political participation marked a turning point in their history, and for the first time they became full-fledged actors in it. Even though the numbers of women activists were not great, they left an indelible mark on the future.

The Mau-Mau Revolt and the "Passive Wing"

Of the many studies of the Mau-Mau rebellion, only one has looked at women.[16] The colonial literature has presented two caricatures of women: ignorant peasants, the victims of bandits' fanaticism, forced by threats to feed the resistance fighters, and urban prostitutes, stripped of tribal affiliation, with nothing left to lose. The reality was more complicated. Women experienced this movement as a major disturbance. Along with the men they had been affected by colonial legislation depriving them of land, because they did most of the agricultural labor for the overpopulated reserves they lived on and were very often used as seasonal workers on the coffee plantations. Being forced to perform communal labor and to pay taxes according to the laws of 1910 and 1934 greatly irritated them. Although political activity was not traditionally Kikuyu women's arena, the first women militants appeared during the 1930s. In 1947 and 1948 they organized several plantation strikes and struggled against being forced to create antierosion terracing in their fields. This was called "the women's war." They also impatiently welcomed the missionaries' dogged assaults on customs affecting women most: bride-prices, initiation rituals, and injunctions against widows' remarrying.

The most famous nationalist woman activist, Rebecca Njeri, was imprisoned in 1952 at the same time as Jomo Kenyatta, and all the women in the country knew this. British power understood the role that women played in what they called the "passive wing" so well that they had prepared a special strategy of propaganda and social measures against it. This strategy was implemented by the Community Development Department, a distant ancestor of the Women's Bureau, and later reinitiated by the government after Kenya's independence.

Women were the main targets of the enforced return to villages from 1954 to 1958, which placed the country under military surveillance to prevent the sharing of food and information with the resistance. These villages were surrounded with barbed wire, and the women were accompanied into the fields by armed guards; a curfew was imposed at four in the afternoon. Several hundred thousand households were displaced and reassembled. The plan was accompanied by social and health programs designed to win women's confidence through child care, milk distribution, and food distribution in cases of starvation. The tool used for this was the Maendeleo ya Wanawake, an association of women's progress clubs that had started at the end of the 1940s and spread in the state of emergency.[17] It is worthwhile to note that during the 1980s these clubs were still the most important women's organizations in Kenya, with more than 6,000 members.

Were peasant women won over to the political ends of the British? Being forced to secrecy left them no choice. The military's partitioning attained its goal of destabilizing the guerrillas. Threatened with deprivation of their lands and condemned to permanent curfew, many women took vows and were considered loyalists. Mentally and socially they remained no less disturbed. Between 1952 and 1958, 35,000 women were arrested and sentenced to prison, including several thousand repeat offenders and among them some armed fighters (10 percent of the total). The British were the first to be surprised. They had been so certain of the women's passivity that they could hardly understand their committed participation, terming it an "unexpected, sudden, and fanatical" reaction. They had also never thought to build women's prisons, which certainly posed logistical problems. Deplorable prison conditions created a scandal in the House of Commons in 1956.

Portuguese African Awakening

In Portuguese-speaking countries, as in French-speaking Guinea, feminist initiative first came from men. After Sékou Touré in Guinea came Amilcar Cabral in Guinea-Bissau. He was born to a family of *assimilados* who had come from Cape Verde and felt particularly strongly about the emancipation of women. In this little country with no other wealth, he had focused his efforts on agriculture and peasants—peasant women. The doctrine of the Parti pour l'Independance de la Guinée et du Cap Vert (PAIGC, the Guinean and Cape Verdean Independence party) gave a very high priority to education, especially for girls, who were almost entirely illiterate. In the labor market, a quota established a minimum number of jobs reserved for women, who had been left out of the market economy. For example, in a tile-manufacturing project initiated in 1976, 40 percent of the jobs had to be offered to women.[18]

But mores are not changed by decree. Women had to be convinced, and they were especially cautious about anything unknown. Men too had to be convinced—it was unthinkable to them to be placed under a woman's command. Some women managed to achieve great popularity. Ernestina (Titina) Silà, an early activist, was born in 1943 in the countryside and sent by Cabral to study in the USSR, whence she returned in 1964. She became a political officer and, when she was killed in a 1973 ambush several days after Cabral's assassination, a national heroine. Francisca Pereira, also a political officer, was the PAIGC's delegate to the Pan-African Women's Organization in Algeria. There were also Teodora Gomes and Carmen Pereira, the latter the daughter of one of the rare Guinean lawyers. Pereira had been to primary school but waited at home, embroidering and sewing, for a husband who himself belonged to the PAIGC. All joined the movement at a young age, around sixteen or seventeen or even ten or twelve, the age at which many married. They were a tiny minority of women. It was all well and good for progress in women's status to be announced after independence with the creation of a women's organization and a law protecting their rights[19]—society's established values took time to change. Education and especially employment remained very male-dominated.

These conclusions are hardly original. If we ignore some exceptional women, we can say the same thing of women's position and role in the liberation wars of other countries—worse, perhaps, because Cabral's attitude toward women's advancement was quite exceptional. This was far less the case in Angola or Mozambique, despite the good intentions of the Front de Liberation du Mozambique (FRELIMO, Mozambique Libration Front). In 1966 its central committee decided to organize women's political and military training "so that at all levels they can take a more active part in the struggle for national liberation."[20] As Mulele established in Zaire around the same time, this small female batallion fought on the front lines and ensured that the rear guard was full. They were given political education and sent on missions but also charged with more traditional tasks, in Western terms, such as organizing the FRELIMO orphanage, teaching in the schools, and giving literacy courses to combat prejudices forbidding girls' education. Most difficult was fighting the traditional division of labor. In effect, everyone in the military, both men and women, was asked to share the burden, including cooking, child care, sowing and harvest. Yet such an undertaking was almost doomed to failure in societies that remained so strongly sex-segregated.

Namibian Women

There was a similar delay in Zimbabwe, where most women intellectuals were colored. In Namibia, however, women advanced very quickly, as they did in South Africa, especially after World War II. The lifestyle imposed on them by men's migration deeply uprooted earlier structures. Charged with almost all the survival work in the Bantustans, few women directly joined the South West African People's Organization (SWAPO)[21] but they were more resolute and more tenacious than the men. As in South Africa, they threw themselves into the struggle against passes for women. In the city, despite or perhaps because of their small number, factory women's and women teachers' union organizing was radical. Women activists in exile in 1956 created a SWAPO Women's Council, "not only to mobilize women to participate in the national struggle but to make them conscious that they have the same right and obligation as men to make decisions concerning their nation's interest; that the woman should therefore develop herself to be a comrade in all aspects and not just a 'homemaker'; that both male and female should understand the system of exploitation and combat it as comrades."[22]

It took ten years for their group to be officially recognized by SWAPO as a full-fledged section. In 1977 actions began in Namibia, where despite repression there were meetings, seminars, and demonstrations that sometimes brought in several thousand women. Their strength lay in a narrow network of relationships between women activists and farmers, in the north and west of the country especially, despite enormous transportation difficulties. But in 1988 only one woman sat on the party's national committee. Much remains to be done, and schools, where attendance has today become almost equal for boys and girls, are starting to change for future generations what has until now been a given.

18

⚡

Sexuality and Emancipation

Socially and politically, women are starting to find their way. Recent changes have sometimes taken place at lightning speed. Today's women are vigorous, creative, and full of promise. African women express themselves in every arena, including the arts (once rare), especially modern art forms and writing. Women are renewing song and dance forms and beginning to move into film. Their very rise and the way in which they—strong women, heads of households in countryside and city, microentrepreneurs and prosperous businesswomen, activists, writers, and artists—are becoming aware of just what is at stake for them, of their struggles and constraints, reveal just how difficult things have become for them.

Sexuality and Social Rituals

African men's way of looking at women and the perception women have of themselves are imprinted with social ideologies that are often still extremely conservative. Social ritual is often long-lived. Anything concerning the essence of the feminine, whether it is little girls' upbringing, young women's initiation, or dominant beliefs about marriage or maternity or even death, is marked by a complicated heritage still felt heavily today. It is perhaps even less possible today than before to speak of "the" African woman. What common denominator is there between a country girl and a city girl, between an educated girl and one who has never seen the inside of a schoolroom, between the woman who works within the capitalist system and one working in the informal sector, between the woman endowed with children and one who is sterile, between the one who uses contraception and AIDS prevention and the woman who is beyond all hope because she lacks the means even to imagine what she might wish for? Diversity in class, culture, religion, and ideology make the problem even more complex. I will try to illuminate certain aspects concretely in areas that have been very insufficiently studied—sexuality and emancipation. They have been too fleetingly examined for reasons that themselves have not been elucidated; men's neglect and even contempt, Western moralizing or guilt, and the viewpoint that, rightly or wrongly, would ignore sex make analysis no easier. Yet it is well to pose a few simple questions on the current evolution in social practices, law, development, and artistic creation and their relations to African women.

From Birth to Marriage and Initiation

We have sufficiently emphasized women's subordinate condition not to need to reemphasize it here. Nonetheless, let us recall that social control of girls does not begin with birth. Like boys', girls' early years are very free. The child breastfeeds whenever she or he wants to, and tenderness and patience are the norm with tiny children; men and women, old and young stop everything to pay immediate attention to a baby when it cries.[1] Some have even tried to explain the often marked absence of combativeness among adults in terms of psychoanalysis: Because the child is free to live exactly as it pleases, sleeping and feeding when it chooses, ever close to its mother's warmth, carried on her back and sleeping with her, it does not need to develop the aggressive qualities against the surrounding world in its early months that would give it the capacity once grown to act as an individual.

This being said, as a general rule girls' education began much earlier than boys'. Boys did not go to be with men until their seventh year. They were and are often still allowed to gambol freely while girls cling closely to their mothers' skirts and are already learning domestic chores, helping to carry water and doing little tasks. Certainly, by five or six a girl is carrying in her turn the next-to-last-born child (displaced from their mother's back by the newest arrival) and supervising the other children who are younger than she is.

In every society, the initiation that comes at puberty was an important ceremony for boys because it was thus that they entered into the world of men and the world of power. Girls' initiation was designed to instruct them sometimes very specifically in sexual games but also in menstruation taboos and the "secrets" of childbirth.

Initiation in most societies lasted several months (at least three), generally during the dry season, because part of the ceremony was to isolate the girls in a savanna or sacred forest far from the village in the company of the older women officiating. The rest of the ceremony consisted of symbolic ritual songs and dances, the eating of certain foods, and even the appearance of masked beings or a trance session (for example, among the Guro). Today it is common for parents to bring their daughters from the city during a school vacation to participate in a ceremony that has been adapted and shortened to three weeks at the most.

Girls' initiations take various forms. Some are fairly agreeable, but most were a pitiless introduction to the life of labor awaiting peasant women.[2] Once again, it is very hard to generalize. In some societies, not all of them Muslim (among the Wolof, true, but also among the Yoruba and the Toro), virginity until marriage was the rule because of customs mainly predating monotheism. In other societies, in contrast, the young woman was not marriageable until she had proven her fertility. Ceremonies initiating the pubescent young woman were thus very diverse, even diametrically opposed to one another.

Among young Peul women, raised to modesty in marriage, the sexual education of girls between ten and twelve or thirteen—the age at which many were married—was mainly left to nature. A girl often openly spent time with boys her own age, so freely that she was not always strong enough to defend herself against assault by a teenage boy older than she was, and her crying in the night worried no one: "The children played yesterday evening," the adults simply commented.[3] Elsewhere, initiation might be more regulated. This was the case for young Guinean Coniagui and Basari women, whose excision ceremony was followed by a retreat lasting several weeks during which the young woman was taught sexual secrets.[4]

We still know little about this type of initiation. The secrets remain well-kept, and women researchers' curiosity has been more limited than regarding boys' initiation. But without its necessarily being as harsh as Tswana initiation, what we do know allows us to imagine an often crude, traumatizing training period in which everything is done to make the young woman submit to men's pleasure.

Once again, we cannot generalize. The very detailed description, almost hour by hour, of the initiation of two young Bemba women (in northern Zambia) shows us how much women of the 1930s preserved of what were ancestral rites in much of central Africa where this form of individual initiation, called *chisungu*, was practiced.[5] Girls seem to have been very frightened by it (but no more than boys during their own rites of passage), even though nothing terrible happened to them; circumcision in particular was hardly practiced. Certainly, during the course of the ceremony, the girls were hurt from time to time, tied or hung in rather acrobatic ways. They were much made fun of, verbally assaulted, and made to cry. They had to stand in front of the other women sometimes entirely naked but usually with their chests uncovered, which was considered very shameful. (But was that not the missionaries' influence?) There was no ritual deflowering or even any simulation of it except by the use of clay figurines and multiple, interminable songs. In short, there was much symbolism and little real violence. Yet what the female anthropologist observer does not emphasize is that this ritual, since it took place normally just before formal marriage, often came after prior sexual relations in which girls had hardly been consulted. This was part of a process that lasted several years. The boy had already performed a series of different kinds of tasks at his mother-in-law's home that were part of the bride-price. Simultaneously his fiancée, a little girl who was not yet marriageable, gradually earned the right to come and clean her fiancé's house and bring him water. The anthropologist adds, "Having gradually won the right to her domestic services, payment gives him the privilege of taking his young bride to sleep with him."[6] Only with the onset of puberty, out of fear of seeing her daughter have a baby before the *chisungu* ceremony took place, did the mother take her daughter back for a while to live with her. Initiation properly speaking was only one stage in a long journey through which the daughter was transferred from one clan to another according to the use men made of her.

Initiation could also take place after marriage rather than before. This was the case among the Haya of northwestern Tanzania, where the young woman—as in other places—was married without being consulted or even having the right to meet her future husband. Throughout the marriage preparations that may last several months or even years, the bride-price was paid and shared among the members of the bride's mother's and father's families. There was no clitoridectomy or special initiation up to this point. As soon as the ceremony was over, however, the young wife was cloistered for long months, sometimes lasting up to a year or two. She had to remain in a dark, isolated corner of the house, without working, barely moving, and speaking to no one. Her mother-in-law was to educate her, and she received only occasional visitors, including her husband and his brothers, who had sexual rights to her. At the end of this long period of seclusion, during which she was to be well fed, supposedly to make her more beautiful, and, in contrast to the rest of her life, was not to work, she was to emerge pregnant. The missionaries long fought this practice, which was still widespread during the 1930s.[7] They considered it immoral and argued that it broke the young woman's spirit, which was shaped from that point on by the desires of her husband and his family.[8]

Sexual relations in initiation could take still more traumatic forms. Young Luo or Luyia girls in western Kenya were "captured" by their fiancé's relatives and dragged screaming to their new homes, where they were to continue to lament noisily. Young Gusii women were supposed to resist as much as possible during the first night of the marriage and to cry during intercourse, which thus became rape.[9]

Several accounts, from one end of the continent to the other, contradict the sweetness and light of the Bemba ritual described above. Some of the worst treatment of women was by the Tswana, whose attitude toward marriage had progressed little by the 1930s.[10] What did change and finally had an impact was the young women's reaction. Unlike their mothers, they had the energy to resist once they learned that there was recourse for what they were enduring. Whenever they could, they began to bring charges of aggression or rape to the colonial courts (not to the native courts, which always found them in the wrong). Some of their accounts make us tremble. Holi Bhembhe, in Swaziland, for example, was carried off by her husband with her own mother's help. He tore off her clothes and raped her even though she had not even reached puberty in the name of the *lobola* (bride-price) that he had paid. The young woman's father testified, "The girl was young, but I was in need." Other girls claimed to have been beaten, forced to endure the marriage ceremony, and then dragged to the husband's house, again because the bride-price had been paid and already spent. One of these young women claimed in 1932 to have been caught and taken back after she fled: "A woman took a cord and they tied me to a tree, and tied my feet to a stake, and laid me down on the ground. The women beat me with big sticks and then beat me on my back, and then did it again when night fell. My brothers gave me to five different men, and only the last one had paid in animals. They starved me."

Another was condemned by the chief to be beaten and dragged over twenty-five kilometers to her husband's house with her arms tied. Another, who had already been beaten with a heavy stick, was then hit and brought by force before the chief. If most of these young victims did not win their cases, they at least had their husbands sentenced to several weeks, even months, of forced labor.

A desperate young woman's reaction could be brutal, and there are several cases of suicide known. But justice was concerned with more aggressive responses: several women, convicted of having poisoned their husbands, were condemned to death. This was no longer murder with the overtones of witchcraft but a quite modern assassination, generally by arsenic, which was easy to procure because it was part of the agricultural technology in use at the time. One of the young women condemned declared that she did not fear execution because nothing could be worse than what she had already endured. These women had believed that their crimes would go unrecognized, not realizing that in the event of an autopsy the diagnosis of poisoning would be obvious.

In 1932 a court's ruling created a scandal. It concerned a girl of sixteen, Sitomiya Kumalo, who had brought a charge of rape. The *lobola* had been paid to her father during her childhood, and she had been locked up against her will for a month with the man to whom she had been promised and then had endured the marriage ceremony. She had then escaped and taken refuge in the police station. The court had dismissed her, arguing that according to custom the girl's consent was not required, that the bride-price had been paid, and that the plaintiff could not furnish proof of the violence she had endured. Its judgment gave rise to numerous protests over the course of months from missionaries and other whites. Even the *Times* took up the problem. The administration concluded that it had to get a judgment condemning forced marriages from Sobhuza, the paramount chief. But his power was fragile, and he disliked imposing such an unpopular measure on his subjects. Therefore he delayed, promising to undertake negotiation and discussion. The circular itself, duly signed by the Swazi National Council, did not come out for several months and finally disappeared into oblivion.[11]

The situation is far from having always been this bad. But without being able to generalize on the basis of these scarce results, we cannot help but notice the docility and passivity that are required of young women regarding their own desires. In the 1960s there was confirmation of this in a fascinating survey on the sexual attitudes of students done under the direction of the headmaster of the Conakry high school in Guinea. Forty-three percent of these educated young women were indifferent to their marital fate, and one-fourth of boys accepted polygamy. The girls, reflecting the dominant ideology, were ignorant about their bodies and their right to think and act for themselves. The passivity of their desire and their submissiveness to boys' sex acts were astonishing; they essentially saw themselves as progenitors and instruments of pleasure for men.[12]

Genital Mutilation

What is left to discuss is the painful subject of female genital mutilation, which is still very much alive in some societies. These practices are part of a phenomenon far from limited to Africa. The suffering once imposed on little Chinese girls to keep their feet from growing or the use of chastity belts, veritable instruments of torture, in Europe during the Crusades are similar, restricting or even stopping women's movements and actions so as to guarantee her husband control of her fertility, until recently confused with her sexuality. In Luganda (a language of central Africa), for example, there was no word meaning "to marry" except *okuwasa*, literally "to make pregnant." It would be worthwhile to pursue the linguistic analysis.

Several degrees of mutilation should be distinguished. The least traumatic is the type known as *sunna*, which means "tradition" in Arabic. The most benign, which probably reflects the Prophet's moderating teachings, consists of removing only the hood of the clitoris, an operation precisely like male circumcision, but ablation of the entire clitoris tends to be performed instead. Excision adds to clitoridectomy the ablation of the labia minora, an operation commonly known as *tahara*, or purification. A particularly perverse form is the incision practiced on little Gishri girls in Hausa country, which makes these barely pubescent girls, purchased at an exorbitant price, capable of being penetrated by cutting their vaginas. They are sometimes seen coming lacerated and bloody to the women doctors' association of Nigeria.

Infibulation, the most mutilating of all, also cuts off the inside of the labia majora and sews together what is left—with silk thread in Sudan and Ethiopia, with acacia thorn in Somalia. This practice also exists in northern Nigeria, parts of Mali, and among certain Tukulor groups. Cauterization is aided by a mixture called *maimai* made of gum and sugar, herbal compresses, or even, in western Africa, ashes and sheep dung or, among the Tukulor, a paste made of resin and blood. The operation closes the vulva almost entirely except for a tiny opening created by inserting a thin stick of wood or a straw to allow urination and menstrual flow. This is done before or sometimes just after the first marriage to guarantee the young girl's virginity. Using a razor blade or something like it, the husband has to reopen the orifice to allow penetration. He thus demonstrates his virility while dramatizing the woman's submission to his desire. This submission is even more obvious because the first acts of sexual intercourse are necessarily painful for her. The operation is done again after childbirth to "restore" the wife's purity.[13] There is no doubt that it is part of the husband's strict control of his wife's sexuality.

The various kinds of clitoridectomy seem even more complex, not only in that the operations are performed at very different ages between birth and puberty but also in that some incisions are made around but do not mutilate the clitoris. In this case, the operation seeks to forge the girl's femininity but to leave the sensitivity of the area intact. These are practices very similar in spirit to facial markings. In context as body markings, we can take them together with other practices that seek to increase the husband's pleasure: clitoral elongation in some Benin societies, elongation of the labia minora by masturbation in interlacustrine societies, enlargement of the vagina with the aid of a stick among the Shona, removal of the uvula in Nigeria, tattooing of the lips and gums with indigo (reportedly very painful) among the Soninke, the insertion of ornaments around the mouth or nostrils, the elongation of the lips or earlobes, and even the obesity obtained by force-feeding young Moorish women.[14]

The World Health Organization estimates that about 40 percent of African women endure these kinds of operations in more than thirty-six nations, extending in a vast belt from Mauritania to the Horn of Africa through parts of Senegal (except for the Wolof and the Serer), Mali (except for the Songhai) and Burkina Faso, crossing from central-northern Africa from west to east via Cameroon, Chad, and the Central African Republic to Egypt, Kenya, and Tanzania. The Congo basin and the area south of the equator are not included, except for a few parts of Botswana, Lesotho, and Mozambique. Although the Islamic areas of Africa are particularly likely to practice these operations, they cannot be identified exclusively with the Arab world; they are unknown in North Africa, Saudi Arabia, and almost 80 percent of the modern Muslim world. The Christian Copts of Egypt and the Jewish Falasha of Ethiopia practice excision, and so the Kikuyu of Kenya whereas their Luo neighbors do not. Similar practices occur in eastern Mexico, Peru, and western Brazil, where they may have been exported during the time of the slave trade.

The origin of female genital mutilation is as vaguely defined as its distribution. It existed well before Islam. Infibulation or "pharaonic circumcision" is perhaps ancient Egyptian in origin, where it may have been practiced on girls of the aristocracy during the first millennium B.C., but analysis of mummies has not been conclusive. The first account known, beyond rare ones on papyrus, is that of Herodotus, in the fifth century B.C., which attributes excision to the Phoenicians, Hittites, Ethiopians, and Egyptians. The Greek geographer Strabo also mentions it in connection with the Egyptians around 25 B.C. Two doctors, Soramus and Aetius, working in Alexandria and Rome in the second and the sixth century A.D., left behind fairly precise descriptions of the operation and the instruments used to perform it. It was thus apparently in Egypt that pre-Muslim Arabs, Jews, and Christians learned clitoridectomy and infibulation. It was widely practiced in Rome, where a fibula was placed on slave boys' foreskins and slave girls' labia majora to keep them from having sex,[15] but the practice may have originated in several places.

Explanations for it are not simple. Some factors were practical: in desertic areas, it has been supposed that pastoral life made men and women who cared for animals more promiscuous. Yet women had to be controlled, so valuable was their virginity, and the rape of young shepherd girls, which was always possible, had to be avoided.

The symbolic meaning of the ritual has been emphasized. Excising the clitoris differentiates the sexes more sharply. This origin comes again from the Egyptians, who believed in the gods' hermaphroditism. Many societies attribute these androgynous qualities to children. The Bambara and Dogon of Mali believe that children have two souls; the female soul of the boy is found in his foreskin, the male soul of the girl in her clitoris. Both are polluted by the foreign element, seat of an evil force or *wanzo* that is hostile to fertility and to the child's entry into the adult world. Female and male circumcision are doubly necessary to affirm sexual identity and destroy evil influences. Among the Soninke, the same word, *salinde*, is used for both operations. Among the Guro of northern Côte d'Ivoire, in contrast, the incisions made around the clitoris instead emphasize a symbolic androgyny.[16] The Mossi of Burkina Faso believe that the clitoris is a dangerous organ that can kill a baby at birth if its head brushes it or make a man impotent if the shaft of his penis touches it.

Popular beliefs on the subject remain fantastic today: that a clitoris that is not eliminated can become as big as a penis, that the larger the clitoris, the dirtier or uglier it is. In Egypt the unexcised girl is called *nigsa*, "unclean"; in Sudan the common word for the operation is *tahur*, "purification"; in Mauritania the word used is *tizian*, "make beautiful." These beliefs are not exclusive to Africa. A Greek doctor of the seventh century A.D., Paul, explained that the operation could have the aesthetic aim of rectifying an enlarged clitoris. He unfortunately failed to provide us his criteria for measurement. More prosaic, in the Middle Ages it was thought that woman's capacity to receive many men denoted an insatiable sexual appetite that had to be controlled. In Europe, even in the nineteenth century, excision was practiced to prevent certain deviations then deemed dangerous, among them masturbation, lesbian tendencies, or other disorders considered female such as nymphomania, hysteria, and even epilepsy or madness.[17]

The ill effects of excision and especially of infibulation need no longer be demonstrated. They are both long- and short-term. In Africa, except when the operation is done in a medical environment, it is done by older women hardly familiar with modern antiseptic technique. In Mali the women who do this are in the caste of blacksmiths. They use unsterilized everyday instruments, and the main risks are hemorrhage, septicemia, and tetanus, to say nothing of painful psychological trauma. Although it is very difficult to measure the consequences of these usually unofficial practices, especially where they are forbidden by law, one report estimates that perhaps a third of little Sudanese girls die of them.[18] Effects can dog the woman all her life: abcesses and cysts, vaginitis and salpingitis, urination problems, repeated infections, and sterility, to say nothing of the frequent need for an episiotomy during childbirth. As this is not usually done ahead of time, the tissues' limited elasticity cause the perineum to rip or even result in a rectal or vaginal fistula. On top of everything else, a woman thus damaged risks being repudiated by her husband.

Yet it is very difficult to fight these practices, to which old women especially, the grandmothers and matrons whose livelihood they are, are very attached. Their daughters-in-law, when they seek to, are not always able to oppose them. The belief runs deep that one is not a real woman without having endured this. In many countries, young unexcised girls remain unmarriageable except in educated urban milieus. Sometimes, as in the *bundu* society of Mende women in Sierra Leone, the ritual is part of the women's secret society, and its sworn secrecy makes any intervention difficult. It is also a celebration that little girls await impatiently because it is a time for fun and gifts and because until they have been initiated their friends will make fun of them and their ignorance.

The ceremony normally took place at the end of the rainy season, a period when, thanks to abundant food, the child was supposed to be in better health. Today she is often brought in during the school vacation, at the height of the rainy season, between June and October. In Sudan, the little girl is decorated like a bride with jewels and henna; after the operation she lies on her couch decorated with red strings and wears a beaded necklace and a scarab supposed to protect her. She receives gold jewelry, money, and cloth. In Somalia, the ceremony is more discreet, and the girl is kept at home afterward for forty days to protect her from the evil spirits or *jinns.* It is exclusively a women's affair (no one talks about it to the husbands), social pressure is very strong, and authoritarian opposition is ineffective. The colonial authorities were particularly reserved on the subject. "Respect for traditions," so poorly understood in the first place, won out. Although Sister Marie-Andrée du Sacré-Coeur, known for her relative feminism, spent three months in Ségou (Mali) in 1936, the White Sisters still pled for excision so that the little girls would be considered normal in their own environment. Britain forbade infibulation in Sudan and Kenya in 1946 but did not touch on the other rituals. The result was mostly that early on the clandestine practices flourished as acts of resistance.

Infibulation declined the most in Egypt and Eritrea, thanks in the first to the social and educational progress achieved under President Gamal Abdel Nasser and in the second to the strength of the Liberation Front, which has recruited many women.[19] The Ethiopian minister of health, a woman, has also worked hard in this direction through the Revolutionary Ethiopian Women's Association. A private hospital with forty beds, specializing in operating on fistulas, has existed in Addis Ababa since 1975. But despite the work of the Somali Women's Democratic Organization and the fact that Somalia is the only country to have assigned a governmental commission to abolish infibulation, there is little reduction of these practices. Instead, husbands have returned to the abandoned custom of "reinfibulating" after childbirth; nearly half of married women have submitted to it. The operation, which consists of making the vagina as narrow as a barely pubescent girl's, is supposed to increase the man's pleasure and in fact possibly the woman's as well. As for Malian girls, the fine and imprisonment for mutilation in France causes more and more immigrant fathers to send their daughters back home to be excised during school vacations. Despite the work of the Union Nationale des Femmes du Mali, the least of the evils remains the presence of in the hospital in Bamako an official excisor who operates on infants to avoid infections. But a family planning center has also been established there.

Anglo-Saxon women's clumsiness has long irritated African women's movements, which have reproached them for meddling, and political men have taken advantage of this to declare that they have other priorities. The World Health Organization's attitude has been slow to take shape. Called to take a position as early as 1958 by the United Nations Economic and Social

Council, it refused the following year, claiming that it was incompetent to do so because "the ritual operations in question arose from a social and cultural context." African women took the offensive themselves in a UN seminar, but the first real action dates only from 1979, with a seminar in Khartoum on traditional practices affecting women's and children's health. Only in 1982 did the World Health Organization declare "that governments should adopt clear national policies to abolish female circumcision, and to intensify educational programs to inform the public about the harmfulness of female circumcision. In particular women's organizations at local levels are encouraged to be involved, since without women themselves being aware and committed, no changes are likely."[20]

The taboo has now been lifted, and young women are turning out to be much less consenting than was supposed. The Senegalese Awa Thiam has created an international organization to abolish genital mutilation that provided an opportunity to address the subject publicly for the first time in Dakar, where, until now, the absence of such practices among the dominant Wolof group had allowed people to avoid the problem.

Modern Polygamy

Traditional-style marriages still often occur, especially in the countryside, but many aspects have disappeared or changed in the past few years, especially favoring the girl's right to make her choice known. Buchi Emecheta's beautiful love story *The Bride-Price*, which tells of the tragic struggle of two young people against custom forbidding marriage between their ethnic groups, takes place in a sufficiently legendary past that mothers still use it to impress their daughters.[21]

Society by society, anthropologists have examined this eminently social act, which reflects so many of a society's codes, beliefs, and desires.[22] This is why we know of so many different kinds of ceremonies and of the long process of exchange between two lineages in which the different elements of wealth in the group, cattle, land, and slaves, come into play. Still considered traditional in style, marriages have changed. First, over the course of the colonial period the bride-price has increasingly been paid in money (large and small amounts) as the money economy has spread to the countryside. In Wolof country, for example, when Senegal had a subsistence economy it was paid in cattle. Aristocratic families might add slaves and, later on, pieces of cloth, anklets, and silver or gold bracelets. Today, the bride-price is set in cattle as a vestige of tradition, but it is most often paid in money. The Wolof say, "We talk about cattle, but we give cash."[23] English differentiates these two stages with two different words; we have gone from the idea of the fiancée's *value* (bridewealth) to the idea of her price (bride-price).

It is commonly said that Western capitalism has caused such inflation in bride-prices that it has become harder and harder for a young man to marry—that boys spent years in the mines or on construction sites to save what was needed, while in the countryside the old chiefs' preference for polygamy had grown because it meant that they could use the labor of their young wives. This dictum is likely and even certainly true in many places, such as the cocoa plantations in southern Cameroon or among the cotton-growing Kasai, although payment of the bride-price in cattle did not make marriage any easier for young people, who were under their elders' control. This is clear among the Mina of southern Togo, where marriage payments had mainly ritual value; they gradually increased with the monetarization of the economy, especially if, for example, the groom was known to have a high social position as an upper-level civil servant or salaried employee.[24] It is more debatable elsewhere, for instance, among the Wolof, where the price was already high several centuries ago,[25] or among the Mkako of northeastern Cameroon, where a mainly endogamous society impeded the course of inflation. There, marriage in fact requires widespread reciprocity, because the price received in exchange for the loss of a sister goes right out again to marry off her brother. Since he has to find a wife as close as possible to the family who is not forbidden to him by incest rules,[26] rapid circulation of marriage payments within a group would make inflation damaging for everyone. In fifty years, it seems that the absolute price has hardly changed.[27] In addition, parents seem to be willing to pay at least for the first wife, who is now chosen earlier and earlier to keep young men from leaving. Once a young man goes to the city, he gains a certain autonomy that removes him from his parents' watchful eye and from exploitation by his future mother-in-law. Once again, wherever we turn, women, young as well as old, are the losers.

What has perhaps most changed in the many societies in which girls' virginity was once required (among the Wolof, the Yoruba, and the Ganda) is sexual experience outside marriage, but this is no guarantee of freedom for girls. Essentially, the woman who has a baby before marriage shows her future husband that she is not sterile, which has no doubt become important because of the spread of sterility caused by venereal disease. The young woman must fight her way out of an insoluble contradiction: satisfying her fiancé and assuring him of her good behavior, which he then requires her to give up.[28]

Marriage has changed in various ways according to whether one is in a Muslim or Christian country. Islam legitimates polygamy while limiting the number of wives for ordinary people to four. For chiefs, polygamy's numbers were limited only by their wealth. Islam also introduced the notion of a certain equality among the wives; before it, the first wife had had more rights. But Islam's effects have sometimes been perverse. Thus among the Wolof the peasant of yesteryear could barely afford to buy two wives, while now the lower-middle-class urbanite wants to demonstrate his having arrived socially by exercising to the letter his rights under Islam.

It is also true that today's women are more ready than women once were to claim their rights to equal treatment. There is no longer any question that they will obey the first wife, even if she is twice their age. Also, there is no question of their all living together under the same roof. The husband gives and supports one household per wife and must respect his days in bed in each one or create serious conflicts.[29] The Senegalese novelist and filmmaker Sembene Ousmane has written a hilarious story on this subject, *Xhala,* in which he describes the misadventures of a middle-class polygamous man of Dakar whose third wife is too young and flirtatious for him.[30]

More generally, polygamous marriage in traditional settings has changed. It is still many poor and illiterate women's fate, and they continue to endure it. A study of Goin women in Burkina Faso shows once again that women's being the means through which matrilineal affiliation is transmitted offers them no economic advantage. On the contrary, their husbands feel that they should not have to feed wives and children not of their lineage throughout the year. Yet the labor of the man's wives is central to his income. A young bachelor has an annual surplus in money of about 20,000 CFA francs; a monogamous man has twice that, and a polygamous man with three wives may reach 120,000 CFA francs annually. In other words, a wife brings her husband about 30,000 CFA francs per year, and her bride-price is "amortized" in about ten years. This is why the price of marriage is comparatively very high, from 300,000 to 500,000 CFA francs in 1986. It is thus very hard for a bachelor to buy a wife, and it takes at least ten years for a monogamous man to procure a second wife. The first wife is a gift from his father and the second from his maternal uncle in compensation for years of work and submission to his elders. But girls, who work at least as hard as their brothers, receive only one piece of cloth per year and do not inherit property, local power, or magical and religious knowledge. The husband basically behaves like a boss who considers his wives a long-term investment and does not hesitate to try to reduce his expenses by asking for a supplement of food from the wife's family. It is true that he is also loaded down with expenses as a father and maternal uncle to young men, to whom he must provide expensive wives, and as a brother to married women, whom he must in part support. A man with two wives must, using the overwork extorted from his wives, pay for a third while also supporting his sons and nephews. The development of the market economy has exacerbated the situation by reserving cash-paid income for men. But women are no longer deceived: An illuminating report on the women of modern Mali showed that peasant women in a forgotten village where fields were still worked with a hoe, questioned by one of their own who had become a doctor, were highly critical of polygamy, which they saw as a source of daily fights ("You can't share a man"), but recognized that they were condemned to it to alleviate their crushing workload.[31]

There are cases in which polygamy can seem a real conflation of interests. The example of a fishing village on the Sierra Leonean coast is typical of this recent renewal of productive polygamy. The village began near Freetown, populated by freed slaves who were Christian and monogamous. Life was poor and the number of inhabitants small. Things changed after World War II, because of the city's growing need for fish. Fish-drying techniques were introduced by experienced fishermen from the Gold Coast. Expelled at the start of the 1960s, they were replaced by Temne immigrants. The village of Tombo, which had 2,500 inhabitants in 1967 during the height of fishing, reached 7,000, mostly Muslim, in 1981.

Production here is organized strictly by household. The husband goes fishing and sells the catch to his first wife, who pays him in cash. She has a little capital and means of production and organizes the drying, transportation, and sale of the fish. It is a labor-intensive industry, because the merchandise is highly perishable, and requires a lot of coordination, with all available hands being put to work: co-wives, children, and relatives. Eighty percent of households are polygamous, usually with two or three wives, who divorce the more easily because their greatest desire, as second and third in line, is to become a head of household in their turn. Eighty-five percent of women of forty or over have been married at least twice. Some have acquired an enviable position in the fish market. In this particular case, economic changes have encouraged polygamy; the productive and reproductive capacities of traditional structures have been integrated and used by modern people. But the women profit little from it, except socially, because they receive very little for their work.[32]

All things being equal, in fact, the process is similar for the Yoruba market woman or the Akan business head who runs her trade as she chooses. She still considers marriage and the children that result from it as the greatest business of her life. And a man's wife wants her husband to help her financially to start up her own business. Once she is married, she wins the right to run her affairs as she sees fit, even including affairs of the heart, without calling her relationship with a polygamous husband into question (although more and more market women divorce).[33] In such a union they can claim to enjoy greater personal autonomy.

Political men may treat marriage as an investment portfolio: The wife or wives remaining on the land (sometimes without having yet entered the market economy) will ensure him the legitimacy and support essential to him in the local voting district at election time, while the educated wife will entertain for him in the city. Here again, some city women may find it a profitable market because they in turn will enjoy a slice of the "national cake," as Nigerians say, in a well-placed husband. It begins to seem that polygamous marriage, as an alliance of individual interests, has little to do with traditional customs, which emphasized alliances between kinship groups.[34]

Finally, it is important to note that in the first five years women's fertility is not affected by the type of marriage. Polygamous wives (48 percent of Senegalese women) have about the same number of children as monogamous women, and divorce in the early years is common only when the wife is sterile.[35] What counts most of all is the way in which the partners cohabit—whether, for example, the husband lives in town and the wife in the village or both live together all the time. There is every possible variation—the husband's sporadic presence, the wife's periodic absences, living separated but in the same village or, more and more often, in the city. In Togo the proportion of wives who do not live with their husbands is higher among young wives—11 percent for women in their first marriages, and 15 percent for those in their second.

In Christian areas, the differences are more marked. The city-dwelling upper-middle class has become monogamous, mainly because of early Victorian pressures to make polygamy illegal in English-speaking colonies on principle. But respect for monogamy is tenuous. A 1929 episode in Lagos shows that already some women unhesitatingly required it but with little success.

This was the case with Bernardina, a market woman selling homemade cookies, the wife of Facundo Paraiso, a middle-class bourgeois Saro of the period and a postal worker. Both were Catholic, and they had been married in church. But Bernardina had had no children, and when she was forty-nine, her husband sought to require her to endure a new wife. For six months he hit her and cut her off financially, forcing her to leave their home. Yet no more than her contemporaries did Bernardina think of bringing her husband before a judge.[36] According to custom, it was the two sides of the family that handled such matters. A number of visits from them took place, and many letters were exchanged among parents, uncles, cousins, and sisters-in-law, from Lagos to Porto Novo, but no one ever reproached Facundo for having a mistress. Instead, he was blamed for his lack of respect for his elders, and for wanting to impose a new wife on the household. Ultimately Bernardina agreed to return to their marital home, where she lived until her death in 1939. History does not tell us what later relations were like between Facundo and his mistress, but there were probably no more problems between the husband and wife.

In French-speaking Africa, the Mandel Decree of 1939 required the consent of both husband and wife, which forbade forced marriage for girls, but did not provide means for its enforcement. Penalties were not added until 1946. The Jacquinot Decree of 1951 authorized monogamous commitment but did not make it compulsory and allowed an adult or divorced woman to marry without a bride-price.[37] Ironically, Côte d'Ivoire was, together with Sékou Touré's Guinea, one of the French-speaking states with the earliest "modern" legislation. Polygamy was officially forbidden there in 1964, but the law as adopted was much less favorable to women than it seemed because of a clumsy transposition from French law. Marriage without contract, by far the most common, was confused with joint-property marriage. Since husbands were the heads of households, this meant that wives lost their property on marriage. Only in 1983 was the option introduced of a contract permitting separation of property, which corresponded much more closely to prior traditions.[38]

The example of Guinea clearly shows how hard it was for a change in mores regarding women to be imposed in an authoritarian way. Through Sékou Touré's efforts, polygamy was abolished in 1968, despite the obvious absence of political support except from a group of feminists called "emancipated militants." Civil marriage was compulsory, and girls could not marry until they were over seventeen, despite men's insistent efforts to lower this to fifteen. Bride-prices were officially set low, and women could obtain a divorce without having to pay them back. When a husband repudiated his wife, he had to provide her financial compensation. Widows could inherit, and fathers became responsible for their illegitimate children.

Immediately, however, consensus twisted the law: The village or neighborhood committee charged with administering local affairs cleverly cheated about a girl's age, or her parents lied about it, or an early birth in a "trial" union, sometimes encouraged by tradition, allowed the terms of the law to be dispensed with. Bride-prices officially set at a maximum of 5,000 Guinean francs were in reality almost 100,000 francs, not including the lavish wedding ceremony itself. The girl's consent to the marriage was obtained by social pressure or exhaustion or even by the actions of an important man who wanted to marry. Yet this part of the law and the components of compulsory civil marriage as set out in 1958 were observed the longest. Polygamy has far from disappeared, although it seldom involves young men, usually more because of their economic difficulties than their beliefs.[39]

Senegal is an example of one ingenious transition. Here Islam predominates: The legal code adopted since independence allows a choice, through contracts signed before marriage, between monogamy and polygamy with up to four wives. Dakar lawyers love to tell about times the husband and wife come to court to record the contract and the judge requires it to be read out loud in the presence of those to be married. It is often only then that women, many still nearly illiterate, learn that their husbands have planned for polygamous marriages without asking them. They become so angry that the men have to back down or risk aborting their marriage plans and losing at least part of the bride-price they have already paid.

Most nations have passed family laws (as in Senegal in 1974)[40] or at least a marriage code that seeks to establish or protect women's rights. Such protection is difficult, because legislators are almost always male and are hardly convinced that it is needed. In Tanzania, where such a law (excluding Zanzibar) was passed in 1971, several deputies refused widows the right to inherit, arguing they had not had that right in the past; others felt that "if a man has to get his wife's consent to a second marriage, the African tradition where man has always been superior to a woman will be endangered. Unless the Law of Marriage Bill intends to change men into women this clause should be removed."[41]

The case of middle-class Krio women in Freetown (Sierra Leone) is extreme. The city was created at the end of the eighteenth century by British humanitarians and was in missionaries' hands from the start. During the nineteenth century, through the contributions of many, a language, Krio, and a culture considered by its members as a model of Westernization were forged. Many members, both men and women, even went to Britain to pursue advanced degrees. And yet a survey of both single university students and high-level professional couples of which the men are lawyers, doctors, and civil servants and their wives have as many degrees as they do and work in professional fields shows an amazing unity between traditional beliefs and customs and Western social conventions. Young people claim the right to choose their partners and reject the notion of bride-price. Husbands generally courted their wives before marriage. The couples had engagements and the traditionally expensive and socially important marriage ceremonies. But the men draw an absolute distinction between the women they marry, who are decent and guaranteed to be faithful, although no longer required to be virgins at marriage (as supposedly they once were), and emancipated women, the "independent" women we have encountered above, who are interesting but not marriageable.[42] A wife's infidelity is an utter crime, to which the only answer is divorce. In contrast, a husband's extramarital relations are almost normal, even encouraged. In fact, one appears to be the corollary of the other. This stereotype seems patterned directly on the Victorian model that won out in the last century and that Luis Buñuel has called "the discreet charm of the bourgeoisie," but it is more complicated than that. Of course, the good-wife stereotype comes straight out of a century of puritanical missionary teaching and its moral discourse.[43] But the more "modern" the couple, the more complex things get, because beliefs about women's power over boys' virility remain strong. A series of taboos about behavior during menstruation, pregnancy, and breastfeeding keep the husband and his wife from having sex for relatively lengthy, frequent periods. It is believed that relations during these periods would be at least as dangerous for the man as for the mother or child. And then there is husbands' reluctance to use contraceptives that might nurture their wives' "bad instincts." Because they are modern, the partners want only three or four children. This creates long interruptions in intercourse in the early years of the marriage and, later, complete interruption, the surest means of avoiding pregnancy if one wants to avoid numerous abortions—a procedure banned from traditional societies but practiced in well-to-do milieus.

In addition, there remains confusion between a man's potency and his fertility. His social class limits the number of his descendents, and therefore the bourgeois man is under very strong pressure from his friends and even his family to prove his virility in other ways: a girlfriend, for example, whom he hides only from his wife. The result is often children born outside his marriage, although these young women do use contraception.[44] The most progressive men in Sierra Leone (as in the rest of West Africa) know almost nothing about male contraception and certainly do not practice it, except for coitus interruptus (which exists in cultural contradiction with the belief that a man's potency is his capacity to impregnate). Men's reluctance has certainly been a cause of delayed AIDS prevention.[45]

Are modern Krio women emancipated? Sexually, women can choose either to be unsatisfied, abandoned wives or the bedmates of polygamous partners. As an old chief who still has twenty wives puts it, needing to prove one's virility is more a burden than anything else. Dakar school counselors today note that children have a difficult time figuring out where they fit within an urban polygamous household (officially so or not), where the old-style decentralized patriarchal home is disappearing, turning each wife and her children into a separate household. The father is usually gone, because he is the rotating head of two or three families—whence the temptation, especially for teenage boys, to play on the void left by paternal power when confronted by their mothers' authority.

Under such conditions, there is nothing surprising about the response of young educated women in societies less Victorian than the Krio, Nigerian, or Ugandan, who ironically claim their right to be "outside wives" after witnessing the unhappy fate of "inside wives." This is a new recognition of polygamy within an officially monogamous setting. The "ring wife," or first wife, the one who believed in monogamous marriage when she contracted for it in church or at city hall, is less and less the envy of today's young women.[46] In Uganda, monogamy was introduced early on because the Ganda king (*kabaka*) converted to Catholicism at the end of the nineteenth century. Yet free marriage or cohabitation is by far the most common form in Ugandan cities today. Neither party will agree to hold property in common. The man will not give the woman any right to his earnings, and the woman does not want her husband to use her earnings to drink and entertain his girlfriends.[47] Their union is often polygamous in practice if not in theory.

Members of this new generation give diverse reasons for their polygamy. They include romantic ones; a man may not have been able to resist his family's pressure to marry someone closer to its own views or its rejection of his choice because the young woman was not of his ethnic group or caste.[48] This is the case for Kiki, a graduate of the University of Ibadan who is being supported by a mother who has herself endured the unhappy fate of the "inside wife." Kiki's father, though opposed to his daughter's misconduct, in fact urges her to behave like a kept woman. In his eyes, recognition of the relationship by her partner would mean that the man would meet his daughter's financial needs, pay her rent, and give her gifts. After all, this is only the local version of Western alimony, the woman being responsible for the children arising from the relationship and the man being expected to do his part. Because such "outside marriage" is not covered legally, it is legitimate for the woman to obtain compensation to help her run her household.

Onome, a scientific researcher in love with her "husband" since childhood, promised herself that she would never see him again after he gave in to his family's demands and agreed to marry the young woman they had chosen for him. This is also the fate of the woman who has arrived socially but has divorced because she was an abandoned wife; she sees her only option in an unofficial union that ensures her independence in a world in which a single woman is still ill-accepted. Temi, a thirty-eight-year-old doctor trained in England ("But I'm not in London anymore, am I?"), divorced from a Christian marriage and already the mother of two children, is now the "wife" of a wealthy Lagos businessman with whom she has had a child.[49] Such a choice ironically conveys a woman's desire for independence. She must brave social taboos, on the one hand, and adopt male behavior, on the other, because having had no religious or civil ceremony allows her to break off the relationship when she chooses.

At other times, instead, a traditional marriage may reinforce formal polygamy as it was in earlier times, notably but not exclusively in Muslim marriage. In any case, highly educated single women who resolutely assert their independence remain an exception today—even more so, no doubt, than working-class women who have gained financial independence.

The notion of an egalitarian relationship between the partners is still a new one. It has developed among young people, especially young women influenced by modern Western Gothic romances, television series, and mass-market novels, but it still seems foreign to most. Young city women's strongest demand of a good husband is that he talk to them—that he keep them apprised of his intentions and plans, still rarely the case. From their perspective men are mute, superior personages whom one serves and who come to one essentially to procreate. Yet there are some militant feminist associations, especially of intellectual women, such as Senegal's Yewwu Yewwi ("Women Stand Up"), that are organizing for women's emancipation and seeking to help women confronting tradition's constraints.

Divorce: Modern Accident or African Legacy?

Divorce was an institution in many African societies. Marriage concluded an alliance between two groups, a political agreement whose goal was to forge an association of interests, and this contract could be broken. Marriage was not sanctified by a monotheistically inspired sacrament. Breaking the contract was not tainted with the usual individualistic Western moralizing. This does not mean that the partners were free. Rather, the group made the decision, and the woman in particular was subject to both her family's and her in-laws' decision. In certain societies, especially strongly patrilineal ones such as the Luo and the Zulu,[50] marriage was supposed to last, and pressure was heavy on the woman to stay with her husband no matter what happened, especially if the bride-price had been high. But in other societies, such as the Wolof, the marriage could be challenged, although the family would intervene to calm things down and preach obedience and patience to the woman. Children belonged to the father, and bride-prices increased with the rise of the market economy, but the maternal family's social role and function as refuge have remained solid.

The longer we study ancient societies, the more we see, if not instability, then at least great fluidity in marriage. This may be true even if only because of demographic fragility and great differences in age between the partners, which meant more widows and the need for women to remarry. In Muslim or matrilineal societies the widow went back to her family (in the former case minus her children); in patrilineal ones the levirate almost automatically meant that the widow went to live with a younger brother or other relative of her deceased husband. Islam did not reduce the frequency of divorce—quite the contrary, husbands could repudiate their wives extremely easily in predominantly Muslim areas.

Among the Fula, for example, marriage is explicitly an individual agreement, not a kinship alliance, but the husband is chosen by the girl's family. Marriages are very unstable. Among Cameroonian Fula, where first marriage is imposed on young women at about fourteen compared with twenty for boys, polygamy is infrequent, and 77 percent of marriages are monogamous. But the number of remarriages is almost three per women. The husband repudiates but generally because his wife has left.[51]

In Lamu (Kenya), a Swahili culture, divorce reached a new record between 1969 and 1978 of 73 percent annually. More than half of women who married during this period were on their second and even their fourth marriages. The first marriage seems to have been a kind of obligatory rite of passage, an initiation into adult life through arrangements made by families when the woman was very young to avoid even the faintest chance that she had already lost her virginity. In the oldest family lines, polygamy is common because men can afford it, and divorces are less frequent because they would upset too many alliances based on mutual interest and convenience. But in working-class environments women live in greater insecurity; according to Swahili proverbs, "A man is just a friend" and "just a straw door made of mats," in other words, insurance of the most fragile kind. The least lapse by the woman—her sterility, of course, an abnormal child, the suspicion of infidelity—is enough to make the man pronounce the sacramental phrase for a repudiation, before witnesses or not. The woman, in contrast, must have serious reasons to divorce, and thus divorce is initiated by women in only 5 percent of cases. Most have no other choice to obtain a divorce than to place themselves in a situation that would cause their husbands to repudiate them: being very unpleasant, refusing to feed him, leaving, or, of course, committing adultery.

Mobility is encouraged by a population imbalance between the sexes. Since slavery was ended in 1897, life in Lamu's archipelago has continued to worsen, causing a significant out-migration of men. The gap has increased because of the arrival in the past several decades of many mostly female refugees from neighboring islands. In this context of economic crisis and demographic imbalance, men and women have turned to serial polygamy; men can no longer afford several wives at once. But since the women do not work for pay, they have to regain the protection of a husband as quickly as possible. This mobility of women engenders a profound shift in their lifestyle. Women help each other more; when a woman acquires a house, she puts up her divorced daughters and even her married ones and their husbands; women with children are beginning to take financial responsibility for them; women are appearing in political and religious demonstrations. Above all, women are learning that many children are not enough to keep a husband; they are reducing the number of their pregnancies without telling their husbands about the contraceptives they have at their disposal. In essence, they are escaping male control.[52]

In matrilineal societies especially, where women continued to depend on their own lineage, mother and brothers, and in fact were required to give them the largest share of their harvest or earnings, there was a strong chance that they would be taken back or supported by their families provided that they made another remunerative match. Observers today complain about the rising divorce rate, repressed by a century of Christian colonization, but it is important to take a closer look, even though it is certainly difficult to do so, given the lack of data available for earlier times.

Today, first marriages—the one in which one doesn't challenge one's parents' decision—are often unstable except if one is a first wife. In this case, a divorce would challenge delicate intra- or interfamilial alliances. But in rural Senegal, more than a third of Wolof women have divorced at least once, usually within the first five years of marriage (i.e., before age thirty) so that they can quickly remarry. The proportion of single women is just 5 percent.

This is where Wolof similarities with Swahili end, because three-fourths of Wolof divorces are requested by women, whose inferior social status often makes them men's victims. The woman wants to free herself by choosing her partner and refusing cruel practices, but she insists on remaining economically dependent on her husband, who she feels should meet her needs (meaning that when it is her "day," he should give her her spending money for food).[53] More than 60 percent of divorces are requested for economic reasons, including the husband's abandoning the marital home. What is new is a wife also claiming her right to pleasure, possibly arguing before the court that her husband is impotent. This is not unusual, because in polygamous cases there may often be a gap of fifty years between the partners. Men most often divorce for adultery, but the opposite is not possible for women because a husband's adultery is considered normal.[54]

In southern Côte d'Ivoire, the fragility of marriage is clear. Marital disputes often lead to physical violence by the husband, especially in the case of adultery by his wife, once severely judged by tradition. To unburden themselves of a weight they less and less accept, women choose escape rather than divorce, which requires them to pay back an often high bride-price. Abandoning the marital home is mainly an urban phenomenon. Husbands' searches for their wives have created their share of colorful newspaper notices with headlines such as "The Flown-Away Wife," "If You See Her, Bring Her Back to Me," "Another Wife Disappears," "The Soldier and the Witch," "A 5,000-Franc Fine for Abandoning Her Home Is Too Low, Helene's Husband Felt," and "A Young Wife Needs a Young Husband."[55]

In southern Togo, almost one-third of women between forty and forty-four have broken off their first marriages. It should be noted, however, that only 11 percent of women in this age-range are in their first monogamous marriages. The Western-style couple remains unusual. Because in this region children over three generally belong to their fathers, the decision to divorce is a serious one for women. Yet they are almost always the ones who take the initiative and are very mobile. Might this be a response to their husband's polygamy? An assertion of their autonomy as wives?[56] In Ghana, the case of the Akan wife (a matrilineal culture) who demanded a divorce because her husband wanted to impose a co-wife on her is not yet commonplace. She had had three children with him, the youngest only five months old. Against the will of the speechless judge, she refused to care for them, even the infant, whom she had weaned: "He has told me that he will take my children, toss me out, leaving me with a baby so no one else will marry me. But I will not take it. Judge, I repeat, I want him to have *all* the children."[57]

Most often, separation is gradual. The woman goes away more and more often on business or for family reasons and then settles elsewhere, leaving room for another woman. But this is less acceptable among the Wolof than among the Ewe and the Akan. The first separation is accepted easily, but a woman who has children from many husbands—three or more—is considered flighty and runs the risk of disapproval from those around her.

Contraception

Most social groups whose incomes are agriculturally and subsistence-based, without powerful technological means, maintain high fertility and assert that this is by choice. Changes in lifestyle that they may want to make have to do with other components of their social structure, particularly migration, and not with the number of descendants they want. This is why any lasting health advances have especially resulted in decreasing mortality and reducing sterility, which increases population, although the drop in infant mortality increases the mean interval between births.

In the cities and some large-scale plantation areas, profound structural transformations are occurring, but they may not necessarily lead to a drop in fertility. On the contrary, the gradual abandoning of the old way of living creates disaffection with the rules and practices of abstinence and prolonged breastfeeding, both elements of natural contraception. The goal of limiting the number of children has been achieved by a minority of women, mainly urban ones. There are few statistics on contraception in Senegal, except for the Cap-Vert peninsula, where 60 percent of the 3,500 women questioned said that they knew of at least one means of contraception but two-thirds of them used traditional methods (abstinence or amulets) and only one-third, mostly younger, knew about modern ones. As one might expect, these differences can be imputed to a woman's degree of urbanization and level of literacy; the ages and number of her children affect her knowledge of contraception only slightly.[58] Women who use birth control both have left traditional parent-child relations behind and use effective techniques, but they are also the same women who have formal or informal jobs and therefore greater ability than others to get household help. They supplement moderately priced domestics' salaries with the many very cheap young female relatives who come from the village to attend school. Thus, bourgeois women feel little need to limit their pregnancies, as they affect their independent aspirations almost not at all and currently pose no problem of paying for school.

In the most open regions, birthrates have either stabilized or even slightly increased in recent years. But there is a growing contradiction between women's often very clearly expressed aspirations to limit their births to some degree and what they do in reality.[59] In Togo, for example, only a tiny minority of highly educated urban women have the number of births they say they want. Especially in Burkina Faso, where the ministry concerned with population has made great efforts at education, officials acknowledge that resolving the problem depends on *men*. As long as their wives cannot get them to come to the educational meetings, there is little hope that attitudes will change in the bedroom.

The typical transitional phase described is almost history in some regions. Recent figures from urban Sierra Leone, for example, with its long creole heritage, clearly show the beginning of a drop in fertility rates. But in most nations, the average number of births per woman remains very high—from five to seven. Change does not seem to be a result of contraceptive campaigns. Fertility rates are among the highest on the continent and just begin to slow down in Kenya, which has, however, made a real effort in this regard. Instead, sociological factors, the economic environment, and ideological and psychological obstacles remain determinative.

Finally, we do not yet know what fertility impact the rapid spread of AIDS will have on young women and their future children, especially in central Africa, which appears the hardest hit. Already in the capital of Rwanda in late 1987, almost 40 percent of young pregnant women examined were seropositive for AIDS.

Culture and Beauty

From Crafts to Popular Art

As in other societies and for the same reasons, the creative powers of African women have historically not been well known. Confined to the domestic sphere, they were the craftswomen of everyday life—pottery, basketry, spinning, and sometimes weaving, though this was also men's work in West Africa. These popular handicraft forms hardly allowed their creativity to develop, except for the delicate techniques of indigo and kola-nut dying to make beautiful cloth. Almost all the craftspeople serving the great chiefs, sometimes extremely talented, were men, whether wood or metal sculptors, religious mask or statue makers, or even, as in ancient Meroe, potters. Women did sometimes make cowry and colored-glass beaded necklaces, but they would still need the means to buy the famous Venetian beads, imported since at least the twelfth century throughout the old Sudan and then in southern Africa by the Portuguese. This was again more of a man's world. If there were women in it, they were exceptional, and no memory of them remains.

Yet there is at least one case in which we can see the history of a women's popular art: the house painting of the Ndebele of southern Transvaal, whose people number 400,000 today. For several centuries—there is an 1820 attestation to it by one missionary[60]—Sotho women have painted their houses, especially the interiors and, most especially, their rooms, using their fingers or feathers and natural paints in red, black, brown, and ochre, derived from whitewash, charcoal, alluvia, and clay mixed with cow dung. Their colors were sober and elegant. When little girls were initiated, they were isolated for several weeks and taught this type of fresco painting along with beadwork, a source of limitless decorative potential in necklaces, aprons, headdresses, and more.[61] Polygamy no doubt inspired co-wives to compete to make their rooms and personal ornaments the most beautiful in the compound. They continue to craft these complex compositions on special occasions—when they marry or a son goes to the veldt for his initiation (*wela*).

Their painting has also begun to show up on the front walls of their homes. The designs are done freehand directly on the wall, without preparatory sketches. The traditional style is handed down from mother to daughter in about a dozen families and features bold lines and abstract strokes in lozenges, squares, chevrons, or circles, inspired by the graphic and geometric shapes of daily life, the designs of beaded jewelry, and ritual objects such as ancient shields.[62]

This art conveys their will to remember the past. This Ndebele group remained unsubdued until 1882 and then became too numerous in the growing twentieth-century urban areas. They were deported in 1955 with a number of other peoples to camps called *kwandebele* ("national homelands") northeast of the capital. In these vast slum neighborhoods they preserved their language and some of their customs against all odds.

In the past few years these women have begun using chemical paints and commercial brushes like the West African fabric dyers. They have also begun painting on exportable canvases. Tourist fashions and nationalist government encouragement have made them bolder. They have begun using brilliant colors and a more literal figurative style. Energetic, colorful designs (enriched in each generation by new themes) depict courtyards, doors, paned windows, and staircases that the women have seen in modern urban villas. Diagonal, horizontal, and vertical stripes trace the shapes of buildings submerged in the daub they are made of. These painters also sometimes take apart the shapes of trees and flowers to elicit new decorative themes. They even ornament their frescoes with lightbulbs and lamp shades, lampposts, and television antennas perched on thatched roofs—drawn as triangles and half-circles, for example. Everything they lack and dream of owning they translate into stylized shapes with their inventive colorations. A razor blade becomes a gigantic design spread across an entire wall, a frenzy of electric blue, bright pink, and black. Every fresco is unique, although they resemble each other. This widespread popular art is clearly modern but also witness of a culture in which women had and certainly still have their piece to speak.

Women Singers

Women's chants and songs are everywhere. In some places they have been collected, for example, among the Bamileke of Cameroon (where the word *nshi* basically means "to dance the song"). This rhythmic poetry should be considered alongside the poetry of the ancient Greek bards and the troubadours of the Middle Ages. Women's songs are full of sayings, maxims, and proverbs but also of their feelings, usually of suffering and despair. There are widows' songs, mourning songs, songs of the sadness of being a childless woman, of the horror of adultery or of illness, a sign of impurity. Yet there are happy songs, wedding songs, and songs for special occasions too.[63]

Women are latecomers to performance. Some unusual characters have become famous soloists, such as the great activist singer Miriam Makeba, who split from the Black City Sisters in the early 1960s and went to live in Sékou Touré's Guinea.

Women griots were not unknown in ancient times, although we have little information about them. Among the Hausa, the 1804 jihad leader Ousmane dan Fodio's own daughter, Nana Asma, was such a person, writing in Arabic, Pular, and Hausa. It is surprising that a society so hostile to women in public life in the past should have produced and continue to produce such diseuses. These women have little education and less Arabic and are considered indecent because they are unmarried and especially because they dare to perform in public. Yet very traditionally, Maizargadi, the widow of a musician in the Kano emir's court, has been the emir's official *zabiya* (griot) for twenty years. More commonly, female singers go from house to house to amuse secluded wives. Modern media allow their art to flourish, and now wives can listen to them at home even in their absence.

Today, more is changing. The very well-known singer Maimuna Coge married a farmer, and he cares for their children while she travels throughout the north to perform on television and radio shows and for audiences such as Kano university students. She has an all-woman band that syncopates her songs with slaps on calabashes. Another older singer mainly goes to political meetings to sing the praises of her candidates, enjoying an obvious autonomy from her younger husband. Yet another, Binta Katsina, became famous for her song calling on women to join in building the nation:

> *You should do every kind of work, you should know every kind of*
> *work*
> *You can write papers, you can pound the typewriter,*
> *You can fly airplanes,*
> *You know how to be in the office,*
> *You could do the government work,*
> *And you could be the police workers,*
> *You could do the customs work,*
> *Let's give you the chance*
> *Women of Nigeria*
> *Women of Nigeria, you know every kind of work.*[64]

The oral tradition is a people's art form. What is new is men's agreeing to publish women's written poetry (*waka*). This genre is relatively rigid because it is spoken in Hausa using the Koranic model, obeys strict rules of rhythm and meter, and aims more to educate than to amuse. The Hausa media began publishing these *waka* in the 1930s and more recently began having them recited live on the radio. Unlike woman singers, women authors of these works are respected, esteemed as knowledgeable Muslims. Two women, Hauwa Gwaram and Hajiya 'Yar Shelo, both almost fifty, managed break into print in 1983,[65] and they are not the first in Islamic areas. Every Swahili poetry anthology features the 1858 poem by Mwana Kupona, a beautiful illustration of the behavior a wife who respects her duties should follow. Hausa women poets persist in this vein. They promote a woman's duty to be decent and her role as guardian of the home, wife, and mother, but they also take on unusual subjects such as health, nutrition, and the care of newborns. In northern Nigeria, simply being published is revolutionary. One can sense a kind of victorious female pride in the lyrics:

> *May God help us to achieve our goals*
> *The women of Kano have been diligent in their work.*
>
> *May God help us to achieve our hearts' desires*
> *The women of Kano persevere in their farming.*
>
> *I will end here, lest you say I have overdone it,*
> *The song on women, who will make our country successful.*[66]

Malian women singers such as Oumou Sangare, singer of Mandingo music, also adopt this traditional approach. But more and more, music is becoming a contemporary art form. The singer Djeneba Diakité replaced the griots' music with *wassoulo,* more melodic and more modern; a trio of singers both gifted and dynamic, the Trois Go, who emerged from the Koteba performing arts troupe of Abidjan triumphed in Bamako's "Discovery" contest in December 1993.

A New Art Form: Literature

Given the constraints of their milieu, it is no surprise to see women preferring a particular art form because it is new and discreet—writing. By definition, women writers are advanced because they are educated. Because of girls' lower educational level, women began writing long after men and are still fewer in number—but what talents!

Sensitive to their sisters' problems, women mainly write about what they know best, what is most important to them and still a battleground—gender. To be truthful, they were preceded by a few male writers, especially in French, who were feminists ahead of their time and energetically condemned women's deplorable status. These works are remarkable for their very high quality. One example is Sembene Ousmane, always ready to sing the courage of working-class women (in *God's Bits of Wood*) and to make fun of men's behavior toward their wives (*Xhala*). The most feminist and most scathing of these writers was Malian Ibrahima Ly (1936–1991), who with passionate violence denounced women's miserable lot both in the time of slavery (*Les noctuelles vivent de larmes*) and in modern times (*Toiles d'araignées*). In the latter his heartrending heroine is a young peasant woman who is to be forcibly married to an old man by the village chiefs. She has been imprisoned by them because she has dared to refuse her husband. "Trampled by life like all our women," she fights to the death to gain the freedom that outdated social conventions stubbornly deny her. The plot comes from a true story the author observed when between 1974 and 1978 he was a political prisoner in Moussa Traoré's jails.

We should also note the great Congolese writer Henri Lopes, who always draws complex female characters that his readers can truly empathize with. Among the many others is the Nigerian writer Chinua Achebe, whose *Things Fall Apart* argues the need to recognize motherhood's heavy burden as at least equal to fathers' role.

It is not surprising that tropical African women writers have flourished in two regions that early had an intellectual class—Igbo country in Nigeria and coastal Senegal. Pioneers in English were Flora Nwapa, who named her novels after her heroines (*Efuru, Idu*), and of course Buchi Emecheta (*The Bride-Price, The Slave Girl, The Joys of Motherhood,* and *Double Yoke*).[67] In French, there was Mariama Bâ (1929–1981), who came from elite Senegalese society, her father serving as minister of health in 1958. She was one of a few girls to graduate from Rufisque's normal school, and her husband was a journalist. There is no doubt that her epistolary novel *So Long a Letter* reflects her own life experiences.

In contrast to men, and except for Flora Nwapa, women writers show little interest in motherhood. They have left the maternal stereotype behind,[68] except to show how empty it is. Unlike Achebe, for whom "mother is supreme," Emecheta has her heroine Nnu Ego survive sterility, the death of her newborn, and finally her children's departure: "I only know how to be a mother. How could I speak to a woman who has no children? Taking my children away from me is like taking a life from me that I never had."[69]

It is not that women reject motherhood but that they find it a natural thing and refuse to turn it into something sacred. They instead treat forced marriage and polygamy in fine novels of disappointed love. More broadly, their subject, a very modern one, is the quest for happinesss. Class and educational level, personality and circumstances combine in the lives of their heroines, caught between her cultural heritage and her desire for change, in very different and circuitous ways. Mariama Bâ tells the story of two married couples of two different generations. The women of the couples are friends. One, Ramatoulaye, had stayed with her husband when he brought his second wife to live with them and ultimately felt that she had been victimized on all counts. The other woman had violated the taboo against

mixed marriage between a low-caste woman and a Tukulor aristocrat and ultimately chose the difficult path of divorce. Neither woman's husband was
able to or wanted to resist the temptations of social pressure. But a new future opens up before them. Ramatoulaye's son-in-law says, "Daba is my
wife. She is not my slave nor my servant," and she says, "I sense the tenderness growing between this young couple, an ideal couple, just as I have always imagined."[70]

In the next generation, women's explorations become more diverse. Not
even counting the political writings by white South African women, there
are black African women's social satires to be enjoyed. *La grève des Bàttu*,
by Aminata Saw Fall, is a harsh depiction of big city beggars and the attempt
of a benighted notable to manipulate them.

Physical Beauty

There is one arena where African women come together with all the women
in the world—beauty. Here men's gaze plays a major role. Recently one
could still see a few gorgeous thin young women in Niamey or Mauritania
begging doctors to fatten them up so that they would fit the traditional
canon of fully fleshed beauty that obtains in desert areas. But the Western
model has weighed more and more heavily since the 1950s, thanks to the
urban media, which started women's pages and even women's magazines in
that era. "Lisette," a young beauty-school student in Dahomey and the first
French-speaking woman to receive a beauty-school scholarship to France,
sells readers of *L'Afrique en Marche* (no. 3, 1957) on straightening their hair.
Skin lighteners were in fashion a few years ago, but the process sometimes
burned faces with permanent spots that disfigured quite a few fashionable
ladies.

In equatorial Africa, elegant ladies' societies first appeared in Brazzaville
after World War II. Popular parlance referred to them by the Lingala term
musiki (in which music's role is clear). These were exclusively female groups
on the order of twenty or so women who were close neighbors in both age
and geography. They gathered at different bars in turn, invited by each of
their different members. The tontines they organized, the new songs they
listened to, and their conversations about fashions were what drew these
women together. The first *musikis* appeared in Leopoldville (across the
Congo River from Brazzaville) in 1954. The gatherings' relative high cost at
first restricted them to women with money—market women, Europeans'
mistresses, courtesans. This was the beginning of the recreational associations that proliferated with the introduction of modern nightclubs. Members
of these groups, in addition to seeking entertainment, solidarity, and mutual
aid, were also often prostitutes or at least B-girls. In Poto-Poto (Brazzaville)
in 1950 there were eight of these associations, with evocative names such as

Violette, Elégance, La Rose, Dollar, Diamant, and Lolita.[71] In Leopoldville Diamant, Rosette, La Lumière, La Beauté, and Reconnaissance arose in the same era. About forty of these associations formed in Coquilhatville (in the old Belgian Congo), among them La Beauté Actuelle, La Fille Gentille, Rosette, La Plus Belle Toilette, and Au Chic.[72] Members would sometimes purchase matching outfits—wrap-skirts, headscarves (*foulards*), and sandals—to show that they belonged and for entering dance, beauty, and "elegance" contests. New styles were launched at big parties, and the fate of a new design depended on the success of the fashion show in which it was launched as well as its adoption by a majority of city women. Legitimate wives tended to imitate trends set by *mwana* (mistresses). Fashions were resolutely non-European in style, and new cuts of blouses and skirts bore evocative names such as King George, Messo ya Putain, Massa ya la Mer, Inzo ya Nzambi, and Marie simba velo.[73]

The most elegant female fashions are now mainly a mix of the two cultures. In Christian central and southern African nations, because of the missionaries' bitter opposition to women's nudity and traditional clothing, Western-style dresses are generally preferred.[74] But in other countries, such as Senegal, the preservation and revival of native clothing was especially in the city considered a badge of identity reclaimed. Only society's educated elite (and even then only on special occasions) would abandon it. During a theatrical gala in Dakar in the 1960s, bourgeois Senegalese women made a point of wearing European dresses while some of the French women attending wore gorgeous boubous. The boubou, an article of clothing as simple as it is elegant, has been popular for a particularly long time with urban working-class women. Until recently, all boubous looked the same except for variations in fabric quality, color, and embroidery.[75] New boubou patterns evolved, however, and by 1993 the original style was scarcely to be seen in the streets of the capital. At the same time, African high fashion, especially from Mali, is exploding internationally.

Ironically, Western canons of beauty hit South Africa the hardest. Beauty pageants are of very special importance in this nation. The trials and tribulations of Miss South Africa 1974, elected Miss World, still make the front pages of South African newspapers. This obsession can be attributed to a sexually hypocritical and highly puritanical society or to enduring South African ideas of women's traditional position and role or even more simply to the absence of a royalty cult and a lack of divas and stars. In 1993 the selection took on a political dimension. In 1992 a colored woman had been named for the first time. The following year, a black woman was named, symbolically very important. Not only was she a beauty but she was intelligent and militant: "If my victory could help put an end to violence in the townships," she told the jury, "I would be very happy. I believe that with

what is now happening in our country, we need someone who knows different cultures. I come from the townships that are prey to violence. I have
lived there."[76]

Officially, the ANC of course rejoiced in her victory as a blow to South
African racism, but more prosaically the election also connoted change in
beauty ideals. Until now fashion designers had deemed the African market
insufficiently profitable. This was a significant obstacle, because the pageant
winner is generally asked during her reign to promote a line of clothing.
Women who might buy the clothing have to be able to identify with the
winner to increase sales. Pessimists would say that black is simply in fashion
because it is profitable today. Let us instead hope, as Palesa Jacquí Mofokeng
does, that the time has come for a universal mixing—not only in gender but
in color.

Conclusion:
The Future

Two themes run through this modern reflection on women in Africa—emancipation and development.

Are women on a path to emancipation? To answer, we have to decide what we mean. After the suffragettes who fought for political rights and the marxists who called for economic equality, feminists, especially Anglo-Saxon ones, gave the term its very individualized sense, in line with the Western human rights tradition. Here it means the right of every woman to claim her autonomy and even her independence, to make her own decisions in her soul and conscience as an individual unto herself, to exercise freedom of choice over her body, her desires, and her aspirations. There has been a lack of understanding between Western women and women from the developing nations, especially African women, no doubt because they have not yet reached this point but especially because the assumptions governing their lives are different. It is especially hard to talk about the struggle as an individual in a society that specifically denies the individual in favor of the group and prefers consensus to freedom of individual choice.

Everything depends on what level of emancipation one means. From a legal perspective, in tradition or in modern legal codes, with few exceptions (mainly in what were the socialist countries) women remain inferior to men on paper even though they have gained the right to vote almost everywhere (only in 1970 in Zaire and in 1977 in northern Nigeria). This is obvious in marriage laws (which generally maintain the notion of a family "head"), in the way in which property and inheritance rights are implemented, and even in the choice of a burial site for one's husband. A 1987 appeals court denied the widow of a renowned Kenyan jurist the right to bury her husband in Nairobi. His Luo family won the case even though culturally he had broken with them. The decree arose from a British legal heritage that cleverly combined "customary" rights—which won out in this case—with imported European ones.[1] In contrast, in Ghana in 1991, modern law and patrilineality won out with the help of the head of state, thanks to the stubbornness of the son of a great anticolonial activist lawyer. Kwame Anthony Appiah was charged by his father with his funeral ceremony at the expense of his father's maternal line, in this case the deceased's sister. An Akan proverb says, "The matriclan loves a corpse." It took all the resources he had to resist his aunt's traditional weight in court; she was none other than the wife of the reigning *asantehene.* In this matrilineal context, the son played the unusual role of leading the entire struggle in his sisters' and his mother's name.[2] Generally speaking, there are cases in which Roman law is superimposed on matrilineal custom and diminishes rather than affirms women's rights.

On the economic level, the degree of women's autonomy remains variable across the continent. Many have the advantage over European women of having long enjoyed separate-property marriages. In particular, African women for centuries have not even understood the possibility of leisure time. Except among the Muslim Hausa and Swahili, there were no stay-at-home wives. Thus opinion is divided on women's recent economic emancipation, whether in the informal sector or the salaried work world, in the countryside or the city. Still, it is commonplace to assert that women's salaries for equal work and qualifications (except in the public sector, and even then) are often lower, sometimes by half, than their male peers'. The law usually makes it hard for them to accumulate capital, and though women are gaining real economic autonomy in the informal sector (which we should really term the "urban popular economy") this is also because they have no access to men's economic world. One remarkable Malian woman entrepreneur, as lively as she is modern, has enjoyed a success that is exceptional even today. Aminata Traoré, a brilliant sociologist and former political official, has established two fine restaurants in Bamako that have become cultural and intellectual meeting places for creative people from the city and elsewhere. She has also organized an artists' studio to exhibit and disseminate the talents of her country's creative craftspeople. Fatou Sylla, as beautiful as her ideas, made the pages of *Ivoire-Dimanche* as a former employee of the Abidjan court who in 1970 became head of a notebook-manufacturing company officially inaugurated by the Planning Ministry itself.[3] These examples represent a fine beginning, but just a beginning.

On the political level, except for a few women who manage to come forward in national struggles and a few flamboyant individuals, participation by women is still the exception. This being said, what is politics, and what is its range? It is doubtless more useful today for determined women to dedicate themselves to improvement in the status of their sisters, respect for a minimum marriage age, and an end to the least acceptable demonstrations of their social inferiority than to perform in the official power comedies with men. Their participation in politics often seems a marginal, very dependent extension of men's. From this perspective, African independence has not necessarily brought an improvement in status for most African women. What seems more important is their integration into the market economy, which began long ago with their work in the informal sector and has since greatly accelerated, more a reflection of the economic crisis than of the twists and turns of political independence.

On the social level especially, cultural constraints weigh heavily on women. The tales women tell about their lives contrast so sharply with the image men have of them that one feels one is hearing about two different categories of female beings. In men's minds, a woman's whole life takes place within marriage or, rather, various marriages and births. Single women are little accepted in even the most Westernized milieus. Men mostly think of women as mothers submerged in traditional families that impose on them women's and children's social circle dominated by male strategies, with the village as the compulsory social and cultural reference point. Yet a woman's life today is actually centered around a small, nuclear family that in the cities no longer obscures the harsh realities of social inequality. The woman is the basic core around whom gather the children of several fathers and even other women who have been her husband's co-wives. An insidious violence, disguised by tradition as "witchcraft business," is still the main means of social action within a way of life that can be characterized as artfully avoiding the worst in order to survive with the hope of exploiting someone else one day—especially another woman.[4] The result is a blend: Independent women can remain so only if they can somehow find a male port in the storm, one they marry late or one they just live with. Sterility is still an absolute evil, except for a few unusual women like Aoua Keita, who transcended her condition through political activity in much the same way as certain rare powerful women before her. This is why the birthrates in Africa remain the highest in the world—not because women, even the poorest and least educated, have not changed in this area. If it were up to them, they would generally have half as many children as they do, but men still refuse virtually any compromise in this area so closely linked with the very conceptual basis of virility.

So—emancipation? Yes, for those women, more and more of them, who have become aware of the constraints described above and begun to fight them. "Bourgeoisified" city women, culturally Westernized, but also more and more working-class women, including women in the countryside, show a real capacity for initiative. They are encouraged by women's organizations, which are much broader and more active than in the West, and follow an old tradition within which they organize among themselves and for themselves, in a view of daily life that includes sharing tasks, concerns, and amusements much more separately among women than women do in the West. These associations are both a strength and a weakness. There is nothing simpler for the powers that be than to limit women to this subsidiary work, controlled by authorities other than they—clearly a case of political affiliation.

It is also the case for development organizations. The phrase "women and development" is on everyone's lips. Works, tracts, and reports on the subject are innumerable. This is in fact the reason I have cited almost none of them in this book,[5] for they still often give one cause for despair. They do demonstrate an awakening to the notion that nonindustrial productive labor (there is little industrial labor done in Africa except in mining areas) is in the hands of women, but they go on to say that therefore we must get to know women and then "sensitize," "awaken," "educate," or "mobilize" them—in short, use them.

We often forget that women must be helped, especially in the countryside, to have their right to participate in decisionmaking accepted by men. It is not enough for women to run for local office—they have yet to be heard at that level, and if they are not, it is not entirely their own fault. It takes a strong will to fly in the face of enduring social and political pressures. At the same time and perhaps even more important, women continue *to have no time.* Crushed under multiple work burdens from morning to night, Rwandan peasant women, for example, have no free time to think about and certainly even less to try out new agricultural techniques that might, in the long run, lighten their load. Yet history shows that we cannot count on men to finance (since it is often in financial terms that the question is posed) or promote improvements that do not first benefit them. Fortunately, we are no longer at the point where men are invited to farming meetings and training while the women go to the fields, as happened not so long ago in Cameroonian villages. But women need development *by* women. The only path is education, if only because many women in the countryside and in poor city neighborhoods do not understand their nation's European lingua franca. The most promising sign is that almost everywhere today the right to parity for girls and boys in schooling is increasingly recognized.

Notes

Introduction

1. Endnotes will give abbreviated references (author, title, publisher, date) for works cited in the bibliography at the end of this volume; the bibliography will not necessarily include all titles cited. For easier reading, a simplified international spelling for African names has been adopted.

2. An expert in psycho-pedagogy of Guinean origin recently interviewed about circumcision in a French periodical described it as an initiation rite whereby the child left his mother to "enter the world of men." It occurred to neither the interviewer nor the interviewee to raise, in this report on "children," the question of *girls'* initiation. *L'Evénément du Jeudi,* no. 472, 1993. Also see J.-C. Muller, "Les deux fois circoncis et les presque excisées," *Cahiers d'Etudes Africaines,* vol. 33, no. 4, no. 132, 1993, pp. 531–544.

3. See the introduction to C. Coquery-Vidrovitch, *Africa: Endurance and Change South of the Sahara,* Berkeley, University of California Press, 1988, and to *Histoires des villes d'Afrique noire des origines à la colonisation,* Paris, Albin Michel, 1993.

4. Early works on women are rare, for example, *Les Abyssiniennes et les femmes du Soudan oriental d'après les relations de Bruce, Browne,* . . . , Turin, Jean Zay, 1876.

5. See Louis Sonolet, *Le parfum de la dame noire: Physiologie humoristique de l'amour africain,* Paris, Libraire F. Juven, ca. 1911.

6. Clara Cahill Park, *Native Women in Africa: Their Hard Lot in the March of Progress,* Boston: Massachusetts Commission for International Justice, 1904.

7. Health Department Archives, thesis in progress by Bérangère Jeannès, Université de Paris 7-Denis Diderot.

8. There are a few exceptions. See Mamadou Diawara, "Femmes, servitude et histoire: Les traditions orales des femmes de condition servile dans le royaume de Jaara du XVᵉ au milieu du XIXᵉ siècle," *History in Africa,* no. 16, 1989, pp. 71–96.

9. Karin Barber, "*Oriki:* History and Criticism," mimeograph, Centre of West African Studies, University of Birmingham, 1987, p. 5.

10. M. Palau-Marty, *Le roi-dieu du Bénin,* Paris, Berger-Levrault, 1964, p. 139.

11. Claude-Hélène Perrot, *Les Ani-Ndenye et le pouvoir aux XVIIIᵉ et XIXᵉ siècles,* Paris, Editions de la Sorbonne, 1982.

12. Diawara, op. cit.

13. Kirk Hoppe, "Whose Life Is It, Anyway? Issues of Representation in Life Narrative Texts of African Women," *International Journal of African Historical Studies,* vol. 26, no. 3, 1993, pp. 623–626.

14. See the bibliography.

15. See Terence O. Ranger, "Religious Movements and Politics in Sub-Saharan Africa," *African Studies Review*, vol. 29, no. 3, 1986, pp. 1–69. Claude Tardits is one of the first anthropologists to have been interested in this subject, notably in *Porto Novo: Les nouvelles générations africaines entre leurs traditions et l'Occident*, Paris-The Hague: Mouton, 1958.

Chapter One

1. This is a birthrate of about 50 births per year per 1,000 inhabitants.

2. Nakanyike B. Musisi, "Women, 'Elite Polygyny,' and Buganda State Formation," *Signs*, vol. 16, no. 4, 1991, pp. 777–779.

3. Claude Tardits, "Aimer, manger et danser: Propos sur la grande polygynie," J. C. Barbier, ed., *Femmes du Cameroun*, Paris, ORSTOM/Karthala, 1985, pp. 119–131.

4. Jan Vansina, *The Children of Woot*, Madison, University of Wisconsin Press, 1978, p. 106.

5. Around Onitsha and in Ika country men worked the fields, but elsewhere men grew only yams. Nina Mba, *Nigerian Women Mobilized*, Berkeley, University of California Press, 1982, pp. 29–30.

6. Marcia Wright, "Technology, Marriage, and Women's Work in the History of Maize-Growers in Mazabuka, Zambia: A Reconnaissance," *Journal of Southern African Studies*, vol. 10, no. 1, 1983, pp. 55–69.

7. Jane I. Guyer, "Female Farming and the Evolution of Food Production Patterns Amongst the Beti of South-Central Cameroon," *Africa*, vol. 50, no. 4, 1980, pp. 341–355, and P. Laburthe-Tolra, *Minlaaba*, Paris, Champion, 1977.

8. Ester Boserup, *The Conditions of Agricultural Growth*, Chicago, Aldine, 1965, and *Women's Role in Economic Development*, New York, Allen and Unwin, 1970. An important detail—"hoe" is a generic term that refers to at least five differently shaped agricultural tools.

9. Watermelon seeds produced a good-quality oil, hence their market value.

10. Margaret Jean Hay, "Kenya: Luo Women and Economic Change During the Colonial Period," E. Etienne and E. Leacock, eds., *Women and Colonization*, New York, Praeger, 1983, pp. 110–124.

11. Carolyn M. Clark, "Land and Food, Women and Power, in Nineteenth-Century Kikuyu," *Africa*, vol. 50, no. 4, 1980, pp. 357–367.

12. The Tswana have been described by missionaries from the first half of the nineteenth century on, because European invasion occurred much earlier in the southern African interior. See Margaret Kinsman, "'Beasts of Burden': The Subordination of Southern Tswana Women, ca. 1800–1840," *Journal of Southern African Studies*, vol. 10, no 1, 1983, pp. 39–54, based on missionary sources from the era.

13. Thomas Hodgson, cited in Kinsman, op. cit., p. 42. The term "owner" was a Eurocentric mistranslation.

14. Robert Moffat, *Missionary Labors and Scenes in Southern Africa*, London, John Snow, 1843, p. 250. Nonetheless, this missionary's successors did say that he exaggerated slightly. Kinsman, op. cit, p. 49.

15. See *Ethnologie régionale*, vol. 1, *Afrique, Océanie*, Paris, La Pléiade, 1972.

16. Jean-Pierre Dozon, *La société bété, Côte d'Ivoire,* Paris, ORSTOM/Karthala, 1985, pp. 153–155.

17. Tardits, "Aimer, manger, danser."

18. Ethel M. Albert, "Women of Burundi: A Study of Social Values," Denise Paulme, ed., *Women of Tropical Africa,* Berkeley, University of California Press, 1963, pp. 179–215.

19. F. S. Arnot, *Garenganze, or Seven Years' Pioneer Mission Work in Central Africa,* London, 1889, p. 194, cited in Marcia Wright, *Strategies of Slaves and Women,* London, James Currey, 1993. Msiri's wives were not only the most numerous and most active of female city dwellers; the great caravans, whose trips to the coast could last several months, included many of these women as well. Slave women portered; wives and others served for cooking, camp making, and sex.

20. Among others see Claude Meillassoux, *Maidens, Meals, and Money,* Cambridge, Cambridge University Press, 1981, and *The Anthropology of Slavery,* Chicago, University of Chicago Press, 1991.

21. Abdoulaye-Bara Diop, *La famille Wolof,* Paris, Karthala, 1985, p. 112.

22. Wright, "Technology, Marriage, and Women's Work."

23. On this topic see the Senegalese film *Hyennes,* by Djibril Diop Mambéty (1992).

24. Personal interview.

25. This is not always the case. In other societies, the birth of twins is considered bad luck, and at least one is sacrificed.

26. Among the Akan of Ghana, where the couple's residence is matrilocal, things are even simpler because the wife continues to live with her family, only going to her husband's for the night. Christine Oppong, *Middle-Class African Marriage,* London, Allen and Unwin, 1974, pp. 32–33.

27. George P. Murdock, *Africa: Its Peoples and Their Culture History,* New York, McGraw-Hill, 1959, quoted in Jean-Claude Muller, *Du bon usage du sexe et du mariage,* Paris, L'Harmattan, 1982, pp. 13–14. The description that follows this assertion concerns very small groups of people (fragmented groups from 1,000 to 150,000 and on average 12,000 to 18,000) that have cultivated their difference in the face of a series of powerful invaders, including the *jihads* (holy wars) of the past century. For the purpose of generalized description, I have synthesized characteristics that in reality vary somewhat from group to group.

28. Melvin L. Perlman, "The Changing Status and Role of Women in Toro (Western Uganda), *Cahiers d'Etudes Africaines,* vol. 6-4, no. 24, 1966, p. 565.

29. See theoretical discussion of this with regard to the Guro of Côte d'Ivoire by Claude Meillassoux, "Essai d'interprétation du phénomène économique dans les sociétés traditionnelles d'auto-subsistance," *Cahiers d'Etudes Africaines,* vol. 1, no. 4, 1960, pp. 38–67. We will return to the subject of marriage in discussion of its recent evolution in the last chapter.

Chapter Two

1. Benedict B.B. Naanen, "Itinerant Gold Mines: Prostitution in the Cross River Basin of Nigeria, 1930–1950," *African Studies Review,* vol. 34, no. 2, 1991, p. 71.

2. Gloria Thomas-Emeagwili, "Class Formation in Pre-Colonial Nigeria," MS, History Department, Ahmadu Bello University, Zaria, ca. 1985, cited in Toyin Falola and Julius O. Ihonvbere, eds., *Nigeria and the International Capitalist System*, Boulder, Lynne Rienner, 1988.

3. Meillassoux, *The Anthropology of Slavery*, using detailed statistical evidence, casts serious doubt on the population increases that can truly be attributed to slave women.

4. Mary Smith, ed., *Baba of Karo*, London, Faber and Faber, 1954, p. 16.

5. Quoted by Claude Meillassoux, "Etat et conditions des esclaves à Gumbu (Mali)," *Journal of African History*, vol. 14, no. 3, 1973, p. 434.

6. Smith, *Baba of Karo*.

7. Ibid.

8. David Eltis and Stanley L. Engerman, "Was the Slave Trade Dominated by Men?" *Journal of Interdisciplinary History*, vol. 23, no. 2, 1992, pp. 237–257, and "Fluctuations in Sex and Age Ratios in the Transatlantic Slave Trade, 1663–1864," *Economic History Review*, vol. 46, 1993, pp. 308–323.

9. In this period 400,000 cowries were about £10.

10. H. C. Marshall, "Notes on the Bamba," 1910, Marshall Papers, Livingstone Museum, quoted by Wright, *Strategies of Slaves and Women*, p. 153.

11. Dugald Campbell, *Ten Times a Slave But Freed at Last: The Thrilling Story of Bwanika, a Central African Heroine*, Glasgow, 1916, cited by Wright, op. cit, pp. 167–168.

12. Marcia Wright, "Women in Peril: A Commentary on the Life Stories of Captives in Nineteenth-Century East Central Africa," *African Social Research*, no. 20, 1975, pp. 800–819; Marcia Wright, *Women in Peril: Life Stories of Four Captives*, Lusaka, Neczam, 1984; and Wright, *Strategies of Slaves and Women*.

13. Sharon Hutchinson, "Relations Between the Sexes Among the Nuer, 1930," *Africa*, vol. 50, no. 4, 1980, pp. 371–388.

14. A turning point was the remarkable thesis of an Ivoirian researcher, Harris-Memel Fote, who demonstrated that even subsistence-, kinship-based, stateless societies were very much dependent on production by slaves in the nineteenth century at least. *L'esclavage dans les sociétés lignagères d'Afrique noire: Exemple de la Côte d'Ivoire précoloniale*, Paris, EHESS, 1988.

15. Robert Shell, "Tender Ties: Women and the Slave Household, 1652–1834," in *Children of Bondage: A Social History of the Slave Society at the Cape of Good Hope, 1652–1838*, Hanover, N.H., University Press of New England, 1994.

16. Hans Heese, *Groep sonder Grense*, Bellville, 1984, especially appendix A, pp. 41–75.

17. Although English law was patrilineal, in the British colony of Virginia matrilineal affiliation was introduced as far as transmission of servile status was concerned, for the obvious purpose of increasing the slave population.

18. "Papers Relative to the Manumission of Steyntje and Her Children, with an Appendix," South African Bound Pamphlets, Cape Town, 1827, cited in Shell, op. cit., p. 4.

19. Afrikander (which became Afrikaner) today refers to whites of Dutch extraction. W. W. Bird, *State of the Cape*, Cape Town, 1966, from the 1823 London edition, pp. 73–74.

Chapter Three

1. Pierre Brasseur and Paule Brasseur-Marion, *Porto-Novo et sa palmeraie*, Mémoires de l'Institut Français d'Afrique Noire, no. 32, 1953; Tardits, *Porto Novo*.

2. Carol P. MacCormack, "Control of Land, Labor, and Capital in Rural Southern Sierra Leone," Edna G. Bay, ed., *Women and Work in Africa*, Boulder, Westview Press, 1982, pp. 35–54.

3. E. Frances White, "Women, Work, and Ethnicity: The Sierra Leone Case," Bay, op. cit., pp. 19–34.

4. Justin Zunon-Gnobo, "Le rôle des femmes dans le commerce précolonial," *Godo-Godo*, no. 2, 1976, pp. 79–105.

5. The kola nut has a slight stimulant effect, similar to that of coffee, and is highly valued in a culture in which theoretically alcohol and tobacco are forbidden.

6. Ph.D. dissertation in progress under the direction of Steve Feierman, University of Florida.

7. L. S. B. Leakey, *The Southern Kikuyu Before 1903*, New York, Academic Press, 1977, p. 491.

8. Joan Vincent, *African Elite: The Big Men of a Small Town*, New York, Columbia University Press, 1971, pp. 187–208.

9. Thomas-Emeagwili, op. cit.

Chapter Four

1. Filomina Chioma Steady, ed., *The Black Woman Cross-culturally*, Cambridge, Mass., Schenkman, 1981.

2. Wright, "Technology, Marriage, and Women's Work."

3. Jean-Claude Barbier, "Mimboo, reine d'Asêm," J.-C. Barbier, ed., *Femmes du Cameroun*, Paris, ORSTOM/Karthala, 1985, pp. 133–150.

4. Christofer Fyfe, *A History of Sierra Leone*, London, Oxford University Press, 1962, p. 19.

5. Carol P. Hoffer, "Mende and Sherbro Women in High Office," *Canadian Journal of African Studies*, vol. 6, no. 2, 1972, pp. 151–164.

6. Fyfe, op. cit.

7. Hoffer, op. cit.

8. Mona Etienne, "Gender Relations and Conjugality Among the Baule (Ivory Coast)," *Culture*, vol. 1, no. 1, 1981, pp. 21–30.

9. J. N. Loucou and F. Ligier, *La reine Pokou, fondatrice du royaume baoulé, XVIIIᵉ siècle*, Paris, ABC, 1975.

10. Bernard Salvaing, "La femme dahoméenne vue par les missionnaires: Arrogance culturelle, ou antiféminisme clérical?" *Cahiers d'Etudes Africaines*, vol. 22, no. 4, 1981, pp. 507–522.

11. John Hunwick, "Songhay, Bornu, and Hausaland in the 16th Century," J.F.A. Adjayi and Michael Crowder, eds., *History of West Africa*, vol. 1, New York, Columbia University Press, 1972, pp. 202–239.

12. Richard Pankhurst, ed., *The Ethiopian Royal Chronicles*, Addis Ababa, Oxford University Press, 1967.

13. Obaro Ikime, "The Changing Status of Chiefs Among the Itsekiri," M. Crowder and O. Ikime, eds., *West African Chiefs*, New York, Africana, 1970, pp. 289–311.

14. Mark R. Lipschutz and R. Kent Rasmussen, *Dictionary of African Historical Biography*, Berkeley, University of California Press, 1989.

15. I. A. Akinjogbin, *Dahomey and Its Neighbors*, Cambridge, Cambridge University Press, 1967.

16. See Mba, *Nigerian Women Mobilized*, pp. 21–26.

17. Kamene Okonjo, "Sex Roles in Nigerian Politics," Christine Oppong, ed., *Female and Male in West Africa*, London, Allen and Unwin, 1983, pp. 218–220.

18. We also find among the Hausa, notably in Katsina and Zaria, the title *iya* given to the king's mother, or if she has died, to a paternal aunt or elder sister. Beverly Mack, "Royal Wives in Kano," C. Coles and B. Mack, eds., *Hausa Women in the 20th Century*, Madison, University of Wisconsin Press, 1991, p. 111.

19. Jacob U. Egharevba, *A Short History of Benin*, Ibadan, Ibadan University Press, 1968, pp. 75–76, cited in Okonjo, op. cit.

20. Translated and published by Frank Heath, Lagos, African Universities Press, 1962.

21. J. H. Speke, *Journal of the Journey to Find the Sources of the Nile*, London, William Blackwood and Sons, 1863.

22. A. T. Bryant, *Olden Times in Zululand and Natal*, London, Longman Green, 1929.

23. Christine N. Qunta, ed., *Women in Southern Africa*, London, Allison and Busby, 1987, pp. 23–76.

24. J. D. Omer-Cooper, *The Zulu Aftermath*, London, Longman, 1966.

25. Gordon M. Haliburton, *Historical Dictionary of Lesotho*, Metuchen, N.J., Scarecrow Press, 1977.

26. Her son finally had to give in to Moshweshwe. D. Sweetman, *Women Leaders in African History*, London, Heinemann, 1984, pp. 55–63.

27. R. Kent Rasmussen, *Mzilikazi of the Ndebele*, London, Heinemann, 1977.

28. Joseph C. Miller, "Nzinga of Matamba in a New Perspective," *Journal of African History*, vol. 16, no. 2, 1975, pp. 201–216.

29. The term "marriage" was interpreted by the Portuguese in the usual sense of the word. Ibid.

30. Dona Barbara died in 1666, and after a period of civil war the Portuguese were temporarily able to control the country through rulers of their choosing. Yet at the start of the eighteenth century all direct contact with the Portuguese ceased until they embarked on the conquest of the country at the start of the twentieth century. Miller, op. cit.; David Birmingham, *Trade and Conflict in Angola*, Oxford, Clarendon Press, 1966; Sweetman, op. cit., pp. 39–47.

31. J. L. Castilhon, *Zingha, reine d'Angola*, Patrick Graille and Laurent Quillerie, eds., Bourges, Ed. G, 1992 (1769).

32. E. J. Krige and J. D. Krige, *The Realm of a Rain-Queen*, London, Oxford University Press, 1943.

33. Sweetman, op. cit., pp. 48–54.

34. *Béatrice du Congo*, Paris, Présence Africaine, 1970. On this subject, see Jean Cuvelier, ed., *Relations sur le Congo du Père Laurent de Lucques (1700–1717)*, Brus-

sels, Institute Royal Colonial Belge, 1953, and Louis Jadin, *Le Congo et la secte des Antonins*, Brussels, Académie Royale des Sciences d'Outre-Mer, 1961.

35. Cf. T. O. Ranger, *Revolt in Southern Rhodesia, 1896–97*, Evanston, Northwestern University Press, 1956, and *The African Voice in Southern Rhodesia, 1898–1930*, London, Heinemann, 1970.

Chapter Five

1. Father Tuillier, missionary to Dahomey, 1867, cited in Salvaing, op. cit.

2. Diawara, op. cit.

3. See Hutchinson, "Relations Between the Sexes."

4. Dozon, op. cit., p. 140.

5. Ife Amadiume, *Male Daughters, Female Husbands*, London, Zed Books, 1987, pp. 99–100.

6. Musisi, op. cit., p. 767.

7. Régine Bonnardel, "Afrique: Les femmes quittent la brousse," *Le Journal de la Paix*, no. 340, 1986, p. 17.

8. H. J. Drewal and M. Thompson Drewal, Gelede: *Art and Female Power Among the Yoruba*, Bloomington, Indiana University Press, 1983.

9. C. Odugbesan, "Femininity in Yoruba Religious Art," M. Douglas and P. Kaberry, eds., *Man in Africa*, New York, Tavistock, 1969, pp. 199–211.

10. M. Wilson and L. M. Thompson, eds., *The Oxford History of South Africa*, Oxford, Oxford University Press, 1969; Monica Wilson, "Mhlakaza," *Les Africains*, Paris, Jeune Afrique, 1977, vol. 5, pp. 203–230.

11. Benetta Jules-Rosette, "Privilege Without Power: Women in African Cults and Churches," R. Terborg-Penn, S. Harley, and A. Rushing, eds., *Women in Africa and the African Diaspora*, Washington, D.C., Howard University Press, 1987, pp. 99–199.

12. A. Roberts, "The Lumpa Church of Alice Lenshina," R. I. Rotberg and A. A. Mazrui, eds., *Protest and Power in Black Africa*, New York, Oxford University Press, 1970, pp. 513–568.

13. Jules-Rosette, op. cit.

14. P. Hazoumé, "Tata Ajaché Soupo Maha Awouiyan," *La Reconnaissance Africaine*, nos. 1–2–3, 1925, p. 7.

15. Quoted by H. d'Almeida-Topor, *Les amazones*, Paris, Rochevignes, 1984, p. 92.

16. Carol Eastman, "Women, Slaves, and Foreigners: African Cultural Influences and Group Processes in the Formation of Northern Swahili Coastal Society," *International Journal of African Historical Studies*, vol. 21, no. 1, 1988, pp. 1–20.

17. Vansina, *The Children of Woot*.

18. The term "creole culture" refers to the mixed culture of the African coasts, the result of syncretism, mostly since the eighteenth century, of Christian European influences and local customs and beliefs. The creoles were a kind of educated local bourgeoisie whose fortune, like that of the Westerners who came through, depended on international trade.

19. George E. Brooks, "*Signares* of Saint-Louis and Gorée: Women Entrepreneurs in 18th-Century Senegal," N. J. Hafkin and E. G. Bay, eds., *Women in Africa,* Stanford, Calif., Stanford University Press, 1976, pp. 19–44.

20. Jean Boulègue, *Les Luso-Africains de Sénégambie, XVIᵉ–XIXᵉ siècles,* Dakar, Institut Fondamental d'Afrique Noire, 1972, pp. 54–55, 61–62, 71–72.

21. In Sahelian Africa there are castes that function similarly to those in India, endogamous groups mainly of professionals whose techniques are passed down from generation to generation: jewelers, ironworkers, shoemakers, dyers, tanners, griots. "Castes" were inferior to "free men" but superior to slaves. This social prejudice persists to this day.

22. John Lindsay, *A Voyage to the Coast of Africa in 1758,* London, 1759, pp. 80 and 89–90.

23. See Régine Bonnardel, *Saint-Louis du Sénégal: Mort ou naissance?* Paris, L'Harmattan, 1992, pp. 38–43.

24. See Raymond Mauny, *Glossaire des expressions et termes locaux employés dans l'Ouest africain,* Dakar, 1952, pp. 37 and 48.

25. Joseph Miller, *Way of Death: Merchant Capitalism and the Angolan Slave Trade 1730–1830,* Madison, University of Wisconsin Press, 1988.

26. Ibid., p. 294. On creolization in the nineteenth century, see Anne Stamm, "La société créole à Saint Paul de Loanda dans les années 1836–1848," *Revue Française d'Histoire d'Outre-Mer,* vol. 59, no. 213, 1972, pp. 578–610.

27. See Coquery-Vidrovitch, *Histoire des villes africaines,* chap. 6.

28. Akintoye, "The Economic Foundation of Ibadan in the 19th Century," I. A. Akinjogbin and S. Osoba, eds., *Topics on Nigerian Economic and Social History,* Ife, Ife University Press, 1980, pp. 55–65.

29. Okonjo, "Sex Roles in Nigerian Politics," p. 216, cited in Saburi O. Biobaku, *The Egba and Their Neighbours, 1842–1872,* Oxford, Clarendon Press, 1957.

30. We also note a second wife in the same region, Ifeyinwa "Olinke," who died at an advanced age in 1909 and who took on family authority because she had become much richer and more popular than her husband. Amadiume, op. cit., pp. 44–49.

31. Perlman, op. cit., p. 567.

32. Marguerite Dupire, "The Position of Women in a Pastoral Society," Paulme, *Women of Tropical Africa,* p. 58.

33. See, for example, B. Larsson, *Conversion to Greater Freedom?* Stockholm/Uppsala, Almqvist and Wiksell, 1991.

Chapter Six

1. Elizabeth A. Eldredge, "Women in Production: The Economic Role of Women in 19th-Century Lesotho," *Signs,* vol. 16, no. 4, 1991, pp. 707–731.

2. K. Vickery, cited in Wright, "Technology, Marriage, and Women's Work."

3. Maud Shimwaayi Muntemba, "Women and Agricultural Change in the Railway Region of Zambia: Dispossession and Counter-Strategies, 1930–1970," Bay, *Women and Work in Africa,* pp. 83–103.

4. Hay, "Luo Women."

5. Susan Martin, *Palm-Oil and Protest: An Economic History of the Ngwa Region, South-eastern Nigeria, 1800–1980*, Cambridge, Cambridge University Press, 1988.

6. Which produced a high-quality oil.

7. Jane Guyer, "Food, Cocoa, and the Division of Labour by Sex in Two West African Societies," *Comparative Studies in Society and History*, vol. 22, no. 3, pp. 355–373.

8. K. Mair, *Anthropology and Development*, London, Macmillan, 1984.

9. Cited in Martin Chanock, "Making Customary Law: Men, Women and Courts in Colonial Northern Rhodesia," M. J. Hay and M. Wright, eds., *African Women and the Law*, Boston, Boston University Press, 1983, p. 63.

10. Cited in Alan R. Booth, "'European Courts Protect Women and Witches,'" *Journal of Southern African Studies*, vol. 18, no. 2, 1992, p. 273.

11. H. Child, *The History and Extent of Recognition of Tribal Law in Rhodesia*, revised edition, Salisbury (Harare), Ministry of Domestic Affairs, 1976.

12. Under the levirate, a widow was inherited by a brother, a son, or even a nephew of the deceased. It was socially beneficial in that the woman continued to be protected by the group for which she worked.

13. Child, op. cit., p. 91, cited in J. May, *Zimbabwean Women in Colonial and Customary Law*, Harare, Mambo Press/Holmes McDougall, 1983, p. 67.

14. Cited in Susie Jacobs, "Women and Land Resettlement in Zimbabwe," *Review of African Political Economy*, nos. 27–28, 1984, p. 45.

15. See D. Jeater, *Marriage, Perversion, and Power: The Construction of Moral Discourse in Southern Rhodesia, 1894–1930*, Oxford, Clarendon Press, 1993.

16. Gordon Wilson, *Luo Customary Law and Marriage Law Customs*, Nairobi, Government Printer, 1968, pp. 122–144. See M. J. Hay, "Women as Owners, Occupants, and Managers of Property in Colonial Western Kenya," Hay and Wright, op. cit., p. 111.

17. Cited in Jean Davison, "'Without Land We Are Nothing': The Effect of Land Tenure Policies and Practices upon Rural Women in Kenya," *Rural Africana*, no. 27, 1987, p. 19.

18. Rayah Feldman, "Women's Groups and Women's Subordination: An Analysis of Policies Towards Rural Women in Kenya," *Review of African Political Economy*, nos. 22–23, 1984, pp. 67–77.

19. This is what the women colorfully call "sitting on a man." J. Van Allen, "Sitting On a Man: Colonialism and the Lost Political Institutions of Igbo Women," *Canadian Journal of African Studies*, vol. 6, no. 2, 1972, pp. 165–181.

20. Andrzej Zajackowski, "La famille, le lignage et la communauté villageoise chez les Ashanti de la période de transition," *Cahiers d'Etudes Africaines*, vol. 1, no. 4, 1960, pp. 99–114.

21. Christine Oppong, Christine Okali, and Beverly Houghton, "Woman Power: Retrograde Steps in Ghana," *African Studies Review*, vol. 18, no. 3, 1975, pp. 71–83.

22. Christine Okali, "Kinship and Cocoa Farming in Ghana," in Oppong, *Female and Male in West Africa*, pp. 170–178.

23. See J. Dey, "Gambian Women: Unequal Partners in Rice Development Projects," *Journal of Development Studies*, no. 17, 1981, pp. 109–122, and "Women in

African Rice Farming Systems," in International Rice Research Institute, ed., *Women in Rice Farming*, London, Gower, 1985.

24. Guyer, "Female Farming."

25. H. R. Barrett and A. W. Brown, "Time for Development? The Case of Women's Horticultural Schemes in Rural Gambia," *Scottish Geographical Magazine*, vol. 106, no. 1, 1989, pp. 3–11.

26. Sam Jackson, "Hausa Women on Strike," *Review of African Political Economy*, no. 13, 1978, pp. 21–36.

27. T. J. Bembridge, "The Role of Women in Agricultural and Rural Development in Transkeï," *Journal of Contemporary African Studies*, vol. 7, nos. 1–2, 1988, pp. 149–182.

Chapter Seven

1. Generally caused by Western capitalism, labor migration occurred early on; one example is the seasonal migratory movements of the *navetanes*, the laborers used in the Senegambian up-country for peanut farming, where export began a generation before colonialism proper. See Philippe David, *Les navetanes: histoire des migrants saisonniers de l'arachide en Sénégambie des origines à nos jours*, Dakar/Abidjan, Les Nouvelles Editions Africaines, 1980.

2. Josef Gugler, "The Second Sex in Town," *Canadian Journal of African Studies*, vol. 6, no. 2, 1972, pp. 289–301.

3. Marcia Wright, "Justice, Women, and the Social Order in Abercorn, Northeastern Rhodesia, 1897–1903," Hay and Wright, *African Women and the Law*, pp. 33–50.

4. Janet Bujra, "Women 'Entrepreneurs' of Early Nairobi," *Canadian Journal of African Studies*, vol. 9, no. 2, 1975, pp. 213–234.

5. Virginity is less and less a requirement. In Wolof families, for example, it is no longer customary to show off a bloody sheet after consummation of the marriage. Abdoulaye-Bara Diop, *Le famille wolof*, Paris, Karthala, 1985.

6. Kenneth Little, *African Women in Town*, Cambridge, Cambridge University Press, 1973, pp. 19–22.

7. Renée Pittin, "Houses of Women: A Focus on Alternative Lifestyles in Katsina City," Oppong, *Female and Male in West Africa*, pp. 291–302.

8. Philip Mayer, *Townsmen or Tribesmen: Conservatism and the Process of Urbanization in a South African City*, Cape Town, Rhodes University/Oxford University Press, 1963, and Ester Boserup, *Woman's Role in Economic Development*, London, Allen and Unwin, 1970, cited in Gugler, "The Second Sex in Town," p. 293.

9. But woman suffrage did not begin in Zaire until 1970. Suzanne Comhaire-Sylvain, *Femmes de Kinshasa hier et aujourd'hui*, Paris/The Hague, Mouton, 1968, p. 229.

10. A. W. Southall, "The Growth of Urban Society," in Stanley Diamond and Fred Burke, eds., *The Transformation of East Africa: Studies in Political Anthropology*, New York/London, Basic Books, 1966.

11. J. C. Caldwell, *African Rural-Urban Migration: The Movement to Ghana's Towns*, London, Hurst, 1969.

12. Wole Soyinka, *The Lion and the Jewel*, London, Oxford University Press, 1963.

13. C. Obbo, "Town Migration Is Not for Women," Ph.D. diss., University of Wisconsin, Madison, 1977.

14. Cherryl Walker, *Women and Resistance in South Africa*, London, Onyx Press, 1982, pp. 40–43.

15. Julia C. Wells, "The History of Black Women's Struggle Against Pass Laws in South Africa, 1900–1956," Hay and Wright, op. cit., pp. 145–168.

16. Between 1921 and 1936, the total number of female city dwellers increased by 142.3 percent compared with 78.4 percent for men. In Johannesburg, the largest city, the corresponding figures were 245 percent and 45 percent. Ibid.

17. D. Gaitskell et al., "Class, Race, and Gender: Domestic Workers in South Africa," *Review of African Political Economy*, nos. 27–28, 1984, p. 99.

18. B. Bozzoli, with Mmantho Nkotsoe, *Women of Phokeng*, London, James Currey, 1991.

19. K.S.O. Beavon and C. Rogerson, "Changing the Role of Women in the Urban Informal Sector of Johannesburg," David Drakakis-Smith, ed., *Urbanisation in the Developing World*, London, Croom Helm, 1986, pp. 205–225.

20. J. Penvenne, *Making Our Own Way: Women Working in Lourenço Marques, 1900–1933*, Boston, Boston University Press, 1986; Mirjana Morokvasic, "Birds of Passage Are Also Women," *International Migration Review*, vol. 18, no. 4, 1984, pp. 886–901.

21. Kubuya Namulemba Malira, "Regard sur la situation sociale de la citoyenne lushoise d'avant 1950," *Likundoli*, no. 2, 1974, pp. 63–71.

22. Census of 1969, in Little, op. cit., p. 10.

23. Ibid.

24. There were 61,000 Merina women compared with 51,000 men. There is the same preponderance of women in the cities of Antsirabe (22,000 inhabitants), Ambatolampy (4,750 inhabitants), and Arivonimamo (3,600 inhabitants), like the capital characterized by remarkably homogeneous immigration. A. Southall, "Madagascar," *African Urban Notes*, vol. 3, no. 1, 1968, pp. 14–22.

25. Thirty percent of the educated female migrants came to the city to find jobs, compared with 4 percent of illiterate women and 5 percent of those with up to four years of education. *Women in the Urban Labor Markets of Africa: The Case of Tanzania*, World Bank Working Paper, no. 380, 1980.

26. See Christine S. Obbo, *African Women*, London, Zed Press, 1980, pp. 70–86.

27. Penvenne, *Making Our Own Way*, and Penvenne, *African Workers and Colonial Racism: Mozambican Strategies and Struggles in Lourenço Marques, 1877–1962*, Portsmouth, N. H., Heinemann, 1995.

28. On Tanzania, see R. H. Sabot, *Economic Development and Urban Migration, Tanzania, 1900–1971*, Oxford, Oxford University Press, 1979; M. Mbilinyi, "Tanzania After Nyerere: Changing Employment Patterns in the 1970s: Casualisation and Feminisation of Labour," photocopy, School of Oriental and African Studies, University of London, 1986.

29. Fifty-three percent compared with 45 percent in western Africa around 1975.

30. Gudrun Ludwar-Ene, "Explanatory and Remedial Modalities for Personal Misfortune in a West African Society," *Anthropos*, no. 81, 1986, pp. 555–565.

31. M. Peil, "Going Home: Migration Careers of Southern Nigerians," *International Migration Review*, no. 22, 1988, pp. 563–585.

32. In Maseru there are 843 men for every 1,000 women. C. R. Wilkinson, "Migration in Lesotho: A Study of Population Movements in a Labour Reserve Economy," Ph.D. diss., University of Newcastle, 1985.

33. Josef Gugler and Gudrun Ludwar-Ene, "Plusieurs chemins mènent les femmes en ville en Afrique subsaharienne," H. d'Almeida-Topor and J. Riesz, eds., *Etudes franco-allemandes sur l'Afrique subsaharienne*, Cahiers Afrique Noire, no. 13, 1989, pp. 1–15. The authors provide a chart of the average sex ratio, urban and nationally, for each nation during the period 1951–1987.

34. Respectively 93 and 92 men per 100 women in the city according to 1975 figures. Aderanti Adepoju, "Patterns of Migration by Sex," Oppong, *Female and Male in West Africa*, pp. 54–65.

35. Bonnardel, *Saint-Louis du Sénégal.*

36. On the order of 867 men per 1,000 women in 1984 (compared with 1,025 men per 1,000 women in the rest of the country). Jose Van Kesteren, "Female Workers in Addis Ababa," *Social Science Research Review*, vol. 4, no. 1, 1988, pp. 17–32.

37. Irving Kaplan, "The Society and its Environment," in Harold D. Nelson and Irving Kaplan, eds., *Ethiopia: A Country Study*, Washington, D.C., U.S. Government Printing Office, 1981, p. 71.

38. The male/female ratio (as much as one can trust statistics) apparently went from 119 to 131 between 1950 and 1963 (compared with a very normal national ratio of 102). Adepoju, op. cit., p. 61.

39. Veena Thadani, "Women in Nairobi: The Paradox of Urban 'Progress,'" *African Urban Studies*, no. 3, 1978–1979, p. 72.

40. Only 15 percent of women workers but 29 percent of women entrepreneurs and 37 percent of office workers claimed this. Adepoju, op. cit.

41. Thirty percent of men claimed that they wanted to remain in the city. Wilkinson, op. cit.

42. British law preferred not to cede the entire property, especially in the city, but to grant emphyteutic leases, generally for ninety-nine years, at the end of which time the property reverted to the crown.

43. Around 1880, more than 3,200 plots were allotted, most of them to men. Kristin Mann, "Women, Land, Property, and the Accumulation of Wealth in Early Colonial Lagos," *Signs*, vol. 16, no. 4, 1991, pp. 682–705.

44. The law giving the wife the right to a share of her husband's wealth dates only from 1979 and was not promulgated until 1985. Study of inheritance trials in 1990 in Brong-Ashanti country (in the heart of the cocoa-growing area) demonstrates that generally a deceased father leaves his farms to his children and that the mother's family (the plaintiffs in these cases) less and less often wins. Gwendolyn Mikell, *Assault on Matriliny: Ghanaian Social Policy and Development*, work in progress.

45. G. Mikell, "Using the Courts to Obtain Relief: Akan Women and Family Courts in Ghana," Princeton Institute Paper, 1992. See *Cocoa and Chaos in Ghana*, Washington, D.C., Howard University Press, 1992.

46. The only recourse is for the husband to give it while he is alive, provided that the matrilineal family does not oppose him. Only 4 percent of the Akan in 1965 were married under the marriage law of 1894 (monogamous, Christian, recorded marriage), which provided that in intestate cases three-ninths of his holdings would go to

the deceased's lineage, four-ninths to his children, and two-ninths to his widow. Oppong, *Middle-Class African Marriage*, pp. 43–45.

47. C. Coquery-Vidrovitch, "Démographie et déstabilisation politique en Afrique occidentale," Eric Vilquin, ed., *Révolution et population: Aspects démographiques des grandes révolutions politiques,* Louvain-la-Neuve, Academia, 1990, pp. 173–202.

Chapter Eight

1. Claire Robertson, *Sharing the Same Bowl,* Bloomington, Indiana University Press, 1984.

2. Sharon B. Stichter and Jane L. Parpart, eds., *Patriarchy and Class,* Boulder, Westview Press, 1988, p. 17.

3. Margaret J. Hay, "Women as Owners, Occupants, and Managers of Property in Colonial Western Kenya," Hay and Wright, *African Women and the Law,* p. 117.

4. Thadani, "Women in Nairobi."

5. Malira, "Regard sur la situation sociale."

6. For example, shoemakers making shoe tongues use plastic materials or old tires. These "Dunlop sandals" may end up for sale at the local supermarket. Similarly, clothing dyers start with cotton fabric that is often imported and then sell it to urban women.

Chapter Nine

1. A. Nyirenda, *African Market-Vendors in Lusaka, with a Note on a Recent Boycott,* Rhodes-Livingstone Journal, no. 22, 1957.

2. René Caillié, *Journal d'un voyage à Toembouctu et à Jenné, dans l'Afrique centrale,* modern edition, 3 vols., Paris, Anthropos, 1965 (1830).

3. All these names correspond to historical linguistic groupings—today manipulated through ethnicity.

4. Robertson, *Sharing the Same Bowl.*

5. Suzanne Comhaire-Sylvain, "Le travail des femmes à Lagos, Nigeria," *Zaire,* vol. 5, no. 2, 1951, p. 169.

6. D. McCall, "Trade and the Role of Wife in a Modern West African Town," A. Southall, ed., *Social Change in Modern Africa,* London: Oxford University Press, 1981, pp. 286–299.

7. Called the Nago along the western coast that they traveled to Abidjan and beyond.

8. Comhaire-Sylvain, op. cit.

9. The sample is representative only of a relatively privileged group, the survey having been conducted in a girls' school and having focused on mothers of girls from twelve to eighteen who were in their last year of primary school or in secondary school, still exceptional at the time.

10. See Chapter 15.

11. See Rita Cordonnier, *Femmes africaines et commerce: Les revendeuses de tissus de la ville de Lomé,* Paris, L'Harmattan, 1987.

12. On the railroad, see Agnès Lambert, "Les réseaux marchands féminins du chemin de fer Dakar-Niger," Chantal Blanc-Pamard, ed., *Politiques agricoles et initiatives locales: Adversaires ou partenaires?* Paris, ORSTOM, 1993, pp. 91–106.

13. Chantal Vléï, "Le Travail salarié des femmes à Abidjan, 1946–1986," Ph.D. diss., University of Paris-7 Denis Diderot, 1994.

14. Nyirenda, op. cit.

15. Marvin Miracle, *Agriculture in the Congo Basin: Tradition and Change in African Rural Economies,* Madison, University of Wisconsin Press, 1967, pp. 333–334, cited in Ilsa Schuster, "Marginal Lives: Conflict and Contradiction in the Position of Female Traders in Lusaka, Zambia," Bay, *Women and Work in Africa,* pp. 105–111.

16. Stanley Pool, now just called "Le Pool," is the wide expanse of water in the middle of the Congo River that separates Brazzaville from Kinshasa. See Didier Gondola, "Migration et villes congolaises au XIXe siècle," Ph.D. diss, Université of Paris-7 Denis Diderot, 1993, p. 126. In 1950 only 15 percent of the women in Kisangani (compared with 50 percent of men) had received any education and only 2 percent (compared with 90 percent of men) were employed in the "modern" (formal economic) sector. V. G. Pons, *Stanleyville: An African Urban Community Under Belgian Administration,* London, Oxford University Press, 1969, pp. 215 and 248.

17. See Gertrude Mianda, *Les femmes maraîchères de Kinshasa et la conquête de l'autonomie: Sexe et pouvoir,* Paris, L'Harmattan, 1994.

18. M. De Young, "An African Emporium: The Addis Markato," *Journal of Ethiopian Studies,* vol. 5, no. 2, 1967, pp. 103–123.

19. About 5,000 licenses are granted annually, but there are 45,000 peddlers, mostly illegal. W. Mitullah, "Hawking as a Survival Strategy for the Urban Poor in Nairobi: The Case of Women," *Environment and Urbanization,* vol. 3, no. 2, 1991, pp. 13–22.

20. In the five main cities of Tanzania, the percentage of city women working, mostly informally, in 1980 was only 21 percent compared with 80 percent of men. *Women in the Urban Labour Markets in Africa: The Case of Tanzania,* World Bank Working Paper, no. 380, 1980; D. W. Drakakis-Smith, "The Changing Economic Role of Women in the Urbanization Process: A Preliminary Report from Zimbabwe," *International Migration Review,* vol. 18, no. 4, 1984, pp. 1278–1291; A. Sporrek, *Food Marketing and Urban Growth in Dar es Salaam,* Lund, Royal University of Lund, 1985.

21. David Simon, "Urban Poverty, Informal Sector Activity, and Intersectorial Linkages: Evidence from Windhoek, Namibia," *Development and Change,* vol. 15, no. 4, 1984, pp. 551–575.

22. Janet McGaffey, "Gender and Class Formation: Businesswomen in Kisangani," *Entrepreneurs and Parasites: The Struggle for Indigenous Capitalism in Zaire,* Cambridge: Cambridge University Press, 1990, pp. 165–183.

23. In the same way, some Zambian women from the Copperbelt specializing in clandestine beer brewing earn as much at one time as their mining husbands in a month. Jane Parpart, "Class and Gender in the Copper Belt: Women in Northern Rhodesian Copper Mining Communities, 1926–1964," Claire Robertson and Iris Berger, eds., *Women and Class in Africa,* London, Africana, 1986, p. 150; Schuster, "Marginal Lives."

24. Alf Schwarz, "Illusion d'une émancipation et aliénation réelle de l'ouvrière zaïroise," *Canadian Journal of African Studies*, vol. 6, no. 2, 1972, p. 187.

25. *Malams* or marabouts are the literate men of Islam and often travel in their work.

26. Enid Schildkrout, "Dependence and Economy: The Economic Activities of Secluded Hausa Women in Kano," Oppong, *Female and Male in West Africa*, pp. 112–127, and "Age and Gender in Hausa Society: Socio-Economic Roles of Children in Urban Kano," Jean S. La Fontaine, ed., *Sex and Age as Principles of Social Differentiation*, London and New York, Academic Press, 1978, pp. 109–137.

27. This unique kind of savings system provides poor people a not insignificant amount of capital.

28. Catherine Coles, "Hausa Women's Work in a Declining Urban Economy: Kaduna, Nigeria, 1980–1985," in Catherine Coles and Beverley Mack, eds., *Hausa Women in the 20th Century*, Madison, University of Wisconsin Press, pp. 163–191.

Chapter Ten

1. Charles Van Onselen, "The Witches of Suburbia: Domestic Service on the Witwatersrand, 1886–1914," *Studies in the Social and Economic History of the Witwatersrand, 1886–1914*, vol. 2, *New Nineveh*, London, Longman, 1982, p. 3.

2. R. Young, *African Wastes Reclaimed: The Story of the Lovedale Mission*, London, J. M. Dent, 1902, pp. 125–126.

3. I. Berger, "Dependency and Domesticity: Women's Wage Labour 1900–1920," *Threads of Solidarity*, Bloomington, Indiana University Press, pp. 16–45.

4. Van Onselen, *New Nineveh*, pp. 54–60.

5. Caused by the massacre of the Xhosa's cattle in a vast messianic movement that, ironically, forced survivors to emigrate to the city to work for white settlers.

6. The South African Union in 1910 included four states: Cape, Natal, Orange Free State, and Transvaal.

7. At the end of the nineteenth century in 1891, only in the Cape colony were black women the majority of domestics: almost 20,000 (compared with 3,600 female whites) and 8,500 men (of whom 1,200 were white). The arrival en masse of poor whites changed this; the number of household employees exploded, including employment of white women. In 1926, out of 13,000 white domestics, 12,000 were women. *Cape of Good Hope Census, 1891*, Cape Town, W. A. Richards and Sons, 1892, p. 316, and *Census of the European Population, 1926*, Union of South Africa Blue Books, 22–31, pt. 11, "Occupations (Europeans)."

8. There were 14,000 African men compared with 5,000 women in Durban, 1,500 compared with 1,000 in Cape Town, and 7,000 compared with 5,000 in Pretoria but 22,000 of both sexes in Johannesburg and only 1,000 men compared with 4,000 women in Port Elizabeth, 1,000 compared with 6,000 in East London, and 500 compared with 2,000 in Kimberley. Gaitskell et al., "Class, Race and Gender."

9. Ibid.

10. Jacklyn Cock, *Maids and Madams*, Johannesburg, Ravan Press, 1980.

11. Which is still only one-tenth of the minimum salary then called for by the Congress of South African Trade Unions (COSATU), the largest South African trade-union federation.

12. Gugler and Ludwar-Ene, "Plusieurs chemins mènent les femmes en ville."

13. In 1983 the official, greatly underestimated figure for domestics alone (unfortunately not separated by gender) was a little over 45,000. Karen Tranberg Hansen, "Gender and Housing: The Case of Domestic Service in Lusaka, Zambia," *Africa*, vol. 62, no. 2, 1992, pp. 248–265.

14. The Dagara live in southwestern Burkina Faso, near the Côte d'Ivoire border.

Chapter Eleven

1. P. Songue, *Prostitution en Afrique: L'exemple de Yaoundé*, Paris, L'Harmattan, 1986.

2. Francis Simonis, "Splendeurs et misères des moussos: Les compagnes africaines des Européens du cercle de Ségou au Mali (1890–1962)," C. Coquery-Vidrovitch, ed., *Histoire africaine du XXᵉ siècle: Sociétés-villes-cultures*, Paris, L'Harmattan, 1993, p. 209.

3. Called the VSN, "volontaires du service national."

4. C. Van Onselen, "Prostitutes and Proletarians, 1896–1914," *Studies in the Social and Economic History of the Witwatersrand, 1886–1914*, vol. 1, *New Babylon*, London, Longman, 1982, pp. 103–161.

5. Of ninety-seven bordellos, two were in a colored neighborhood, locations for twenty-two were not given, and all the others were in European neighborhoods; 222 full-time prostitutes were recorded, of whom only 48 (a scant 22 percent) were black, 91 white, and 83 colored. Ibid., p. 111.

6. In 1897 only 12 percent were married with their families living with them (mainly white salaried workers); this percentage rose to 42 percent in 1912.

7. Bujra, "Women 'Entrepreneurs' of Early Nairobi"; Luise White, *The Comforts of Home*, Chicago, University of Chicago Press, 1990.

8. Janet M. Bujra, "Production, Property, Prostitution: 'Sexual Politics' in Atu," *Cahiers d'Etudes Africaines*, vol. 17, no. 1, 1977, pp. 13–40.

9. Ronald Hyam, "Empire and Sexual Opportunity," *Journal of Imperial and Commonwealth History*, vol. 14, no. 2, 1986, p. 36.

10. Okonjo, "Sex Roles in Nigerian Politics."

11. "Combien tu m'offres?" Renée Pittin, "Migration of Women in Nigeria: The Hausa Case," *International Migration Review*, vol. 18, no. 4, p. 1301.

12. Pons, op. cit., p. 219.

13. Jean La Fontaine, "The Free Women of Kinshasa: Prostitution in a City in Zaire," J. Davis, ed., *Choice and Change: Essays in Honour of Lucy Mair*, London, Athlone Press, 1974, p. 99.

14. J. Maquet, *The Premise of Inequality in Ruanda*, Oxford, Oxford University Press and IAI, 1969, p. 78; J. Beattie, *The Nyoro State*, Oxford, Oxford University Press, 1971, p. 144.

15. Title of a work by Georges Balandier (*Sociologie des Brazzavilles noires*, Paris, A. Colin, 1955).

16. Manijke Vandersypen, "Les femmes libres de Kigali," *Cahiers d'Etudes Africaines*, vol. 17, no. 65, 1967, pp. 95–120.

17. The Belgians imposed monogamy, although several kinds of marriage—civil, religious, and "customary" (supposedly traditional)—were recognized. Monogamy was required, for example, to qualify for a loan for construction or to buy a parcel of land or a house. Family assistance, health insurance, and pensions were allowed only for the sole legal wife. La Fontaine, op. cit., pp. 89–113.

18. A term from Songue, op. cit.

19. Schwarz, op. cit., pp. 196–197.

20. Naanen, "Itinerant Gold Mines."

21. In 1985, as the pimping trials of the past ten years in Abidjan attest. K. Goli, *La prostitution en Afrique: Un cas, Abidjan,* Abidjan, Les Nouvelles Editions Africaines, 1986. The work is especially well researched because Goli was police commissioner of Abidjan.

Chapter Twelve

1. See Simonis, *Les Français à Ségou.*

2. In the case of a Kinshasa textile mill, 91 percent of women were not or no longer officially married; 45 percent were unlucky former market women, 72 percent had been prostitutes, and 85 percent were permanent partners of men and teenage mothers responsible for 178 natural children at the time of the study. Schwarz, op. cit., pp. 195 and 204.

3. Excerpted from interviews gathered in Kinshasa in 1965. Schwarz, op. cit., pp. 202–203.

4. Boserup, *Women's Role in Economic Development.*

5. In 1981 the maximum was 31 percent of female salaried workers in Liberia (a high figure no doubt due to the very particular history of this country of creolized emigrants from the United States) and 28 percent in Swaziland, but it dropped to 22 percent in Botswana, 16.9 percent in Kenya and Zimbabwe, 11.2 percent in Mali, and less than 10 percent elsewhere. The percentage of factory workers was much lower: 23.4 percent in Swaziland and 18 percent in Botswana but only 13.4 percent in Liberia, 11.3 percent in Mali, 8.5 percent in Kenya, 7.2 percent in Zimbabwe, and less than 6 percent everywhere else. Statistics come from the International Labour Organisation. See J. M. Bujra, "Urging Women to Redouble Their Efforts: Class, Gender, and Capitalist Transformation in Africa," Robertson and Berger, *Women and Class in Africa,* pp. 117–140.

6. Interviews collected by Jan Vansina in Congo.

7. In 1924 one-fourth of Ngoni adult men were absent from their villages. Deborah Fayi Bryceson, "The Proletarianization of Women in Tanzania," *Review of African Political Economy,* no. 17, 1980, pp. 4–27.

8. In Tanzania, women went from being 7 percent of all salaried workers in 1969 to 9 percent in 1974. Ibid., p. 20. Malawi had the most female agricultural salaried workers, with almost one-third of women (29 percent), according to the International Labour Organisation, 1981.

9. An amendment to the Natives' Urban Act of 1923. Berger, *Threads of Solidarity,* chap. 3. From the 1950s on, apartheid prohibited blacks from sleeping in white neighborhoods without special authorization. Exceptions were made for domestics

on the condition that they did not sleep under the same roof. The nationalists, who were as narrow-minded as they were well-organized, created lean-tos attached to houses with a break in the roofline to respect this law, which of course did not improve living conditions for their personnel of color (personal survey).

10. Fifteen shillings weekly in the textile industry. *Guardian,* February 27, 1941.

11. Berger, *Threads of Solidarity,* pp. 230–231.

12. A study of East London shows that two-fifths of women born in the city were heads of families, of whom a fourth were unmarried mothers. In the Eastern Bantu Township (an old Johannesburg suburb) up to 41 percent of women were heads of households. Berger, *Threads of Solidarity,* p. 226.

13. Section 10 of the Urban Area Act prohibited Africans regardless of gender from being in the city for more than seventy-two hours unless they belonged to one of four well-defined categories of birth, length of residency, and length of time with the same employer.

14. Joanne Yawitch, "The Incorporation of African Women into Wage Labour, 1960–1980," *South African Labour Bulletin,* vol. 9, no. 3, 1983, pp. 85–86.

15. The total of Asian or colored active workers only doubled and the percentage of white women workers dropped by half (agricultural workers were counted no longer as "workers" but as "housewives"). Gertruida Prekel, "Black Women at Work, Progress Despite Problems," *South African Labour Bulletin,* vol. 6, no. 3–4, 1982, pp. 65–82.

16. Being banished meant being barred from any meeting of more than two persons and outlawed by society.

17. The *Report on the Commission of Inquiry into Labor Legislation* by the Wiehahn Commission (Pretoria, 1981) called for an end to sex discrimination in salaries and for job security in the event of pregnancy, among other things.

18. An hourly wage of 42 shillings for men and 32 shillings for women.

19. Two-thirds of women workers (63 percent) are independent women, most often heads of families, although they represent only one-fourth of working women aged fifteen to fifty-four years old in Dar es Salaam.

20. Thirty-five percent of women workers were born in Kinshasa compared with only 2.3 percent of men in 1958 and 3.6 percent in 1966. More than one-third of the female workers questioned (162) had arrived in the capital when they were younger than ten. Most were cut off from their rural roots; almost half had never left Kinshasa and 16 percent had been to the village just once, with 6 percent maintaining continuous contact. Schwarz, op. cit., pp. 191–193.

21. Elementary form 7.

22. Nine hundred out of 1,260.

23. In the same way, the Kenya Cashew Nuts Company appreciates its female workers, who are "more careful and faster than the men." Bujra, "Urging Women to Redouble Their Efforts," p. 132.

24. Fairly expensive because it represents up to a fifth of their own salary, 40–60 shillings compared with 300 shillings.

25. "Mimi ni bendera nafuata upepo." Bryceson, "The Proletarianization of Women in Tanzania."

26. The women were younger than the men; 70 percent were under twenty-five. Carolyn Dennis, "Capitalist Development and Women's Work: A Nigerian Case Study," *Review of African Political Economy*, nos. 27–28, 1984, pp. 109–119.

27. Forty-three percent of men and 33 percent of women had been to secondary school. Only among the men was a tiny minority of illiterates found (1 percent).

28. Renée Pittin, "Gender and Class in a Nigerian Industrial Setting," *Review of African Political Economy*, no. 31, 1984, pp. 70–81.

Chapter Thirteen

1. Benoît Verhaegen, "La famille urbaine face à la polygamie et la prostitution," in C. Coquery-Vidrovitch, *Processus d'urbanisation en Afrique*, pp. 124–130, and *Femmes zaïroises de Kisangani*, Paris, L'Harmattan, 1992.

2. R. Bonnardel, "Saint-Louis du Sénégal: Le règne des femmes dans les petites activités," C. Coquery-Vidrovitch, *Processus d'urbanisation en Afrique*, pp. 150–168, and C. Coquery-Vidrovitch, *Saint-Louis du Sénégal*, op. cit.

Chapter Fourteen

1. As it was, for example, among the Haya of northwestern Tanzania, on the edge of Lake Victoria. See Larsson, *Conversion to Greater Freedom?*

2. At independence, 77 percent of Congolese students (a total of 1.6 million) were in Catholic schools, compared with 19 percent in Protestant and only 4 percent in secular ones.

3. Regarding all this, see Barbara A. Yates, "Colonialism, Education, and Work: Sex Differentiation in Colonial Zaire," Bay, *Women and Work in Africa*, pp. 127–152.

4. Simonis, *Les Français à Ségou*, citing the Ségou mission diary.

5. Fewer than 1,000 girls out of 29,000 high-school students, or less than 1.5 percent of school-age girls (fifteen to nineteen years old, school ages in Africa usually being older than in the West).

6. There were 350,000 girls in primary school and fewer than 10,000 everywhere else; 430 were divided among seven "female" vocational schools, 350 among sixteen hospital schools, and 200 in secondary schools, mostly in Leopoldville and Elisabethville.

7. Compared with 136 male health assistants, 250 agronomist's assistants, and 15 veterinary assistants.

8. See Chapter 11.

9. Methodist missions in 1844 had enrolled 2,500 girls compared with only some 1,900 boys. In 1851 there were 9,800 boys and 9,275 girls in the Cape colony, and in 1930 there were almost 80,000 educated African girls compared with almost 60,000 boys. Only at the turn of World War II was the percentage briefly reversed by efforts to promote education generally. J. Cock, *Maids and Madams*, chap. 8, "Education for Domesticity."

10. Cherryl Walker, *Women and Resistance in South Africa*, Cambridge, Mass., Onyx Press, 1982, p. 161.

11. There were 280,000 white girls compared with 305,000 boys at the beginning of college but 21,000 white girls with B.A.'s compared with 52,000 boys, 1,253 girls with Master's degrees compared with 6,156 boys, and 334 female Ph.D.'s compared with 3,335 male. *Population Census*, 1970, cited by Cock, *Maids and Madams*.

12. There were 116,000 compared with 98,000 boys in class 1 (the youngest) and 26,000 compared with 24,000 in class 3 but less than 8,000 compared with 11,000 in class 4 and 3,300 compared with 5,700 in class 5. *Blue Book*, 1977, cited by Cock, *Maids and Madams*.

13. Shula Marks, ed., *Not Either an Experimental Doll*, Bloomington and Indianapolis: Indiana University Press, 1987.

14. A declaration by an Afrikaner member of parliament, quoted in the *Eastern Province Herald*, June 2, 1977. Although this is certainly an exaggeration, this is not to say that pregnancy rates in black South African schools are not extremely high, contraceptive use being neither taught nor available to young people.

15. In 1841 the Lovedale seminary (founded by Scots Presbyterians) had twenty boy students, eleven African and nine white.

16. Since the end of the nineteenth century: 66 in 1873, 67 in 1883, 137 in 1893, 156 in 1903, 210 in 1923, and 281 in 1939, these last two figures including nursing students. Cock, *Maids and Madams*.

17. This latter, created in 1853, was exclusively for vocational training and trained girls only for household tasks. In 1856 alone, girls at the school produced six hundred pieces of needlework.

18. From the end of the nineteenth century on, the inhabitants of Saint-Louis and Gorée and then of Rufisque and Dakar could elect representatives to the French parliament. This right, limited to the colonies of the old regime, was ratified in 1916 by giving their inhabitants French nationality. The latter was negotiated by Blaise Diagne (the first black deputy, elected in Dakar in 1914) in exchange for his active assistance in recruiting black soldiers in the countryside, which was a protectorate.

19. A girl had to have a father who was himself educated. M. J. Mbilinyi, "The 'New Woman' and Traditional Norms in Tanzania," *Journal of Modern African Studies*, vol. 10, no. 1, 1972, pp. 79–81.

20. Claude Rivière, "La promotion de la femme guinéenne," *Cahiers d'Etudes Africaines*, vol. 8-3, no. 31, 1968, pp. 406–427.

21. Seventeen mothers out of a hundred had been to primary school, and ten had had some secondary education. Diana L. Barthel, "The Rise of a Female Professional Elite: The Case of Senegal," *African Studies Review*, vol. 18, no. 3, 1975, pp. 1–15.

22. In 1961, out of 600,000 children in school only 38 percent were girls. Lois Weis, "Some Problems of Assessing Change: Women and Education in Ghana," *International Journal of Women's Studies*, vol. 3, no. 5, 1980, pp. 431–453.

23. Sir Akitoye Ajasa was a Saro (descended from a freed slave from Sierra Leone) from Dahomey, a member of the long-lived Christian elite, an intimate friend of Lord Lugard, and the publisher of the journal *The Nigerian Pioneer*. He was viewed as a conservative. Cheryl Johnson, "Grass Roots Organizing: Women in Anticolonial Activity in Southwestern Nigeria," *African Studies Review*, vol. 25, nos. 2 and 3, 1982, pp. 137–157.

24. There were 1,599 girls—only 125 in the north, 477 in the east, and 997 in the west (i.e., for these last two regions, infinitely fewer than the demand). Cheryl John-

son, "Class and Gender: A Consideration of Yoruba Women During the Colonial Period," Robertson and Berger, *Women and Class in Africa*, pp. 237–253.

25. Freetown was created in 1786 on Granville Sharp's utopian notion of freed blacks' returning from Britain, Canada, and the Caribbean. It became a crown colony in 1807. This first group, to which was added blacks freed by antislavery British groups throughout the nineteenth century, gave birth to a language, Krio, a product of this mixed cultural origin.

26. The Maroons were fugitive slaves from the Caribbean. Some well-organized Maroon groups were sent to join in the creation of Freetown.

27. Adelaide M. Cromwell, *An African Victorian Feminist: The Life and Times of Adelaide Smith Caseley Hayford, 1868–1960*, London, Frank Cass, 1986.

28. Johnson, "Class and Gender."

29. Ten shillings for the first two classes of elementary school but £1 for classes 1 to 4, £6 for class 5, and £8 for class 6. Mba, op. cit., pp. 118–134.

30. Schildkrout, "Dependence and Economy."

31. In Tanzania in 1970, the illiteracy of women, always very high, varied considerably by age: 90 percent of women aged thirty to thirty-four compared with 58 percent of men of that age-group had never been to school and still 79 percent compared with 46 percent of men in the twenty- to twenty-four-year-old age-range. The ratio in primary school remained much in boys' favor: 1.55 boys to each girl. Mbilinyi, "The 'New Woman,'" p. 63.

32. Rivière, "La promotion de la femme guinéenne," pp. 426–427.

33. Claire Robertson, "Women's Education and Class Formation in Africa, 1950–1980," Robertson and Berger, *Women and Class in Africa*, p. 97.

34. Overall, 88.5 percent of women were illiterate in 1960, 82.4 percent in 1970, and still 72.8 percent in 1980, compared respectively with 73.4 percent, 58.3 percent, and 48 percent of men.

35. In 1918 her younger brother left on the first civilian ship for school in France. This story was told me by Mme. Diop in 1975.

36. Esther Ogunmodede, *New African*, April 1983.

37. Bujra, "Women 'Entrepreneurs,'" p. 136.

38. Between 1957 and 1965 240,000 jobs were counted in Uganda, and the figure slowly rose only to 257,000 in 1967 with a population of 8.5 million. The only women present in numbers worth analyzing were in the health sector (75–90 percent of nursing personnel, according to educational level), teaching, and administration, with women holding 17 percent of jobs in these three sectors (8,500 out of 51,000); 30 percent of them were teachers (more than honorable at the time in Africa) and 27 percent low-level typists but only 8 percent telephone operators at a level slightly higher. David R. Evans, "Image and Reality: Career Goals of Educated Ugandan Women," *Canadian Journal of African Studies*, vol. 6, no. 2, 1972, pp. 213–232.

39. The survey was done in the six secondary schools for girls, and at least half of the students responded. Ibid.

40. See Chapter 15.

41. Judith Van Allen, "Memsahib, *militante, femme libre*: Political and Apolitical Styles of Modern African Women," Jane S. Jaquette, ed., *Women in Politics*, London, Wiley, 1974, pp. 304–321.

42. Aoua Keita, *Femme d'Afrique*, Paris, Présence Africaine, 1975. See Chapter 15.

Chapter Fifteen

1. Thirteen percent of Lagos market women were Igbo in 1921.

2. See Catherine Coquery-Vidrovitch, *Africa South of the Sahara: Endurance and Change,* Berkeley, University of California Press, 1988.

3. Counting, which is almost reflexive in the West, is in Africa considered a bad omen. Thus one never gives the precise number or age of one's children for fear of provoking the dangerous powers that might cause some of them to disappear.

4. Mba, op. cit., p. 91.

5. The finance law of April 1956 in the southeastern provinces exempted farming women and market women in rural areas but required the taxation of city women and all salaried women workers earning more than £100 a year. Mba, op. cit., p. 102.

6. The taxable minimum was raised, and children over sixteen were deductible.

7. As a child, Wole Soyinka was touched by Yoruba women's poverty and resistance to the tax (see above), and swore to himself, "When I am grown, no khaki-clad civil servant will get a single shilling in taxes from my hard-earned salary." *Ake: The Years of Childhood,* New York, Random House, 1981. The colonial era made it very hard for people to think of the state as representing public welfare.

8. Cited in Mba, op. cit., p. 205. Her funeral procession in 1951 was followed by 25,000 people, among them all the market women, the markets having been closed for the occasion.

9. The *ilu* was the urban Yoruba community.

10. G. O. Olusanya, *The Second World War and Politics in Nigeria, 1939–1953,* Lagos, University of Lagos/Evans Brothers, 1973, pp. 64–65.

11. Mrs. Obasa answered in 1924 that the "age is now past when a maternity hospital should be considered a luxury" (quoted in Mba, op. cit., p. 216). Mrs. Obasa was the daughter of a large-scale Sierra Leonean businessman, Richard Blaize, who came to Lagos in 1862 and became printer to the government. Like her mother, Mrs. Obasa had completed her education in England. In 1908 she married the founder of the first Nigerian political party, the People's Union, created to fight water taxes. Mba, op. cit., pp. 219–220.

12. The population of Lagos was about 100,000 in 1921, in an era in which the male/female ratio was already very slightly in favor of women. In 1963 there were almost 190,000 women in Lagos.

13. See the party's constitution, cited in Mba, op. cit., p. 222.

14. Very limited voting rights had begun to be accorded Lagos men over twenty-one who owned property valued at more than £225 or rented at more than £15 per year, but it was only in 1949 that the right to vote (also based on property) was first extended citywide to some women in Port Harcourt. The Lagos council was elected by universal franchise (i.e., with women voting) starting in 1950. Later, women in the south received the right to vote if they paid the tax (from which they were generally exempted). In the eastern region, the universal franchise was established in 1954 by federal elections. It spread throughout the south in 1959, but in the north it continued to be only men who paid the tax who had the right to vote.

15. That is, a slave off a ship stopped by the antislave-trade squad. These Christian ex-Sierra Leoneans who had returned were called Saros in Nigeria.

16. Reverend I. O. Ransome-Kuti attended the Abeokuta high school (where he became headmaster during World War II) in the year it began, 1908. He himself was a militant nationalist. In 1931 he helped to found the multiethnic Nigerian Teachers' Union, and in Abeokuta he led the regional section of the Nigerian Youth Movement. Johnson, "Grass Roots Organizing." Also see Mba, op. cit., chap. 5.

17. First in Ijebu-Ode, not far from Abeokuta, where she lived after her marriage in 1925. Wole Soyinka tells in very lively fashion how her initiative, which started in an informal way with a suggestion from Reverend Ransome, enjoyed renewed popularity during World War II, once the "women in dresses" (bourgeois women) understood the importance of solidarity with the "women in cloth" (working-class women, farmers, and market women). As a boy of about ten, Soyinka himself, just before entering Ibadan's national high school, participated in a women's literacy program. Soyinka, *Ake,* pp. 245–305.

18. Soyinka's father directed an Anglican mission school, and his mother was an Abeokuta market woman who had a shop not far from the palace. He called her "wild Christian," although she was one of the more moderate of the women behind the movement. Soyinka's first-person perspective beautifully complements research on the subject.

19. Soyinka, *Ake,* p. 211.

20. Ibid., p. 223.

21. Quoted by Mba, op. cit., pp. 150 and 153. Two hundred eighteen songs of this kind have been counted in the Kuti archives.

22. In November 1950 of the following year, despite the AWU's hostility, Ademola was brought back again by a narrow majority on the condition that he respect a constitutionally elected government. The Abeokuta council membership was increased by at least a third, but of its fifty-two elected members the number of women remained stable at four. Their presence on the regional council was even disapproved by the majority of non-city-dwelling Egba, which demonstrates the existence of a fundamental gendered division in the sharing of power.

23. The 1951 constitution established regional legislative assemblies and a national electoral system founded on male suffrage qualified by property. In theory, only men who paid the tax could vote, but gradually, as we have seen (n. 14), there were salutary lapses. The constitutional congress of 1958 forecast universal suffrage except for women in the north, where the Northern People's Congress, including the female head of the party's women's section, resolutely opposed it. It was not until 1977 that northern women were allowed to vote.

24. In 1963 Mrs. Kuti and Mrs. Ekpo went to the World Women's Congress in Moscow.

25. During the war she was adjunct price inspector and was regularly featured in the newpapers of Nnamdi Azikiwe (the NCNC) and of Chief Obafemi Awolowo (the Action Group). She joined the NCNC in about 1950. Mba, op. cit. p. 181.

26. Several women, including Mrs. Ekpo, were, however, elected to the executive committee. Regional women officers began to appear in 1961.

27. See Chapter 14.

28. Named by the government of the western province.

29. Mrs. Alaga, born in 1907, began on a small scale. In 1932 she was the first woman to open a shop in Ibadan. Although she was illiterate, she supervised some 150 retailers and employed a large staff.

30. Little, *African Women in Town*, p. 212.

31. See Chapter 14; see LaRay Denzer, "Women in Freetown Politics, 1914–61," *Africa*, vol. 57, no. 4, pp. 438–456.

32. *Sierra Leone Weekly News*, January 27, 1923, cited in Denzer, op. cit., p. 441.

33. Those who paid income tax or owned property.

34. Messam Aduayom, "Un prélude au nationalisme togolais: La révolte de Lomé, 24–25 janvier 1933," *Cahiers d'Etudes Africaines*, vol. 24, no. 93, 1984, pp. 39–50; S. d'Almeida-Ekoué, *La révolte des Loméennes, 24–25 janvier, 1933*, Lomé, Les Nouvelles Editions Africaines du Togo, 1992.

35. Jane Parpart, *Working-Class Wives and Collective Labor Action in the Northern Rhodesian Copperbelt, 1926–1964*, Boston, African Studies Center, Boston University, 1985.

36. One was let go because of her youth; the other three were sentenced to two months in prison on December 28. H. Diabaté, *La marche des femmes sur Grand-Bassam*, Dakar, Les Nouvelles Editions Africaines, 1975.

37. Her father was born in Kouroussa, Guinea, and her mother was a Diula from northern Côte d'Ivoire.

38. Keita, *Femme d'Afrique*, p. 32. I was aided in my analysis by my graduate students, especially by the paper written by Nathalie Saint-Marc, Université de Paris-7. Also see J. Turrittin, "Aoua Keita and the Nascent Women's Movement in the French Sudan," *African Studies Review*, vol. 36, no. 1, 1993, pp. 39–99.

39. Diawara later had two young co-wives.

40. She later remarried Mahamane Alassane Haidara, who in 1942 was elected senator to the French National Assembly to represent the people of the upper bend of the Niger River. He remained senator until 1959.

41. Keita, *Femme d'Afrique*, p. 121. Some have remarked that the art of electoral fraud, widespread in independent Africa, was learned from earlier masters.

42. Keita, *Femme d'Afrique*, p. 161.

43. This was the abortive federation attempted between Senegal and the French Sudan, which became the Republic of Mali in 1960.

44. Keita, *Femme d'Afrique*, p. 113.

45. Danielle Bazin-Tardieu, *Femmes du Mali*, Ottawa, Léméac, 1975.

46. Cited by Rivière, "La promotion de la femme guinéenne," p. 408, and Claude Rivière, *Mutations sociales en Guinée*, Paris, M. Rivière, 1971.

47. See Chapter 18.

Chapter Sixteen

1. Joseph-Desiré Mobutu, speech to the Third Congress of the Mouvement Populaire de la Révolution, December 1982. Katherine Newbury, "*Ebutumwa bw'emiogo*, the Tyranny of Cassava: A Women's Tax Revolt in Eastern Zaire," *Canadian Journal of African Studies*, vol. 18, no. 1, 1984, p. 53.

2. Ludo Martens, *Une femme du Congo*, Brussels, Editions Presses Ouvrières, 1991.

Chapter Seventeen

1. What Afrikaners still refer to as "race."

2. See Penelope Hetherington, "Women in South Africa: The Historiography in English," *International Journal of African Historical Studies*, vol. 26, no. 2, 1993, pp. 241–269.

3. The two groups together (both colored and Asian, because the law distinguished between them) made up about 30 percent of the total population.

4. See Berger, *Threads of Solidarity;* Bettie du Toit, *Ukubamba Amadolo: Workers' Struggles in the South African Textile Industry,* London, Onyx Press, 1978; Dave Kaplan, ed., *Women and Squatters in the Western Cape: The Vigilance Committee of the Garment Workers' Union, 1940–1943,* Randebosch, South Africa, University of Cape Town, 1986; and *Housing, Hotels, and Women Garment Workers in the Western Cape and the South African Peace Council, 1951–1956,* Randebosch, South Africa, University of Cape Town, 1984.

5. In 1924–1925 there were only 709 African women factory workers out of a total of 15,000 women working in the industry, or less than 5 percent. With very rough figures of course being much higher, the percentage of African women working in factories remained very low until after 1970: 1 percent of the workforce in 1946, 2 percent in 1960, and 7 percent in 1970. Walker, *Women and Resistance in South Africa,* pp. 58, 127.

6. About 147,000 women. The percentage rose to a little over 10 percent in 1936.

7. On Tomana, see interviews conducted by Walker, *Women and Resistance in South Africa,* p. 12. On Ntantala, see *A Life's Mosaic: The Autobiography of Phyllis Ntantala,* Berkeley, University of California Press, 1992.

8. Bozzoli, *Women of Phokeng.*

9. She even spoke in public in 1921 at the invitation of a white suffragettes' club in Pretoria, the Women's Reform Club. This was probably the only time that such a thing happened. Walker, *Women and Resistance in South Africa,* p. 38.

10. Palmer called herself "colored" but was married to a black man and lived in the African neighborhood.

11. Josette Cole, *Crossroads: The Politics of Reform and Repression, 1976–1986,* Johannesburg, Ravan Press, 1987.

12. The first president was a black American woman, Madie Hall-Xuma, the wife of the president of the ANC at the time and full of an Anglo-Saxon-style feminism based more on morals than on politics, with many socially conservative elements.

13. Walker, *Women and Resistance in South Africa,* pp. 115–122.

14. Unregistered unions were not necessarily forbidden but were very vulnerable because they were merely tolerated.

15. South African society is reported to be one of the most sexist in the world. It was not until 1953 that "Bertha's Bill," freeing white wives from measures making them legal minors in relation to their husbands, barely survived a vote by members of parliament (all but three male).

16. See Cora Ann Presley on the women of this 1950s Kenyan rebellion: *Kikuyu Women, the Mau Mau Rebellion, and Social Change in Kenya,* Boulder, Westview Press, 1992.

17. In 1956 almost 50,000 women were members of about six hundred clubs.

18. Stephanie Urdang, *Fighting Two Colonialisms,* New York: Monthly Review Press, 1979.

19. The law recognizes the legality of traditional marriage (which means that a man married traditionally must divorce if he wants to get rid of his wife) and gives children born outside the marriage the same rights as legitimate children (which prevents the father from ignoring them).

20. Cited by Van Allen, "Memsahib, *militante, femme libre,* " p. 315.

21. In the early part of the century, in the war of near-extermination against the Herero led by the Germans, women instituted a Lysistrata-style resistance to force their husbands to take up arms against the colonizers and then for a long time refused to serve as nannies to the white settlers. Tessa Cleaver and Marion Wallace, *Namibia Women in War,* London, Zed Books, 1990, pp. 80–82.

22. SWAPO, *To Be Born a Nation,* London, Zed Press, 1981, p. 291.

Chapter Eighteen

1. Dupire, "The Position of Women in a Pastoral Society," p. 57.

2. As we have already seen with regard to young Tswana women in Chapter 1.

3. Dupire, op. cit., p. 61.

4. Monique Gessain, "Femmes Coniagui (Guinée)," Paulme, *Femmes d'Afrique Noire,* pp. 30–35.

5. The anthropologist invited in 1931 to watch these ceremonies warns us that, for one thing, the rituals that took place over a month had been greatly shortened (according to the women they had once lasted six months). At the same time, the fact that a European woman was watching incited the group to add to what it usually did and emphasize aspects that were dying out because of constant battles with colonial authorities and missionaries. Finally, despite the women's obvious goodwill, the researcher did not observe everything. She did not join the girls secluded in the forest, an important part of the ritual. What exactly happened there? A. Richards, *Chisungu: A Girl's Initiation Ceremony Among the Bemba of Zambia,* 2nd edition, London, Tavistock, 1982 (1st edition, 1956).

6. Richards, op. cit., p. 45.

7. But seclusion was then only two or three months long instead of a year or more.

8. Larsson, *Conversion to Greater Freedom?* pp. 57–70.

9. Robert LeVine and Barbara A. LeVine, *Nyansongo: A Gusii Community in Kenya,* New York, Wiley, 1966, p. 54.

10. As we have seen in Chapter 1.

11. See Booth, " 'European Courts Protect Women.' "

12. Survey by P. Henry in 1964 of 522 students in the upper grades of a mixed high school, published as *La sexualité en Guinée* by Editions Berger-Levrault.

13. But this custom applied only to first marriages, not to remarried divorced women. Raqiya Abdalla, *Sisters in Affliction,* London, Zed Press, 1982.

14. In addition to Esther K. Hicks, *Infibulation,* London, Transaction Publishers, 1993, and Fran P. Hosken, *The Hosken Report,* Lexington, Mass., Women's International Network News, ca. 1993, I was helped by research by Claire Lamb, graduate

student in history at Princeton University, and Edvige Bilotti, graduate student in sociology at Binghamton University in 1992 and 1993.

15. Thus the gladiator avoided wasting his strength, the young virgin was worth more, and the male domestic slave could not impregnate his female partners (or, more likely, sin with the lady of the house). Infibulation was also reputed to protect male actors' and singers' voices. Hosken, *The Hosken Report.*

16. Ariane Deluz, "Social and Symbolic Values of Feminine Kne Initiation Among the Guro of the Ivory Coast," D. Parkin and D. Nyamwaya, eds., *Transformations in African Marriage,* Manchester, Manchester University Press, 1987, pp. 113–115.

17. Lilian P. Sanderson, *Against the Mutilation of Women,* London, Ithaca Press, 1981, p. 29.

18. Hanny Lightfoot-Klein, "Pharaonic Circumcision of Females in the Sudan," *Medicine and Law,* vol. 2, 1983, pp. 353–360.

19. The Egyptian Feminist Union was founded in 1920 by Hoda Shaarawi.

20. Quoted by Bilotti, op. cit., pp. 44–45.

21. Custom held that the disobedient young woman would die in her first labor. This was unfortunately the heroine's fate. Ironically, her struggle for freedom was undermined by the story's upholding traditional beliefs.

22. See, for example, Paulme, *Women of Tropical Africa;* Marie-José Tubiana, *Des troupeaux et des femmes,* Paris, L'Harmattan, 1985; Adam Kuper, *Wives for Cattle,* London, Routledge and Kegan Paul, 1982.

23. Diop, *La famille wolof,* p. 112.

24. Thérèse Locoh, *Fécondité et famille en Afrique de l'ouest: Le Togo méridional contemporain,* Paris, Presses Universitaires de France, 1985, p. 70.

25. There are midseventeenth-century reports of a great number of oxen and goats. Already in 1905, a council of officials had set up a fee schedule to combat rising prices. Diop, *La famille wolof,* pp. 112–113.

26. Which are quite far-reaching—the boy being forbidden female descendants of each of his four grandparents and the direct exchange of sisters being prohibited. Elisabeth Copet-Rougier, "L'antilope accouche toujours de l'eléphant: Etude de la transformation du mariage chez les Mkako du Cameroun," Parkin and Nyamwaya, op. cit., pp. 75–92.

27. In Senegal the price remains high. The total cost of required marriage gifts is often over 2,000 CFA francs in rural areas, where the annual average salary of a peasant in 1985 was around 80,000 francs (100 CFA francs were worth 2 French francs until January 1994 and 1 franc thereafter). Family laws limiting the cost of the gifts are hardly followed. In Cameroon, Mkako bride-prices in 1973 were around 15,000 francs, whereas income from tobacco might amount to only 38,000 francs per year. This was still better than for their nearest neighbors, whose bride-prices might reach 80,000 or 100,000 francs. Across Africa one finds every gradation along a spectrum of variables that include the society's kinship system, development level, and position of women.

28. See Wambui Wa Karanja, "Outside Wives and Inside Wives in Nigeria: A Study of Changing Perceptions in Marriage," Parkin and Nyamwaya, op. cit., pp. 247–262.

29. Diop, *La famille wolof.*

30. *Xhala* in Wolof means "impotent," and the hero becomes so and is the laughingstock of the neighborhood. The novelist made an excellent film from his book.

31. "Mali: La part des femmes," *Géopolis*, France 2 (television channel), October 16, 1993.

32. Filomena Chioma Steady, "Polygamy and the Household Economy in a Fishing Village in Sierra Leone," Parkin and Nyamwaya, op. cit., pp. 211–232.

33. The same shift toward divorce is happening in the Temne village mentioned above, where wives' faithfulness is a strict requirement and some wives try to escape this constraint.

34. I. M. Lewis, "Foreword," Parkin and Nyamwaya, op. cit., p. xiv.

35. Yves Charbit, Lamine Gueye, and Salif Ndiaye, eds., *Nuptialité et fécondité au Sénégal*, Paris, Presses Universitaires de France, 1985, pp. 59–72.

36. Of 380 civil trials listed in Lagos, a survey of 1885, 1895, and 1905 revealed only 4 that concerned domestic trouble of this kind. Kristin Mann, "Women's Rights in Law and Practice: Marriage and Dispute Settlement in Colonial Lagos," Hay and Wright, op. cit., pp. 151–171.

37. Marc Dumetz, *Le droit du mariage en Côte d'Ivoire*, Paris, Libraire Générale de Droit et de Jurisprudence, 1975; Mamadou Niang, "L'évolution du statut juridique, politique et social de la femme en Afrique traditionnelle et moderne," *Bulletin de l'IFAN-B*, vol. 38, no. 1, 1976, pp. 32–66.

38. Vléï, "Le travail salarié des femmes à Abidjan 1946–1986."

39. Rivière, "La promotion de la femme guinéenne."

40. The Senegalese legal code outlaws repudiation and authorizes separation only through a divorce awarded by the court.

41. *The Standard*, Dar Es Salaam, January 22, 1971, cited in Mbilinyi, "The 'New Woman,'" p. 67.

42. As in Western societies, the requirement of virginity has practically disappeared in every society, either discreetly (among the Wolof and Hausa) or in very open fashion (for example, among the Yoruba and the Ganda). Girls' freedom increased especially during the 1950s, when many began to go to school and when they discovered that they could use the courts to defend themselves as men did. See Nicole Echard, "De la prohibition à la prescription: Sens et non-sens de la virginité des filles (Afrique de l'ouest)," N. Echard, ed., *La première fois: Le roman de la virginité à travers les siècles et les continents*, Paris, Ramsay, 1981, pp. 337–395.

43. See Jeater, *Marriage, Perversion, and Power*.

44. The survey was done about fifteen years ago. Barbara E. Harrell-Bond, *Modern Marriage in Sierra Leone*, Paris/The Hague, Mouton, 1976. So many illegitimate births gave rise in 1965 to an unsuccessful attempt to have the rights of these children recognized equally with the rights of legitimate children. Such equality was imposed by Sékou Touré in Guinea in the early 1960s and passed in 1979 in Nigeria, to the great chagrin of the women's associations, whose members were mainly legitimate wives. Fear of inheritance quarrels caused men to accept and even encourage contraceptive use by their girlfriends.

45. Men have, however, practiced coitus interruptus for a long time among the Ganda and in the Bas-Zaire region, where apparently 30 percent of men do so. Dominique Tabutin, ed., *Population et sociétés en Afrique au Sud du Sahara*, Paris, L'Harmattan, 1988, pp. 156–160.

46. There is a heartrending description of the experience of polygamy in S. Fainzang and O. Journet, *La femme de mon mari*, Paris, L'Harmattan, 1988.

47. Christine Obbo, "The Old and the New in East African Elite Marriage," Parkin and Nyamwaya, op. cit., pp. 263–282.

48. The social weight of traditional structures and the historical differentiation between free people, low-caste people (usually artisans), and slaves, especially in Sahelian societies (including Senegal), can still be very strong and discourages mixed alliances.

49. Karanja, op. cit.

50. Max Gluckman, "Kinship and Marriage Among the Lozi of Northern Rhodesia and Zulus of Natal," A. R. Radcliffe-Brown and D. Forde, eds., *African Systems of Kinship and Marriage*, London, Oxford University Press, 1967, pp. 252–254.

51. Martine Quéchon, "L'instabilité matrimoniale chez les Foulbé du Diamaré," Barbier, *Femmes du Cameroun*, pp. 299–312.

52. Françoise Le Guennec-Coppens, "L'instabilité conjugale et ses conséquences dans la société Swahili de Lamu," Parkin and Nyamwaya, op. cit., pp. 233–245.

53. The husband is also supposed to buy most of the wife's and the children's clothing.

54. Diop, *La famille wolof*, chap. 8.

55. Laurence Jolfre, "La condition féminine en Côte d'Ivoire à travers les médias, 1951–1970," D.E.A. thesis, Université Paris 12, 1992.

56. Forty-seven percent of men aged fifty to fifty-nine are polygamous. Locoh, op. cit., p. 77.

57. Mikell, "Using the Courts to Obtain Relief."

58. Taking urbanization into account cuts the literacy factor in half. Charbit, Gueye, and Ndiaye, pp. 137–140.

59. Locoh, op. cit., pp. 20–24.

60. John Campbell describes the nearby city of Zurrichane, where he did a series of sketches. The houses were painted in lively colors, yellows and reds, and ornamented with sculpted clay pillars with human figures painted in various colors on them, especially on the side facing the house. Buildings grouped together and enclosed by a low wall are an arrangement still visible today. John Campbell, *Travels in South Africa (Second Journey)*, London, London Missionary Society, 1822, vol. 1, pp. 220–227.

61. But the depression helped replace embroidery on animal skins with plastic beads on cotton fabrics during the 1950s.

62. M. Courtney-Clarke, *Ndebele: The Art of an African Tribe*, New York: Rizzoli, 1986.

63. L. M. Ongoum, "Femmes Bamileke," Barbier, *Femmes du Cameroun*, pp. 284–297. We should also note the very old songs of San and Pygmy women.

64. Quoted in Beverly M. Mack, "Songs from Silence: Hausa Women's Poetry," Carole Boyce Davies and Anne Adams Graves, eds., *Ngambika*, Trenton, N.J., Africa World Press, 1986, p. 185.

65. *Alkalami a hannun matu* (A Pen in Women's Hands), Zaria, 1983.

66. Quoted in Mack, "Songs from Silence," p. 188.

67. The title *The Joys of Motherhood* is probably an allusion to the heroine of Nwapa's *Efuru*, who had never experienced the joy of motherhood.

68. Almost always apparent in the men's works, except in the work of Abdoulaye Ly, who speaks of mothers "whose children . . . rivet them to the home as chains attach a criminal to a post." *Toiles d'araignées,* Paris, L'Harmattan, p. 102.

69. Buchi Emecheta, *The Joys of Motherhood: A Novel,* New York, G. Braziller, 1979, p. 222.

70. Mariama Bâ, *So Long a Letter,* London, Heinemann, 1981, p. 73.

71. Balandier, *Sociologie des Brazzavilles noires,* p. 146.

72. Didier Gondola, *Villes miroirs: Migration et identités urbaines à Brazzaville et Kinshasa 1930–1970,* Paris, L'Harmattan, 1996.

73. "Slut's Eyes," "Sea Waters," "God's House," "Marie Goes Biking."

74. The first Senegalese girls admitted to the renowned Dakar Sisters' secondary school still remember the Sisters' struggle to prevent them from wearing traditional wrap-skirts, considered a sign of savagery and rebellion, even in the early 1960s.

75. These are simply generous rectangles of various widths with a circle at the top to admit the head and neck. The skirt-cloth knotted around the waist is still worn in the countryside and at home and about in the city.

76. Palesa Jacquí Mofokeng, quoted in *Afrique Magazine,* no. 106, September 1993.

Conclusion

1. Patricia Stamp, "Burying Otieno: The Politics of Gender and Ethnicity in Kenya," *Signs,* vol. 16, no. 4, 1991, pp. 808–845. See also David W. Cohen, *Burying SM: The Politics of Knowledge and the Sociology of Power in Africa,* Portsmouth, N.H., Heinemann, 1992.

2. Appiah tells this story in *In My Father's House,* New York, Oxford University Press, 1992, pp. 181–195. Recently, a talented female Ghanaian writer argued that he might rather claim his British mother's than his Ghanaian father's heritage, according to his matrilineal references. Nkiru Nzegwu, "O Africa: Gender Imperialism in Academia," Obioma Nnoemeka and Oyeronke Oyewumi, eds., *African Women and Imperialism,* Trenton, N.J., Africa World Press, 1996.

3. Cited in C. Vidal, *Sociologie des passions,* Paris, Karthala, 1991, p. 147.

4. B. Jewsiewicki, ed., *Naître et mourir au Zaïre,* Paris, Karthala, 1991, pp. 52–54.

5. Nonetheless worth reading are: J. L. Parpart, ed., *Women and Development in Africa: Comparative Perspectives,* Lanham, Md., University Press of America, 1989; the special issue on this theme in *Review of African Political Economy,* nos. 27–28, 1984; and the newsletter of the Women and Development network established by ORSTOM and the French Cooperation Ministry around 1985.

Bibliography: African Women in Modern History

Les Abyssiniennes et les femmes du Soudan oriental d'après les relations de Bruce, Browne, Caillaud, Gobat, Dr Cuny, Lejean, Baker, etc. Turin: Jean Gay, 1976.

Aduayom, Messam. Un prélude au nationalisme togolais: La révolte de Lomé, 24–25 janvier 1933. *Cahiers d'Etudes Africaines*, 1984, 24-1(93):39–50.

Afshar, Haleh. *Women, Work, and Ideology in the Third World.* London: Tavistock, 1985.

Afshar, Haleh; Dennis, Caroline, eds. *Women and Adjustment Policies in the Third World.* New York: St. Martin's Press, 1992.

Aina, O. I. Mobilizing Nigerian Women for National Development: The Role of the Female Elite. *African Economic History*, 1993, 21:1–20.

Albert, Irène. *Des femmes, une terre: Une nouvelle dynamique sociale au Bénin.* Paris: L'Harmattan, 1993.

Allman, Jean. Rounding Up Spinsters: Gender, Chaos, and Unmarried Women in Colonial Asante. *Journal of African History*, 1996, 37(2):195–214.

d'Almeida-Topor, Hélène. *Les Amazones: Une armée de femmes dans l'Afrique précoloniale.* Paris: Rochevignes, 1984.

d'Almeida-Ekoué, S. *La révolte des Loméennes, 24–25 janvier 1933.* Lomé: Les Nouvelles Editions Africaines du Togo, 1992.

Amadiume, Ifi. *Male Daughters, Female Husbands: Gender and Sex in an African Society.* London: Zed Books, 1987.

Antoine, Philippe; Nanitelamio, Jeanne. *La montée du célibat féminin dans les villes africaines: Trois cas, Pikine, Abidjan et Brazzaville.* Paris: Centre Français sur la Population et le Développement (CEPED), 1990.

Antoine, Philippe; Nanitelamio, Jeanne. *Peut-on échapper à la polygamie à Dakar?* Dossiers du CEPED, no. 32, 1995.

Appiah, Anthony. *In My Father's House: Africa in the Philosophy of Culture.* New York: Oxford University Press, 1992.

Appleton, Simon; Collier, Paul; and Horsnell, Paul. *Gender, Education, and Employment in Côte d'Ivoire.* Washington, D.C.: World Bank, 1990.

Ba, Ginette. Women and Feminine Experience in Lessing's *The Four-Gated City* (1969). *Annales de la Faculté des Lettres et Sciences Humaines* (Dakar), 1989, (19):83–94.

Bâ, Mariama. *So Long a Letter.* Translated from the French by Modupe Bode-Thomas. London: Heinemann, 1989.

Barber, Karin. *I Could Speak Until Tomorrow. Oriki, Women, and the Past in a Yoruba Town.* Washington, D.C.: Smithsonian Institution Press, 1991.

Barbier, Jean-Claude, ed. *Femmes du Cameroun: Mères pacifiques, femmes rebelles.* Paris: ORSTOM/Karthala, 1985.

Bardouille, Raj. *Research on Zambian Women in Retrospect and Prospect: An Annotated Bibliography.* Lusaka: Swedish International Development Agency, 1992.

Bardouille, Raj. The Sexual Division of Labour in the Urban Informal Sector: The Case of Some Townships in Lusaka. *African Social Research,* 1981, (32):29–53.

Barrett, H. R.; Browne, A. W. Time for Development? The Case of Women's Horticultural Schemes in Rural Gambia. *Scottish Geographical Magazine,* 1989, 106(1):4–11.

Barrett, Jane; et al. *South African Women on the Move.* Toronto: Between the Lines, 1985.

Barthel, Diane L. The Rise of a Female Professional Elite: The Case of Senegal. *African Studies Review,* 1975, 18(3):1–15.

Baumgardt, Ursula. La représentation de l'Autre: L'exemple du répertoire d'une conteuse peule de Garoua (Cameroun). *Cahiers d'Etudes Africaines,* 1994, 34-1-3(133–135):295–311.

Bay, Edna G. Belief, Legitimacy, and the *Kpojito:* An Institutional History of the "Queen Mother" in Precolonial Dahomey. *Journal of African History,* 1995, 36(1):1–28.

Bay, Edna G., ed. *Women and Work in Africa.* Boulder: Westview Press, 1982.

Bay, Edna; Hapkin, Nancy, eds. *Women in Africa.* African Studies Review, 1975, 18(3).

Bazin-Tardieu, Danielle. *Femmes du Mali: Statut, image, réaction au changement.* Ottawa: Léméac, 1975.

Beavon, K.S.O.; Rogerson, C. The Changing Role of Women in the Urban Informal Sector of Johannesburg. In: Drakakis-Smith, David, ed. *Urbanisation in the Developing World.* London: Croom Helm, 1986, 205–225.

Belloncle, G. *Femmes et développement en Afrique sahélienne.* Paris: Editions Ouvrières, 1980.

Beneria, Lourdes. Conceptualizing the Labor Force: The Underestimation of Women's Economic Activities. *Journal of Development Studies,* 1981, 17(3):10–28.

Berger, Iris. *Sources of Class Consciousness: The Experience of Women Workers in South Africa 1973–1980.* Boston: Boston University Press, 1982.

Berger, Iris. *Threads of Solidarity: Women in South African Industry, 1900–1980.* Bloomington: Indiana University Press/London: James Currey, 1992.

Biesele, Megan. *Women Like Meat: The Folklore and Foraging Ideology of the Kalahari Ju/'hoan.* Bloomington and Indianapolis: University of the Witwatersrand and Indiana University Press, 1993.

Biondi, Jean-Pierre. *Saint-Louis du Sénégal: Mémoires d'un métissage.* Paris: Denoël, 1987.

Bivens, Mary Wren. "Women, Ecology, and Islam in the Making of Modern Hausa Cultural History." Ph.D. diss., Michigan State University, 1994.

Blier, Susan Preston. The Path of the Leopard: Motherhood and Majesty in Early Danhomè. *Journal of African History,* 1995, 36(3):391–418.

Bonnardel, Régine. Afrique: Les femmes quittent la brousse. *Le Journal de la Paix,* 1986, (340):16–21.

Bonnardel, Régine. *Saint-Louis du Sénégal: Mort ou naissance?* Paris: L'Harmattan, 1992.

Booth, Alan R. "European Courts Protect Women and Witches": Colonial Law Courts as Redistribution of Power in Swaziland 1920–1950. *Journal of Southern African Studies*, 1992, 18(2):253–275.

Boserup, Ester. *Woman's Role in Economic Development.* London: Allen and Unwin, 1970.

Bozzoli, Belinda. Marxism, Feminism, and South African Studies. *Journal of Southern African Studies*, 1983, 9(2):139–171.

Bozzoli, Belinda, with the assistance of Mmantho Nkotsoe. *Women of Phokeng: Consciousness, Life Strategy, and Migrancy in South Africa, 1900–1983.* London: James Currey/Portsmouth, N.H.: Heinemann, 1991.

Briefings. *Review of African Political Economy*, 1984, (27–28): 120–163.

Bryceson, Deborah Fahy. The Proletarianization of Women in Tanzania. *Review of African Political Economy*, 1980 (17):4–27.

Bryson, Judy C. Women and Agriculture in Sub-Saharan Africa: Implications for Development (An Exploratory Study). *Journal of Development Studies*, 1981, 17(3):30–45.

Bujra, Janet. Women "Entrepreneurs" of Early Nairobi. *Canadian Journal of African Studies*, 1975, 9(2):213–234.

Bukh, J. *The Village Women in Ghana.* Uppsala: Scandinavian Institute of African Studies, 1978.

Buvinic, Marya; Lycette, Margaret; and McGreewey, Paul W., eds. *Women and Poverty in the Third World.* Baltimore: Johns Hopkins University Press, 1983.

Callaway, H. *Gender, Culture, and Empire: European Women in Colonial Nigeria.* London: Macmillan, 1987.

Callaway, Barbara J. *Muslim Hausa Women in Nigeria: Tradition and Change.* Syracuse: Syracuse University Press, 1987.

Callaway, Barbara; Creevy, Lucy. *The Heritage of Islam: Women, Religion, and Politics in West Africa.* Boulder: Lynne Rienner, 1994.

Caplan, Pat. Development Policies in Tanzania: Some Implications for Women. *Journal of Development Studies*, 1981, 17(3):98–107.

Castilhon, J. L. *Zingha, reine d'Angola: Histoire africaine.* Patrick Graille and Laurent Quillerie, eds. Bourges: Ed. G, ca. 1990 (1769).

Centre for Social Development and Humanitarian Affairs, United Nations. *Women in Politics and Decision-making in the Late Twentieth Century.* Dordrecht and Boston: M. Nijhoff, 1992.

Charbit, Yves; Gueye, Lamine; and Ndiaye, Salif, eds. *Nuptialité et fécondité au Sénégal.* Paris: Presses Universitaires de France, 1985.

Charlton, Sue Ellen M. *Women in Third World Development.* Boulder: Westview Press, 1984.

Chauduri, Nupur; Strobel, Margaret, eds. *Western Women and Imperialism: Complicity and Resistance.* Bloomington and Indianapolis: Indiana University Press, 1992.

Chauncey, George, Jr. The Locus of Reproduction: Women's Labour in the Zambian Copperbelt, 1927–1953. *Journal of Southern African Studies*, 1981, 7(2): 135–164.

Chemain-Degrange, Arlette. *Emancipation féminine et roman africain.* Dakar: Les Nouvelles Editions Africaines, 1980.

The Civilization of the Woman in African Tradition. Paris: Présence Africaine, 1975.

Clark, Caroline. Land and Food, Women and Power in Nineteenth-Century Kikuyu. *Africa,* 1980, 50(4):357–367.

Cleaver, Tessa; Wallace, Marion. *Namibia Women in War.* London: Zed Books, 1990.

Cock, Jacklyn. *Maids and Madams: A Study in the Politics of Exploitation.* Johannesburg: Ravan Press, 1980.

Cohen, David William. *Burying SM: The Politics of Knowledge and the Sociology of Power in Africa.* Portsmouth, N.H.: Heinemann, 1992.

Cole, Josette. "When Your Life Is Bitter You Do Something": Women and Squatters in the Western Cape, Tracing the Origins of Crossroads and the Role of Women in Its Struggle. In: Dave Kaplan, ed., *South African Research Papers.* Cape Town: University of Cape Town, 1986, 4–63.

Coles, Catherine; Mack, Beverly, eds. *Hausa Women in the 20th Century.* Madison: University of Wisconsin Press, 1991.

Comhaire-Sylvain, Suzanne. *Femmes de Kinshasa, hier et aujourd'hui.* Paris/The Hague: Mouton, 1968.

Comhaire-Sylvain, Suzanne. *Femmes de Lomé.* Bandundu: Ceeba, 1982.

Comhaire-Sylvain, Suzanne. Le travail des femmes à Lagos, Nigéria. *Zaïre,* 1951, 5(2):169–187, 475–502.

Cooper, Barbara M. Cloth, Commodity Production, and Social Capital: Women in Maradi, Niger, 1890–1989. *African Economic History,* 1993, (21):51–71.

Cooper, Barbara M. *Marriage in Maradi, 1900–1989: Contestations and Contradictions.* London: Heinemann, 1996.

Cooper, Barbara M. Reflections on Slavery, Seclusion, and Female Labor in the Maradi Region of Niger in the Nineteenth and Twentieth Centuries. *Journal of African History,* 1994, 35(1):61–78.

Cooper, Barbara M. Women's Worth and Wedding Gift Exchange in Maradi, Niger, 1907–89. *Journal of African History,* 1995, 36(1):121–140.

Cooper, Frederick, ed. *Struggle for the City: Migrant Labor, Capital, and the State in Urban Africa.* Beverly Hills, Calif.: Sage, 1983.

Coquery-Vidrovitch, Catherine. *Histoire des villes africaines des origines à la colonisation.* Paris: Albin Michel, 1993.

Coquery-Vidrovitch, Catherine. The Urbanization Process in Africa from the Origins to the Beginning of Independence. *African Studies Review,* 1991, 34(1):1–98.

Cordonnier, Rita. *Femmes africaines et commerce: Les revendeuses de tissu de la ville de Lomé (Togo).* Paris: L'Harmattan, 1987.

Courtney-Clarke, Margaret. *Ndebele: The Art of an African Tribe.* New York: Rizzoli, 1986.

Couturier, Lucie. *Mes inconnus chez eux: Mon amie Fatou, citadine.* Paris: Rieder, 1925.

Creevey, Lucy E. *Women Farmers in Africa: Rural Development in Mali and the Sahel.* Syracuse: Syracuse University Press, 1986.

Cromwell, Adelaide M. *An African Victorian Feminist: The Life and Times of Adelaide Smith Casely Hayford 1868–1960.* London: Frank Cass, 1986.

Current Research on African Women. *Canadian Journal of African Studies*, 1988, 22(3):409–682.

Dacher, Michèle; Lallemand, Suzanne. *Prix des épouses, valeur des soeurs, suivi de Les représentations de la maladie: Deux études sur la société Goin, Burkina-Faso*. Paris: L'Harmattan, 1992.

Davies, Carole Boyce; Graves, Anne Adams, eds. *Ngambika: Studies of Women in African Literature*. Trenton, N.J.: Africa World Press, 1986.

Davison, Jean. "Without Land We Are Nothing": The Effect of Land Tenure Policies and Practices upon Rural Women in Kenya. *Rural Africana*, 1987, (27):19–33.

Davison, Jean, with the Women of Mutira. *Voices from Mutira: Lives of Rural Gikuyu Women*. Boulder: Lynne Rienner, 1989.

Davison, Jean, ed. *Agriculture, Women, and Land: The African Experience*. Boulder: Westview Press, 1988.

Day, Linda L. The Evolution of Female Chiefship During the Late 19th-Century Wars of the Mende. *International Journal of African Historical Studies*, 1994, 27(3):481–503.

Deere, Carmen Diana. Rural Women's Subsistence Production in the Capitalist Periphery. *Review of Radical Political Economy*, 1976, 8(1):9–17.

Deluz, A.; Lecour-Grandmaison, C.; and Retel-Laurentin, A. *La natte et le manguier*. Paris: Mercure de France, 1978.

Deniel, Raymond. *Femmes des villes africaines*. Abidjan: Inades, 1985.

Dennis, Carolyn. Capitalist Development and Women's Work: A Nigerian Case Study. *Review of African Political Economy*, 1984, (27/28):109–119.

Dennis, Carolyn. Women and the State in Nigeria: The Case of the Federal Military Government 1984–1985. In: Haleh, Afshar, ed., *Women and the State*. London: Tavistock, 1987.

Dennis, Carolyn. Women in African Labour History. *Journal of Asian and African Studies*, 1988, 23(1–2):125–140.

Denzer, LaRay. Women in Freetown Politics, 1914–1961: A Preliminary Study. *Africa*, 1987, 57:438–456.

Denzer, LaRay. Yoruba Women: A Historiographical Essay. *International Journal of African Historical Studies*, 1994, 27.

Des femmes sur l'Afrique. *Cahiers d'Etudes Africaines*, 1977, 19(65):5–194.

Désalmand, Paul. *L'émancipation de la femme en Afrique et dans le monde: Textes et documents*. Abidjan: Les Nouvelles Editions Africaines, 1977.

Diabaté, Henriette. *La marche des femmes sur Grand-Bassam*. Dakar: Les Nouvelles Editions Africaines, 1975.

Diarra, Fatoumata A. *Femmes africaines en devenir: Les femmes Zarma du Niger*. Paris: Anthropos, 1971.

Diawara, Mamadou. Femmes, servitude et histoire: Les traditions orales des femmes de condition servile dans le royaume de Jaara (Mali) du XIVᵉ au milieu du XIXᵉ siècle. *History in Africa*, 1989, 16:71–96.

Diop, Abdoulaye Bara. *La famille wolof*. Paris: Karthala, 1985.

Dirasse, Laketch. *Reaching the Top: Women Managers in Eastern and Southern Africa*. Nairobi: ESAMI Printing Press, 1991.

Drakakis-Smith, D. W. The Changing Economic Role of Women in the Urbanization Process: A Preliminary Report from Zimbabwe. *International Migration Review*, 1984, 18(4):1278–1290.

Drewal, Henry John; Drewal, Margaret Thompson. *Gelede: Art and Female Power among the Yoruba*. Bloomington: Indiana University Press, 1983.

Droy, Isabelle. *Femmes et développement rural*. Paris: Karthala, 1990.

Druve, Nell; Hammand, Jenny. *Sweeter Than Honey: Ethiopian Women and Revolution, Testimonies of Tigrayan Women*. Trenton, N.J.: Red Sea Press, 1990.

Duman, Ernest. Commodity Queens and the Distributive Trade in Ghana: A Sociohistorical Analysis. *African Urban Studies*, 1982, (12):27–41.

Eastman, Carol M. Women, Slaves, and Foreigners: African Cultural Influences and Group Processes in the Formation of Northern Swahili Coastal Society. *International Journal of African Historical Studies*, 1988, 21(1):1–20.

Eldredge, Elizabeth A. *A South African Kingdom: The Pursuit of Security in Nineteenth-Century Lesotho*. Cambridge: Cambridge University Press, 1993.

Elson, Diane; Pearson, Ruth. The Subordination of Women and the Internationalisation of Factory Production. In: Young, Kate; Wolkowitz, Carol; and McCullagh, Roslyn, eds. *Of Marriage and the Market: Women's Subordination in International Perspective*. London: CSE Books, 1981.

Emecheta, Buchi. *The Bride-Price*. New York: George Braziller, 1976.

L'emploi et les conditions de travail des femmes africaines: Deuxième conférence régionale africaine, Addis-Ababa. Geneva: International Labour Organisation, 1964.

Enfants et femmes du Mali: Une analyse de situation. Paris: UNICEF/L'Harmattan, 1989.

Epprechts, Marc. Domesticity and Piety in Colonial Lesotho: The Private Politics of Basotho Women's Pious Associations. *International Journal of African Historical Studies*, 1993, 19(2):202–224.

Epprecht, Marc. Women's "Conservatism" and the Politics of Gender in Late Colonial Lesotho. *Journal of African History*, 1995, 36(1):29–56.

Erlich, Michel. *La femme blessée: Essai sur les mutilations sexuelles féminines*. Paris: L'Harmattan, 1986.

Etats généraux du féminisme: Exposition coloniale internationale de Paris. Paris: Conseil National des Femmes Françaises, 1931.

Etienne, Mona. Gender Relations and Conjugality Among the Baule (Ivory Coast). *Culture*, 1981, 1(1):21–30.

Etienne, Mona; Leacock, Eleanor. *Women and Colonization: Anthropological Perspectives*. New York: Praeger, 1983.

Etonde-Ekoto, Grace. La femme et la libération de l'Afrique: Quelques figures culturelles. *Présence Africaine*, 1986, (140):140–153.

Fainzang, S.; Journet, O. *La femme de mon mari: Anthropologie du mariage polygamique en Afrique et en France*. Paris: L'Harmattan, 1988.

Family, State, and Economy in Africa. *Signs*. 1991, 16(4).

Feldman, Rayah. Women's Groups and Women's Subordination: An Analysis of Policies Towards Rural Women in Kenya. *Review of African Political Economy*, 1984, (22–23):67–77.

La femme dans la société francophone traditionnelle. Rennes: Université de Rennes-2, 1978.

La femme dans les sociétés coloniales. Aix-en Provence/Groningen/Amsterdam: Institut d'Histoire des Pays d'Outre-Mer, 1984.

La femme noire dans la vie moderne: Images et réalités. *Présence Africaine,* 1987, (142–143).

Femmes dakaroises: Rôles traditionnels féminins et urbanisation. Annales de l'Université d'Abidjan, 1972, F(4).

Femmes et politiques alimentaires. Paris: ORSTOM, 1985.

Ferguson, Anne E.; Katundu, Beatrice Liatto. Women in Politics in Zambia: What Difference Has Democracy Made? *African Rural and Urban Studies,* 1994, 1(2):11–30.

Fields, Karen. *Revival and Rebellion in Colonial Central Africa.* Princeton: Princeton University Press, 1985.

Fisher, Humphrey J. Slavery and Seclusion in Northern Nigeria: A Further Note. *Journal of African History,* 1991, 32(1):123–135.

Frank, Odile. *The Childbearing Family in Sub-Saharan Africa: Structure, Fertility, and the Future.* World Bank Working Paper 509, 1990.

Freeman, Donald B. Survival Strategy or Business Ground? The Significance of Urban Agriculture for the Advancement of Women in African Cities. *African Studies Review,* 1993, 36(3):1–22.

Gable, Eric. Woman, Ancestors, and Alterity Among the Manjaco of Guinea-Bissau. *Journal of Religion in Africa,* 1996, 26(2):104–121.

Gaitskell, Deborah; Kimble, Judy; et al. Class, Race, and Gender: Domestic Workers in South Africa. *Review of African Political Economy,* 1984, (27–28):86–105.

Geiger, Susan N. *TANU Women: Gender, Culture, and Politics in Tanganyika.* London: Heinemann, 1996.

Geiger, Susan N. Women in Nationalist Struggle: TANU Activists in Dar es Salaam. *International Journal of African Historical Studies,* 1987, 20(1):1–26.

The Gendered Politics of the Land. *Southern African Feminist Review,* 1995, (1).

Glassman, Jonathan. *Feasts and Riots: Rivalry, Rebellion, and Popular Consciousness on the Swahili Coast, 1856–1888.* New York: Heinemann, 1995.

Goebel, Allison; Epprecht, Mark. Women and Employment in Sub-Saharan Africa: Testing the World Bank and WID Models with a Case Study. *African Studies Review,* 1995, 38(1):1–22.

Goli, Kouassi. *La prostitution en Afrique: Un cas, Abidjan.* Abidjan: Les Nouvelles Editions Africaines, 1986.

Gondola, Didier. *Villes miroirs: Migration et identités urbaines à Brazzaville et Kinshasa, 1930–1970.* Paris: L'Harmattan, 1996.

Goodwin, June. *Cry Amandla: South African Women and the Question of Power.* New York: Africana, 1984.

Gordon, Elizabeth. An Analysis of the Impact of Labour Migration on the Lives of Women in Lesotho. *Journal of Development Studies,* 1981, 17(3):59–76.

Gordon, Robert J. The Venal Hottentot Venus and the Great Chain of Being. *African Studies,* 1992, 51:185–202.

Goutalier, Régine. Les états généraux du féminisme à l'Exposition coloniale 30–31 mai 1931. *Revue d'Histoire Moderne et Contemporaine,* 1989, 36:266–284.

Greene, Sandra E. *Gender, Ethnicity, and Social Change on the Upper Slave Coast: A History of the Anlo-Ewe.* London: Heinemann, 1996.

Grier, Beverly. Pawns, Porters, and Petty Traders: Women in the Transition to Cash Crop Agriculture in Colonial Ghana. *Signs,* 1992, 17(2):304–328.

Gugler, Josef. The Second Sex in Town. *Canadian Journal of African Studies,* 1972, 6(2):289–302.

Gugler, Josef; Ludwar-Ene, Gudrun. Plusieurs chemins mènent les femmes en ville en Afrique subsaharienne. In: d'Almeida-Topor, Hélène; Riesz, Janos, eds., *Etudes franco-allemandes sur l'Afrique subsaharienne.* Cahiers Afrique Noire, Laboratoire Tiers-Monde, Afrique, no. 13. Paris: L'Harmattan, 1992, 1–15.

Guyer, Jane I. Female Farming and the Evolution of Food Production Patterns Amongst the Beti of South-Central Cameroon. *Africa,* 1980, 50(4):341–356.

Guyer, Jane I. Food, Cocoa, and the Division of Labour by Sex in Two West African Societies. *Comparative Studies in Society and History,* 1970, 22(3):355–373.

Guyer, Jane I. Household and Community in African Studies. *African Studies Review,* 1981, 24(2–3):87–137.

Guyer, Jane I. *Money Matters: Instability, Value, and Social Payments in the Modern History of West African Communities.* London: James Currey/Portsmouth, N.H.: Heinemann, 1994.

Guyer, Jane I.; Peters, Pauline E., eds. Conceptualizing the Household: Issues for Theory and Policy in Africa. *Development and Change,* 1987, 18(2).

Hafkin, N. J. *Women and Development in Africa: An Annotated Bibliography.* Addis Ababa: United Nations Economic Commission for Africa, 1977.

Hafkin, N; Bay, E., eds. *Women in Africa: Studies in Social and Economic Change.* Stanford, Calif.: Stanford University Press, 1976.

Hakansson, Thomas. *Bridewealth, Women, and Land: Social Change Among the Gusii of Kenya.* Stockholm: Graphic System, 1988.

Hansen, Karen Tranberg, ed. *African Encounters with Domesticity.* New Brunswick, N.J.: Rutgers University Press, 1992.

Hansen, Karen Tranberg. *Distant Companions: Servants and Employers in Zambia, 1900–1985.* Ithaca: Cornell University Press, 1989.

Harrell-Bond, Barbara E. *Modern Marriage in Sierra-Leone: A Study of a Professional Group.* Paris/The Hague: Mouton, 1975.

Hay, Margaret Jean; Stichter, Sharon, eds. *African Women South of the Sahara.* London: Longman, 1984.

Hay, Margaret Jean; Wright, Marcia, eds. *African Women and the Law: Historical Perspectives.* Boston: Boston University Press, 1982.

Hetherington, Penelope. Women in South Africa: The Historiography in English. *International Journal of African Historical Studies,* 1993, 26(2):241–269.

Hicks, Esther K. *Infibulation: Female Mutilation in Islamic Northeastern Africa.* London: Transaction Publishers, 1993.

Hirschmann, David. Urban Women, Civil Society, and Social Transition in the Eastern Cape, South Africa. *African Rural and Urban Studies,* 1994, 1(2):31–48.

Hishongwa, Ndentale Selma. *Women in Namibia: The Changing Role of Namibian Women from Traditional Precolonial Times to the Present.* Paris: L'Harmattan, 1983.

Histoire des femmes en Afrique. Cahiers Afrique Noire, Laboratoire Tiers-Monde, Afrique, no. 11. Paris: L'Harmattan, 1987.

Hoffer, Carol P. Mende and Sherbro Women in High Office. *Canadian Journal of African Studies,* 1972, 6(2):151–164.

Hollos, Marida. Migration, Education, and the Status of Women in Southern Nigeria. *American Anthropologist,* 1991, 93(4):852–870.

Hoppe, Kirk. Whose Life Is It, Anyway? Issues of Representation in Life Narrative Texts of African Women. *International Journal of African Historical Studies,* 1993, 26(3):623–636.

Horn, Nancy E. *Cultivating Customers: Market Women in Harare, Zimbabwe.* Boulder: Lynne Rienner, 1994.

Hosken, Fran P. *The Hosken Report: Genital and Sexual Mutilation of Females.* Lexington, Mass.: Women's International Network News, ca. 1993.

Housing, Hotels, Women Garment Workers in the Western Cape and the South African Peace Council 1951–56. Rondebosch, South Africa: University of Cape Town, 1984.

Hyslop, Jonathan. White Working-Class Women and the Invention of Apartheid: "Purified" Afrikaner Nationalist Agitation for Legislation Against "Mixed" Marriages, 1934–9. *Journal of African History,* 1995, 36(1):57–82.

Ismail, Ellen; Makki, Maureen. *Femmes du Soudan.* Paris: L'Harmattan, 1990.

Jackson, Sam. Hausa Women on Strike. *Review of African Political Economy,* 1978, (13):21–36.

Jacobs, Susie. Women and Land Resettlement in Zimbabwe. *Review of African Political Economy,* 1984, (27–28):33–49.

Jeater, Diana. *Marriage, Perversion, and Power: The Construction of Moral Discourse in Southern Rhodesia 1894–1930.* Oxford: Clarendon Press, 1993.

Jewsiewicki, Bogumil, ed. *Naître et mourir au Zaïre: Un demi-siècle d'histoire au quotidien.* Paris: Karthala, 1993.

John, C. B.; Webster, Ellen Low, eds. *The Church and Women in the Third World.* Philadelphia: Westminster Press, 1985.

Johnson, Cheryl. Grass Roots Organizing: Women in Anticolonial Activity in Southwestern Nigeria. *African Studies Review,* 1982, 25(2–3):137–155.

Journet, Odile. Rôles et statuts des femmes dans la société Diola (basse Casamance). Ph.D. diss., Université Lyon-2, 1976.

Jules-Rosette, Benetta. Cultural Ambivalence and Ceremonial Leadership: The Role of Woman in Africa's New Religions. In: John, C. B.; Webster, Ellen Low, eds. *The Church and Women in the Third World.* Philadelphia: Westminster Press, 1985, 88–104, 160–164.

Jules-Rosette, Benetta. Privilege Without Power: Women in African Cults and Churches. In: Terborg-Penn, Rosalynn; Harley, Sharon; and Rushing, Andrea, eds., *Women in Africa and the African Diaspora.* Washington, D.C.: Howard University Press, 1987, 99–119.

Kabira, Wanjiku Mukabi; Nzioki, Elizabeth Akinyi. *Celebrating Women's Resistance.* Nairobi: African Women's Perspectives, 1993.

Kalu, Anthonia C. Those Left in the Rain: African Literary Theory and the Re-invention of the African Woman. *African Studies Review,* 1994, 37(2):77–96.

Kane, Mohamadou. Le féminisme dans le roman africain de langue française. *Annales de la Faculté des Lettres et Sciences Humaines* (Dakar), 1980, (10):141–200.

Kaplan, Dave, ed. *Women and Squatters in the Western Cape: The Vigilance Committee of the Garment Workers' Union, Cape Province, 1940–1943.* Randebosch, South Africa: University of Cape Town, 1986.

Keita, Aoua. *Femme d'Afrique: La vie d'Aoua Keita recontée par elle-même.* Paris: Présence Africaine, 1975.

Kenyon, Susan M. *Five Women of Sennar: Culture and Change in Central Sudan.* Oxford: Clarendon Press, 1991.

Kimble, Judy. Runaway Wives: Basotho Women, Chiefs, and the Colonial State, c. 1890–1920. Paper presented at Women in Africa Seminar, School of Oriental and African Studies, London, June 17, 1983.

Kinsman, Margaret. "Beasts of Burden": The Subordination of Southern Tswana Women, ca. 1800–1840. *Journal of Southern African Studies,* 1983, 10(1):39–53.

Kisekka, Mere. Research on the Status of Women, Development, and Population Trends in Africa: An Annotated Bibliography. In: Little, Kenneth L., ed. *Sociology of Urban Women's Images in African Literature.* London: Macmillan, 1980, 41–66.

Knibiehler, Yvonne; Goutalier, Régine. *La femme au temps des colonies.* Paris: Stock, 1985.

Konaré, Adam Ba. *Dictionnaire des femmes célèbres du Mali: Des temps mythico-légendaires au 26 mars 1991, précédé d'une analyse sur le rôle et l'image de la femme dans l'histoire du Mali.* Bamako: Jamana, 1993.

Koso-Thomas, Olayinka. *The Circumcision of Women: A Strategy for Eradication.* London: Zed Books, 1987.

Krige, E. J.; Comaroff, J. L., eds. *Essays on African Marriage in Southern Africa.* Cape Town: Juta, 1981.

Kuper, Adam. *Wives for Cattle: Bridewealth and Marriage in Southern Africa.* London: Routledge and Kegan Paul, 1982.

Kurwijila, Rosebud; Due, Jean M. Credit for Women's Income Generation: A Tanzanian Case Study. *Canadian Journal of African Studies,* 1991, 25(1):90–103.

La Fontaine, Jean. The Free Women of Kinshasa. In: Davis, John, ed. *Choice and Change: Essays in Honour of Lucy Mair.* London: Athlone, 1974, 89–113.

LaDey, Jennie. Gambian Women: Unequal Partners in Rice Development Projects? *Journal of Development Studies,* 1981, 17(3):110–122.

Ladipo, Patricia. Developing Women's Cooperatives: An Experiment in Rural Nigeria. *Journal of Development Studies,* 1981, 17(3):124–135.

Larsson, Birgitta. *Conversion to Greater Freedom? Women, Church, and Social Change in North-Western Tanzania Under Colonial Rule.* Stockholm/Uppsala: Almqvist and Wiksell International, 1991.

Lawson, Lesley. *Working Women in South Africa.* Johannesburg: Raven Press/Oxford: Pluto Press, 1985, 1986.

Leach, Melissa. *Rainforest Relations: Gender and Resources Among the Mende of Gola, Sierra Leone.* Edinburgh: Edinburgh University Press for the International African Institute, 1994.

Le Cour-Grandmaison, Colette. Activités économiques des femmes dakaroises. *Africa,* 1969, 39:138–151.

Le Cour-Grandmaison, Colette. *Femmes dakaroises: Rôles traditionnels feminins et urbanisation.* Annales de l'Université d'Abidjan, series F, 4, 1972.

Lemaire, Charles-François Alexandre. *Africaines: Contribution à l'histoire de la femme en Afrique.* Brussels: Imprimerie Scientifique, 1897.

Lightfoot-Klein, Hanny. *Prisoners of Rituals: An Odyssey into Female Genital Circumcision in Africa.* New York: Haworth Press, 1989.

Little, Kenneth L. *African Women in Town: An Aspect of Africa's Social Revolution.* Cambridge: Cambridge University Press, 1973.

Little, Kenneth L., ed. *The Sociology of Urban Women's Image in African Literature.* London: Macmillan, 1980.

Little, Kenneth. Some Methodological Considerations in the Study of African Women's Urban Roles. *Urban Anthropology,* 1975, 4(2):107–121.

Locoh, Thérèse. *Fécondité et famille en Afrique de l'ouest: Le Togo méridional contemporain.* Paris: Presses Universitaires de France, 1984.

Lovett, Margot. On Power and Powerlessness: Marriage and Political Metaphor in Colonial Western Tanzania. *International Journal of African Historical Studies,* 1994, 27:273–301.

Ly, Madina; Achola, O. Pala. *La femme africaine dans la société précoloniale.* Paris: UNESCO, 1979.

Lydon, Ghislaine. The Unraveling of a Neglected Source: Women in Francophone West Africa in the 1930s. *Cahiers d'Etudes Africaines,* forthcoming.

McCaffrey, Kathleen M. Images of Women in West African Literature and Film: A Struggle Against Dual Colonization. *International Journal of Women's Studies,* 1980, 3(1):76–88.

McCall, D. Trade and the Role of Wife in a Modern West African Town. In: Southall, A., ed. *Social Change in Modern Africa.* London: Oxford University Press, 1981, 286–299.

McCann, James C. *Peoples of the Plow: An African Agricultural History of Ethiopia, 1800–1990.* Madison: University of Wisconsin Press, 1995.

McGaffey, Janet. Gender and Class Formation: Businesswomen in Kisangani. In: *The Struggle for Indigenous Capitalism in Zaïre.* Cambridge: Cambridge University Press, 1989, 165–183.

Mackintosh, Maureen. *Gender, Class, and Rural Transition: Agrobusiness and the Food Crisis in Senegal.* London: Zed Books, 1989.

Malira, Kubuya Namulemba. Regard sur la situation sociale de la citoyenne lushoise d'avant 1950. *Likundoli,* 1974, 2(1):63–71.

Manceaux, Michèle. *Les femmes du Mozambique.* Paris: Mercure de France, 1975.

Mandala, E. Capitalism, Kinship, and Gender in the Lower Tehiri Valley of Malawi 1860–1960. *African Economic History,* 1984, (13):137–170.

Manicom, Linzi. Ruling Relations: Rethinking State and Gender in South African History. *Journal of African History,* 1992, 13(3):441–465.

Mann, Kristin. *Marriage, Status, and Social Change Among the Educated Elite in Colonial Lagos.* Cambridge: Cambridge University Press, 1985.

Marks, Shula, ed. *Not Either an Experimental Doll: The Separate Worlds of Three South African Women.* Bloomington and Indianapolis: Indiana University Press, 1987.

Martens, Ludo. *Une femme du Congo.* Brussels: EPO, 1991.

Martin, Susan. Gender and Innovation: Farming, Cooking, and Palm Processing in the Ngwa Region, South-Eastern Nigeria, 1900–1930. *Journal of African History,* 1984, 25.

Mascarenhas, Ophelia; Mbilinyi, Marjorie. *Women in Tanzania. An Analytical Bibliography.* New York: Africana, 1983.

Massoz, Michel. *Les femmes bantoues du XXe siècle.* Liège: M. Massoz, 1991.

Mathabane, Mark. *African Women: Three Generations.* London: HarperCollins, 1994.

Matsepe, Ivy F. African Women's Labour in the Political Economy of South Africa 1880–1970. Ph.D. diss., Rutgers University, 1984.

May, Joan. *African Women in Urban Employment: Factors Influencing their Employment in Zimbabwe.* Gwelo: Mambo Press, 1979.

May, Joan. *Zimbabwean Women in Colonial and Customary Law.* Harare: Mambo Press/Holmes McDougall, 1983.

Mazire, Dominique. Une organisation de femmes au Kenya: Maendeleo Ya Wanawake. *Politique Africaine,* 1994, 53:139–142.

Mba, Nina. *Nigerian Women Mobilized: Women's Political Activity in Southern Nigeria 1900–1965.* Berkeley: University of California Press, 1982.

Mbilinyi, J. Marjorie. The "New Woman" and Traditional Norms in Tanzania. *Journal of Modern African Studies,* 1972, 10(1):57–72.

Mbilinyi, J. Marjorie. The State of Women in Tanzania: "Work by Everyone and Exploitation by None?" *Canadian Journal of African Studies,* 1972, 6(2):371–377.

Mbilinyi, J. Marjorie. Tanzania After Nyerere: Changing Employment Patterns in the 1970s: Casualisation and Feminisation of Labour. Photocopy, School of Oriental and African Studies, University of London, 1986.

Meillassoux, Claude. *Maidens, Meals, and Money: Capitalism and the Domestic Community.* Cambridge: Cambridge University Press, 1981.

Mianda, Gertrude D. M. Dans l'ombre de la démocratie au Zaïre: La remise en question de l'émancipation mobutiste de la femme. *Canadian Journal of African Studies,* 1995, 29(1):51–78.

Michel, A.; Agbessi-Dos Santos, H.; and Diarra, Fatoumata, eds. *Femmes et multinationales.* Paris: Karthala, 1981.

Mickelwait, Donald R. *Women in Rural Development: A Survey of the Role of Women in Ghana, Lesotho, Kenya, Nigeria, Bolivia, Paraguay and Peru.* Boulder: Westview Press, 1976.

Mignot-Lefebvre, Yvonne, ed. *La sortie du travail invisible:* Les femmes dans l'économie. *Revue Tiers-Monde,* 1985, 26(102).

Mikell, Gwendolyn, ed. *African Women: States of Crisis.* Forthcoming.

Mikell, Gwendolyn. Culture, Law, and Social Policy: Changing the Economic Status of Women in Ghana. *Yale Journal of International Law,* 1991, 17(1):225–239.

Mikell, Gwendolyn. Filiation, Economic Crisis, and the Status of Women in Rural Ghana. *Canadian Journal of African Studies,* 1984, 18(1):195–217.

Miller, J. C. Nzinga of Matamba in a New Perspective. *Journal of African History,* 1975, 16(2):201–216.

Miller, Joseph C. *Way of Death: Merchant Capitalism and the Angolan Slave Trade 1730–1830.* Madison: University of Wisconsin Press, 1988.

Mirabel, Rogus. *The Black Sash: The Story of the South African Women's Defence of the Constitutional League.* Johannesburg: Rotonews, 1956.

Miracle, M.; Miracle, D. S.; and Cohen, L. Informal Savings Mobilization in Africa. *Economic Development and Cultural Change*, 1980, 28(4):701–724.

Mirza, Sarah; Strobel, Margaret, eds. *Three Swahili Women: Life Histories from Mombasa, Kenya.* Bloomington: Indiana University Press, 1989.

Mitullah, Winnie. Hawking as a Survival Strategy for the Urban Poor in Nairobi: The Case of Women. *Environment and Urbanization*, 1991, 3(2):13–22.

Momsen, Janet Henshall. *Women and Development in the Third World.* London/New York: Routledge, 1991.

Montgomery, Barbara. The Economic Role of the Ivoirian Woman. Photocopy, Center for Research on Economic Development, University of Michigan, 1977.

Moore, Henriette L.; Vaughan, Megan. *Cutting down Trees: Gender, Nutrition, and Agricultural Change in the Northern Province of Zambia, 1890–1990.* London: James Currey/Portsmouth, N.H.: Heinemann,1994.

Morokvasic, Mirjana. Birds of Passage Are Also Women. *International Migration Review*, 1984, 18(4):886–901.

Muller, Jean-Claude. *Du bon usage du sexe et du mariage: Structures matrimoniales du haut plateau nigérien.* Paris: L'Harmattan/Montréal: Serge Fleury, 1982.

Muntemba, Maud Shimwaayi. Women and Agricultural Change in the Railway Region of Zambia: Dispossession and Counterstrategies, 1930–1970. In: Bay, Edna G., ed. *Women and Work in Africa.* Boulder: Westview Press, 1982, 83–111.

Murro, Assury. Women Commodity Producers and Proletariats: The Case of African Women. In: Kiros, Fassil G., ed. *Challenging Rural Poverty.* Trenton, N.J.: Africa World Press, 1985.

Musisi, Nakanyike B. Women, "Elite Polygyny," and Buganda State Formation. *Signs*, 1991, 16(4):757–785.

Nath, Kamla. *Women and Technological Change in the Gambia: A Case Study of the Salt Industry.* Boston University Papers no. 107, 1985.

Nelson, Nici. How Women and Men Get By: The Sexual Division of Labour in the Informal Sector of a Nairobi Squatter Settlement. In: Bromley, R.; Gerry, C., eds. *Casual Work and Poverty in Third World Cities.* London: Wiley, 1979.

Nelson, Nici. Mobilising Village Women: Some Organisational and Management Considerations. *Journal of Development Studies*, 1981, 17(3):46–57.

Newbury, Catharine. Ebutumwa bw'emiogo, the Tyranny of Cassava: A Women's Tax Revolt in Eastern Zaire. *Canadian Journal of African Studies*, 1984, 18(1):35–54.

Ntantala, Phyllis. *A Life's Mosaic: The Autobiography of Phyllis Ntantala.* Berkeley: University of California Press, 1992.

Nyirenda, A. African Market-Vendors in Lusaka, with a Note on a Recent Boycott. *Rhodes-Livingstone Journal*, 1957, 22.

Nzegwu, Nkiru. O Africa: Gender Imperialism in Academia. In: Nnaemeka, Obioma; Oyewumi, Oyeronke, eds. *African Women and Imperialism.* Trenton, N.J.: Africa World Press, 1996.

O'Barr, Jean F., ed. *Perspectives on Power: Women in Africa, Asia, and Latin America.* Durham: Duke University Press, 1982.

Obbo, Christine S. *African Women: Their Struggle for Economic Independence.* London: Zed Press, 1980.

Obbo, Christine S. Town Migration Is Not for Women. Ph.D. diss, University of Wisconsin, Madison, 1977.

Oboler, Regina Smith. *Women, Power, and Economic Change: The Nandi of Kenya.* Stanford, Calif.: Stanford University Press, 1985.

O'Brien, Colleen. The Search for Mother Africa: Poetry Revises Women's Struggle for Freedom. *African Studies Review,* 1994, 37(2):147–156.

Ogundipe-Leslie, Morala; Davies, Carole Boyce. Women as Oral Artists. *Research in African Literatures,* 1994, 25(3).

Ogunsheye, F. A. Formal Education and the Status of Women in Nigeria. In: Ogunsheye, F. A., et al., eds. *Nigerian Women and Development.* Ibadan: Ford Foundation, 1982.

Okeyo, Achola Pala. Daughters of the Lakes and Rivers: Colonization and the Land Rights of Luo Women. In: Etienne, Mona; Leacock, Eleanor, eds. *Women and Colonization: Anthropological Perspectives.* New York: Praeger, 1980, 186–213.

Oppong, Christine, ed. *Female and Male in West Africa.* London: Allen and Unwin, 1983.

Oppong, Christine, ed. *Middle-Class African Marriage: A Family Study of Ghanaian Senior Civil Servants.* London: Allen and Unwin, 1974.

Oppong, Christine; Abu, Katharine. *Seven Roles of Women: Impact of Education, Migration and Employment on Ghanaian Mothers.* Geneva: International Labour Organisation, 1987.

Oppong, Christine; Okali, Christine; and Houghton, Beverly. Woman Power: Retrograde Steps in Ghana. *African Studies Review,* 1975, 18(3):71–83.

Ormerod, Beverly; Volet, Jean-Marie. *Romancières africaines d'expression française: Le sud du Sahara.* Paris: L'Harmattan, 1994.

Pankhurst, Helen. *Gender, Development, and Identity. An Ethiopian Study.* London: Zed Press, 1992.

Park, Clara Cahill. *Native Women in Africa: Their Hard Lot in the March of Progress.* Boston: Massachusetts Commission for International Justice, 1904.

Parkin, D.; Nyamwaya, D., eds. *Transformations in African Marriage.* Manchester: Manchester University Press, 1987.

Parpart, Jane. Where Is Your Mother? Gender, Urban Marriage, and Colonial Discourse on the Zambian Copperbelt. *International Journal of African Historical Studies,* 1994, 27(2):241–271.

Parpart, Jane L., ed. *Women and Development in Africa: Comparative Perspectives.* Lanham, Md.: University Press of America, 1989.

Parpart, Jane L. *Working-Class Wives and Collective Labor Action in the Northern Rhodesian Copperbelt, 1926–1964.* Boston: African Studies Center, Boston University, 1985.

Parpart, Jane L.; Staudt, Kathleen A., eds. *Women and the State in Africa.* Boulder/London: Lynne Rienner, 1989.

Paulme, Denise, ed. *Women of Tropical Africa.* Berkeley: University of California Press, 1963.

Peil, Margaret. Female Roles in West African Towns. In: Goody, J., ed. *Changing Social Structure in Ghana.* London: International African Institute, 1975.

Pellow, Deborah. *Women in Accra: Options for Autonomy.* Algonac, Mich.: Reference Publications, 1977.

Penvenne, Jeanne. *Making Our Own Way: Women Working in Lourenço Marques, 1900–1933.* Boston: Boston University Press, 1986.

Perlman, Melvin L. The Changing Status and Role of Women in Ttoro (Western Uganda). *Cahiers d'Etudes Africaines,* 1966, 6-4(24):564–591.

Person, Yves. La femme dans l'histoire africaine. *Godo-Godo* (Abidjan), 1975, (1):33–66.

Phiri Kings, M. Some Changes in the Matrilineal Family System Among the Chewa of Malawi Since the 19th Century. *Journal of African History,* 1983, 24(2):257–274.

Pittin, Renée. Gender and Class in a Nigerian Industrial Setting. *Review of African Political Economy,* 1984, (31):71–81.

Pittin, Renée. Migration of Women in Nigeria: The Hausa Case. *International Migration Review,* 1984, 18(4):1293–1313.

Porter, Gina. A Note on Slavery, Seclusion, and Agrarian Change in Northern Nigeria. *Journal of African History,* 1989, 30(3):487–491.

Power, Joey. "Eating the Property": Gender Roles and Economic Change in Urban Malawi, Blantyre-Limbe 1907–1953. *Canadian Journal of African Studies,* 1995, 29(1):79–109.

Preiswerk, Yvonne; Milbert, Isabelle, eds. *Femmes, villes et environnement.* Geneva: Institut Universitaire d'Etudes du Développement, 1995.

Presley, Cora Ann. *Kikuyu Women, the Mau Mau Rebellion, and Social Change in Kenya.* Boulder: Westview Press, 1992.

Prinz, Manfred. "Maïmouna" d'Abdoulaye Sadji, roman initiatique et féministe. *Annales de la Faculté des Lettres et Sciences Humaines* (Dakar), 1987, (17):55–69.

Prussin, Labelle, ed. *African Nomadic Architecture: Space, Place, and Gender.* Washington, D.C.: Smithsonian Institution Press, 1995.

Qunta, Christine. *Women in Southern Africa.* London: Allison and Busby, 1987.

Radcliffe-Brown, A. R.; Forde, Daryll, eds. *African Systems of Kinship and Marriage.* New York: Oxford University Press, 1950.

Ravololomanga, Bodo. *Etre femme et mère à Madagascar (Tañala d'Ifanadiana).* Paris: L'Harmattan, 1992.

Redding, Sean. Legal Minors and Social Children: Rural African Women and Taxation in the Transkei, South Africa. *African Studies Review,* 1993, 36(3):49–74.

Riss, Marie-Denise. *Femmes africaines en milieu rural.* Paris: L'Harmattan, 1989.

Rivière, Claude. La promotion de la femme guinéenne. *Cahiers d'Etudes Africaines,* 1968, 8-3(31):406–427.

Rivière, Claude. *Union et procréation en Afrique: Rites de la vie chez les Evé du Togo.* Paris: L'Harmattan, 1990.

Roberts, Richard. Women's Work, Household Social Relations, and the Maraka Textile Industry: A Social History. Paper presented at the conference "African Women in History," University of Santa Clara, May 1981.

Robertson, Claire. Invisible Workers: African Women and the Problem of the Self-Employed in Labour History. *Journal of Asian and African Studies,* 1988, 23(1–2):180–195.

Robertson, Claire. *Sharing the Same Bowl: A Socio-economic History of Women and Class in Accra.* Bloomington: Indiana University Press, 1984.

Robertson, Claire; Berger, Iris, eds. *Women and Class in Africa.* London/New York: Africana, 1986.

Robertson, Claire; Klein, Martin, eds. *Women and Slavery in Africa.* Madison: University of Wisconsin Press, 1984.

Rogers, B. *The Domestication of Women.* New York: St. Martin's Press, 1980.

The Role of African Women: Past, Present, Future. *Canadian Journal of African Studies,* 1972, 5(2).

Romero, Patricia. *Life Histories of African Women.* London: Ashfield Press, 1987.

Romero Curtin, Patricia. Wedding in Lamu, Kenya: An Example of Social and Economic Change. *Cahiers d'Etudes Africaines,* 1984, 24-2(94):131–155.

Rondeau, Chantal. *Les paysannes du Mali: Espaces de liberté et changements.* Paris: Karthala, 1995.

Rosaldo, Michelle Zimbalist; Lamphere, Louise, eds. *Women, Culture, and Society.* Stanford, Calif.: Stanford University Press, 1974.

Rouch, Jean; Bernus, E. Note sur les prostituées "toutou" de Treichville et d'Adjamé. *Etudes Eburnéennes,* 1959, (6):231–242.

Ruelland, Suzanne; Caprile, Jean-Pierre. *Contes et récits du Tchad: La femme dans la littérature africaine.* Paris: Conseil International de la Langue Française, 1993.

Rural Africa. *Sage: A Scholarly Journal on Black Women,* 1990, 7.

Rybalkina, I. G. Women in African History. *African Quarterly,* 1990, 29(3–4):83–91.

du Sacré Coeur, Soeur Marie-André. *La femme noire en Afrique occidentale.* Paris: Payot, 1939.

Sadie, Y.; van Aardt, M. Women's Issues in South Africa: 1990–1994. *Africa Insight,* 1995, 25(2):80–90.

Salvaing, Bernard. La femme dahoméenne vue par les missionnaires: Arrogance culturelle, ou antiféminisme clérical? *Cahiers d'Etudes Africaines,* 1981, 21-4(4) (84):507–522.

Samb, Babacar. L'évolution du statut social de la femme dans l'Islam. *Annales de la Faculté des Lettres et Sciences Humaines* (Dakar), 1991, (21):155–168.

Savané, Marie-Angélique, ed. *Femmes et développement en Afrique de l'Ouest: Incidences des transformations socio-économiques sur le rôle et le statut des femmes.* Geneva: United Nations Research Institute for Social Development, 1986.

Scarnecchia, Timothy. Poor Women and Nationalist Politics: Alliance and Fissures in the Formation of a Nationalist Political Movement in Salisbury, Rhodesia, 1950–6. *Journal of African History,* 1996, 37(2):283–310.

Schildkrout, Enid. Age and Gender in Hausa Society: Socio-economic Roles of Children in Urban Kano. In: La Fontaine, Jean S., ed. *Sex and Age as Principles of Social Differentation.* London/New York: Academic Press, 1978, 109–137.

Schipper, Mineke, ed. *Unheard Words: Women and Literature in Africa, the Arab World, Asia, the Caribbean, and Latin America.* London: Allison and Busby, 1985.

Schlyter, Ann. Women in Harare: Gender Aspects of Urban-Rural Interaction. In: Baker, Jonathan. *Small-Town Africa: Studies in Rural-Urban Interaction.* Uppsala: Scandinavian Institute of African Studies, 1990, 182–191.

Schmidt, Elizabeth. *Peasants, Traders, and Wives: Shona Women in the History of Zimbabwe, 1870–1939.* Portsmouth, N.H.: Heinemann, 1992.

Schuster, Ilsa. Perspectives in Development: The Problem of Nurses and Nursing in Zambia. *Journal of Development Studies,* 1981, 17(3):78–97.

Schwarz, Alf. Illusion d'une émancipation et aliénation réelle de l'ouvrière zaïroise. *Canadian Journal of African Studies*, 1972, 6(2):183–212.

Scobie, Alaster. *Women of Africa.* London: Cassel, 1960.

Scully, Pam. *Liberating the Family? Gender, Labor, and Sexuality in the Rural Eastern Cape, South Africa.* London: Heinemann, 1996.

Seager, Joni; Olson, Ann. *Women in the World: An International Atlas.* London/Sydney: Pan Books, 1986.

Sefa Dei, George I. The Women of a Ghanaian Village: A Study of Social Change. *African Studies Review*, 1994, 37(2):121–145.

Seibert, Jutta. Changement des structures familiales et leurs conséquences sur les stratégies de vie des femmes: Le cas de Lomé. In: d'Almeida-Topor, Hélène; Riesz, Janos, eds. *Etudes franco-allemandes sur l'Afrique subsaharienne.* Cahiers Afrique Noire, Laboratoire Tiers-Monde, Afrique, no. 13. Paris: L'Harmattan, 1992.

Sembene, Ousmane. *Gods' Bits of Wood.* London: Heinemann, 1970.

Seyni Ndione, Emmanuel. *L'économie urbaine en Afrique: Le don et le recours.* Paris: Karthala/Environnement et Développement en Afrique, 1994.

Shell, Robert. *Children of Bondage: A Social History of the Slave Society at the Cape of Good Hope 1652–1838.* Hanover, N.H.: University Press of New England, 1994.

Shostak, Marjorie. *Nisa: The Life and Words of a !Kung Woman.* New York: Vintage Books, 1983.

Shrire, Carmel. *Digging Through Darkness: Chronicle of an Archeologist.* Johannesburg: University of Virginia Press and Witwatersrand University Press, 1995.

Simon, David. Responding to Third World Urban Poverty: Women and Men in the "Informal Sector" in Windhoek, Namibia. In: Momsen, Janet Henshall; Townsend, Janet, eds., *Women's Role in Changing the Face of the Developing World.* Durham: Institute of British Geographers, 1984, 95–130.

Simone, Abdoumaliqalim. From Reproduction to Reinvention: Women's Roles in African Cities. *Africa Insight*, 1995, 25(1):4–14.

Simonis, Francis. *Les Français à Ségou.* Paris: L'Harmattan, forthcoming.

Smith, Joan; Wallerstein, Immanuel; and Evers, Hans-Dieter, eds. *Households and the World Economy.* Beverly Hills: Sage, 1984.

Smith, Mary, ed. *Baba of Karo, a Woman of the Muslim Hausa.* London: Faber and Faber, 1954.

Smith, Regina Oboler. *Women, Power, and Economic Change: The Nani of Kenya.* Stanford, Calif.: Stanford University Press, 1985.

Snyder, Margaret; Zenebeworke, Tadesse. *African Women and Development: A History.* London: Zed Books, 1976.

Songue, Paulette. *Prostitution en Afrique: L'exemple de Yaoundé.* Paris: L'Harmattan, 1986.

Sonolet, Louis. *Le parfum de la dame noire: Physiologie humoristique de l'amour africain.* Paris: Librairie F. Juven, ca. 1911.

Southall, A. W. The Pattern of Migration in Madagascar and Its Theoretical Implications. Paper presented at the annual meeting of the African Studies Association, 1967.

Sow, Fatou. La femme dans l'économie et la culture au Sénégal (Emploi; nuptialité, fécondité; pêche et division sexuée du travail; projets d'énergie et travail féminin;

bilan de la décennie 1975–85). Photocopy, Institut Fondamental d'Afrique Noire, Dakar, 1991.

Staudt, K. A. Rural Women Leaders: Late colonial and Contemporary Contexts. *Rural Africana*, 1978–1979, (3):5–22.

Staunton, Irene, ed. *Mothers of the Revolution: The War Experiences of Thirty Zimbabwean Women*. Bloomington: Indiana University Press, 1991.

Steady, Filomina Chioma, ed. *The Black Woman Cross-culturally*. Cambridge, Mass.: Schenkman, 1981.

Steady, Filomina Chioma. *Female Power in African Politics: The National Congress of Sierra Leone*. Pasadena, Calif.: California Institute of Technology, 1975.

Stichter, Sharon B.; Parpart, Jane L., eds. *Patriarchy and Class: African Women in the Home and the Workforce*. Boulder: Westview Press, 1988.

Stichter, Sharon B.; Parpart, Jane L., eds. *Women, Employment, and the Family in the International Division of Labor*. Philadelphia: Temple University Press, 1990.

Strang, Jessica. *Working Women: An Appealing Look at the Appalling Uses and Abuses of the Feminine Form*. London: Johnson Editions, 1984.

Strobel, Margaret. African Women: A Review. *Signs*, 1982, 8(1):109–131.

Strobel, Margaret. *European Women and the Second British Empire*. Bloomington: Indiana University Press, 1991.

Strobel, Margaret. *Muslim Women in Mombasa 1890–1975*. New Haven/London: Yale University Press, 1979.

Strobel, Margaret, ed. and transl. *Three Swahili Women: Life Histories from Mombasa, Kenya*. Bloomington: Indiana University Press, 1989.

Sullerot, Evelyne, ed. *Le fait féminin: Qu'est-ce qu'une femme?* Paris: Fayard, 1978.

Swantz, Marja-Liisa. *Women in Development: A Creative Role Denied? The Case of Tanzania*. New York: St. Martin's Press, 1985.

Sweetman, David. *Women Leaders in African History*. London: Heinemann, 1984.

Tadani, Veena. Women in Nairobi: The Paradox of Urban Progress. *African Urban Studies*, 1978–1979, (3):67–83.

Tardits, Claude. Aimer, manger et danser: Propos sur la grande polygynie. In: Barbier, Jean-Claude, ed. *Femmes du Cameroun*. Paris: ORSTOM/Karthala, 1985, 119–131.

Tardits, Claude. *Porto-Novo: Les nouvelles générations africaines entre leurs traditions et l'Occident*. Paris/The Hague: Mouton, 1958.

Tardits, Claude. Réflexions sur le problème de la scolarisation des filles au Dahomey. *Cahiers d'Etudes Africaines*, 1962, 3(10):266–281.

Tarrab, Gilbert; Coëne, Chris. *Femmes et pouvoirs au Burkina-Faso*. Paris: L'Harmattan/Québec: G. Bermette, 1989.

Terborg-Penn, Rosalyn; Harley, Sharon; and Rushing, Andrea Benton, eds. *Women in Africa and the African Diaspora*. Washington, D.C.: Howard University Press, 1989.

Tesfagorgis, Abeba. *A Painful Season and a Stubborn Hope: The Odyssey of an Erithrean Mother*. Trenton, N.J.: Red Sea Press, 1992.

Thadani, Veena. Women in Nairobi: The Paradox of Urban "Progress." *African Urban Studies*, 1978–1979, (3):67–83.

Thiam, Awa. *Continents noirs*. Paris: Tierce, 1987.

Thiam, Awa. *La parole aux négresses*. Paris: Gonthier Denoël, 1978.

Thomas-Emeagwili, Gloria. Class Formation in Pre-Colonial Nigeria. MS, History Department, Ahmadu Bello University, ca. 1985.

Tripp, Aili Mari. Gender, Political Participation, and the Transformation of Associational Life in Uganda and Tanzania. *African Studies Review*, 1994, 37(1):107–132.

Tubiana, Marie-José. *Des troupeaux et des femmes: Mariage et transferts de biens chez les Beri (Zaghawa et Bideyat) du Tchad et du Soudan.* Paris: L'Harmattan, 1985.

Tumbo-Masabo, Zubeida; Liljeström, Rita. *Chelewa-Chelewa: The Dilemma of Teenage Girls.* Uppsala: Nordiska Afrikainstitutet, 1994.

Turrittin, Jane. Aoua Keita and the Nascent Women's Movement in the French Sudan. *African Studies Review*, 1993, 36(1):39–99.

Turshen, Meredith, ed. *Women and Health in Africa.* Trenton, N.J.: Africa World Press, 1991.

Urdang, Stephanie. *Fighting Two Colonialisms: Women in Guinea-Bissau.* New York: Monthly Review Press, 1979.

Van Allen, Judith. Memsahib, *militante, femme libre:* Political and Apolitical Styles of Modern African Women. In: Jaquette, Jane S., ed. *Women in Politics.* London: Wiley, 1974, 304–321.

Van Allen, Judith. "Sitting on a Man": Colonialism and the Lost Political Institutions of Igbo Women. *Canadian Journal of African Studies*, 1972, 6(2):165–182.

Van Kesteren, Jose. Female Workers in Addis Ababa. *Social Science Research Review*, 1988, 4(1):17–32.

Vansina, Jan. *The Children of Woot.* Madison: University of Wisconsin Press, 1978.

Vaughan, Megan. *The Story of an African Famine: Gender and Famine in Twentieth-Century Malawi.* Cambridge: Cambridge University Press, 1987.

Vaughan, Megan; Whitehead, Rachel, eds. *Marriage, Sexuality, and Colonial Discourse: The Crisis over Marriage in Colonial Africa.* London: Zed Books, forthcoming.

Verhaegen, Benoît. *Femmes zaïroises de Kisangani: Combats pour la survie.* Paris: L'Harmattan, 1990.

Verhaegen, Benoît. La famille urbaine face à la polygamie et à la prostitution: Le cas de Kisangani au Zaïre. In: Coquery-Vidrovitch, Catherine, ed. *Processus d'urbanisation en Afrique*, vol. 2. Paris: L'Harmattan, 1988.

Vidal, Claudine. L'intérêt des passions: Côte d'Ivoire. In: *Sociologie des passions.* Paris: Karthala, 1991, 131–178.

La ville africaine et ses urgences vitales. Kinshasa: Faculté Catholique, 1991.

Vincent, Jeanne-Françoise. *Femmes africaines en milieu urbain.* Paris: ORSTOM, 1966.

Vincent, Jeanne-Françoise. *Traditions et transitions: Entretiens avec des femmes Beti du Sud-Cameroun.* Paris: ORSTOM/Berger-Levrault, 1976.

Visages des conditions de travail des femmes au Mali. In: *Le Mali: Les défis du développement à la base.* Montréal: SUCO, 1990, 72–76.

Vléï, Chantal. Le travail salarié des femmes à Abidjan, 1946–1986. Ph.D. diss., Université Paris-7, 1994.

Vuorella, Ulla. *The Women Question and the Modes of Human Reproduction: An Analysis of a Tanzanian Village.* Monographs of the Finnish Society for Development Studies, no. 1; Transactions of the Finnish Anthropological Studies, no. 20. Helsinki: Lamakepenatus and the Scandinavian Institute of African Studies, 1987.

Walker, Cherryl. *Women and Resistance in South Africa.* Cambridge, Mass.: Onyx Press, 1982.

Walker, Cherryl, ed. *Women and Gender in Southern Africa to 1945.* London: James Currey, 1990.

Ware, Helen. *Women, Education, and Modernization of the Family in West Africa.* Canberra: Department of Demography, Australian National University, 1981.

Weis, Lois. Women and Education in Ghana: Some Problems of Assessing Change. *International Journal of Women's Studies,* 1980, 3(5):431–453.

Weiss, Ruth. *The Women of Zimbabwe.* London: Aldgate Press, 1986.

Wells, Julia C. The History of Black Women's Struggle Against Pass Laws in South Africa, 1900–1956. In: Hay, Margaret; Wright, Marcia, eds. *African Women and the Law.* Boston: Boston University Press, 1982, 145–168.

Werner, Jean-François. *Marges, sexe et drogue à Dakar: Enquête ethnographique.* Paris: Karthala/ORSTOM, 1994.

White, E. Frances. *Sierra Leone's Settler Women Traders: Women on the Afro-European Frontier.* Ann Arbor: University of Michigan Press, 1987.

White, Luise. Anthologies About Women in Africa. *Canadian Journal of African Studies,* 1994, 28(1):127–133.

White, Luise. *The Comforts of Home: Prostitution in Colonial Nairobi.* Chicago: University of Chicago Press, 1990.

White, Luise. Separating the Men from the Boys: Constructions of Gender, Sexuality, and Terrorism in Central Kenya, 1939–1959. *International Journal of African Historical Studies,* 1990, 23(1):1–25.

Women and African Cinema. *Matatu,* 1996, Spring.

Women and Development. *Review of African Political Economy,* 1984, (27–28).

Women's History. *Journal of Southern African Studies,* 1983, 10(1).

Wright, Marcia. Autobiographies, histoires de vie et biographies de femmes africaines en tant que textes militants. *Cahiers d'Etudes Africaines,* 1988, 28-1(109):45–58.

Wright, Marcia. Consciousness and Protest Among Slave Women in Central Africa, 1886–1911. In: Robertson, Claire; Klein, Martin, eds. *Women and Slavery in Africa.* Madison: University of Wisconsin Press, 1983, 246–270.

Wright, Marcia. Justice, Women, and the Social Order in Abercorn, Northeastern Rhodesia, 1897–1903. In: Hay, M. Jean; Wright, Marcia, eds. *African Women and the Law: Historical Perspectives.* Boston: Boston University Press, 1982, 33–50.

Wright, Marcia. *Strategies of Slaves and Women: Life-Stories from East Central Africa.* London: James Currey, 1993.

Wright, Marcia. Technology, Marriage, and Women's Work in the History of Maize-Growers in Mazabuka, Zambia: A Reconnaissance. *Journal of Southern African Studies,* 1983, 10(1):55–69.

Wright, Marcia. Women in Peril: A Commentary on the Life Stories of Captives in Nineteenth-Century East-Central Africa. *African Social Research,* 1975, (20):800–819.

Yates, Barbara A. Colonialism, Education, and Work: Sex Differentiation in Colonial Zaire. In: Bay, G. Edna, ed. *Women and Work in Africa.* Boulder: Westview Press, 1982, 127–152.

Young, Kate; Wolkowitz, Carol; and McCullagh, Roslyn. *Of Marriage and the Market: Women's Subordination in International Perspective.* London: CSE Books, 1981.

Zeleza, Tiyambe. Gendering African History. *Africa Development,* 1993, 18(1):99–117.

Zunon-Gnobo, J. Le rôle des femmes dans le commerce précolonial. *Godo-Godo,* (Abidjan), 1976, (2):79–105.

About the Book and Author

Over the last century, the social and economic roles played by African women have evolved dramatically. Long confined to home and field, overlooked by their menfolk and missionaries alike, African women worked, thought, dreamed, and struggled. They migrated to the cities, invented new jobs, and activated the so-called informal economy to become Africa's economic and social focal point. As a result, despite their lack of education and relatively low status, women are now Africa's best hope for the future.

This sweeping and innovative book is the first to reconstruct the full history of women in sub-Saharan Africa. Tracing the lot of African women from the eve of the colonial period to the present, Catherine Coquery-Vidrovitch explores the stages and forms of women's collective roles as well as their individual emancipation through revolts, urban migrations, economic impacts, social claims, political strength, and creativity. Comparing case studies drawn from throughout the region, she sheds light on issues ranging from gender to economy, politics, society, and culture. Utilizing an impressive array of sources, she highlights broad general patterns without overlooking crucial local variations. With its breadth of coverage and clear analysis of complex questions, this book is destined to become a standard text for scholars and students alike.

Catherine Coquery-Vidrovitch is professor of contemporary history and head of the Graduate Studies Program on the Third World and Africa at the University of Paris-7 Denis Diderot. A renowned historian of sub-Saharan Africa, she has taught at most of the French-speaking African universities and has held visiting positions at Princeton and Binghamton University. Among her many publications, *Afrique noire: Permanences et Ruptures* (also published in English as *Africa: Endurance and Changes South of the Sahara*) was awarded the Aumale prize of the Academie des Sciences Morales et Politiques.

Index

CPSIA information can be obtained at www.ICGtesting.com
Printed in the USA
LVOW06s0135180714

394832LV00002B/82/A